Vibrant Virginia

Vibrant Virginia

Engaging the Commonwealth to Expand Economic Vitality

Edited by Margaret Cowell and Sarah Lyon-Hill

Virginia Tech Center for Economic and Community Engagement

Blacksburg, Virginia

This book was peer-reviewed by two expert practitioners prior to publication by Virginia Tech Publishing.

Copyright © 2022 Margaret Cowell and Sarah Lyon-Hill
Individual chapters © 2022 respective authors

First published 2022 by Virginia Tech Publishing.for Virginia Tech Center for Economic and Community Engagement

Virginia Tech Publishing
University Libraries at Virginia Tech
560 Drillfield Drive
Blacksburg, VA 24061

Virginia Tech Center for Economic and Community Engagement
702 University City Blvd. (Mail Code 0373)
Blacksburg, VA 24061

 This work is licensed under the Creative Commons Attribution-NonCommercial-NoDerivatives 4.0 International License. To view a copy of this license, visit http:/creativecommons.org/licenses/by-nc-nd/4.0/ or send a letter to Creative Commons, PO Box 1866, Mountain View, California, 94042, USA. Note to users: This work may contain components (e.g., photographs, illustrations, or quotations) not covered by the license. Every effort has been made to identify these components but ultimately it is your responsibility to independently evaluate the copyright status of any work or component part of a work you use, in light of your intended use.

Cataloging-in-Publication Data

Vibrant Virginia: engaging the Commonwealth to expand economic vitality / edited by Margaret Cowell and Sarah Lyon-Hill.

Includes bibliographical references.

ISBN: 978-1-949373-85-1 (paperback)
ISBN: 978-1-957213-00-2 (PDF)
ISBN: 978-1-949373-86-8 (epub)
DOI: https:/doi.org/10.21061/cowell

1. Rural-urban relations—Virginia. 2. Urbanization—Virginia. 3. Rural development—Virginia. 4. Cities and towns—Virginia. 5. Virginia—economic conditions. I. Cowell, Margaret. II. Lyon-Hill, Sarah.

Contents

List of Figures	vii
Acknowledgments	ix
Introduction	1

Part I	Unpacking the Urban-Rural Divide	
Chapter 1	Defining Virginia's Urban-Rural Continuum	17
Chapter 2	Declining Rural Influence in Virginia Politics	41
Chapter 3	State Policy to Bridge Economic Development Divides	59

Part II	Vibrant and Connected Economies	
Chapter 4	Bridging the Urban-Rural Economic Divide through Regional Connectivity	83
Chapter 5	Connecting Entrepreneur Ecosystems across Urban and Rural Regions	101
Chapter 6	Advancing STEM Educational Opportunities for All Virginians	121
Chapter 7	Achieving Competitive Advantage through Expanded Virginia Broadband	139

Part III	Vibrancy of Place and Creative Placemaking	
Chapter 8	Arts, Culture, and Community Building in Rural Virginia	165
Chapter 9	Enhancing Place through Public Art in the Metropolitan Exurbs	181
Chapter 10	Creating Vibrant Main Streets throughout Virginia	197
Chapter 11	Preserving Virginia's Scenic Beauty	215

Part IV	**Vibrant, Healthy, and Connected Communities**	
Chapter 12	Supporting Refugee, Migrant, and Community Partnerships	237
Chapter 13	Responding to the Addiction Crisis through University-Community Collaboration	255
Chapter 14	Local Policy Agenda and Public Health Priorities	277
Chapter 15	Improving Regional Air Service in a Rural-Metropolitan Area	297

Conclusion	317
Works Cited	323
Index	365
Contributors	379

Figures

I.1	Vibrant Virginia Program Activities	5
1.1	Virginia's metropolitan statistical areas	19
1.2	Census urban-rural continuum	20
1.3	USDA rural-urban typology	21
1.4	Select regions of Virginia	22
1.5	Virginia population growth, 1820–2019	24
1.6	Virginia population growth by Census-defined urban cores, urban clusters (suburb), and rural counties	27
1.7	Virginia population by race	28
1.8	Virginia land reserved for state and national parks, and conservation easements	29
1.9	Households with broadband, satellite, or cellular internet in Virginia	31
1.10	Households with/without internet by region type	31
1.11	Percent of households with housing costs more than 30% of income	32
1.12	Medically underserved areas by level of rurality	32
1.13	K–12 education spending per pupil by county	33
1.14	Virginia poverty by county	33
1.15	Virginia employment, 1969–2018	35
1.16	Per Capita Income by rural, urban, and suburb region types	35
1.17	Net tax revenue and distribution by Virginia county	36
1.18	Level of fiscal stress by Virginia county	37
2.1	Net change in support for Warner 2001 to 2020	52
2.2	Net change in support for Warner 2001 to 2020	53
3.1	Employment growth since 2008 by community type, United States	61
3.2	Change in population since 1950	69
3.3	Virginia's certified and characterized sites	77

7.1	Policy barriers to municipal broadband expansion	151
9.1	Virginia's Gateway Region, 2016	183
9.2	"The Return" in Hopewell, VA	189
9.3	"Washington Street Bridge Gateway" in Petersburg, VA	189
9.4	"The Gardens at Exit 45" in Prince George County	190
9.5	"The Return"	193
9.6	"Washington Street Bridge Gateway"	194
9.7	"The Gardens at Exit 45"	195
10.1	Virginia Main Street communities	205
11.1	Dogwood Lane	216
11.2	McAfee Knob Clouds	221
11.3	James River	223
11.4	Thames River	223
11.5	Viewshed schematic	228
11.6	The ConserveVirginia 2.0 Scenic Preservation Map	230
14.1	Representation of health issues in rural and urban jurisdictions	283
14.2	Distribution of political commitments in urban and rural jurisdictions	285
15.1	Shenandoah Valley	301
15.2	Shenandoah Valley Regional Terminal	303

Acknowledgments

An edited book like this one is a collaborative endeavor that takes years to complete and with scores of debts accumulated along the way. First, we want to thank Dr. John Provo for conceiving of Vibrant Virginia and entrusting us with the book component of the much broader initiative. Throughout, we have had the support and encouragement of our colleagues in Virginia Tech's Center for Economic and Community Engagement, notably Scott Tate, Conaway Haskins, Julia Kell, Doris Waddell, and Albert Alwang. We are indebted to our Virginia Tech colleagues on the senior leadership team for Vibrant Virginia, including Drs. Guru Ghosh, Ed Jones, Karen Roberto, Karen Ely Sanders, Susan Short, and Anne Khademian (now with Universities at Shady Grove). We thank Neda Moayerian, Abigail Sale, and Hye-Jeong Seo for their excellent research assistance. Extensive feedback and suggestions for improving the manuscript were provided by Liz Povar and Sheila Martin. We are also grateful to Jessica Ryan for careful editing and to Peter Potter, Caitlin Bean, and others at Virginia Tech Publishing for helping us to cross the finish line and share this work with the world. We are also thankful for financial support provided by the Policy Destination Area and Virginia Tech's Institute for Society, Culture, and Environment. Finally, the editors recognize and are humbled by the immense support provided by their respective families.

Introduction

Margaret Cowell and Sarah Lyon-Hill

On November 13, 2018, Amazon announced that one of its second headquarters (HQ2) would be located in Arlington, Virginia. As part of the deal, the company announced a $2.5 billion investment and the promise of 25,000 full-time, high-paying jobs. That same day, nearly 250 miles to the south, the City Council in Martinsville, Virginia, discussed a proposed list of projects to be included in their 2019 Comprehensive Economic Development Strategy (CEDS) being prepared for the US Economic Development Administration (EDA). Among the items listed were an $800,000 proposal to purchase blighted properties and a $100,000 proposal to recruit manufacturers of clean energy components to Martinsville's Enterprise Zone. And eighty miles to the west of Martinsville, the Blue Ridge Crossroads Small Business Development Center announced on their Facebook page that same day the grand opening of The Graceful Goose, a fine décor and gifts shop on South Main Street in Galax, Virginia. Meanwhile in Virginia Beach that day, city leaders joined Grammy Award–winning musician and hometown hero Pharell Williams to announce a new music festival called "Something's in the Water," which would aim to unite the Hampton Roads region, confront racial tensions, and spur economic growth.

While the nature and scale of the investments being made in these areas is obviously quite different, leaders in all four of these places presumably have the same goal: to promote opportunities for local residents and firms to advance and thrive. Whether it's high-tech jobs with Amazon in Arlington, blight removal and clean energy expansion in Martinsville, small business development in Galax, or cultural development in Virginia Beach, this snapshot of one single day in the Commonwealth of Virginia reminds us that the opportunities and challenges we face across our urban and rural areas are unique but also in many ways universal. Our goal in this book is to explore cases across the urban-rural continuum, looking at connections and disconnects, documenting similarities and differences, all with an eye toward highlighting opportunities for community stakeholders from all sectors to address regional challenges.

Never have these opportunities and solutions seemed more important than they do now, as we begin to dig out from and adjust to economic devastation and political divisiveness unlike anything in modern history. It is true that some parts of Virginia were buffered from the brunt of the 2020 economic fallout from COVID-19 because of their ties to state, federal, and other anchor institutions, which remained largely unaffected. But it is also true that other parts of Virginia's Commonwealth were simply devastated when the floor fell out from underneath the low-wage service workers who are disproportionately employed in retail, passenger transportation, arts and entertainment, accommodation, restaurant and bars, and other personal services that depend on face-to-face interactions. There are also many places in between; including a cross-section of mid-sized Virginia towns and cities that, even before the pandemic, were working tirelessly to repurpose existing assets and talent, cultivate a more diverse economic base, and undo the lasting effects of generations of segregation and concentrated poverty.

We know that the work of community and economic development is not facile, especially in the present environment. We also know that it will not necessarily be easy to convince skeptics that there are lessons we can learn from one another. Nevertheless, we aim to try. The divisive 2016 and 2020 presidential elections reminded us just how big the chasms have become between the haves and the have-nots, the right and the left, the urban and the rural. The unfortunate reality is that sustainable and equitable economic growth has eluded many rural parts and some urban areas of our Commonwealth and those who stay in lagging regions find it more difficult to access the wealth-creating opportunities that generally are found in more prosperous areas. Still, while we might be tempted to point to Virginia's declining rural areas as proof of an urban-rural schism, leaders in lagging metropolitan regions like Hampton Roads would probably argue that urban areas can also be left behind. Their 2020 State of the Region report noted, "While Virginia was 'open for business,' it seemed that Hampton Roads was on the outside, looking in" (42). Other urban areas, including much of Northern Virginia, faced their own challenges related to economic success, including exacerbated issues of affordability, congestion, and increasingly longer commutes.

No one could blame the person who concludes that Virginia is a commonwealth of extremes, with each end of the continuum far too afield to peacefully coexist or to perhaps learn something from one another. How can a place like southwest Virginia, with its close economic and cultural ties to Appalachia and its history of coal and tobacco production, possibly relate to a place like Richmond, home to a Federal Reserve Bank and an economic base that is supported by law, finance, and government? While there are certainly distinguishing features that make these places unique, there are also many ways in which they are similar. Both are grappling with how to reinvent themselves, embrace (and sometimes encourage) dynamic change, and manifest what their own version of the creative or innovation economy will look like.

It seems possible then that certain challenges and opportunities might be universal for all Virginia localities. After all, aren't we all interested in seeking knowledge about how to cultivate strong, vibrant, and inclusive communities? Who among us is not concerned with cultivating capacity to take advantage of emerging opportunities or at the very least embrace economic change? And who would turn down an offer to procure the resources needed to enact changes that will further contribute to the strong, vibrant, and inclusive economy they have imagined?

THE VIBRANT VIRGINIA INITIATIVE

We launched Vibrant Virginia in 2017 in order to create a space in which we could explore answers to these and other questions. Drawing on scholarship, practice, and outreach from Virginia Tech faculty, staff, and students, as well as myriad partners from across the Commonwealth with which we regularly work, we have examined an array of issues impacting the quality of life across the urban and rural regions of the Commonwealth of Virginia. We have tackled cross-cutting topics such as expanding K–12 education reform, supporting entrepreneurial ecosystems, and growing advanced manufacturing to context-specific concerns such as coastal resilience, unmanned systems, and mine-land reclamation. Our broad, but inclusive focus reflects that, from the onset, our Vibrant Virginia team has committed to elevating the voices of community leaders, local governments, small businesses, nonprofits, and K–12 and university educators.

The idea for Vibrant Virginia was conceived of by Dr. John Provo, director of Virginia Tech's Center for Economic and Community Engagement (CECE). Inspired by our colleagues in Oregon—who embarked on a similar journey with their book, *Toward One Oregon* (Oregon State University Press, 2011)—Dr. Provo assembled a core leadership team to shape our own initiative in Virginia. The senior leadership team from Virginia Tech includes Guru Ghosh, Ed Jones, Karen Roberto, Karen Ely Sanders, Susan Short, and Anne Khademian (now with Universities at Shady Grove). Within the CECE, we were assisted greatly by the efforts of Albert Alwang, Conaway Haskins, Julia Kell, Neda Moayerian, and Scott Tate, some of whom have contributed chapters to this book. Early conversations led to the realization that, in order for the initiative to be successful, Vibrant Virginia would have to emphasize equal and engaged partnerships among university faculty and communities for the purpose of imagining possibilities and co-creating solutions to economic and social challenges.

To facilitate these partnerships and to encourage greater university engagement across Virginia, the Vibrant Virginia initiative evolved into a multipronged approach that would ultimately include:

- community conversations where faculty traveled to regions across the state to listen to community stakeholders and their needs;
- campus conversations where groups of Virginia Tech faculty, staff, and students met to discuss connections, challenges, and opportunities related to scholarship and outreach across the Commonwealth;
- seed grants to students and faculty who wished to partner with community actors to address a challenge facing rural and urban communities in the Commonwealth; and

- this book and its related website (https://cece.vt.edu/VibrantVirginia.html), both of which offer chapter authors and community stakeholders the opportunity to voice their perspectives and reflect on both the formal submissions related to Vibrant Virginia as well as their own ideas about what makes for a vibrant Virginia.

An essential element to the Vibrant Virginia initiative, the community conversation series brings together a diverse group of local stakeholders to discuss pertinent issues facing the Commonwealth's regions. From K–12 educators to entrepreneurs, manufacturers to university faculty, farmers to nonprofits, these conversations connect community members to Virginia Tech faculty and resources. Since 2018, fifteen conversations have been held in places such as Saint Paul, Newport News, Farmville, South Boston, South Hill, Danville, and Arlington. These community conversations will continue for the foreseeable future. Figure I.1 shows the geographic scale and locations of these conversations as of 2021.

The campus conversations provide an opportunity for the Virginia Tech community to connect with one another and share research, outreach, and teaching developments in topics related to Vibrant Virginia. A typical conversation would include updates from stakeholders, presentations from seed-funding recipients, and announcements from funders, including USDA Rural Development and the Virginia Department of Housing and Community Development.

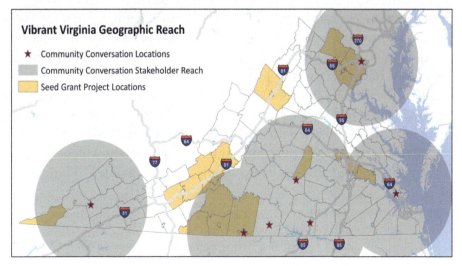

Figure I.1. Vibrant Virginia Program Activities

Seed funding began in spring 2018, when four projects were awarded funding from an applicant pool of fifteen proposals. A second round was awarded to three additional projects in 2019. In total, applications came from all of Virginia Tech's nine colleges. The modest seed funding has allowed faculty, staff, and graduate students to dive deeper and look into new research projects that align with the Vibrant Virginia goals. Many of these funded projects are represented in this book, including the projects described in chapters written by Rebecca J. Hester, Katrina M. Powell, and Katherine Randall; Phyllis L. Newbill, Susan G. Magliaro, Kerry O. Cresawn et al.; and Max Stephenson, Jr., Lara Nagle, and Neda Moayerian.

The final piece of the Vibrant Virginia initiative is this book, which represents the culmination of Vibrant Virginia's early efforts. For this edited collection, we solicited contributions that would investigate the ties that bind us across the urban-rural continuum. Our goal was to curate a collection of writings that would include both practical experiences and scholarly contributions related to Vibrant Virginia; seek to "connect the dots" between learning, discovery, and engagement; advance the important work being done at Virginia Tech and other colleges and universities in Virginia; and celebrate the communities, stakeholders, and government officials with which we regularly collaborate. We humbly assert that, with this book, we have succeeded in doing so.

Vibrant Virginia, the book, starts from the fundamentally optimistic premise that a vibrant Virginia is possible. While our contributors highlight divergences, inequities, and tensions between urban, rural, and the places in between, they also help us to highlight the opportunities that are afforded by a more holistic understanding of the urban-rural continuum. Though it may seem easier to focus on the chasms that exist in this wonderfully diverse amalgamation of counties, towns, and cities, doing so would mean that we missed an opportunity to collectively think about, work on, and actualize solutions with benefits that are broadly realized.

For some readers, this leap may initially seem insurmountable. If you fall into that category, let us begin simply, by conceiving of Virginia as:

- a commonwealth full of places that are economically, conceptually, and physically interdependent;
- a place that is full of opportunities and challenges; and

- a dichotomy, but one that is bounded by common laws and institutions.

If we believe these ideas to be tenable, then we can begin to unpack the more complex notions of a vibrant Virginia, many of which are highlighted in the chapters that are included herein.

The chapters that follow offer a multifaceted glimpse into the many ways that Virginia's communities and regions are working to cultivate a strong, vibrant, and inclusive economy. As you will read, their efforts are not without difficulty, as evidenced by the many challenges the authors describe throughout the book. Still, stories of the wins and the losses provide ideas for those who wish to replicate successful efforts or avoid mistakes that have already been attempted. Moreover, these stories remind us that the Commonwealth of Virginia is full of places that are economically, conceptually, and physically interdependent. They also describe the bridges that exist between these places as being both tenuous and also resilient. Our hope is that Virginia's leaders—including local, regional, state, federal, private sector, and nonprofit partners—will consider the sound advice provided by the authors in this book to help the Commonwealth achieve its promise of an even stronger, more vibrant, and increasingly inclusive economy.

OVERVIEW OF THE BOOK

The first section delves into Virginia's urban-rural divide. It urges us to consider what comes to mind when we think of an urban place. What does it mean to live or work in a rural area? How do statewide politics and public policy affect the urban-rural divide in Virginia? These and other questions are the focus of part I, which includes an overview of Virginia across the urban-rural spectrum, a look at how changing demographics have shaped Virginia politics, and an overview of how the Commonwealth has employed state policy to shape economic development outcomes. Together, these chapters set the stage for a candid conversation about what a truly vibrant Virginia might look like and how the very nature of vibrancy might vary from place to place.

In chapter 1, Sarah Lyon-Hill and John Provo challenge us to think critically about existing definitions of urban and rural places. The authors describe ongoing conversations among federal and state agencies working to understand how changing demographics affect how we categorize places and their residents. They then hone in on Virginia to remind us that urban, rural, and other places also differ in terms of their social, environmental, and economic characteristics. Finally, and perhaps most important, the authors remind us of the importance of thinking about both the interdependence and nuance of place and provide a host of Virginia examples to illustrate these important ideas.

In chapter 2, Stephen J. Farnsworth, Stephen Hanna, and Kate Seltzer discuss Virginia's changing political landscape. More specifically, they compare county-level voter support for Mark Warner's 2001 campaign for governor versus his 2020 reelection campaign for senator. The comparison is astutely used as a proxy to illustrate how rural influence in Virginia politics has declined over the last two decades, as fewer Democratic officials have been elected to represent rural areas. The authors offer four key interlocking reasons why rural influence has declined and conclude with some thoughtful considerations for how rural Virginia might engender a revived political influence in coming years.

Continuing with the exploration of statewide effects on urban and rural places, chapter 3 presents a thorough discussion of how state economic development policy is being leveraged to bridge Virginia's divides. Stephen Moret offers insights into how the Virginia Economic Development Partnership and key partners are utilizing state-level policies to encourage employment growth in smaller metro and rural regions. Recognizing that many of these same areas have been disproportionately affected by the COVID-19 pandemic, Moret bluntly reminds us of the new challenges we face in the economic recovery of areas that had already been struggling with a lack of economic opportunity. He concludes with an optimistic discussion of the Rural Think Tank's policy recommendations to advance a rural growth agenda.

Part II focuses on the importance of cultivating a vibrant and connected economy. When we think about the vibrancy of a place, we often think about its economy and the employment opportunities available to the people who call it home. Continuing our exploration of what a vibrant Virginia looks like, the chapters in this section offer a glimpse into the workforce and economic development challenges and opportunities that exist within the Commonwealth of Virginia.

Chapter 4 introduces the concept of regional connectivity and the importance of re-casting the way we think about industry clusters. In the past, most discussions of industry clusters have focused on agglomerations, knowledge spillovers, networks of businesses, and labor pools within concentrated urban areas. Christiana K. McFarland and Erica Grabowski propose an alternative way of thinking about industry clusters and do so in a way that disabuses us of the notion that clusters only exist in denser areas or that they are incapable of spanning jurisdictional boundaries. The authors challenge us to think about the idea of regional connectivity with a new focus on cluster-based strategies that may help us to bridge the urban-rural divide, especially in rural and lagging regions looking to identify potential industrial pathways.

Thinking creatively about ways to grow and diversify regional and local economies, particularly rural areas, is the focus of chapter 5. In it Scott Tate and Erik R. Pages describe how two Virginia regions have embraced entrepreneurship as a means to build connections that will facilitate better linkages between small towns, urban centers, and large anchor institutions. They begin their chapter with an astute overview of how economic development policies and priorities have shifted in recent decades and discuss the implications of new statewide programs like GO Virginia, which is a bipartisan, business-led economic development initiative to diversify the economy and create more high-paying jobs through incentivized collaboration between business, education, and government. The authors end the chapter with some promising lessons, which will likely be of use to other communities seeking to enhance their region's entrepreneur ecosystem and connect rural areas to regional assets.

Chapter 6 emphasizes the important role that higher education plays in facilitating workforce development and STEM education opportunities. Phyllis L. Newbill, Susan G. Magliaro, Kerry O. Cresawn, Lindsay B. Wheeler, Elizabeth W. Edmondson, Albert Byers, and Padmanabhan Seshaiyer discuss the importance of developing a statewide STEM network in order to grant access and opportunity for high-quality STEM learning across the Commonwealth. Their chapter proposes a blueprint for a strategic, multisector STEM network to promote STEM literacy and expertise across the Commonwealth and describes efforts to build a statewide collaborative of partners working to do so. The chapter ends with strategic recommendations that will likely prove useful to both Virginia stakeholders and people working elsewhere to support STEM networks.

Chapter 7 by Erv Blythe and James Bohland includes a compelling argument for why broadband connectivity is essential to any understanding of a vibrant and equitable Virginia, while also acknowledging "last mile" challenges and ways to overcome them. An important argument is made in this chapter when the authors critique what they describe as a dominant legacy coalition and policy framework that supports corporate providers over community-oriented solutions designed to bridge the broadband gap. Given the strength of this coalition, the authors ask whether community broadband initiatives can be successful in Virginia. In their answer, the authors point to a few successful community-based efforts across the Commonwealth. They end with a series of recommendations for how we might increase broadband connectivity and a reminder that the future viability of rural communities and some urban communities will depend on our success in doing so.

Virginia is a commonwealth made up of dynamic public spaces, vibrant imaginaries, and historic towns and cities. The importance of these places and the people who live and work within them is the focus of the chapters in part III. Together, they describe the diversity of experiences, opportunities, and challenges affecting communities across Virginia. The authors herein remind us that the vibrancy of Virginia should be measured not only in economic terms but also in terms of the relationships that are built, the histories preserved, and the continued well-being of communities therein.

Patrick County in the West Piedmont region of Virginia is the focus of the work described in Max Stephenson Jr., Lara Nagle, and Neda Moayerian's chapter on arts, culture, and community building. In chapter 8, they describe their work with community members in Patrick County to explore the ways that community cultural development (CCD) strategies—including story circles, workshops, and surveys—can be used to encourage individual and social learning. The authors provide great insights into their longtime engagement with Patrick County as members of Virginia Tech's Institute for Policy and Governance (VTIPG) and shed light on adaptations made necessary by the COVID-19 pandemic. They end the chapter with a poignant discussion of how social imaginaries can help community members uncover shared understandings of how they belong and how they can create change.

Chapter 9 takes a deeper look at a specific placemaking initiative in the Tri-Cities region of Virginia. Conaway Haskins describes how the Southside Community Gateway Project came to be, how it was funded, and how a regional foundation worked with local governments to facilitate public art that would enhance several strategically important highway intersections across three localities: the cities of Hopewell and Petersburg and the county of Prince George. In doing so, Haskins provides a detailed case study showing how small cities and the suburban and peri-urban communities that surround them can use public art to advance economic development via creative placemaking. The chapter ends with an important reminder that although the Gateway Project has generally been well received, such public art interventions inherently exist within contested spaces and cannot be thought of as stand-alone strategies to bridge the many divides that exist within regions.

A shared understanding of place is central to the argument that John Accordino and Kyle Meyer develop in chapter 10, which highlights Virginia's historic cities and towns. Focusing on downtown commercial areas, the authors describe the evolution of these places from their development as regional centers, to their decline after World War II, and to their recent efforts to make these communities more hospitable to entrepreneurs looking to live and work in these areas while also tapping into regional or broader networks of innovation and commerce. Their chapter provides insights into how the Commonwealth of Virginia and local partners are helping to facilitate these efforts. They end with an important reminder about interjurisdictional conflict and ultimately point to a few examples we might use as inspiration.

Public engagement efforts are also front and center in the work of Scenic Virginia, whose leadership in founding a scenic viewshed register is highlighted in chapter 11 by Leighton Powell, Lynn M. Crump, Richard G. Gibbons, Lisa Dickinson Mountcastle, Patrick A. Miller, and Jisoo Sim. The authors begin with a history of Virginia's programs for scenic resource recognition and preservation. They follow up with an overview of the public engagement activities and programs that they helped develop to promote scenic beauty across the Commonwealth. A unique collaboration between Virginia Tech and Scenic Virginia is described, most notably the development of a tool that would act as a "defensible decision framework for identifying and assessing the characteristics of a scenic viewshed" (223). The authors conclude with a discussion of the growing importance of scenic resources during the COVID-19 pandemic and the looming threats of sea level rise and climate change.

A focus on vibrant, healthy, and connected communities is the focus of part IV. Across the entirety of the urban-rural spectrum, families and communities rely on public health, social service, and transportation entities for assistance. The importance of these institutions has never been clearer, given the overlapping threats from COVID-19, economic upheaval, regional inequalities, and racial injustice that have challenged communities across the Commonwealth in recent years. The chapters in this section offer several examples that highlight the importance of collaboration when it comes to promoting vibrant, healthy, and connected communities.

Ongoing and acute challenges related to refugee resettlement are the focus of chapter 12. Rebecca J. Hester, Katrina M. Powell, and Katherine Randall describe a pilot study in southwest Virginia involving several nonprofits, service provider organizations, and newly resettled refugee partners. Using interview and focus group data, the authors focus largely on refugee resettlement policy implementation in rural areas. Their writing reminds us of the importance of social networks in rural communities, particularly for newcomers seeking to comply with the sometimes daunting expectations of integration. Their work ends with a discussion of the newly founded Virginia Consortium for Refugee, Migrant, and Displacement Studies (VCRMDS).

In chapter 13, Mary Beth Dunkenberger, Sophie Wenzel, and Laura Nelson discuss the important university and community collaborations that can support communities in their responses to substance use disorder (SUD) and opioid use disorder (OUD). The authors point to the overlapping public health, economic, and law enforcement issues that converged in recent years to exacerbate the crisis. Given the interdependent nature of these challenges, the authors offer lessons from their work in Roanoke and the New River Valley, illustrating how communities can develop a coordinated response that includes proactive leadership from these and other sectors.

In chapter 14, Stephanie L. Smith, Abdulilah Alshenaifi, Elizabeth Arledge, et al. turn toward locally elected governing bodies with the authority to enact health-promoting ordinances to examine which diseases, risks, and other health issues reach the agendas of city councils and boards of supervisors in both urban and rural areas of Virginia. While there are some differences across urban and rural areas, the authors find that noncommunicable diseases and related risks, mental health, and broader healthy community initiatives appear frequently across all communities. The chapter ends with a discussion of implications for those engaged in health policymaking, including a reminder about the risks associated with coercive financial incentives and entrepreneurial grantmaking.

As Nicholas J. Swartz, Justin Bullman, and Jordan Hays remind us in chapter 15, transportation is another form of infrastructure necessary for dynamic communities and connected economies. The authors discuss the importance of regional air service, especially in rural metropolitan areas like the Shenandoah Valley, where members of the Shenandoah Valley Regional Airport (SHD) and James Madison University (JMU) partnered to form the Fly SHD Community Air Service Task Force. The chapter provides a rich description of how the task force came to be and general lessons for other places looking to bolster their own regional airports and for other groups looking to engage in community-based efforts and initiatives.

The book concludes with reflections from us, the editors, on findings from the book as well as the broader Vibrant Virginia initiative. We conclude with a brief reminder about contested narratives of vibrancy, the interconnectedness and embeddedness of localities and regions, the inertia of investment, and the power of place. In doing so, we remind ourselves that a quick glance across the United States reveals that Virginia is not alone in its extremes. States across the country simultaneously grapple with acute growth in some areas and lagging regions in others. The inequities that result can be astonishing, but so too can the opportunities, especially when we consider creative ways to bridge the gap. As the chapters that follow illustrate, Virginia is replete with examples of communities that have found ways to integrate opportunities across the urban-rural continuum. We hope you enjoy exploring these stories with us.

Part 1

Unpacking the Urban-Rural Divide

Chapter 1

Defining Virginia's Urban-Rural Continuum

Sarah Lyon-Hill, John Provo, and Margaret Cowell

This chapter provides an introductory overview of the urban-rural continuum and what it means for Virginia and its many regions. The authors begin by examining the varied definitions of "urban" and "rural," including the cultural stereotypes associated with these two concepts. Like most states, Virginia is a mix of urban and rural localities, each with its own distinct history, economy, and culture. This chapter continues by exploring historical trends across the regions of the state, including population shifts, migration, economic transitions, and the manifestation of micropolitan and metropolitan regions. The resources and infrastructure present in different parts of the state affects economic and community vibrancy, regardless of urban and rural characteristics. In conclusion, although it can be simple to identify data that illustrates a distinct urban-rural divide, depending on where one is situated, an urban or rural community can mean very different things. The characterization of urban and rural as a continuum helps distinguish certain transitional places, for example, smaller metro areas that are often identified as rural but are clearly urbanizing.

Urban and rural as a binary has often been a contentious topic of discussion. When conceiving of urban and rural as two bifurcated concepts, it is easy to notice the distinct differences and characteristics separating these two types of places. However, this perspective may also limit people's understandings of how these places are connected, their varied approaches to community and economic development, and their imaginations of what these places could be.

This chapter explores the challenge of defining urban and rural and offers a more nuanced understanding of those terms in public policy. Different definitions and usages by the US Census, US Department of Agriculture, and other federal and state agencies all serve specific purposes but complicate peoples' understanding of urban and rural. Perhaps urban and rural are best understood and analyzed not as discrete concepts, but as a continuum, a range of places characterized by their relative density. The sections below first examine the different definitions of urban and rural according to both academics and federal agencies. The chapter then explores how urban and rural manifest socially, environmentally, and economically within the Virginia context. Virginia's regions have evolved over time and illustrate how the urban-rural continuum is not only nuanced but also interdependent.

Defining Urban and Rural in Virginia

Government entities have taken steps to create definitions that distinguish between urban and rural locales. In thinking about methodology, Hailu and Wasserman (2016) recommend that researchers consider three factors when determining urban-rural classification: the unit of geography (for which data is available), interest in a level of geography, and comparability among other states and the nation. Using county-level data, for example, the US Census Bureau often uses metropolitan statistical areas (MSAs) as proxies for urbanized clusters. The census defines metropolitan statistical areas as having at least one urbanized core of 50,000 or more in population, along with adjacent territory that is socially and economically integrated with the core, as measured by commuting patterns. Christiana K. McFarland and Erica Grabowski discuss these economic interdependencies in greater detail in chapter 4. Meanwhile, rural is "defined as all population, housing, and territory not included within an

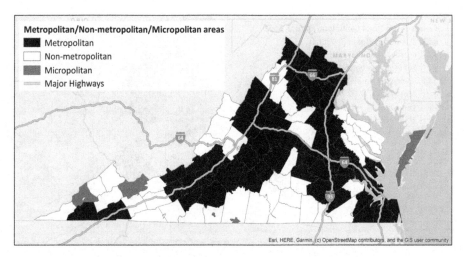

Figure 1.1. Virginia's metropolitan statistical areas

urbanized area or urban cluster" (Ratcliffe et al. 2016, 3), making it so that rural areas range from dense, small towns to remote, less populated areas.

Virginia is a largely metropolitan state. Of Virginia's 133 counties and independent cities, 80 are located within census-designated MSAs, or 88% of Virginia's population. As seen in figure 1.1, MSAs cover a contiguous portion of the north, central, and eastern parts of the state. This includes the Virginia portion of the Washington, DC suburbs; the central area surrounding the state capital of Richmond; and to the east Hampton Roads, whose urban core is defined by a major shipyard, naval bases, and one of the largest ports on the East Coast. Several smaller MSAs run along the western part of the state. Blacksburg, Bristol, Charlottesville, Harrisonburg, Lynchburg, Roanoke, and Staunton all feature institutions of higher education or healthcare. As Stephen Moret discusses in chapter 3, several of these areas have grown enough during the last quarter-century to be recategorized as urban areas.

Virginia's nonmetropolitan pockets include several micropolitan areas, which are similar to metropolitan areas except their core is more than 20,000 but fewer than 50,000 in population. In southwest Virginia, Big Stone Gap in Wise County and Bluefield in Tazewell County are micropolitan areas. Both are historically connected to the coal industry. Danville and Martinsville in southern Virginia are micropolitan areas that grew up around tobacco and textile manufacturing. Truly rural areas are scattered around all parts of the state, including Virginia's Eastern Shore

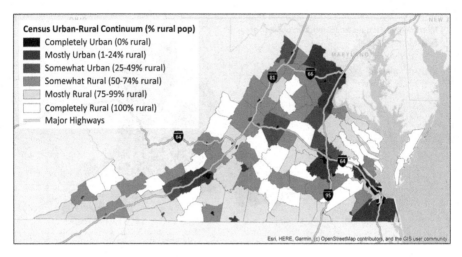

Figure 1.2. Census urban-rural continuum

and other coastal areas, best known for agriculture, aquaculture, and tourism. Between the West Virginia border and the several metropolitan areas along I-81 is the Alleghany Highlands, a rural area that is home to major wood products manufacturing sectors.

As black and white as metropolitan and nonmetropolitan definitions may seem, they are not meant to represent urban or rural. In more recent years, the census and other federal offices have developed urban-rural classifications that offer a more integrated approach to understanding this continuum. Census typology understands urban and rural in terms of population density of census tracts and block groups (smaller than counties), labeling a census tract or block group "urban" or "rural" based on its density. Examining the larger county geography, the census then calculates the percentage of the population within these census tracts or block groups that are designated as rural. Counties are then placed within a six-category range from completely rural to completely urban (see figure 1.2). By categorizing counties along an urban-rural spectrum, urban residents may be part of nonmetropolitan areas, while more rural residents may be included in metropolitan areas. Isserman (2005) urges readers to acknowledge these nuances because failing to do so may lead to the "misunderstanding of rural conditions, the misdirection of federal programs and funds, and a breakdown of communication that confuses people" (465).

These kinds of blurred lines are certainly evident across the commonwealth. As shown in figure 1.2, the north, central, and eastern parts of Virginia are more thoroughly urbanized, with cities and urbanized counties shown as the darkest pockets, representing the core of the metropolitan areas described above. You can see each of those metro areas is also surrounded by less urbanized communities (less than 50% rural). The western metro area's urban cores are much smaller, often only the central city, and encompass somewhat more rural areas (50–74% rural). The nonmetropolitan areas, micropolitan and rural, include some very small urbanized areas but are all quite rural in composition (75–100% rural).

Other systems that can be used to classify urban and rural include the US Department of Agriculture-Economic Research Service (USDA-ERS) Rural-Urban Continuum Codes (RUCC), and Urban Influence Codes (UIC) as well as the US Health Resources and Services Administration–Federal Office of Rural Health Policy Rural Urban Commuting Areas (RUCA) (Hailu and Wasserman 2016). The USDA classification bases its categories on metro-nonmetro categorization and population counts. As figures 1.2 and 1.3 demonstrate, these different definitions can have a substantial and visually striking effect on how localities across Virginia are classified.

Though technical definitions can be helpful in both research and policy, many people have lived experiences and observations that more directly contribute to their understanding of what makes a place urban or rural. In practice, the terms urban and rural may be understood best as perceptions constructed by society as much as anything else. The

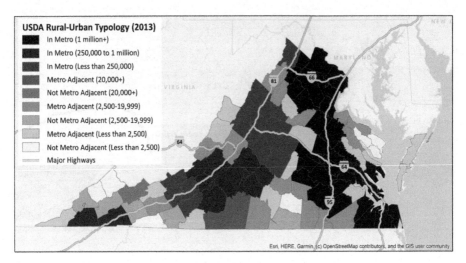

Figure 1.3. USDA rural-urban typology

economic, environmental, and social features observed by a place in relation to other communities are how most people would identify an urban or rural place. Scott, Gilbert, and Gelan (2007), for instance, identify stereotypes and dimensions used to define rural: "(i) negative, i.e., not urban; (ii) low population density; (iii) extensive land use; (iv) primary economic activity and employment; and (v) community cohesion and governance" (4). Noting that rural tends to be a more complex concept, they also acknowledge that urban areas are generally seen as "freestanding, densely occupied and developed with a variety of shops and services" (4). When using traditional descriptive and sociocultural methods of urban-rural classification, Halfacree (1993) proposes that much of the literature does not properly conceptualize space in rural areas, ignoring the difference between rural as a "distinctive type of locality and the rural as a social representation" (34).

The following sections describe the evolution of social, environmental, and economic characteristics of the urban-rural continuum through the lenses of different institutional and cultural definitions. Figure 1.4 shows the more colloquial regions of the state. These different vantage points allow us to identify clear urban-rural trends and to distinguish nuance; for instance, certain smaller metros that often are identified as rural are clearly urbanizing.

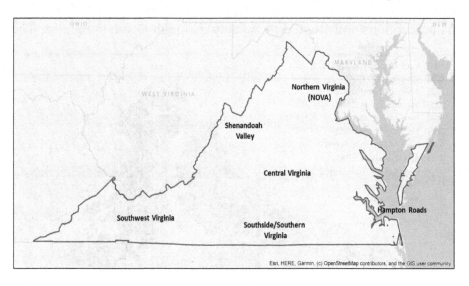

Figure 1.4. Select regions of Virginia

Population Shifts and Urbanization, 1820–1970

Like the United States, the urbanization of Virginia is certainly a long-term phenomenon with diverse economic and social roots. Observing population growth across the state since 1820 allows for the exploration of a few of those roots (see figure 1.5). It is important to note, however, that African Americans were enslaved until the end of the Civil War in 1865 and were not fully counted or named in the US Census until 1870. Therefore, the first three maps in figure 1.5 are distinctly misrepresentative of the entire population during those periods.

Since its colonial days, Virginia steadily grew in population across its varied geography, with different social phenomena promoting population change in different regions of the state. In 1820, two decades after the Revolutionary War ended, Virginia and its frontier had a population of 904,000 people who were more or less evenly distributed across the state's counties. By the beginning of the Civil War in 1861, however, urban growth could be seen in different regions. The tobacco industry in southern Virginia drove the development of urban centers in Pittsylvania and Halifax Counties. The cities of Harrisonburg and Charlottesville represented new urban cores around which farms, mills, and institutions like the University of Virginia thrived. The state's capital of Richmond and localities near the Port of Virginia in Hampton Roads also grew thanks to government and trade.

Following the Civil War and into the early twentieth century, advances in technology pushed the country's transportation network ahead and facilitated industrialization, which offered new opportunities for urbanization. Travel times from New York to Virginia improved from two to seven days in 1830 to two to three days by 1857. In the same period, travel times from New York to Chicago improved from three weeks to two days (Cronon 1991). Virginia's approach to legacy infrastructures, such as limited rail mileage or improved roads, was "pay-as-you-go" fashion, which limited growth during that time (Heineman 1996). The McCormick Reaper, invented in Virginia's Shenandoah Valley, resulted in major improvements in the harvesting of wheat. It was later commercialized in the burgeoning industrial center of Chicago, Illinois, in 1902 by the company that would later become known as International Harvester (Cronon 1991).

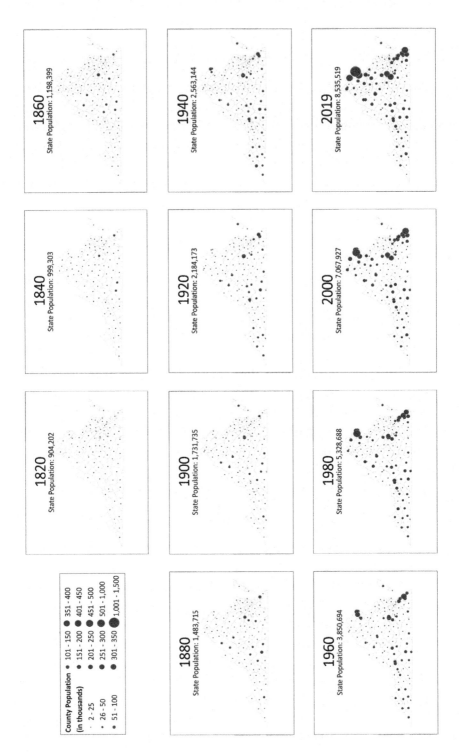

Figure 1.5. Virginia population growth 1820–2019

The state's population saw moderate growth between 1880 and 1940, with growth ranging between 17% and 26% every twenty years (US Census 1860, 1940). However, regions of the state saw different levels of growth and contraction. Far southwest Virginia counties experienced a population boom in the late nineteenth and early twentieth centuries due to the growing demand for coal. Many prosperous mining towns burst into life and thrived at this time (Eller 2008). With consumer demand going hand in hand with increased mechanization and train logistics, southern Virginia's tobacco and textile manufacturing caused a boom in areas around Danville and Martinsville. Meanwhile, what would become the urban crescent, or the three largest metropolitan regions in the state (Hampton Roads, Richmond, and Washington, DC), initially experienced population retractions as people moved west in the nineteenth century. That trend quickly shifted as government and industrial entities expanded in the twentieth century.

The twentieth century marked the beginning of the urban-rural divide narrative as many Americans conceive of it today. After World War I, Sophie Tucker asked vaudeville audiences, "How you gonna keep 'em down on the farm?" (Holsinger 1999). Tucker was singing about returning doughboys exposed to European cities. From 1900 to 1920, just after World War I, many urban centers exploded with residents. The cities of Portsmouth, Norfolk, and Newport News in the Hampton Roads region grew their populations by 212%, 148% and 81% respectfully, gaining populations of 54,000, 116,000, and 36,000 by 1920. The City of Richmond, the largest urban core at the time, grew by 102% to about 172,000 residents. In the growing coalfields, Wise County (47,000), Russell County (27,000), and Lee County (25,000) grew by 137%, 49%, and 27%, respectively (US Census 1900, 1920). As Holsinger (1999) describes in the Sophie Tucker song, exposure to European cities during World War I was one factor contributing to the migration to more population-dense towns and cities.

Another contributing factor was the Great Migration of African Americans, which began around 1915 and lasted over six decades. By 1970, more than six million African Americans moved from the rural South to northern, midwestern, southern, and West Coast cities (Wilkerson 2010). In Virginia, this outmigration from the rural south was felt particularly hard in rural southern or Southside Virginia, where the mechanization of harvesting for cotton and other crops was thought to be a driving force for migration to the North. However, Wilkerson (2010) argues that many rural regions did not mechanize their farming until the Great Migration was well underway, and many migrants cited other reasons for moving away from the rural South, including Jim Crow and the dream of new opportunities. Similarly, Appalachian regions experienced outmigration during and after World War II. After the Second World War, demand for coal dwindled, mining technology evolved, and many Appalachians began to migrate to the Midwest for more economic opportunities (Eller 2008).

Connections between urban cores and their rural hinterlands had always existed through shared foodsheds. Historically, a city would be fed by its rural hinterlands. This kind of interdependence, essential to the life of both the city and countryside, has long been broken. Changes in food production, specialization, and scale allow food to be shipped year-round over great distances (Cronon 1991). These connections shifted further when exurban housing became appealing and white Americans fled to the suburbs. As jobs followed people to the suburbs, the dispersal of manufacturing, for instance, and concentration of professional and technical jobs at the urban center, created spatial mismatches. Commuting patterns extended and shifted, causing more diversification of suburban/exurban populations and relocation for rural populations (Persky and Weiwel 2000; Stoll, Holzer, and Ihlanfeldt 2000; Weitz 2003; Wilson 1987, 1997).

By the 1970s, highways, developers, and white flight drove growth in the suburbs surrounding the urban cores. It was during this period when Northern Virginia counties began to grow rapidly around Washington, DC, and counties around Richmond grew substantively. Even counties around smaller urban cores, such as Lynchburg and Roanoke, grew, contributing to the creation of metropolitan areas dotted across Virginia (US Census Bureau 1960–2000).

VIRGINIA DURING THE PAST FIFTY YEARS

In 1970, Virginia's population was approximately 4.66 million people. Suburban counties accounted for 59% of that population, urban core counties accounted for 21%, and rural counties accounted for 19%. By 2018, Virginia's 8.52 million population was 66% suburban, 21% urban, and 12% rural. Rural population numbers have remained

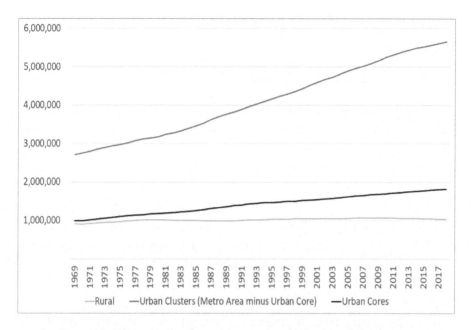

Figure 1.6. Virginia population growth by census-defined urban cores, urban clusters (suburb), and rural counties (BLS 1969–2017)

relatively stagnant since the 1980s (BEA 1969–2018). Moreover, when distinguishing between counties that the 2010 census designated as urban cores (urban), those that are in metropolitan areas but outside the urban core (suburban), and those outside metropolitan areas altogether (rural), one will see that suburban counties have continued to outpace rural and urban counties in growth (BEA 1969–2018).

Table 1.1. Virginia Population Change by County Type			
	Rural counties (%)	Suburban counties (%)	Urban Core counties (%)
1970–1975	7	8	11
1975–1980	4	7	6
1980–1985	−1	9	7
1985–1990	−1	11	11
1990–1995	4	9	6
1995–2000	2	9	4
2000–2005	1	8	6

2005-2010	1	7	5
2010-2015	-2	5	5
Source: Bureau of Economic Analysis, 1969-2018			

These population shifts become more nuanced when viewing them through the lenses of age and race. In rural counties, middle-aged and older populations continued to increase 18.5% on average during the decades since 1970, while younger populations declined. Starting in 1970, the nineteen and under age group declined 2–17% each decade. Beginning in 1980, young professionals ages twenty to thirty-four declined 6–13% each decade. Between 2000 and 2010, rural counties saw a 5% decline in adults aged thirty-five to fifty-four (US Census Bureau 1970–2010).

Meanwhile, rural counties saw relative population stagnation among white and Black residents between 1980 and 2017, and only small increases among other race or ethnic groups. Urban core populations grew across every race demographic except white residents during the past fifty years. The proportion of African Americans residing in rural counties constituted the largest shift for the demographic group. In 1970, 43% of Black Virginian residents lived in a rural county; by 2010, only

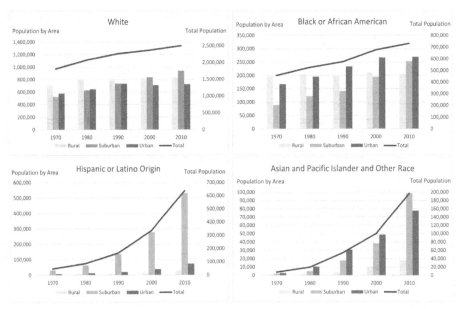

Figure 1.7. Virginia population by race (US Census Bureau 1970–2010)

28% of Black residents lived in rural Virginia. Proportionally, most had migrated to the suburbs. The largest overall population increases between 1970 and 2017 were among Asian and Hispanic groups, who moved to metropolitan regions of Virginia, particularly counties surrounding the urban cores, such as Northern Virginia, the suburbs of Richmond, and the chain of urban islands that make up Hampton Roads (US Census Bureau 1970–2010). Chapter 12 of this volume describes how more rural and urban communities are handling the influx of migrants and immigrants.

Regardless of how regions have changed in the past century and a half, and no matter the pace at which they have changed, the ways in which our communities and local and regional institutions have adapted to these changes have shaped the urban-rural dynamic across Virginia. Communities see and address these changes using different lenses, such as economic development, community development, or social services. Regional institutions, such as Planning District Commissions, Economic and Industrial Development Authorities, Workforce Development Areas, and now GO Virginia regions, also take different approaches in adapting to changing population and economic demographics. Many of these institutions attempt to influence those demographic and economic changes through policy. In chapter 8, Max Stephenson Jr., Lara Nagle, and Neda Moayerian argue for a community cultural development approach when facing dramatic demographic, social, and economic

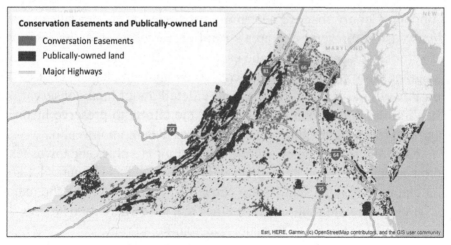

Figure 1.8. Virginia land reserved for state and national parks, and conservation easements

change. In chapter 2, Stephen J. Farnsworth, Stephen Hanna, and Kate Seltzer speak to politics across Virginia, and how political phenomena shape and are shaped by different regions across the urban-rural continuum.

Resources, Infrastructure, and Expenditures

Not only are regions influenced by political and programmatic structures, they are also shaped by the natural resources and infrastructure developed within them. Infrastructure is varied and covers many topics from education to water quality. Nicholas J. Schwartz, Justin Bullman, and Jordan Hays, for example, describe the importance of airport infrastructure for rural and urban regions alike in chapter 15. While this volume does not address every natural resource or type of infrastructure, a handful of examples are discussed in this chapter and elsewhere in the book.

The Commonwealth of Virginia is a vast territory, which includes myriad ecosystems across almost 43,000 square miles of land. Far southwest Virginia's mountainous topography continues along the state's northwest border, eventually evening out in the farmlands of southern and central Virginia. As figure 1.8 illustrates, much of the publicly owned land in Virginia can be found along Appalachia's mountain ridges. A plethora of conservation easements also makes up a portion of the more rural county land in Virginia, particularly in areas like Loudoun County that are near more urbanized areas but whose residents wish to preserve the area's rural character. Despite its purportedly "urban" characteristics, the eastern part of the state contains small geographies of publicly owned, conserved land. In chapter 11, Leighton Powell and colleagues offer more detail about land conservation in Virginia, both urban and rural, and the efforts to preserve historic and culturally significant viewsheds across the commonwealth.

As with most settlements worldwide, Virginia's cities and towns tend to run along waterways or roadways. Hence, you'll find in figures 1.1 and 1.3 that metropolitan regions are conveniently located along the major US highways within the state. Counties that are largely rural are mostly located outside the range of major water and road routes.

Other types of infrastructure and amenities also shape the lives of people in these regions and often help to characterize the quality of

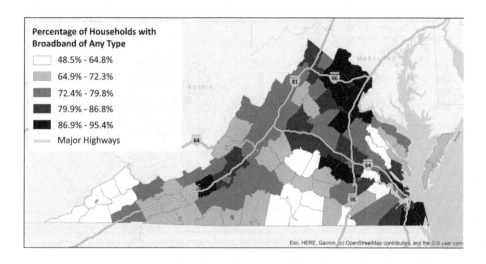

Figure 1.9. Households with broadband, satellite, or cellular internet in Virginia

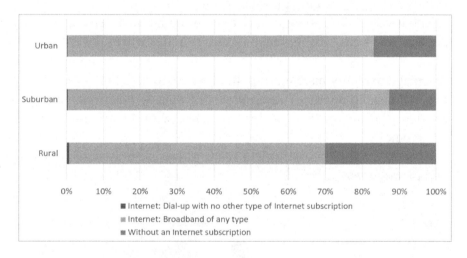

Figure 1.10. Households with/without Internet by region type
(ACS 2019 5-year estimates)

life in urban and rural areas. Politicians, media, and others go so far as to stereotype rural and urban regions based on the quality of these resources, whether warranted or not. With the COVID-19 pandemic keeping most families in their homes in 2020 and 2021, for instance, the question of internet access across the urban-rural continuum has been a very salient topic. In chapter 7, Erv Blythe and James Bohland talk

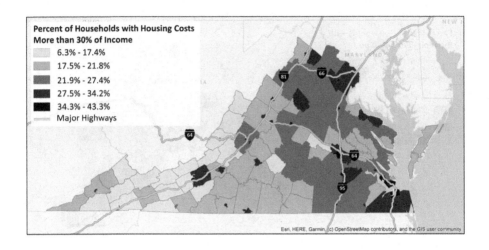

Figure 1.11. Percent of households with housing costs more than 30% of income

about the challenges and opportunities for broadband access across the commonwealth, describing how access to the internet depends heavily on where one lives. In Virginia, there are counties where fewer than half of households have subscriptions to internet services, including a small percentage that only have dial-up. In other counties, as many as 95% of households have internet subscriptions. Similar to other resources, the prevalence of internet access does correlate with the urban-suburban-rural typology.

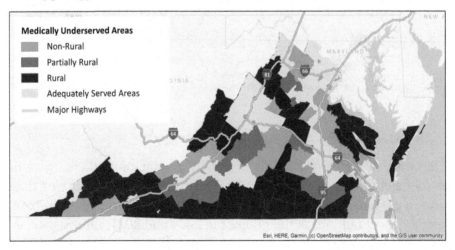

Figure 1.12. Medically underserved areas by level of rurality (HRSA 2017)

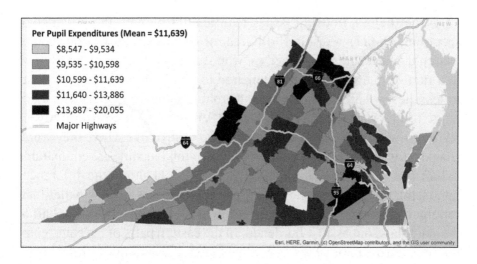

Figure 1.13. K-12 education spending per pupil by county

Another infrastructure topic that is often categorized in terms of urban and rural is housing stock. Aging housing stock and a lack of affordable housing are common challenges for most areas. They may manifest in different ways for places depending on where they are along the urban-rural spectrum. For instance, on the far ends of each spectrum, very rural or very urban areas may both face aging housing infrastructure. Typically, newer suburban neighborhoods may be more concerned with affordability challenges.

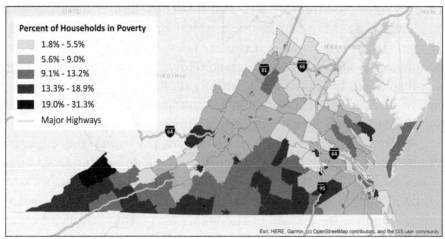

Figure 1.14. Virginia poverty by county (ACS 2018 5-year estimates)

Nevertheless, housing issues manifest throughout the urban-rural spectrum, often as a result of different or lack of land use controls. For example, Blacksburg, Virginia, in Montgomery County is a small town in a rural-esque metro when compared to places like Richmond, Charlottesville, or Fairfax; however, affordable housing is a serious challenge to incoming faculty and staff at Virginia Tech, new employees in the growing tech sector, and others who wish to live where they work. Blacksburg housing costs as a percentage of total income are comparable to Fairfax County and Virginia Beach. Figure 1.11 shows the differences in housing prices across the state. Core communities in the smaller metropolitan and micropolitan regions of the less developed western half of the state stand out as cost-burdened. In the eastern parts of the state, communities across parts of the more developed regions show as moderately to severely cost-burdened.

Healthcare infrastructure is also front and center because of the COVID-19 pandemic, not to mention the ongoing challenge of a large and aging baby boomer population. As figure 1.12 illustrates, many regions across Virginia are medically underserved in terms of having too few primary care providers, high infant mortality, high rates of poverty, and/or a high elderly population (HRSA 2017). These metrics help to highlight areas of the state that have vulnerable populations and limited physical or financial access to medical care.

Many rural counties are faced with an aging population, higher poverty rates (see figure 1.14), and distinctly farther distances that residents must drive to reach a hospital or physician (US Census Bureau 1970–2010). It is little wonder that these counties are designated as medically underserved. However, counties within metropolitan areas, both urban and partially rural, are also challenged by a lack of medical infrastructure and vulnerable populations. In this case, the challenges may come in the form of limited transit to medical facilities, limited finances, or too few physicians per capita. Indeed, community and economic developers alike continue to gain understanding of how access to medical and public healthcare greatly influence economic and community vibrancy throughout the state. While many public health issues exist in the state, Mary Beth Dunkenberger, Sophie Wenzel, and Laura Nelson discuss and highlight the challenges of the opioid crisis in the Commonwealth in chapter 13. In chapter 14,

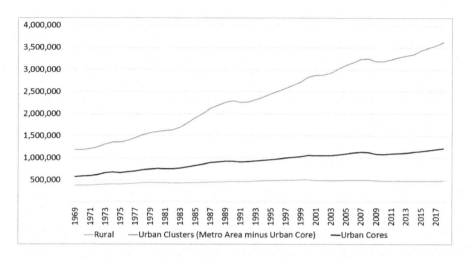

Figure 1.15. Virginia employment (BEA 1969–2018)

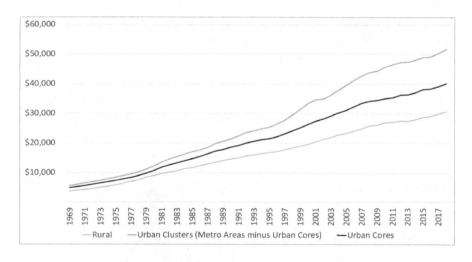

Figure 1.16. Per capita income by rural, urban, and suburb region types (BEA 1969–2018)

Stephanie L. Smith and colleagues examine if and how different types of public health issues appear on county-level policy agendas.

Finally, education and workforce infrastructure vary across regions. For instance, per-pupil expenditures by county do not fall neatly into urban or rural categories (figure 1.13). In fact, counties that invest the most in their students can be found in some of the most urbanized and some of the more rural areas of the state. Nor do financial input measures necessarily align with workforce or economic outcomes. Certain counties in far southwest Virginia have some of the highest standards of learning test scores. Yet, poverty rates remain higher in those same counties as well (see figure 1.14). Chapter 6 addresses some of these workforce disparities, illustrating how STEM education opportunities may address workforce outcomes.

Urban-Rural Economic Interdependence

This chapter has explored our understanding of the urban-rural continuum in Virginia and the challenges in addressing that through the shifting lens of regions. Harvard Business School's Michael Porter long ago convinced most economic policymakers that our nation and states are essentially collections of regions, urban or rural, whose fate is bound together. If one is to believe Porter's argument, should these collections of regions see the economic fate of our urban and rural places move closer together or farther apart?

Macroeconomic indicators tend to follow the urban-suburban-rural trend seen in population growth rates. These regions are distinct. Since 1969, major employment clusters continued to grow in urban areas but increased substantially in the counties surrounding urban cores. Rural counties remained relatively stagnant over time (see figure 1.15). Per

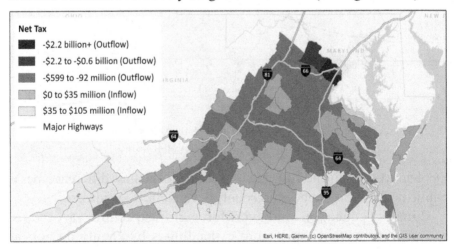

Figure 1.17. Net tax revenue and distribution by Virginia County (Auditor of Public Accounts 2017; Virginia Department of Taxation 2017)

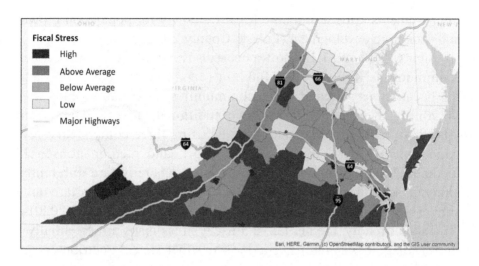

Figure 1.18. Level of fiscal stress by Virginia County (DHCD 2020)

capita income increased for all region types, with suburban counties outpacing urban counties, and urban counties outpacing rural counties (see figure 1.16). Poverty rates across these regions were also distinct. Metropolitan (12%) and nonmetropolitan (29%) poverty rates diverged by seventeen percentage points according to the 2018 American Community Survey 5-Year Estimates. When comparing urban, suburban, and rural counties, the poverty rates were 29% in rural counties, 16% in urban core counties, and 11% in suburban counties (ACS 2018 5-Year estimates).

As these distinctions have become more pronounced, they may have a great impact on tax systems. Virginia's tax system, like many states, places a tremendous local burden on property taxes. It also allows for a locally levied machine and tools tax and other smaller levies. Localities additionally receive a share of state-levied sales tax. While income taxes are not levied locally in Virginia, they do represent a major part of the state tax base. At the local level, tax capacity and the level of effort to assess taxes are wildly divergent. Some redistribution between localities takes place through complex formulas, such as formulas for education and roads. Complaints from more prosperous jurisdictions, that are net contributors, about the willingness of more distressed jurisdictions to tax themselves are perhaps not surprising. There are a number of rural communities that passed new levies or bond issues by popular vote in 2020 (*Roanoke Times* 2021a). For example, Pulaski County funded school improvements critical to their "40×30" strategy for population growth and economic development (Pulaski County 2021).

Figures 1.17 and 1.18 show a net redistribution of revenue between communities through state funding (e.g., schools and roads) and the fiscal stress status of these communities. Fiscal stress measures the ability of a county to generate additional local revenues from a tax base relative to the state average using three components: revenue capacity per capita, revenue effort, and median household income. Urbanized and rural communities generally fare differently, although several of Virginia's landlocked independent cities fare quite similarly to challenged rural communities. (APA 2017; DHCD 2020)

Taken broadly, the net tax and fiscal stress maps are essentially a mirror image of each other. The localities that are net contributors are generally experiencing low fiscal stress and the net receiving communities are generally experiencing high fiscal stress. The state's redistributive choices appear to ask those with the opportunity to aid those with need, and localities in need across the state are both urban and rural. Is this interdependence politically or economically sustainable?

Orfield (1997, 2002) advocated for legislative coalitions between economically challenged cities and inner suburbs as a model for sustaining political support for tax-base sharing. The Virginia experience with coalitions between individual urban and rural communities of need has had limited traction in the legislature (*Roanoke Times* 2021b; Schneider 2018). Thus, while these macro characteristics of urban-rural-suburban are distinct, these categories may limit approaches to supporting communities in need.

If states are vessels for regional economies, as argued by Porter (2004) and others, then this angle may shed better light on opportunities for supporting communities of all types. As illustrated, regions are a mix of urban, rural, and suburban. From this point of view, addressing regional needs may present a better strategy for building coalitions that cross the urban and rural continuum of Virginia. And while it is generally accepted that urban communities and some of their rural hinterlands have become more disconnected, as some rural regions have grown to micropolitan or metropolitan scale their fates are more clearly linked to larger urban centers.

The growth of regional industry clusters has supported the growth of these new MSAs, and today a cluster's "health" serves as one indicator for overall regional health (Porter 2004). Industry clusters across Virginia were analyzed at the regional level in the state's GO Virginia Growth and Diversification plans. The program is organized in nine regions, several of which are primarily urban (Northern Virginia, Richmond, Hampton Roads), three that are significantly more rural than others (southwest Virginia, southern Virginia, and the Shenandoah Valley), and three that are mixed between small metropolitan areas and adjacent rural areas (Blacksburg-Roanoke-Lynchburg; Fredericksburg and the Northern Neck/Middle Peninsula; and Charlottesville). There are common industry clusters across all nine regions, but unique flavors in the very urban (IT/cyber/federal), in the rural (agricultural/related), and in the mixed regions (higher ed–influenced technology sectors) (Virginia Department of Housing and Community Development 2021).

The GO Virginia plans also include situational analysis of opportunities and challenges in each region. Common concerns across urban, rural, and mixed regions have been the availability of talent (in terms of raw numbers and specific skills) and the capacity of our educational systems at all levels to promote talent. Not surprising, following the release of these plans, more than half the investments through the GO Virginia program have focused on developing skilled talent. As discussed by Stephen Moret in chapter 3, additional state investment has flowed in this area, sometimes explicitly crossing urban, rural, and mixed regions. Different regions have also turned to strategies that encourage entrepreneurship and small business development as seen in chapter 5 by Scott Tate and Erik R. Pages. Still, additional support has moved to rural broadband—as Blythe and Bohland describe in chapter 7—and some rural regions have pursued population stabilization as a goal (Virginia Department of Housing and Community Development 2021).

Conclusion: It All Depends on Where You Sit

While urban and rural are often described in very dichotomous ways, we hope that this chapter illustrates the true murkiness of this distinction. Indeed, in many cases, depending on where one is situated, an urban or rural community can mean very different things. The characterization of urban and rural as a continuum helps distinguish certain transitional places, smaller metro areas that are often identified as rural but are clearly urbanizing. Designing policy with this continuum in mind could clarify opportunities and challenges.

While the contributors to this book conceive of urban, rural, and the urban-rural spectrum in a variety of ways, the editors are grateful for the nuanced descriptions and analyses they provide. These divergences serve as explorations that engage both the technical definitions noted above and the less tangible, and sometimes fuzzy, understandings of where one falls within the urban-rural spectrum. As our Oregon colleagues remind us in *Toward One Oregon*, "we need to update our stories to arrive at new 'truths' if we are to write the next chapters of our shared history in a constructive, sustainable, and satisfying way" (14). We, the editors, are humbled by the contributors' efforts to help us update our shared stories and collectively write Virginia's important next chapters.

Chapter 2

Declining Rural Influence in Virginia Politics

Comparing Mark Warner's 2001 and 2020 Elections

Stephen J. Farnsworth, Stephen Hanna, and Kate Seltzer

This chapter traces the declining influence of rural Virginia through a comparison of statewide election results nearly two decades apart: 2001 and 2020. The authors compare Mark Warner's 2001 election as governor, which included significant rural support, and his 2020 senate campaign, which did not. Although both contests involved victorious statewide campaigns by the same Democratic candidate, the political and cultural changes that have taken place in Virginia over this period could suggest something comparable to two different states: the Virginia of 2001 and the Virginia of 2020. As this chapter shows, the Virginia political environment of 2020 was far different from the environment of 2001—and those differences were not advantageous for the advancement of rural interests.

Recent decades have been tough on rural influence in Virginia politics. Two decades ago, Virginia Democratic candidates hoping to win statewide elections had to win a larger share of the rural vote than is necessary for Democratic candidates to win statewide elections today. Democratic candidates seeking to compete in rural areas in previous elections emphasized issues of particular importance to rural areas, where the region's once-leading industries, including agriculture, mining, textiles, and manufacturing, had seen better days.

The substantial population growth in Virginia cities and suburbs over the past two decades, together with the increasing tendency of suburban voters to reject Republican candidates, have far overshadowed the growing Republican voting trend in more rural areas, where many communities have seen little if any increase in population and political clout in Virginia elections (Farnsworth and Hanna 2013, 2017a, 2017b, 2018a, 2018b).

At the same time that rural political influence has been in decline in Virginia and elsewhere, the challenges found in rural America have increased. As other chapters in this book point out, rural areas can suffer from a host of challenges, including low wages, economic stagnation, youth outmigration, limited access to healthcare and transit, as well as increasing community problems relating to chemical addictions (Egan 2002). Also increasing has been the belief of some who live in rural areas that their ways of life are under threat from more populous areas and modern culture (Cowell, Eckerd, and Smart 2020; Monnat and Brown 2017). Plans to improve the fortunes of rural communities exist, including via land use policies, tele-work, rural investment, and the promotion of tourism (Bascom 2001). But any such ideas to revive rural areas may languish if political clout increasingly flows to urban and suburban areas, as has been the case in Virginia in recent years (Lewis 2019; Masket 2017).

These factors occur in conjunction with a growing cultural polarization and resentment among some in rural America (Lichter and Ziliak 2017; G. McKee 2020; Rodden 2019; Scala and Johnson 2017). Some rural voters have developed a collective group consciousness that explains support for small government conservatism among residents of relatively low-income communities (Walsh 2012). While higher levels of government support for the less affluent may be in their economic self-interest, rural residents in an interview project objected to a large federal government assistance role because they believed any expanded federal programs would be controlled by urban political elites who disrespected them (Walsh 2012). Perceived liberal contempt (or actual contempt, if one prefers) is a key factor in explaining the rise of pro-Republican sentiments from low-income and rural voters who might benefit from the expanded government programs promoted by Democratic candidates (Johnston, Jones, and Manley 2019; S. McKee 2008; Walsh 2012).

The rural-suburban-urban dynamics in Virginia come into focus via a comparison of Mark Warner's electoral victories in 2001 and 2020. To place those two elections into context, we first discuss the historical dynamics of rural political influence in Virginia. Starting with the end of Reconstruction and for nearly a century thereafter, Virginia was ruled by a conservative Democratic oligarchy that provided outsized influence for political figures from outside the most populated regions of the Commonwealth. That advantaged rural interests, as did the transition of many of those conservative Democratic-elected officials and like-minded voters into the Republican Party during the final decades of the twentieth century, a time of peak Republican influence in Virginia. The declining rural electoral influence in Virginia becomes apparent through an analysis of two twenty-first-century elections, Mark Warner's 2001 victory as governor and his 2020 re-election to the US Senate. We then conclude with a discussion of how this comparison offers insights for the future of rural political influence in Virginia.

The Changing Nature of Virginia Politics

From its colonial roots, the influence of rural Virginians on the Commonwealth's politics has been immense. At times, rural interests in Virginia diverged, as they did during the early nineteenth century. Communities in the Tidewater, where slavery was relatively common, were sometimes at odds with the more sparsely populated western mountainous regions, where slavery was relatively uncommon. Those differences declined in importance in the wake of the political and economic transformations brought about by the Civil War and its aftermath, including the end of slavery, the departure of many of the mountain counties that became West Virginia, and the postwar US military occupation. Taken together, these developments reduced the salience of antebellum policy disputes among white rural Virginians of the mountains and the Tidewater (Dabney 1971). As Virginia industrialized in the late nineteenth and early twentieth centuries and as the urban jurisdictions of Hampton Roads, Northern Virginia, and Richmond grew and prospered, urban voters remained less influential than their growing populations might suggest, given the continuing control of Virginia by a white rural elite. More than half a century ago, V. O. Key Jr. (1949, 19) famously described Virginia as a "political museum piece." He further observed, "Of all the American states, Virginia can lay claim to the most thorough control by an oligarchy."

While more urbanized states, including New York, Massachusetts, Illinois, and Missouri, had powerful urban political organizations that wielded statewide and sometimes national influence, rural voices dominated Virginia's most influential political machine throughout much of the nineteenth and twentieth centuries. The "Organization" began to dominate the state in the late nineteenth century and rose to its greatest prominence during the twentieth century under Harry F. Byrd Sr. of Clarke County, a newspaper publisher, apple baron, governor, and highly influential US senator (Medvic 1999). As the national Democratic Party realigned itself in a more liberal direction to take account of the very different electorate that emerged following the Civil Rights Act and the Voting Rights Act of the 1960s, the Byrd Organization had little interest in an inclusive approach and suffered politically as a result (Sabato 1977). Meanwhile, the previously tiny Republican Party of Virginia, which fought the Byrd Organization without success for decades, managed to elect the state's first Republican governor of the twentieth century in 1969. That reform-oriented governor, Linwood Holton, favored school desegregation and opposed welcoming members of the Byrd Organization into the GOP, but Holton's moderate vision of Republicanism fell out of favor as white rural conservative voters and "Organization" politicians increasingly made the Republican Party their new home (Atkinson 2006).

The 1980s and 1990s were a period of great tumult in Virginia. Voters narrowly elected L. Douglas Wilder (D) governor in 1989, making him Virginia's first and to date the Commonwealth's only African American chief executive. His years in office were followed by significant Republican gains. Republicans won the Virginia gubernatorial elections of 1993 and 1997, and after George Allen's 2000 US Senate victory, both US Senate seats from Virginia were also in Republicans hands. Republicans had become dominant in the legislature as well, winning majority control of the Senate of Virginia in 1995 and majority control of the Virginia House of Delegates in 1999 after decades in the minority in both chambers (Atkinson 2006). Democratic congressman Rick Boucher continued to hang onto power in the largely rural "Fighting Ninth" congressional district in Virginia's southwest, and his victories were one of the few bright spots for Democratic candidates in rural Virginia during this era. But his days were numbered as well, as Boucher lost his bid for a fifteenth term in 2010 (Samuelsohn 2011).

For Virginia Democrats, the statewide political landscape at the dawn of the twenty-first century looked bleak. Even as suburban areas of the Commonwealth enjoyed massive population growth, a majority of suburban voters frequently joined with a majority of rural voters in supporting Republican candidates, leading to a series of statewide defeats for the Democratic Party (Atkinson 2006). Urban areas were also gaining population, but those increases likewise were not enough to overcome Republican strengths elsewhere. No Democratic presidential candidate had won Virginia's electoral votes between 1964, when Lyndon Johnson narrowly prevailed in the Commonwealth, and 2008, when Barack Obama's victory in Virginia started a string of Republican presidential candidate losses in Virginia. Even Bill Clinton, himself a populist Southern governor, did not make Virginia a priority during his 1992 and 1996 presidential campaigns, although he did make some campaign appearances on behalf of Mark Warner's 1996 US Senate campaign (Atkinson 2006). Democratic prospects across the South during the early twenty-first century seemed so bleak that some political observers encouraged the party to focus elsewhere (Schaller 2006).

While many of these same forces were at play here in Virginia, there are nuanced differences that can be observed in comparing two statewide elections involving Mark Warner that occurred nearly two decades apart. Together, these elections illuminate the changing nature of Virginia politics over the past two decades. This comparison also illustrates how Democratic candidates can respond to the changing composition of the Virginia electorate and the Democratic electoral coalition, including a shift among many rural voters toward Republican candidates.

MARK WARNER'S ELECTIONS: COMPARING THE 2001 AND 2020 CONTESTS

Before he was a candidate for office, Mark Warner made a fortune as a technology entrepreneur. He managed L. Douglas Wilder's 1989 successful gubernatorial campaign and then became Virginia's Democratic Party chair. As the head of the state party organization, he launched strident attacks against George Allen, the Republican candidate for governor in 1993 (Atkinson 2006). Allen's conservative, partisan attacks on the

Democrats secured his election that year. Starting in the 1980s and 1990s, attack ads increasingly became the norm for both parties competing in Virginia elections. As Virginia Republicans became more conservative and Virginia Democrats became more liberal, members of these redefined political parties sought to distinguish themselves ideologically in the political marketplace, with partisan vitriol that had previously been more common in Washington than in the Commonwealth (Farnsworth 2005).

Mark Warner first campaigned for a statewide elected office in 1996, challenging incumbent Republican US senator John Warner. The challenger focused on his centrist credentials and his years as a successful entrepreneur. Mark Warner also emphasized his relative youth when he jogged along a Labor Day parade route in Buena Vista, sweat pouring off him as he shook hand after hand in that community in rural Virginia (Black and Black 2002). John Warner, who had not faced a serious general election challenge in years, was re-elected narrowly, with 52% of the vote, a better-than-expected showing for the Democratic challenger (Black and Black 2002). In an effort to secure a greater share of rural votes than Democratic candidates had been receiving, a key Mark Warner line of attack that year was to broadcast that John Warner had voted to cut Medicare and increase Medicare premiums, matters of great importance to many voters found in aging, rural electorates (Atkinson 2006).

In the years between 1996 and 2001, Mark Warner methodically worked his way into the governor's office, focusing on expanding technology in education in rural areas and seeking to apply his private sector management skills to managing the budget in Richmond (Beiler 2001/2002). He also commissioned a NASCAR driver to advertise his campaign at the Bristol Motor Speedway (among others) and a bluegrass singer to describe his commitment to rural Virginia in down-home musical terms (Bai 2002; Warner 2001).

The power of an original song is something that Steve Jarding, former campaign manager for Sen. Mark Warner's successful 2001 gubernatorial campaign, knows well. Jarding commissioned a campaign song from a supporter and popular bluegrass singer in the Roanoke Valley, Dave Saunders. The folksy song used an old tune with new, pro-Warner, lyrics. "Part of the lyrics suggested that the people in the mountains in Virginia should embrace this guy," said Jarding. "People would play it on radio stations. They would start playing the song as if it were put out by an artist, as opposed to the campaign," he said. "We ran ads with it as our theme music, and we would have people say, 'I can't get that stupid song out of my head!'" (Glass and Phillip 2009).

The Warner campaign's rural outreach in 2001 was not just catchy songs and race cars, though. The campaign also created a "Sportsmen for Warner" organization that plastered distinctive orange yard signs around the state. The campaign touted Mark Warner's pro-gun stance so aggressively that the National Rifle Association decided not to endorse Mark Earley, the Republican candidate in the 2001 race (Bai 2002).

During his four years as governor and beyond, Mark Warner continued to bolster his image as a centrist businessman who could connect with rural voters as he sought to set the stage for his next elective office (Hebel 2005; Peirce 2005). Political observers considered him presidential material, describing him as the next centrist Democratic presidential candidate cut from the Bill Clinton mold (France 2005; Graff 2006; Starobin 2006). In the end, John Warner decided to retire from the US Senate, and Mark Warner turned his sights away from the Iowa Caucus and returned to Virginia to contest another statewide election.

Warner easily won the 2008 Senate election, a dozen years after he first sought that seat. He defeated former governor Jim Gilmore by a nearly two-to-one margin, securing 65% of the vote. Six years later, Warner secured a tougher-than-expected re-election victory over Republican Ed Gillespie in 2014, a tough year for Democratic candidates around the country (Vozzella, Portnoy, and Weiner 2014). The results of the 2014 election demonstrated that Warner's traditional centrist approach failed to have the traction it once did in rural areas of Virginia. That moderate approach also failed to generate all that much excitement with urban and suburban voters (Farnsworth, Hanna, and Hermerding 2014).

During these years, Republicans increased their support in rural areas by emphasizing cultural differences over issues like abortion and guns, thereby reducing the ability of Democratic candidates—even those with a history of doing well with rural voters—to secure all that many votes beyond urban and suburban jurisdictions (Bai 2002; Walsh 2012). In 2020, Mark Warner faced an easier road to re-election, winning 55% of the vote against Republican Daniel Gade, a first-time Senate candidate (Leahy 2020).

Table 2.1 shows the political jurisdictions with the greatest decline in support for Mark Warner between his 2001 and 2020 elections. Overall,

Warner won the 2001 race with 52.16% of the vote and the 2020 race by 56.02% of the vote, a gain of 3.85 percentage points over those nineteen years. Presidential elections have higher turnout than state elections, and Virginia's population has grown substantially over the past twenty years, so the discussion below focuses more on percentages than raw vote totals. Raw vote numbers are not as useful for comparing the very different electorates of these two contests: Warner was elected governor in 2001 with just under a million votes, while he received more than 2.4 million votes in 2020.

Table 2.1. Jurisdictions with Greatest Decline in Support for Warner						
County	Support for Warner 2001		Support for Warner 2020		Change in % of votes cast for Warner	Change in % of votes cast
	Vote	%	Vote	%		
Buchanan	2,522	65.65	3,746	25.90	−39.75	70.63
Russell	3,288	60.36	4,507	24.84	−35.52	77.27
Wise	4,128	58.48	5,509	25.41	−33.06	72.43
Dickenson	2,052	61.03	2,907	28.49	−32.54	51.21
Tazewell	4,504	54.34	5,250	23.03	−31.31	102.43
Lee	2,240	53.30	2,923	22.74	−30.56	79.61
Norton	591	67.57	773	37.33	−30.24	38.37
Bland	732	48.15	835	21.62	−26.54	95.27
Giles	2,713	56.54	3,071	30.06	−26.47	66.15
Craig	757	50.30	918	24.09	−26.22	72.22
Alleghany	2,822	58.97	3,018	35.30	−23.67	56.21
Patrick	2,310	48.35	2,651	25.11	−23.24	67.75
Smyth	3,973	51.38	4,691	28.38	−23.00	53.35
Scott	2,191	42.77	2,877	20.38	−22.39	59.82
Grayson	1,946	46.68	2,507	24.56	−22.12	47.55

Buena Vista City	1,020	58.63	853	37.13	−21.49	88.80
Wythe	4,043	48.57	3,822	27.24	−21.33	88.61
Bath	744	51.77	804	30.57	−21.20	56.73
Appomattox	2,741	51.31	2,268	30.26	−21.05	104.91
Henry	10,616	61.37	9,872	41.32	−20.06	59.74
State of Virginia	*984,177*	*52.16*	*2,467,409*	*56.02*	*3.85*	*133.47*

The jurisdictions with the twenty largest declines, as measured by percentage of the vote cast for Warner, are all rural counties or cities located in rural areas, with many of them located in the southwest corner of Virginia. Of those twenty jurisdictions, fifteen of them provided Warner with at least 50% of the vote in 2001, while Warner received at least 40% of the votes in the other five counties on the 2001 list. In 2020, only one of these twenty jurisdictions provided Warner with at least 40% of the vote, Henry County, which is by far the largest county by population on this list of the twenty largest percentage declines for Warner.

Among these twenty counties and cities listed in table 2.1, Henry cast 10,616 votes (61%) for Warner in 2001—no other jurisdiction on the list cast more than 5,000 votes for Warner that year, though a few had higher percentages of votes cast for the Democratic candidate. Warner's outreach in the years leading up to that election clearly generated significant rural support, as he received some significant margins in some of these jurisdictions. Warner won more than 60% of the vote in 2001 in Norton City and the counties of Henry, Buchanan, Russell, and Dickenson.

Of these twenty jurisdictions, seven of them saw percentage declines in the vote for Warner of greater than 30 points between the two elections. Ranking first in the movement away from Warner, with a 39.75-point decline, is Buchanan County, while Russell County and Wise County ranked second and third. Two other southwest Virginia counties, Dickenson and Tazewell, ranked fourth and fifth.

Table 2.2 lists the top twenty jurisdictions in Virginia that saw the greatest increase in the percentage of the vote cast for Mark Warner between the 2001 and the 2020 elections. The list includes many of the fast-growing suburban communities in Northern Virginia and in the

Richmond area. While many of the largest percentage point gains were found in northern Virginia cities, including Manassas Park, Fairfax, Manassas, and Falls Church, this list of greatest percentage gains for Warner includes some of the state's largest jurisdictions, including the counties of Fairfax, Prince William, Loudoun, Arlington, Henrico, and Chesterfield as well as Richmond City. While Warner also won many of the Hampton Roads jurisdictions, only Newport News City saw a percentage point gain for Warner large enough to place it among the top twenty jurisdictions with the greatest increase in support for the Democratic candidate.

Some of the places that were very pro-Warner in 2001 were notably more so in 2020. In the City of Richmond, for example, Warner won 73% of the vote in 2001 and won 83% of the vote in 2020. Voters in the City of Charlottesville cast nearly 73% of their ballots for Warner in 2001, increasing to 85.76% support for Warner in 2020.

Table 2.2. Jurisdictions with Greatest Increase in Support for Warner					
County	Support for Warner 2001		Support for Warner 2020		Change in % of votes cast for Warner	Change in % of votes cast
	Vote	%	Vote	%		
Manassas Park (City)	691	46.25	4,084	67.86	21.61	302.81
Harrisonburg (City)	3,083	47.67	11,116	66.30	18.63	159.23
Prince William	27,792	46.79	144,162	64.24	17.45	284.65
Fairfax (City)	3,478	51.73	9,179	68.88	17.15	98.20
Manassas City	2,992	45.73	10,547	62.82	17.10	156.58
Loudoun	20,907	45.84	137,814	61.80	15.97	388.90
Fairfax	146,537	54.47	415,791	69.89	15.42	121.15
Falls Church (City)	2,623	65.82	7,016	79.95	14.12	120.23
Henrico	42,089	51.39	117,119	65.07	13.68	119.75

Charlottes-ville (City)	6,781	72.87	20,672	85.76	12.89	159.03
Williamsburg (City)	1,475	57.48	4,811	70.33	12.84	166.60
Chesterfield	33,810	41.95	107,568	53.67	11.72	148.67
Danville (City)	7,346	53.50	12,519	65.16	11.66	39.93
Alexandria (City)	23,739	68.21	65,071	79.37	11.16	135.56
Arlington	35,990	68.27	102,880	79.37	11.10	145.88
Albemarle	14,891	56.35	42,730	67.31	10.96	140.22
Newport News (City)	21,318	56.97	53,265	67.61	10.64	110.54
Hopewell (City)	2,467	49.40	5,695	59.64	10.24	91.21
Richmond (City)	35,558	73.26	91,222	83.27	10.01	125.71
Emporia (City)	912	59.41	1,618	69.38	9.97	51.92
State of Virginia	*984,177*	*52.16*	*2,467,409*	*56.02*	*3.85*	*133.47*

Comparing these two tables demonstrates the limited value that rural Republican votes have for a Democratic candidate in a statewide contest taking place in 2020. Losing 30 percentage points of support in rural counties between 2001 and 2020 may not be desirable for a candidate, but the impact is minimized when those percentage declines are occurring in jurisdictions where at most 25,000 votes are cast. Had those rural counties at the top of table 2.1 continued to support Warner in 2020 by the percentage they had supported him in 2001, each of those counties would have contributed no more than several thousand additional votes to Warner's statewide total. In other words, those "lost" Democratic votes (so to speak) between 2001 and 2020 in these rural counties are not all that significant when compared to the huge percentage gains Warner

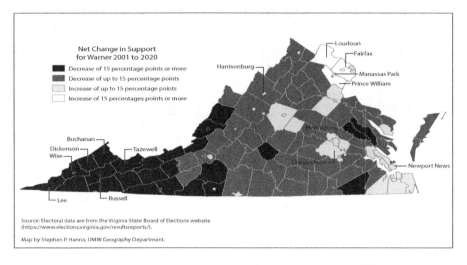

Figure 2.1. Net change in support for Warner 2001 to 2020

secured in the electorates of Fairfax, Loudoun, or Prince William over that same time period.

Figure 2.1 allows us to take a larger perspective of the gains and losses statewide for Warner when comparing the 2001 and the 2020 elections. In this illustration, the darkest counties are those where Warner lost the greatest percent of votes over that nineteen-year period. Warner's gains are shaded lighter, with Warner's greatest percentage gains colored white. This illustration does not mark which candidate won a given jurisdiction, rather the colors illustrate percentage gains and losses between those two election years.

As expected from the previous tables, Warner's support fell by the greatest percentages in southwest Virginia, with his greatest gains in the state's urban and suburban areas. Along the I-95 corridor, where there has been particularly strong population and economic growth, Warner fared particularly well. He gained in urban and suburban areas near Washington, DC, and Richmond, as well as in the fast-growing Fredericksburg region, which includes Stafford and Spotsylvania Counties. Warner also registered some of his stronger gains in the Hampton Roads area, in the Charlottesville-Albemarle area, and some of the individual independent cities in more conservative parts of the state, including Winchester and Harrisonburg along the I-81 corridor, which connects Republican counties along the western edges of the Commonwealth.

Of course, a traditional election map like figure 2.1 illustrates jurisdictions by physical size, not by population. As such, compact places

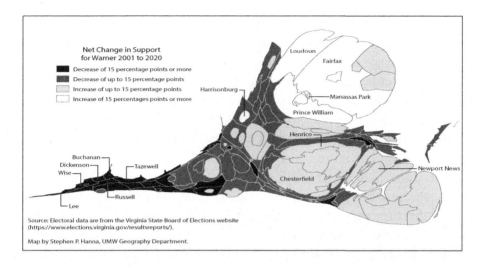

Figure 2.2. Net change in support for Warner 2001 to 2020, jurisdictions sized by population

like Arlington County are barely visible compared to large counties like nearby Fauquier, which has a notably smaller population. To compensate for the fact that physical size may be misleading when talking about electoral influence, social scientists often employ a cartogram, which resizes political jurisdictions by the number of votes cast. This allows one to see an electorate as it really exists (Hanna and Farnsworth 2013). After all, people vote, acres do not. Cartograms are commonly employed, for example, in maps of the Electoral College, where the most populous states, like California, expand, and the most rural states, like Wyoming or Alaska, shrink in accordance with the relatively few electoral votes allocated to states with small populations.

Figure 2.2 employs this same cartogram technique for political jurisdictions in Virginia, adjusting the acreage-based image in figure 2.1 to account for population. We use the same color coding for both illustrations: the darker counties are where Warner lost the greater percentage of votes, and the lighter ones are where he gained the greatest percentage of votes. The result looks like a pair of scissors, where the more populated counties and cities of the I-95 and I-64 corridors expand to take account of the larger numbers of votes cast in that part of the Commonwealth. Nearly all of the counties where Warner lost the most ground, marked in black, shrink in response to the relatively small number of votes cast there.

For Democratic statewide candidates in Virginia looking at the Commonwealth's electorate, the implications are clear: the first rule of electoral politics is to pay attention to where the votes are. That means focusing on the most populous areas, of course, but it also means focusing on those areas where one's prospects of connecting with persuadable voters are greatest. The more rural jurisdictions are not particularly compelling campaign venues for Democratic candidates given the fact that so many rural jurisdictions turned away from Warner, one of the more moderate Democratic candidates to win statewide office over the past two decades. As such, rural interests are not likely to obtain the attention or the focus today that they previously received from Democratic candidates. Democrats instead are more likely to focus on connecting with and addressing the needs of newer citizens in the rapidly diversifying suburbs, where their prospects are brighter (Olivo 2018, 2019, 2021). Given these political incentives for Democratic candidates running statewide in Virginia, the urban-rural divide seems more likely to widen than to narrow in the years ahead.

Discussion

The fact that rural Virginia, and rural America, is turning redder, and suburban Virginia, and suburban America, is turning bluer is not a new story. Indeed, in recent years many elected officials of both parties, including former president Trump, sought to intensify those existing geographical cleavages and convert them to electoral advantage (Dionne, Ornstein, and Mann 2017; Farnsworth 2018).

What is going on in Virginia, a state with a population that has been growing at a rate faster than the national average, represents a particular challenge for the retention of rural influence. The fact that the statewide electorate here is rapidly becoming increasingly Democratic (Republicans lost every statewide election between their victories in 2009 and 2021) makes the challenge doubly difficult for rural interests.

In the short term, rural Virginians who are seeing centuries of political dominance evaporate have turned to gerrymandered legislative districts as a key means of maximizing Republican influence (Farnsworth 2002a, 2002b). Given that the rural areas of the state nearly always elect Republicans to the legislature, those rural lawmakers end up with great influence when Republicans control the Virginia House of Delegates or the Senate of Virginia (Farnsworth 2002a, 2002b). When Democratic majorities rule Richmond, the pro-Republican voting patterns of rural areas leave them with few seats at the table, and far less influence.

Sometimes circumstances can work out to the benefit of rural areas, even though few Democratic officials are elected outside of districts dominated by urban and suburban voters. The Medicaid expansion debate in Virginia is an example of how this process can play out in policymaking. Rural areas were among the parts of Virginia with the highest levels of uninsured people in the years after the adoption of the Affordable Care Act. Hospitals doing business in rural Virginia were also facing financial pressures because of the high levels of uncompensated care they needed to provide in their communities. So even though Medicaid expansion would help rural voters and rural healthcare systems avoid bankruptcy over unpaid healthcare bills, most Republican-elected officials dared not face the wrath of partisan electorates critical of a Democratic president's healthcare initiative (Farnsworth 2015b). Medicaid expansion passed eventually, as Democratic lawmakers and a few Republicans who voted with them, delivered additional healthcare support to rural areas as part of a statewide policy change that would also benefit poor voters in urban areas (Farnsworth and Engel 2018).

The current conservative political environment of skepticism if not hostility to the federal government is a longtime Republican political message that can connect with many rural voters (Gingrich 1995). Research demonstrates that an antifederal government view has taken root in both national and Virginia public opinion (Farnsworth 2015a; Hood, Kidd, and Morris 2015). Unfortunately for Virginia Republicans and for the rural elected officials who are a key part of the party's caucus in Richmond, the small government message that works so well in more conservative parts of the Commonwealth puts a low ceiling on support for the party in the Washington suburbs, which contain large numbers of people working for the federal government or for federal government contractors.

So what, then, can rural Virginians do to increase their influence in this increasingly less favorable political environment? Well, one has to start with the observation that rural interests are unlikely to ever dominate state politics in the way they have over nearly all of the Commonwealth's first two and a half centuries. There are now simply too many suburban and urban voters with different priorities, and who recognize the ever-increasing influence of their regions in Virginia politics, to allow rural interests to turn back the clock. As shown in the above tables and figures, the Commonwealth is unlikely to restore a county courthouse–based statewide political organization that told urban and suburban areas how things were going to work in the Old Dominion.

Majority power brings great influence. Without the votes, little influence exists. That political reality has long worked to the advantage of Virginia's rural interests, but it no longer does so.

Gerrymandering, a traditional mechanism that could help rural areas by packing urban voters into overwhelmingly pro-Democratic districts, also is likely to be of less use to conservatives in the future than it has in the past. The continuing population growth of urban and suburban areas means that rural areas will lose additional legislative seats in the 2021 redistricting cycle, the latest in a long line of districts that have migrated eastward and northward in Virginia over recent decades (Farnsworth and Hanna 2018b). In addition, in 2020 Virginia voters approved a constitutional amendment designed to reduce the ability of elected officials to shape the legislative maps for partisan advantage (Barakat 2021). For these reasons, the reconfiguration of the legislature in 2021 and in the years ahead is unlikely to provide disproportionate advantage to rural interests.

These days, few Democratic candidates succeed in rural areas of Virginia, though some individuals can be convinced to run in regional contests in districts that favor Republicans (Grim and Gray 2018; Schneider 2018a). Unfortunately for rural interests, electoral defeats do not endear a region to the partisan power brokers who gain their majorities elsewhere. As long as rural voters reject Democratic candidates, and as long as Virginia as a whole elects Democratic governors and Democratic legislative majorities, the prospects are not great for rural interests to secure much influence in policymaking. There are significant partisan divisions these days, and those divisions work against the dominant party paying much attention to the interests of the voices who are not part of the majority party. The Democratic majority caucus elected to the House of Delegates in 2019 was more liberal any Democratic caucus in Virginia's history. It was also less dependent on rural votes than ever before. Those trends are not good news for rural interests whenever Republicans are in the minority.

Compromise is, of course, a potential response. The ability of some rural lawmakers to compromise with lawmakers from more populated areas over Medicaid expansion is a sign that rural interests can sometimes prevail even as conservative voices lose influence in Virginia. Similarly, the economic and healthcare crisis created by COVID-19 also offer opportunities for compromise. Environmental issues, like healthcare matters, might also lend themselves to compromises that can benefit rural areas as well as less rural places. Programs that help farming families to stay in farming across generations could both help keep rural areas vibrant and retain Virginia's vibrant tourism economy, for example.

Of course, such efforts at bipartisan compromise may be difficult in times of strong ideological divisions. That takes us to perhaps the best scenario for a revived political influence for rural Virginia, a revived Republican Party. If the Republican Party can secure a majority in both chambers of the legislature in the coming years, that political development would generate significant influence for rural lawmakers. Rural lawmakers are a key part of the Republican coalition and with a future Republican majority would come committee chairmanships, leadership positions, and other opportunities for rural interests to be more prominent in policymaking. That, of course, would require a Republican Party able to compete more effectively in those suburban areas where they have lost seats in recent years. It would require a more inclusive message than that offered by the party that has been losing ground in the suburbs for more than a decade and has also failed to win a statewide election during that same time frame. Fortunately for the future of real political influence, Virginia politics can be very fluid, and so such modifications of Republican messaging to woo the suburbs may be an appealing path forward. No party wants to stay in the minority forever, after all. Doing better in the suburbs is the Republican Party's best chance for majority status and revived influence for the rural lawmakers within the party caucus.

Thanks to the Center for Leadership and Media Studies at the University of Mary Washington for financial assistance and the editors for their helpful suggestions. All errors remain the authors' responsibility.

Chapter 3

State Policy to Bridge Economic Development Divides

Stephen Moret

This chapter describes how state leaders in Virginia are working to position every region of the Commonwealth for growth. The author describes the rural-urban economic divide and its underpinnings in the US, as well as details state-level efforts being pursued in Virginia to help position smaller metros and rural regions for employment growth. It concludes with a brief discussion of emerging challenges associated with economic recovery from the COVID-19 pandemic.

With stagnant or declining employment and population, many rural communities across the United States—like their counterparts across the Commonwealth of Virginia—have been struggling with a lack of economic opportunity (Porter 2018; Swenson 2019), persistent outmigration of talent (Swenson 2019), hospital closures (Saslow 2019), school closures (Bosman 2018), aging populations (Van Dam 2019), and a devastating opioid crisis (Macy 2018), among other challenges. Success stories are few and far between (Krugman 2019). Indeed, the shared challenges rural communities face are so great that some have suggested the very notion of healthy economic growth in many, if not most, rural areas is basically a lost cause (Krugman 2019; Swenson 2019; see also Porter 2018).

Despite the economic headwinds facing rural communities across the country, state leaders in Virginia have adopted an ambitious goal to position every region of the Commonwealth for growth. This chapter describes the rural-urban economic divide and its underpinnings in the US, as well as details state-level efforts being pursued in Virginia to help position smaller metros and rural regions for employment growth. The chapter ends with a section highlighting emerging challenges associated with economic recovery from the COVID-19 pandemic.

AMERICA'S RURAL-URBAN ECONOMIC DIVIDE: NATIONAL CONTEXT

The growing economic divides among rural localities, cities, and metro areas span many forms of measurement, including but not limited to growth (or decline) in jobs, population, and earnings. These divides largely are the result of massive economic shifts that have occurred over the last several decades—shifts that have continued and strengthened with the passage of time. The central driver of these shifts has been the economic triumph of cities and the metro areas in which they are situated, as cities and their metros have been well positioned to benefit from industry sector changes, globalization, immigration, and technology in ways that nonmetro rural localities simply have not.

The Brookings Institution recently published a troubling analysis highlighting an expanding economic divide between metro areas (especially large ones) and rural areas in the US, as large metro areas have enjoyed considerably faster growth than smaller metros and rural localities, as illustrated in figure 3.1 (Arnosti and Liu 2018).

In general, rural, nonmetro areas face substantially worse economic, education, and health outcomes than their urban and metro counterparts. For example, in rural (nonmetro) areas, poverty, unemployment, and food insecurity rates tend to be substantially higher while educational attainment levels tend to be substantially lower than in urban (metro) areas (Community Strategies Group 2019). Health insurance coverage rates are lower in rural areas than urban areas (Day 2019). Labor force participation rates are substantially lower in nonmetro areas than in metro areas, even for prime-working-age cohorts (Economic Research Service 2019). In the wake of declining economic prospects and spiraling opioid abuse, the violent crime rate in rural communities recently rose above the national average (Greenblatt 2018). Even highly educated workers face economic challenges in rural areas, as the college earnings premium tends to be much higher in metro areas than in rural, nonmetro areas (Moret 2016).

For many years, corporate executives in the US have favored cities and metro areas for most new economic development projects. For example, the Virginia Economic Development Partnership (VEDP), which is the state economic development authority for the Commonwealth of Virginia, recently performed an analysis of a comprehensive national announcements database, which revealed that, in the four years through FY18 (the latest time period VEDP analyzed), 76% of rural localities in the United States (using the US Census definition of rural localities) did not secure a single new economic development project in any of those four years, excluding expansions of existing establishments (S. Hartka, personal communication, 27 January 2021). Additionally, the same analysis indicated that, in a typical year, more than 90% of rural localities in the US did not secure a single new economic development project (S. Hartka, personal communication, 27 January 2021). Such areas represent the bulk of Virginia's geography—and that of the US overall—and they often are desperate for more economic development. Additionally, over the decade through 2018, site consultants increasingly have favored

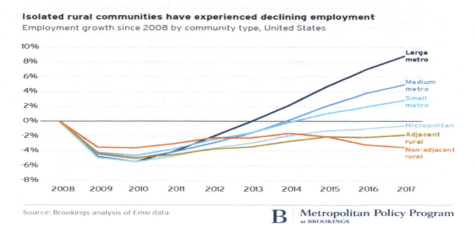

Figure 3.1. Employment growth since 2008 by community type, United States

proximity to major markets (i.e., larger metro areas), as that particular criterion increased from the eighth most important site-selection factor in 2008 to tied for most important in 2018 (Gambale 2009, 2019). Indeed, the two additional factors tied for most important in 2018—availability of skilled labor and highway accessibility—also tend to favor metro areas, especially large ones. While rural leaders in many states often feel left behind by state leaders (Community Strategies Group 2019), the reality is that there are simply far more rural localities in need of new employment opportunities than there are companies with economic development projects willing to consider rural localities—especially those located in regions with a small labor force.

While the real rural-urban economic divides are stark, quirks of metro area classification make the growth rates of rural localities seem worse than they really have been over time (Van Dam 2019). The reason is that, as many rural localities have grown and become more densely populated over time, they have been (appropriately) reclassified as part of a metropolitan area, meaning they no longer are included in analyses of rural locality growth rates (Van Dam 2019). Van Dam (2019) illustrated this phenomenon, stating that:

> According to the United States' original 1950 urban classifications, rural America is crushing it. It's home to about as many people as urban America, and it's growing faster. So why do headlines and statistics paint rural areas as perpetually in decline?
>
> Because the contest between rural and urban America is rigged. Official definitions are regularly updated in such a way that rural counties are continually losing their most successful places to urbanization. When a rural county grows, it transmutes into an urban one.
>
> In a way, rural areas serve as urban America's farm team: All their most promising prospects get called up to the big leagues, leaving the low-density margins populated by an ever-shrinking pool of those who couldn't qualify. (paras. 1–3)

Over the long arc of time (i.e., decades), one might consider that an often-missed problem facing rural America (and rural Virginia) is that its challenges look worse because of its successes, as high-growth rural localities eventually lose their rural classification, making the remaining rural localities look worse by comparison.

In the midst of a worrying national context for rural communities, state, regional, and local leaders in Virginia have embraced a relatively radical goal—to position every region of the Commonwealth for economic growth. To achieve that ambitious objective, rural development leaders and stakeholders across Virginia collaborated to craft a set of high-impact initiatives that are now being at least partially implemented, such as rural broadband deployment, world-class custom workforce solutions, and development-ready sites.

THE CASE FOR A REGIONAL APPROACH

Since a strong majority of US localities do not experience any project wins in a typical year, regular success at the local level would require a vastly greater (and unprecedented) economic development effort in any state. In contrast, the vast majority of Virginia's regions already experience one or more project wins each year. Further, based on employment forecasts by Moody's Analytics, virtually all Virginia regions could be positioned for net growth with no more than a few hundred additional jobs on average each year—an addressable gap for VEDP and its partners. When every region adds employment, workers in every locality will benefit from regional job opportunities within a reasonable commuting distance. VEDP's regional approach is reinforced by region-led efforts (e.g., marketing efforts of regional economic development organizations) and state-level initiatives focused on regions (e.g., many grant and/or service programs focus on regions, such as state-funded growth and diversification plans through GO Virginia and its associated investments in sites, workforce, and cluster scale up and entrepreneurial ecosystems) in Virginia and has been embraced as one of five transformational goals for economic development in the Commonwealth of Virginia ("Every region wins") (Virginia Economic Development Partnership 2017).

The importance of positioning each region of Virginia (or any state) for at least a little growth each year is reinforced by recognizing the implications of not doing so. All across the country, regions that have experienced even small, but sustained, annual declines in employment and population have tended to lose critical anchor institutions over time, such as hospitals (Saslow 2019) and grocery stores (Simpson 2019), while having to close or consolidate public schools (Bosman 2018). As these institutions close or consolidate, rural areas become less attractive for remaining residents as well as for potential new residents. Even a small amount of growth each year would go a long way toward enabling these critical institutions to remain open, sustaining rural communities for growth opportunities not currently envisioned that could emerge in the future.

STATE-LEVEL RURAL DEVELOPMENT INITIATIVES IN VIRGINIA

In 2017, VEDP collaborated with hundreds of local, regional, and state partners to craft the first comprehensive Strategic Plan for Economic Development of the Commonwealth of Virginia. The Strategic Plan put forth five transformational goals for Virginia and VEDP, including a relatively radical goal to enable each region of Virginia to experience growth in employment and median earned income (VEDP 2017). In practice, such a goal would mean positioning smaller metro areas and rural regions for growth, since the large metro areas representing the bulk of Virginia's so-called urban crescent (i.e., the Northern Virginia localities included in the Washington, DC, metropolitan area, the Greater Richmond MSA, and the Virginia Beach–Norfolk-Newport News MSA) already were expected to experience relatively consistent, if not always impressive, growth. To formalize this transformational goal, VEDP now measures its success based not just on the amount of jobs and capital investment it helps secure but also on how many of Virginia's regions experience employment growth each year.

Faced with many years of stagnant or negative growth in much of rural Virginia, economic conditions recently exacerbated by the decline of coal and natural gas extraction activity in southwest Virginia (and previously exacerbated by sharp declines in the textiles, tobacco, and furniture sectors in southern Virginia and beyond), rural development stakeholders in Virginia formed a "Rural Think Tank" group in 2017 to collaboratively identify, prioritize, and advocate for the top things Virginia could do (that it wasn't already doing) to position the Commonwealth's smaller metros and rural regions for growth.

Members of the group were encouraged that each small metro area and rural region in Virginia needs just 100–300 additional jobs annually above forecasts to position every region of the Commonwealth for sustained employment growth. That meant (and means) that rural growth in Virginia is an achievable, albeit difficult, goal. After evaluating current and past rural development initiatives as well as exploring what other states and communities have done, the think tank group prioritized several high-impact, interdependent initiatives. The group's top priority initiatives, ranked in order, appear below (note there has been a tie for the top priority).

1. Ubiquitous broadband access: Leverage public-private partnerships and/or state and local incentives to achieve ubiquitous broadband coverage in Virginia within five to seven years.
2. Rural marketing initiative: Brand rural Virginia as the most attractive, most competitive location in the US for manufacturing and other sectors (e.g., business process outsourcing, data centers, distribution) open to rural locations.
3. Expanded [business-ready] sites inventory: Dramatically expand competitive site inventory, ranging from mega sites to business parks, depending on the regional strategy.
4. Customized workforce program: Create a world-class, turnkey, customized workforce development incentive program for competitive economic development projects to build confidence that a high-quality, trained workforce can be secured.
5. Partnerships to fund transformational projects: Partner with the Tobacco Commission, the Virginia Coalfield Economic Development Authority, and other economic development funding sources in rural Virginia to target and attract high-impact projects to rural Virginia communities through private capital investment partnership opportunities.
6. Tax/incentive changes: Encourage state and local leaders to work together in a bipartisan fashion to make state and/or local tax changes to ensure that Virginia's tax burden rankings for new, job-creating investments (either

expansions of existing firms or new firms) are no worse than those for existing firms.
7. Community competitiveness support: Bring back some form of a community competitiveness/readiness index.
8. Civic leadership cultivation: Rebuild civic leadership with the next generation in rural Virginia.

From late 2017 through late 2020, these top priorities and their order have remained unchanged through many meetings of the Rural Think Tank group. Thanks to the support of Virginia's executive and legislative branch leaders, substantial progress is being made on several of these initiatives, as detailed below.

Ubiquitous Broadband Access (tied for priority initiative no. 1)

In Virginia, as in other states across America, there is a large gap between broadband access levels in urban and rural communities (Perrin 2019). In recent years, state leaders in Virginia have embraced near-ubiquitous rural broadband access as a top priority, recognizing that it is as essential to the full development of rural communities in the twenty-first century as electricity or telephone access was in the twentieth century. Indeed, broadband access is not just about economic development—it is also essential for education (Coleman 2019; Fishbane and Tomer 2019; Vogels et al. 2020), healthcare (Rheuban 2019), social connectivity (Fishbane and Tomer 2019), and agriculture (Scott and Shaw 2020), among other domains.

A recent study found that access to broadband throughout Virginia could empower growth in rural and small businesses, which would add as much as $1.3 billion to gross state product and create more than 9,400 new jobs, resulting in around $452.4 million in new annual wages (Technology Engagement Center 2019). Such an infusion in economic activity would result in tens of millions of dollars in new annual state income tax revenues.

The impact of near-ubiquitous broadband access on the agricultural economy in Virginia promises to be even greater. A recent study found that full deployment of connected agriculture technologies could increase agricultural output by 18% (US Department of Agriculture 2019), which in Virginia would mean the agriculture sector, currently generating $70 billion in economic activity, could grow by $12.6 billion, potentially yielding tens of millions more in new annual state tax revenues.

Households and local budgets may also see significant gains from expanding broadband access, considering estimates suggesting that property values are higher for rural homes that have broadband access (Whitacre and Deller 2019).

In pursuit of expanding broadband access, the Commonwealth created the Commonwealth Connect initiative, with an interagency effort coordinated by a chief broadband advisor in the governor's office, directing policy changes, supporting local and regional planning efforts, and making capital grants to public/private partnerships to make the construction and operation of broadband infrastructure profitable in less-dense regions.

In recent years, state investments in rural broadband access in Virginia have grown exponentially, and rural broadband deployment is accelerating. Since 2017, Virginia's annual public investments in broadband grants have grown from $1 million per year to over $80 million in 2020 alone. While the results of that $80 million can't be perfectly projected, the Commonwealth's previous deployment of $44 million led to the connection of over 108,000 homes and businesses. Further, in 2021, Virginia allocated $700 million from the American Rescue Plan Act to the Commonwealth's broadband program, accelerating the timeline for universal coverage to 2024. It is highly likely that, under the next Governor, Virginia will be the first large state, or at least among the first large states, to close its rural/urban digital divide.

Rural Marketing Initiative (tied for priority initiative no. 1)

As previously noted, there are many more rural communities seeking quality economic development opportunities than there are good economic development projects open to locating in such areas. Virginia's rural communities were doubly challenged in competing for economic development projects a few years ago, as Virginia was one of the only states in America without a marketing budget for economic development, other than for tourism. State leaders have now embraced a goal to brand and expand national awareness of what is already true of rural Virginia: it is a highly compelling business investment destination and one of the most attractive and competitive locations in the US for manufacturing and other sectors interested in rural locations (e.g., business process outsourcing, data centers, distribution facilities, and onshore IT delivery centers). With a wide array of stunning landscapes, impressive outdoor recreation assets, and world-class employers, as well as some of America's best public schools and thriving downtowns, rural Virginia has a strong foundation to build upon. Funding is now being provided for targeted marketing initiatives to help ensure corporate executives and top site-selection consultants across the US—and in key markets around the world—are aware of these distinctive assets in Virginia's predominantly rural regions.

VEDP's marketing efforts place a special emphasis on rural communities and smaller metro areas. For example, more than half of the partner mentions on VEDP's Twitter account over the past two years were of a rural locality or region. These and other social media efforts highlight regional assets, key companies, project announcements, available properties, executive quotes, company case studies, education and workforce development programs, and more. Each issue of Virginia Economic Review (VEDP's quarterly publication sent to thousands of executives and site-selection consultants across the country) provides an inside look at Virginia's economy, its diverse array of world-class companies, its amazing talent, and its stunning natural beauty, as well as insights from national thought leaders. Rural content is integrated into each issue of the publication, and the Q3 2019 issue was dedicated to Virginia's rural advantages and opportunities. VEDP also coordinates a variety of inbound site consultant and media familiarization tours with regional partners each year, many of which are conducted in predominantly rural regions.

Thanks in large part to national marketing and lead generation efforts launched since 2018, Virginia's position in state business climate rankings, based on perceptions of corporate executives and/or site-selection consultants, has improved, and the number of VEDP-generated leads each year has roughly doubled. That has resulted in more opportunities for rural areas and smaller metros to compete for economic development projects. Nevertheless, with a total state marketing budget much smaller than those of top competing states, Virginia's smaller communities still struggle to stand out in the competitive economic development landscape.

Expanded Business-ready Sites Inventory (priority initiative no. 3)

In recent years, the lack of a prepared site was one of the most common reasons that rural Virginia communities missed out on high-impact advanced manufacturing and distribution projects. Analysis of competitive project losses by VEDP indicated that billions of dollars in new capital investment and many thousands of new jobs were lost over the last few years primarily due to a lack of prepared sites.

In 2019 and 2020, with $2 million in funding from the Virginia General Assembly, VEDP collaborated with more than 100 local partners and three engineering firms to characterize every identified development site in Virginia of twenty-five acres or larger (466 sites in total), enabling the state and its local partners to understand the preparedness level of each site, as well as the investments necessary to make them competitive as locations for quality economic development projects. Moreover, the state has begun investing to help prepare these sites through the GO Virginia grant program, the Tobacco Region Revitalization Commission (a regional economic development agency), and the Virginia Business-Ready Sites Program managed by VEDP. Each of these grant programs provide matching state funds to prepare identified development sites to be competitive.

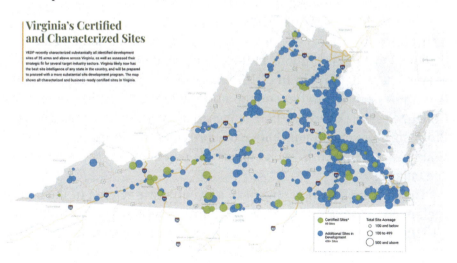

Figure 3.2. Virginia's certified and characterized sites (VEDP 2020)

A fully funded site development program for Virginia would require roughly $20–30 million annually plus matching funds from localities. The return on investment would be substantial: thousands of additional jobs and billions in additional capital investment each year that would be secured with a more competitive portfolio of prepared sites in place. More specifically, VEDP has estimated a robust site development program as described here would result in approximately 28,000 to 49,000 additional direct jobs in manufacturing and supply chain projects over a decade, which collectively would yield roughly $128–272 million per year in new state general fund revenues. Most of these wins would occur in and/or directly benefit Virginia's rural regions and localities.

Custom Workforce Program (priority initiative no. 4)

One of the biggest obstacles to attracting economic development projects to smaller metros and rural regions is the concern many executives have about being able to attract a qualified, well-trained workforce in those smaller labor markets. States like Georgia and Louisiana have addressed this challenge, in part, by offering world-class customized workforce recruitment and training programs (e.g., the Georgia Quick Start program and the FastStart program in Louisiana).

Prior to 2019, Virginia lacked a turnkey, custom workforce recruitment and training incentive program, even as it boasted some of the best higher education institutions in the country and the highest educational attainment in the South. In 2019, with support from the governor and General Assembly, and in collaboration with the Virginia Community College System (VCCS), VEDP launched the Virginia Talent Accelerator Program, a job-creation incentive that provides training and recruitment solutions customized to each company's unique processes, equipment, and culture.

Building on the appointment of a twenty-year veteran of the highly acclaimed Georgia Quick Start program, as SVP of Talent Solutions, VEDP assembled one of the best custom workforce teams in America. The leadership team of the Virginia Talent Accelerator Program includes highly experienced functional leaders with expertise in talent acquisition, video services, visualization services (e.g., graphics, animation), instructional design, learning technologies, manufacturing technologies, and organizational development. As 2020 ended, the full team totaled about twenty talented professionals. This team delivers comprehensive workforce solutions, including recruitment and screening of talent, as well as development and delivery of customized onboarding and training programs.

The Virginia Talent Accelerator Program team's work received rave reviews on their initial projects. For example, the head of R&D for the Americas of GSK, a leading global pharmaceutical company, said, "the [Virginia Talent Accelerator Program] team on the ground is absolutely top notch." Executives of Morgan Olson, a leading producer of delivery vans, were amazed by the comprehensiveness, quality, and speed of the team's work, which helped the company launch production faster and with much lower turnover than expected for their new 700-job delivery van assembly facility in rural Pittsylvania County.

VEDP is well on the way toward reaching its ultimate goal of having the best custom workforce program in America by 2023. In less than two years from its launch, the Virginia Talent Accelerator Program has already helped Virginia advance in both national rankings of top workforce development programs, moving from number 7 to number 4 in area development and from number 7 to number 3 in business facilities. With one of America's best custom workforce programs, Virginia will be able to secure more significant economic development wins—particularly in smaller metros and rural areas.

Partnerships to Fund Transformational Economic Development Projects (priority initiative no. 5)

Recognizing the unique challenges facing smaller metros and rural communities, state executive and legislative leaders recently prioritized special initiatives to secure high-impact, quality economic development projects. For example, VEDP is collaborating with its state, regional, and local partners to implement a rural and small metro technology centers initiative that is working to attract top tech companies interested in locating domestic software development and tech services operations in lower-cost markets outside of big cities. Through this new initiative, the Commonwealth is leveraging a statewide investment in computer science education of up to $1.1 billion through the Tech Talent Investment Program (TTIP) to more than double the production of computer science degrees—a historic investment in tech talent that was the result of Virginia's novel (and successful) bid for the Amazon HQ2 project. Much attention has been given to Virginia Tech's new Innovation Campus in Northern Virginia, but most of the Commonwealth's new computer science investments being funded by the TTIP will occur in other smaller communities in Virginia, such as Blacksburg (Virginia Tech), Charlottesville (University of Virginia), Harrisonburg (James Madison University), Petersburg (Virginia State University), Radford (Radford University), and Williamsburg (The College of William & Mary), as well as other smaller communities that host a community college, enabling big increases in the tech-talent pipeline inside or nearby nearly every smaller metro and rural region of Virginia. GO Virginia has also funded a variety of grants across Virginia to improve site preparedness and build workforce pipelines, investments that help position participating regions for success in securing major economic development projects.

Additionally, through VEDP-initiated custom programs, Virginia committed $2.5 million in new higher education programs at Blue Ridge Community College and James Madison University to secure a $1 billion Merck investment in Rockingham County that will create 100 high-quality jobs. Many other manufacturers in the area will benefit from those new higher education programs. With VEDP assistance and a custom performance grant, the Commonwealth also collaborated with local partners to secure a $400 million expansion of the largest Volvo Group plant in the world, which will result in 777 new advanced manufacturing jobs in Pulaski County.

Targeted Tax/Incentive Changes (priority initiative no. 6)

A competitive analysis performed by McKinsey & Company indicates that Virginia typically offers considerably smaller incentive packages than do competing states, such as Georgia, North Carolina, South Carolina, Tennessee, and West Virginia (Buescher and Duvall 2018). Further, combined state-and-local tax burdens in Virginia for new or expanding businesses often are higher than in most other states (Tax Foundation 2015), largely because many competing states offer by-right tax exemptions or credits to encourage new job creation and/or capital investment. While tax and incentive considerations usually are not the most important site-selection factors used by companies to select investment locations

(Gambale 2019), they often play a material role once a firm has narrowed down its list of candidate sites to those in a small number of states with otherwise comparable location advantages. Sometimes states will even be eliminated early in the site-selection process due to uncompetitive state/local tax burdens for a particular project type, meaning a customized, project-specific solution to address a particular tax competitiveness issue (e.g., relatively high local property taxes on machinery and tools) won't ever be considered by the prospect.

VEDP has identified a number of targeted initiatives to address Virginia's tax and incentive competitiveness challenges, such as property tax changes to attract capital-intensive manufacturing projects that often consider locating in rural communities, as well as job creation payroll rebates to encourage projects to locate in economically distressed areas. Additionally, VEDP and its partners have suggested that state and local leaders encourage the formation of start-up firms by delaying the imposition of locally imposed taxes, including Business, Professional, and Occupational License (BPOL) and machinery-and-tools (M&T) taxes in the first three years, as well as reducing the state/local regulatory burden during that time frame.

To date, VEDP and Virginia's Major Employment and Investment Project Approval Commission (MEI Commission), consisting of Administration and General Assembly leaders, have collaborated to offer competitive incentive packages for very large economic development projects. However, little progress has been made to date on Virginia's tax and incentive competitiveness for more typical economic development projects (i.e., the more than 95% of project opportunities that aren't big enough to qualify for MEI consideration), and there has not been an appetite in Virginia to tackle business tax reform that would address some of Virginia's long-standing weaknesses. Virginia economic development veteran Liz Povar has emphasized the importance of proactively involving local leaders in discussions about potential tax changes that would impact local revenue sources, noting, "Engaging local elected leadership in these discussions is important to help them understand the overall impact to business expansion and attraction, and to be able to identify solutions that reduce the perceived (and sometimes real) fear of revenue loss" (personal communication, 7 February 2021).

Community Competitiveness Support (priority initiative no. 7)

A major challenge facing rural communities in need of economic growth is that they often lack the resources necessary to adequately fund and staff their economic development efforts. Indeed, many rural localities in Virginia do not have a single full-time staff member focused on economic development. Many years ago, Virginia had a certified-communities program that helped communities understand how to position themselves to attract more economic development projects. Members of the Rural Think Tank envisioned an opportunity for VEDP to bring back some form of a community competitiveness initiative or economic development readiness index. In response, VEDP crafted a Local and Regional Competitiveness Initiative (LRCI) to assist local and regional partners working to be better prepared for economic development success.

VEDP launched the LRCI in January 2020 with a self-assessment tool sent to all local and regional economic development organizations in Virginia. The content in the self-assessment tool was developed by VEDP's Economic Competitiveness division following a thorough review of economic development best practices and discussions with subject matter experts. The self-assessment was divided into two major categories.

The first category considers organizational capacity characteristics of each economic development office, such as budgets, staffing levels, and professional development. The second category encompasses the geographic and economic diversity of the state by looking at the distinct goals of each locality, along with the strategies and resources they employ to achieve those goals. This information will help VEDP and its partners to better understand regional and statewide trends regarding economic development organizations.

The results of this self-assessment exercise have been incorporated into a report shared with each Virginia economic development organization that participated. The reports were individualized for each respondent and showed how each locality scored compared to a set of peer localities. The report also contained detailed information on each of the organization and strategy indicators in the self-assessment. The best-practice descriptions of the indicators provided localities a path forward for those that want to improve their programs, highlighted resources that provide further information or financial support, and gave localities talking points on why a strategy or organizational component is critical for the community. Ultimately, VEDP hopes that these digestible, comprehensive reports will act as a reference point for economic development practitioners as they champion economic development in their community.

Following the release of the report, VEDP began looking for opportunities to directly support localities, with special consideration for rural localities that want to strengthen their organization or pursue new strategies to enhance their community impact. Preliminary analysis has revealed that rural communities face capacity gaps in organizational staffing and budgets that directly impact the quantity and quality of the economic development programs that they are able to pursue. VEDP envisions working with those specific communities that are understaffed and/or underfunded, as well as other interested communities, to creatively address identified capability gaps. Potential support opportunities include VEDP-provided technical support or matching funding for third-party support for resource-intensive projects, such as strategy development or target industry analysis, among others.

As the world economy becomes more sophisticated and competitive, Virginia's economic development efforts will have to rise to meet those challenges. Armed with this comprehensive data, Virginia's local and regional economic development practitioners will be better able to advocate and guide activities across the Commonwealth to ensure that each locality's potential is optimized, and that prosperity can be spread across Virginia.

Civic Leadership Cultivation (priority initiative no. 8)

With aging populations and persistent out-migration, many rural localities face challenges with building their next generation of civic and public leadership. Additionally, a long-term trend of corporate headquarters shifting away from smaller communities to bigger markets has left many rural localities with branch plants that serve as stepping stones for rising executives whose departures, often after relatively short tenures, further limit local leadership capacity (L. Green, personal communication, 29 January 2021).

Transitioning to the next generation of leaders is critical for rural communities that need to maximize their potential amid challenging economic headwinds. With this challenge in mind, members of the Rural

Think Tank agreed that rebuilding civic leadership with the next generation in rural Virginia represents a critical opportunity to help position rural regions and smaller metro areas for success. Fortunately, the Virginia Rural Center (VRC) also recognized the importance of civic leadership and has been acting to address this critical issue.

Civic leadership has been well documented as a driver of community strength. The training of civic leaders as a method to build vibrant communities has been extensively studied, and it is understood that for a community to grow and thrive, it must develop opportunities to engage potential leaders. One of the shortcomings of some rural communities is a lack of leadership programs and identifiable ways for rural citizens to develop the skills learned through leadership positions—and that are needed for effective leadership. VRC is the established voice for rural localities throughout the Commonwealth and is launching the Virginia Rural Leadership Institute (VRLI), whose mission will be to create and grow leaders to empower them to become highly valuable citizens within their communities.

The VRLI will provide specific curricula needed by rural leaders to address unique challenges to their area. Research has been conducted at Appalachian State University by a contracted employee of the VRC to identify the specific skills that rural civic leaders need to address current and future challenges. These findings, along with input from rural stakeholders and partners such as the Rural Think Tank, will inform curriculum development of VRLI by identifying the skills that are important for rural civic leaders. Activities involved in the development, planning, and implementation of the VRLI will be led by the VRC with significant input from key rural stakeholders and partners.

Outcomes each year would include graduating twenty to thirty leaders with (1) increased knowledge in the areas of leadership, community, and economic development, (2) the implementation of a participant community impact project (a component of VRLI curriculum), and (3) the construction of statewide, uniquely rural networks among participants. The VRC has been actively planning VRLI since 2019 and has the funding in place to launch the first year's program. Prior to COVID-19 the plan was to launch VRLI in 2021, however, the timing and overall implementation of the program will be adjusted as needed to ensure the health and safety of participants as the VRC continually monitors the uncertainty associated with the pandemic.

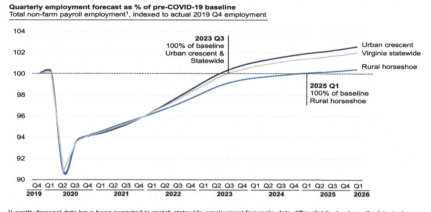

Figure 3.3. Total nonfarm payroll employment in Virginia by quarter

COVID-19 AND THE RURAL-URBAN DIVIDE

As if the prepandemic challenges facing rural regions were not enough, COVID-19 resulted in large job losses across rural Virginia. Further, as illustrated in figure 3.3, employment forecasts by Moody's Analytics prepared in late 2020 suggested that Virginia's rural regions and small metros would take considerably longer to recover than those regions that comprise the urban crescent (i.e., Northern Virginia, Hampton Roads, and Greater Richmond). While Virginia as a whole was expected to recover its prepandemic employment by mid-2023, rural Virginia wasn't expected to recover until 2025. This new economic divide made Virginia's rural development efforts even more urgent than before.

With the rapid shift to remote work experienced by most professionals during the pandemic, some have suggested (or hoped) that a postpandemic increase in remote work could result in new opportunities for population migration that would benefit rural regions and smaller metros (Mannheimer 2020; Repp 2020). Unfortunately, while there likely will be a large, permanent increase in remote work, much of it may be a hybrid form where workers continue to travel to the office regularly even as they work from home more frequently than in the past. Accordingly, new rural growth opportunities associated with remote work may not be as large as many had hoped during the pandemic. As vaccines were beginning to become widely available in early 2021, VEDP was working to assess the size of the postpandemic remote work opportunity, as well as the location preferences and site-selection considerations of professionals across the country who may be interested in a permanent relocation following the pandemic.

With many vibrant downtowns, an excellent quality of life (rated no. 1 nationally by Forbes), a mild, four-season climate, and a lower cost of living, rural Virginia communities likely will be well positioned to attract new remote workers currently living in higher cost metros who want to relocate to a more rural setting. The Commonwealth's attractiveness for such relocating professionals is being strengthened by the Virginia Main Street Program, administered by the Virginia Department of Housing and Community Development, a placemaking tool that helps revitalize downtowns in small communities across Virginia, making them more attractive to existing and new residents alike (E. Johnston, personal communication, 28 January 2021).

Conclusion

No state has cracked the code on addressing America's rural growth challenge, but Virginia seeks to be one of the first to do so. With a wide array of beautiful landscapes and leading employers, some of America's best public schools and thriving downtowns, and, importantly, a cadre of policy leaders focused on the issue, rural Virginia has a relatively strong foundation to build upon. Working together, state, regional, and local leaders are leveraging those strengths and others to position rural Virginia to buck national trends. Our sustained focus will be essential for meaningful progress to occur. Time will tell whether these efforts will be implemented at their envisioned scale—and, if so, whether they will succeed—as well as what lessons other states and regions may be able to draw from Virginia's experience.

This chapter draws from the author's previous writing—in particular the Q3 2019 issue of Virginia Economic Review, which focused on America's rural growth challenge and the various ways in which state, regional, and local leaders in the Commonwealth are working to position Virginia's smaller metro areas and rural regions to buck national trends. Also included are selected passages from the author's doctoral dissertation (Moret 2016) related to the seemingly magical properties of metropolitan areas, as described by Moretti (2013). Drafts of several paragraphs were provided by VEDP staff or VEDP partners. Passages drawn from previous writing and draft paragraphs provided by VEDP staff or partners have not been separately cited in this chapter, except where the original passage cited a third party (e.g., Moretti).

Part 2

Vibrant and Connected Economies

Chapter 4

Bridging the Urban-Rural Economic Divide through Regional Connectivity

Christiana K. McFarland and Erica Grabowski

This chapter explores the viability of a new regional connectivity framework to foster cluster-based strategies to help bridge the urban-rural divide in Virginia. The authors propose a place-based, intra-regional economic connectivity solution focused on developing the industrial base of lagging Virginia communities. The analysis finds that jobs in Virginia localities grow faster when they are part of regional industry clusters and that the magnitude of the relationship between growth and connectivity varies along the urban-rural hierarchy. The chapter concludes by discussing implications for economic development policy.

The urban-rural divide has become one of the most preeminent economic issues of our time. Once characterized by steady convergence, in which market forces rectified regional economic disparities, the past forty years have witnessed a shift in the trajectory of the US economy toward divergence (Ganong and Shoag 2017). The rapid rise of highly concentrated urban agglomeration economies, coupled with significant technological advances and the decline in manufacturing, has left many rural and less talent-rich places behind. Noted economic geographer Enrico Moretti (2012) describes a "winner-takes-all economy" where "winners tend to become stronger and stronger, as innovative firms and innovative workers keep clustering there, while losers tend to lose further ground" (79). The result is extreme growth in a handful of high-tech and coastal regions, while others, namely rural and heartland regions, experience historic levels of brain drain, poverty, drug abuse, and unemployment (Parker et al. 2018).

These characterizations of the urban-rural divide are familiar to Virginia. Broader trends in urbanization and the declining coal industry have weakened the economies of many rural parts of the state. This divide has only intensified since the Great Recession. According to the Commonwealth Institute, "In 2016, there were 3.2% more occupied jobs in metro areas than in 2007. But in non-metro areas, there were 6.3% fewer filled jobs than before the recession" (Warren and Goren 2018). In addition to employment differentials, rural areas also see lower wages, educational attainment, broadband access, and healthcare access and quality than their urban counterparts.

Despite the magnitude of the challenges posed by the growing urban-rural divide, as well as the substantive research and evidence documenting its underlying causes, solutions for effective economic revitalization in lagging communities have been hard to come by. Recommendations range from people-based, mobility strategies that assist population migration away from declining places toward opportunity-rich places to broader strategies to rebuild foundational assets such as healthcare access, workforce skills, infrastructure, and housing stock. While investments in these assets are critical for renewed growth, they fall short of providing strategic direction for developing new economic drivers in lagging places. For example, workforce development programs can develop skills, but for which industries?

This chapter proposes a place-based, intra-regional economic connectivity solution focused on developing the industrial base of lagging Virginia communities. Specifically, it calls attention to the potential benefits to local communities of fostering connections to industry clusters and economic specializations that are already present in their broader regions. Connectivity to industry clusters in the regional economy can offer direction and prospects for local growth by broadening the asset base available to communities from which to build anew. This chapter discusses how different types of urban and rural communities can leverage connectivity for growth. A Virginia-focused analysis finds that jobs in Virginia localities grow faster when they are part of regional industry clusters and that the magnitude of the relationship between growth and connectivity varies along the urban-rural hierarchy. Implications for economic development policy are discussed.

REGIONAL CONNECTIVITY AS AN ECONOMIC DEVELOPMENT FRAMEWORK

This chapter explores the viability of a new regional connectivity framework to foster cluster-based strategies to help bridge the urban-rural divide in Virginia. A regional connectivity framework suggests that local economic growth can be spurred by tapping and nurturing economic specializations that are present outside of the locality and in the broader region, even spanning urban and rural areas. This approach contrasts traditional notions of cluster development, which tend to focus on agglomeration within concentrated urban areas.

Two proven features of regional economies support a regional connectivity approach to local growth and bridging the urban-rural divide: first, most regions are composed of a diverse array of local communities along the urban and rural spectrum; and second, the drivers of regional economies are industry clusters, or networks of businesses, labor pools, and so forth, whose linkages often cross local jurisdictional boundaries. In terms of the first feature, studies of regional economic diffusion and concentration often suggest an antagonistic relationship between urban and rural communities within the same regions, specifically that urban economic growth weakens surrounding rural communities, leading to further divergence and backwash effects (Lewin, Weber, and Holland 2013; Myrdal 1957). However, economic geography studies offering a more contextual perspective, particularly when accounting for proximity to urban agglomeration, confirm economic opportunities for rural areas (Barkley, Henry, and Bao 1996; Partridge et al. 2008). For example, Partridge et al. (2008) examine how proximity of rural communities to urban cores affects population and employment growth in rural areas over the period of 1950–2000. They find that rural counties near urban areas have stronger job and population growth. The authors attribute the benefits of proximity to the ascendance of agglomeration economies and the ability of outlying counties to provide services and quality of life to regional industries and workers.

A second foundational feature of regions is that the drivers of regional economies are industry clusters, or firms in related industries that are geographically concentrated and leverage the benefits of their proximity, including knowledge spillovers, thick labor markets, and specialized suppliers. For industry clusters to provide a development pathway for disparate parts of regions, however, the spatial scale of their linkages must be regional. The industry cluster literature discusses the spatial implications of these linkages noting that innovation and knowledge-based activities are associated with greater urban density, while other activities such as supply chain relationships and commuting exhibit a broader regional, including rural, footprint (Dabson 2011; Feser and Isserman 2009; Jaffe, Trajtenberg, and Henderson 1993; Rosenthal and Strange 2001). Overall, the literature suggests that linkages and spatial scales vary by cluster, indicating that some clusters are better suited as targets for bridging the urban-rural divide than others.

Additionally, Porter (2003) and Delgado, Porter, and Stern (2010, 2014) examine regional economic performance, the composition of regional economies, and the role of industry clusters in the economy measuring clusters at the spatial scale of broad regions inclusive of highly urban and highly rural places (economic areas). They find that key indicators of regional economic performance at this scale, including wages, wage growth, employment growth, and innovation, are strongly and positively influenced by the strength of each region's clusters. Overall, studies of industry clusters suggest the power of intra-regional cluster connectivity at a scale spanning urban and rural but lack clarity on how different clusters are situated within their regions or the prospects for connectivity to positively impact different parts of regions.

Delgado and Zeuli (2016), however, offer one of the few studies specifically exploring the impact of industry cluster linkages within regions on local economic outcomes. The authors examine whether inner-city industry connections to metropolitan regional clusters impact inner-city employment growth. This connectivity between local employment and regional clusters indicates that the mechanisms of agglomeration, such as skilled labor, sophisticated and demanding local customers, niche markets, suppliers, and related industries, are at work regionally and have an influence on local development. The authors find that the strength of the cluster in the metropolitan region is positively associated with employment growth in the inner-city cluster. In doing so, Delgado and Zeuli (2016) offer an intra-regional connectivity framework, which this analysis extends in order to examine the urban-rural divide.

Speaking to the interaction of rural development, industry type, and regional context, Tandoh-Offin (2010) notes:

> [R]ural development strategies must be based on a realistic assessment of opportunities and constraints, which will determine whether improving integration with the urban economy through infrastructure improvements and supply chain management are the right priorities. . . . Areas of focus in this regard could include fostering urban-rural interaction around policy decision points where there seem to be a convergence in the interests of the two constituencies. (343)

One measure of "convergence of interest" is urban and rural employment growth generated by mutual support of regional industry clusters through mechanisms such as market expansion, entrepreneurship, and supply chains. For example, in a study of urban-rural connections in Oregon, Martin (2011) finds that rural hops growers leverage nearby urban markets to test and refine their products before taking them to the global market. Additionally, in a study of European rural entrepreneurship, Mayer, Habersetzer, and Meili (2016) find that rural entrepreneurs benefit from proximity to urban cores because they can access urban knowledge and markets while profiting from the typically lower production costs in their peripheral location.

Likewise, Mayer and Provo (2007) investigate the potential of domestic outsourcing, or "farmshoring," from urban firms to drive economic connectivity and growth in more rural areas of Virginia "driven by needs like lower costs, data security, skilled and stable labor forces, and geographic constraints" (3). The authors go on to note that the benefits of farmshoring will only be realized if broader state and regional efforts are in place to create interfaces between urban and rural areas. These interfaces allow local and regional leaders and businesses to share information about local assets, as well as industry sectors, products, and processes that may be candidates for farmshoring.

In addition to rural linkages to urban clusters, rural-focused clusters can also drive growth via connectivity with urban economies. For example, in an analysis of urban-rural economic divides within states, McFarland (2018) finds that urban traded sector businesses such as legal, financial, trade, and transportation thrive as a result of providing economic support to rural-based clusters. In a study examining the interdependence between Minnesota's urban and rural areas, Searls (2011) finds that urban regions receive substantial economic benefits from improved prosperity in rural areas. Every $1 billion increase in rural manufacturing output produces a 16% increase in urban jobs, significant additional business-to-business transactions, and statewide consumer spending and investment. Similarly, a study of the Sacramento, California, region finds that most jobs and economic activity resulting from the region's rural food, agriculture, and processing cluster occurs in urban parts of the region (Sacramento Area Council of Governments 2008).

These examples highlight the potential of a regional connectivity framework for promoting economic development and bridging the urban-rural divide through regional markets, entrepreneurship, and supply chains. The remainder of the chapter offers an analysis of the relationship between intra-regional economic connectivity and growth across urban and rural communities.

Evaluating Connectivity

This analysis assesses whether economic connectivity, defined as cluster strength at different levels of geography, contributes to growth as a result of industry linkages through inputs, outputs, and skills that support competitiveness (Delgado and Zeuli 2016). Specifically, the authors explore the extent to which intra-regional economic connectivity influences county employment growth, and how the relationship between economic connectivity and growth varies along the urban-rural spectrum. This analysis determines whether connectivity, indicated by county participation in regional industry clusters, is associated with employment growth in Virginia counties between 2010 and 2016. Results for Virginia are compared with those for the broader US.

To test the hypothesis that intra-regional economic connectivity is associated with greater growth of county employment, this analysis determines:

- all economic specializations, or industry clusters, that are present outside of each county but within the county's broader economic region (2010);
- the extent to which the county itself participates in those regional clusters, indicated by county-level specialization in those industry clusters (2010); and
- the county annualized employment growth rate for the cluster (2010–2016).

The study evaluates connectivity using standard county definitions, regions that are inclusive of both urban and rural communities as defined by the US Bureau of Economic Analysis (economic areas), traded sector industry cluster definitions developed by the US Cluster Mapping Project, and county rurality categories developed by the USDA (which are aggregated to four categories of metropolitan, micropolitan, rural adjacent, and rural remote). This analysis utilizes traded sector clusters (vs. local clusters), or those industries that serve markets beyond their regions, since they are highly concentrated in a few regions with specific competitive advantages and drive high levels of overall regional economic performance (Ketels 2017).

The observations or units of analysis are "county-clusters," or traded sector industry clusters with at least ten jobs in the county and a cluster location quotient greater than one in the economic region outside of/excluding the county ("rest of region" location quotient). A location quotient greater than one for an area indicates a higher employment concentration and greater economic specialization than the national average. This calculation across all US counties and economic area regions results in 35,107 county-cluster observations, 1,337 of which are in Virginia.[1] The county-level observations represent those clusters that are viable candidates for connectivity. For example, the Danville, Virginia, furniture county-cluster, with a location quotient of 6.34 in the rest of the Greensboro economic area region and employment of 410 in Danville, is an observation in this analysis.

Since all observations are characterized by regional cluster strength, the extent of connectivity between the region and locality is determined by the level of county specialization in the cluster, or the county-cluster location quotient. For example, Danville's "connectivity" to the regional

---

1. In Virginia, independent cities are treated as counties.

furniture cluster is indicated by the Danville-furniture county-cluster location quotient of 7.24. The model analyzes annualized county-cluster employment growth between 2010 and 2016 as a function of the strength of the county-cluster (county-cluster location quotient). It controls for the initial size of the cluster within the county (as a share of county traded sector employment) and the initial size of the cluster in the region (cluster employment in the economic area), as well as overall county employment growth and national cluster growth with the inclusion of county and cluster fixed effects. The specific growth time frame of 2010–2016 allows for an examination of the economic recovery period following the 2008 Great Recession and reflects the most recent data available on industry cluster employment.

Table 4.1 summarizes the dependent and independent variable data for all observations in our analysis, those county-clusters in the US with at least ten jobs and a rest of region location quotient greater than one. Of note, annualized employment growth for county-clusters overall declined, on average, from 2010–2016.

Table 4.1. Dependent and Independent Variable Summary Table (35,107 Observations)					
	Minimum	Maximum	Median	Mean	Standard deviation
Annualized employment growth rate	−100	201.490	0.000	−7.380	30.361
County-cluster location quotient	0.003	976.186	1.322	5.772	22.811
County-cluster share of employment (%)	0.002	100	1.695	4.940	8.828
Regional cluster size	10	518,647	4,230	15,634	42,838

Because a location quotient is a ratio of the specialization in a county relative to specialization across the US, the county-cluster location quotient variable has no maximum value. For example, in Aleutians East Borough, Arkansas, 93% of 2010 traded sector jobs in the county were part of the Fish and Fishing Products cluster, whereas on average, other counties had a concentration of less than 1% for this cluster, resulting in a location quotient of 976.2 for the Aleutians East Borough, Arkansas-Fish and Fishing Products county-cluster. There is no upper limit for location quotients, therefore, this analysis log transforms the independent variable "county-cluster location quotient" and interprets the percentage change rather than absolute value change.

THE IMPORTANCE OF REGIONAL LINKAGES

Our analysis indicates that job growth in Virginia localities increases when the connectivity between those jobs and regional industry clusters is stronger. This finding holds for county-clusters throughout the US and is an even greater predictor of growth in Virginia. In Virginia, cluster connectivity together with the initial size of the cluster in the county and in the region explain 21.6% of the variation in annual job growth for county-clusters ($R2 = .2156$, $F(1,337) = 2.997$, $p < .05$) (see table 4.2). Holding constant the initial size of the county-cluster and size of cluster in the region, as well as overall county growth and national cluster growth, for every 10% growth in a Virginia county's cluster specialization, the county-cluster annualized employment growth rate increases by about 0.3 percentage points.[2]

Table 4.2. Virginia Connectivity Effect on Growth	
Dependent variable	Employment growth rate, 2010–2016
Variables	
Log (county-cluster location quotient)	2.997**
	(1.414)
Percent of county traded employment	−0.0052
	(0.1494)
Region-cluster size	−1.17 × 10⁻⁵
	(1.87 × 10⁻⁵)
Fixed-Effects	
Industry cluster	Yes
County	Yes

2. To find the expected change in y for a 10% increase in the coefficient of x, we multiply the coefficient by log(1.1) (Benoit 2011). The expected difference in county-cluster annualized employment growth rate for a 10% increase in log(county-cluster location quotient) is 2.997 log(1.1), which equals 0.286 percentage points, or about 0.3.

Fit statistics	
Observations	1,337
R^2	0.21568
Within R^2	0.01239

Note: One-way (Industry Cluster) standard-errors in parentheses.
Signif. Codes: **: 0.05; *: 0.1

The same predictors explain 16.5% of the variation in county-cluster growth across the US ($R2 = .1647$, $F(35,107) = 1.018$, $p < .001$) (see table 4.3). Holding constant the initial size of the county-cluster and size of the cluster in the region, as well as overall county growth and national cluster growth, for every 10% growth in a county's cluster specialization, the county-cluster annualized employment growth rate increases by 0.01 percentage points.

Table 4.3. US Connectivity Effect on Growth

Dependent variable	Employment growth rate, 2010–2016
Variables	
Log (county-cluster location quotient)	1.018**
	(0.4044)
Percent of county traded employment	0.1205**
	(0.0454)
Region-cluster size	-2.71×10^{-5}***
	(9.43×10^{-6})
Fixed-Effects	
Industry cluster	Yes
County	Yes
Fit statistics	
Observations	35,107
R^2	0.16475
Within R^2	0.00500

Note: One-way (Industry Cluster) standard-errors in parentheses.
Signif. Codes: ***: 0.01; **: 0.05; *: 0.1

These findings suggest that regional economic connectivity drives growth in the US overall, and even more so in Virginia localities. The relationship between connectivity and growth is further bolstered when examining employment growth patterns in communities along the urban-rural hierarchy—from very urban to the most rural—within economic regions (see table 4.4). When the data are disaggregated by county type (metropolitan, micropolitan, rural adjacent, and remote rural), the results suggest that all types of communities benefit from connectivity, but that the magnitude of the relationship between connectivity and growth varies based on rurality. In an analysis of growth and connectivity in US county-clusters, the greatest relationship is evident in remote rural counties. Comparisons to Virginia cannot be made due to the limited number of county-clusters.

Table 4.4. US Connectivity Effect on Growth by County Type

Dependent variable	Employment growth rate, 2010–2016			
	Metropolitan	Micropolitan	Rural Adjacent	Remote Rural
Variables				
Log (county-cluster location quotient)	0.4349	1.805***	2.642***	3.472***
	(0.4673)	(0.5591)	(0.8832)	(0.8275)
Percent of county traded employment	0.1180*	−0.0284	−0.0054	−0.0469
	(0.0650)	(0.0664)	(0.0792)	(0.0574)
Region-cluster size	−1.87 × 10^{-5}**	−1.51 × 10^{-5}	7.17 × 10^{-6}**	−8.71 × 10^{-6}**
	(7.61 × 10^{-6})	(1.15 × 10^{-5})	(1.69 × 10^{-5})	(2.27 × 10^{-5})
Fixed-Effects				
Industry cluster	Yes	Yes	Yes	Yes
County	Yes	Yes	Yes	Yes
Fit statistics				
Observations	16,356	8,013	5,858	4,880
R^2	0.14433	0.15516	0.19087	0.23663
Within R^2	0.00222	0.00542	0.00838	0.01034

Note: One-way (Industry Cluster) standard-errors in parentheses.
Signif. Codes: ***: 0.01; **: 0.05; *: 0.1

For every 10% increase in a metropolitan county's cluster specialization, this model predicts a 0.041 percentage point increase in the employment growth rate. For every 10% increase in a micropolitan county's cluster specialization, this model predicts a 0.17 percentage point increase in the employment growth rate. For every 10% increase in a rural adjacent county's cluster specialization, this model predicts a 0.25 percentage point increase in the employment growth rate. The largest effect is seen in remote rural counties, where for every 10% increase in a remote rural county's cluster specialization, the model predicts a 0.33 percentage point increase in the employment growth rate.

The finding regarding high growth potential of connectivity for rural remote communities runs counter to previous studies of regional development, which concluded that backwash effects, like brain drain, characterize the impact of regional economic activity on remote rural areas (Barkley, Henry, and Bao 1996; Partridge et al. 2008). Although it may be true that very rural and remote communities are more challenged to connect regionally, and likely that proximity to urban agglomeration is a factor, our analysis indicates that when they are connected, the benefits are material. COVID-19 and job shifts to remote work underscore the importance of internet connectivity and device access, in particular, for regional integration. Indeed, Partridge et al. (2008) find that for remote rural communities, the most critical factor contributing to regional connectivity is infrastructure, namely high-speed internet, that allows for remote work. The findings demonstrate that metropolitan areas also reap benefits from broader regional connectivity, which can incentivize urban leaders to work regionally with their rural counterparts.

Of course, not all industry clusters respond to or rely on connectivity in the same way. As noted, the spatial scale of cluster linkages varies. Those with greater innovation and knowledge-based activities are typically associated with greater urban density, while other activities such as supply chain relationships and commuting exhibit a broader regional, including rural, footprint (Audretsch and Feldman 2004; Dabson 2011; Feser and Isserman 2009; Jaffe, Trajtenberg, and Henderson 1993; Rosenthal and Strange 2001). To understand which clusters may be candidates for an intra-regional economic connectivity approach, the analysis compares the average annualized growth rates of each type of industry cluster under both connected (industry cluster has a location quotient greater than one in both the county and the rest of the region) and not connected (industry cluster has a location quotient greater than one in the rest of region but not the county) conditions in metropolitan, micropolitan, rural adjacent, and rural remote communities.

Table 4.5 summarizes initial findings regarding those clusters in which greater annual employment growth is evident and most significant under connected conditions by county type. County employment growth in these clusters is stronger when the cluster is also present in the rest of the region, suggesting that certain industry clusters are more poised to benefit from connectivity in different county types. The largest number of clusters benefitting from connectivity are present in remote rural counties.

Table 4.5. Industry Clusters Exhibiting Statistically Significant Greater Annualized Employment Growth Rates (2010–2016) Under Connected (vs. Not Connected) Conditions, by County Type in US

Metropolitan	Micropolitan	Rural Adjacent	Rural Remote
Agricultural Inputs and Services	Automotive	Biopharmaceuticals	Education and Knowledge Creation
Automotive	Coal Mining	Distribution and Electronic Commerce	Fishing and Fishing Products
Education and Knowledge Creation	Furniture	Education and Knowledge Creation	Furniture
Insurance Services	Insurance Services	Fishing and Fishing Products	Hospitality and Tourism
Jewelry and Precious Metals	Metalworking Technology		Metalworking Technology
	Wood Products		Oil and Gas Production and Transportation
			Performing Arts
			Production Technology and Heavy Machinery

Economic developers can strengthen these clusters by working regionally to ensure that necessary cluster assets, from talent to supply chain, are coordinated and bolstered. Further analysis that controls for other pertinent factors such as size of the cluster will confirm which clusters benefit from the agglomeration effects that reach beyond their local borders.

Policy Implications

A regional connectivity framework for economic development provides a new way to approach economic and cluster-based development. Specifically, state, regional, and local policy leaders and practitioners can "map the cluster composition of [their location] and nearby region, identifying strong and emerging clusters in the region that have some strength in the [locality]" (Delgado and Zeuli 2016, 132). In other words, what clusters are present in the county that are also strong in the broader region? Or what assets and industries are present in the locality that can support regional clusters? Using data provided by this research, economic development organizations can identify how connectivity is likely to impact local growth and select those clusters with predicted positive impact. Once those clusters are narrowed, policy leaders and practitioners can work to build economic connections within the region via an adapted cluster upgrading strategy.

In Virginia, the Virginia Economic Development Partnership has established key industries for growth and development within the state, including Corporate Services, Food & Beverage Processing, Information Technology, Life Sciences, Manufacturing, Supply Chain Management and Unmanned Systems. These are roughly inclusive of the following traded sector clusters: Distribution and Electronic Commerce, Water Transportation, Wood Products, Forestry, Financial Services, Business Services, Automotive, Agricultural Inputs and Services, Transportation and Logistics, Food Processing and Manufacturing, Aerospace Vehicles and Defense, Biopharmaceuticals, Medical Devices, and Information Technology and Analytical Instruments. To apply a regional connectivity framework to these target clusters, economic developers in Virginia, whether local, regional, or state, can:

1. identify those regions with a specialization in the cluster (see appendix);

2. assess which county type(s) are best positioned to benefit from connectivity within the cluster (see table 4.4); and
3. begin to scope out counties and local assets within the region for additional investments to bolster the cluster and strengthen linkages between the cluster in the locality and the broader region.

Applying this approach to grow the Distribution and Electronic Commerce cluster in Virginia, for example, the US Cluster Mapping Project identifies the Johnson City–Kingsport–Bristol (Tri-Cities), TN-VA Economic Area as a region with a high specialization in the cluster (see appendix). The most significant growth in this cluster in the region is in the Electronic and Catalog Shopping and the Warehousing and Storage industries. As noted in the analysis of types of US counties, rural adjacent counties are well positioned to grow the Distribution and Electronic Commerce via connectivity. Therefore, one path for growing the Distribution and Electronic Commerce cluster in Virginia is to further examine the potential of rural remote parts of the Johnson City–Kingsport-Bristol (Tri-Cities), TN-VA Economic Area, such as Lee County, Virginia, as candidates for targeted cluster connectivity investments. These investments can range from collective marketing of a region's cluster specialties and providing firms and entrepreneurs with local services, such as financial advice, marketing, and design, to identifying weaknesses in existing cluster value chains, attracting investors and businesses to fill those gaps, aligning industry needs and workforce programs, and streamlining the regulatory environment (Cortright 2006; Delgado and Zeuli 2016).

Conclusion

Examples from all parts of the country, from California and Oregon to Minnesota and Virginia, underscore how robust linkages within regions, often between urban and rural communities, provide the fuel that drives business innovation, competitiveness, and growth. In the current environment, significant global supply chain disruptions bring to light the importance of connected regional economies and the value of rural communities to economic resilience. A recent McKinsey study found that due to pandemic-related disruptions, 93% of supply chain leaders are prioritizing resiliency with strategies such as near-shoring and regionalizing supply chains (Alicke, Gupta, and Trautwein 2020). This pivot provides opportunities for growth and recovery in smaller and rural communities that, through greater regional connectivity, have the potential to offer cost savings, enhanced data security, and workforce stability to industries located in more urban areas (Mayer and Provo 2007).

Indeed, this analysis of county employment growth from 2010–2016 reveals that communities with industries that are integrated across urban and rural areas within economic regions grow more quickly than those that are not. These findings are particularly pronounced for communities in Virginia as well as more broadly for rural communities across the US. This suggests that coordinated regional economic development approaches across jurisdictions and sectors are promising for rural development. While economic connectivity is a potential strategy for communities with nearby regional economic strengths, there are communities whose entire regions are economically challenged and for which this approach may not present a viable path. Connectivity is not a prescription but reflects how competitive regions and industry clusters within them can leverage a broader range of assets in urban and rural communities from talent and critical infrastructure to specialized suppliers and niche customers. The application of a regional connectivity framework can help practitioners and policymakers identify potential industry pathways for rural and lagging communities and prioritize investments to support growth and development that narrows the urban-rural divide.

This chapter is an adaptation of McFarland, C., and Grabowski, E. (2021). Local Employment Impacts of Connectivity to Regional Economies: The Role of Industry Clusters in Bridging the Urban-Rural Divide. Manuscript submitted for publication.

APPENDIX

Table 4.6. Strongest Traded Sector Industry Clusters in Virginia Economic Area	
Economic area	Industry clusters
Dover, DE*	Livestock Processing, Fishing and Fishing Products, Distribution and Electronic Commerce, Hospitality and Tourism

Greensboro-Winston-Salem-High Point, NC	Education and Knowledge Creation, Textile Manufacturing, Furniture, Plastics, Construction Products and Services, Downstream Chemical Products, Printing Services, Wood Products, Paper and Packaging, Apparel
Harrisonburg, VA	Livestock Processing, Wood Products, Nonmetal Mining
Johnson City–Kingsport-Bristol (Tri-Cities), TN-VA	Distribution and Electronic Commerce, Coal Mining, Plastics, Communications Equipment and Services, Construction Products and Services, Printing Services, Wood Products, Nonmetal Mining
Raleigh-Durham-Cary, NC	Education and Knowledge Creation, Information Technology and Analytical Instruments, Marketing, Design, and Publishing, Livestock Processing, Biopharmaceuticals, Performing Arts
Richmond, VA	Business Services, Financial Services, Insurance Services, Marketing, Design, and Publishing, Tobacco, Performing Arts
Roanoke, VA	Business Services, Education and Knowledge Creation, Insurance Services, Printing Services
Virginia Beach–Norfolk-Newport News, VA-NC	Business Services, Water Transportation, Insurance Services
Washington-Baltimore-Northern Virginia, DC-MD-VA-WV	Business Services, Education and Knowledge Creation, Financial Services, Marketing, Design, and Publishing, Communications Equipment and Services

Note: This table lists all economic areas with Virginia counties. Some economic areas cross state boundaries. For example, Northampton County, Virginia, and Accomack County, Virginia, are in the Dover, Delaware, economic area.
Source: US Cluster Mapping Project, Institute for Strategy and Competitiveness, Harvard Business School, 2017.

Chapter 5

Connecting Entrepreneur Ecosystems across Urban and Rural Regions

Scott Tate and Erik R. Pages

This chapter explores evolving approaches to entrepreneurship in two Virginia regions, each anchored by one or more higher education institutions and including a mix of rural, suburban, and more metropolitan municipalities. The chapter includes a rich description of the state-wide GO Virginia program, a discussion of the important role of entrepreneurship as a regional growth strategy, and an overview of the contours of the innovation and entrepreneurship climate in both case study regions. The chapter concludes with a synthesis discussion of lessons learned, including implications and recommendations for state, regional, local, and institutional policymakers and leaders.

In recent years, the theory and practice of economic development has shifted to be more inclusive of a more diverse mix of strategies designed to attract, retain, and grow new businesses as a means to create new jobs, new wealth, and community prosperity. The emergence of this more holistic understanding of economic development is fostering significant changes in how Virginia communities invest in local and regional economic development. In particular, entrepreneurship is now considered an even more vital component of strategies and policies to grow and diversify regional and local economies.

This chapter explores evolving approaches to entrepreneurship in two Virginia regions, each anchored by one or more higher education institutions and including a mix of rural, suburban, and more metropolitan municipalities. With support from new state initiatives, especially the GO Virginia program, regions are pioneering new approaches to business creation, while also strengthening intra-regional connections that link small towns to urban centers and to larger anchor institutions, especially major colleges and universities.

The chapter begins by reviewing recent changes in economic development policies and priorities, with a particular focus on the important role of entrepreneurship as a regional growth strategy. Virginia's rural regions have suffered from a loss of jobs and income in traditional core sectors, such as coal mining, agriculture, and manufacturing. Entrepreneurship promotion offers one means to combat this economic decline, while also allowing rural communities to create local jobs, develop and retain local talent, and diversify the economy to become less dependent on large employers or declining industry sectors.

The chapter then reviews how two Virginia regions have embraced these new approaches and considers the extent to which the initiatives are spurring economic growth and increasing capacity across the regions, from more rural communities to urban centers such as Charlottesville, Lynchburg, and Roanoke. These case studies offer useful lessons not only for effective economic development practices but also for how rural and urban places are interconnected and interdependent. The chapter traces the contours of the innovation and entrepreneurship climate in each region and explores some recent strategies and activities through the lens of the statewide GO Virginia program. The chapter concludes with a synthesis discussion of possible lessons learned, including implications and recommendations for state, regional, local, and institutional policymakers and leaders.

DEVELOPING AN ECOSYSTEM

Entrepreneur ecosystems are a hot topic for economic development practitioners and researchers today (Ewing Marion Kauffman Foundation 2020; Pages 2018; Stangler and Masterson 2015). However, there remains no singular, widely accepted definition. A 2018 meta-analysis of research literature concerning entrepreneur ecosystems found that most definitions highlighted the presence of networks, producing values or activities that supported business start-up activity in some way (Malecki 2018).

The ecosystem concept emphasizes that supporting entrepreneurship is not about a single economic development program but instead relies on a complex mix of local assets, programs, policies, and business practices. Critical ecosystem components include:

- Capital: Providing diverse sources of capital to help firms start and grow
- Workforce/Human Capital: Building a regional talent base
- Business Assistance: Providing easy access to technical assistance
- Specialized Infrastructure and Facilities: Meeting the unique space needs of entrepreneurs
- Community Culture: Honoring and embracing entrepreneurship
- Effective Regulation: Cutting red tape and promoting flexibility
- Market Access: Helping entrepreneurs identify, access, and succeed in new markets

Places with strong entrepreneur performance typically enjoy strong capabilities in these critical areas, with effective programs, organizations, and supportive policies. No community excels in all areas, but robust ecosystems typically offer easier access to these critical services.

Unique Issues for Rural Places and Mixed Urban-Rural Regions

Ecosystem building depends on similar ingredients, regardless of whether activities are underway in an urban, suburban, or rural setting. Successful ecosystems emerge in places where the local business culture encourages risk-taking and innovation, where capital and other resources are available to fuel business growth, where new ideas and innovations are shared across collaborative networks, and where local people and businesses can easily access support and encouragement. These attributes may be more commonly found in denser urban areas where the levels of local resources and capital are higher, where networks are nearby and easier to access, and where the sheer number and density of entrepreneurs is larger. Because less populated rural locations may lack these naturally occurring attributes, ecosystem building in these places requires a more conscious and focused commitment.

Several unique factors influence ecosystem policy and program development in rural locations (Pages 2018). Self-employment rates in rural areas are higher than in urban locations. In addition, rural firms are more stable and less likely to fail, with rural business survival rates slightly higher than those found in cities. However, many rural firms fail to achieve high growth and thus do not generate major impacts in terms of new job and wealth creation. These rural firms must also contend with constraints related to distance to markets, fewer networking options, and a shallow local talent base. Rural entrepreneurs are also more likely to operate in a few core industries or clusters, with higher concentrations of newer firms operating in manufacturing, agriculture, and tourism-related sectors. As we will see below, these descriptions also characterize firms operating in more mixed rural-urban regions as well.

Ecosystem Building in Virginia Regions: Two Case Studies

Many rural parts of Virginia have been making major investments to spur entrepreneurship for several years. Examples include Opportunity Southwest Virginia, which has been working since 2012 to advance a blueprint plan for entrepreneurial development in far southwest Virginia. There are other examples of towns and counties like Floyd, which has supported a local economic gardening program since 2014, and Staunton, where the Staunton Creative Community Fund has supported local business owners since 2008. These types of grassroots efforts have enjoyed great success and have been greatly accelerated thanks to new state initiatives like GO Virginia, which is a collaborative, public-private, regionally focused state economic development initiative that seeks to grow quality jobs across the Commonwealth.

The GO Virginia Board has prioritized entrepreneurship as a core component of the program. The board directed state staff to engage a consultant, TEConomy Partners LLC, to provide each region with an outside, objective assessment of its entrepreneur ecosystem and the needs and opportunities to strengthen the environment for regional entrepreneur growth. Thanks to investment and technical assistance provided by GO Virginia, most regions in the Commonwealth are now developing or implementing new entrepreneurship-related programming.

The focus here is on two regions in particular, GO Virginia Regions 2 and 9. Both regions not only include one or more metropolitan statistical areas (MSAs) but also include large swaths of rural land and rural features (such as the presence of agriculture and natural resources and amenities). Both regions include a major public research university as an innovation ecosystem anchor and both are beginning to work collaboratively and intentionally to strengthen its entrepreneur ecosystem.

Case Study #1: The Region 2 Entrepreneur Ecosystem

Region 2 of GO Virginia spans three metropolitan statistical areas (MSAs) and regional commissions in western Virginia: the Lynchburg, New River Valley (including Blacksburg and Christiansburg), and Roanoke-Alleghany regions. In total, Region 2 comprises eighteen jurisdictions including thirteen counties and five independent cities. State Route 460, an east-west highway, transects much of the region.

While the region is home to three MSAs—including the hubs of Roanoke-Salem, the City of Lynchburg, and the towns of Blacksburg and Christiansburg—the region contains large areas that are predominantly rural, including the one-stoplight agrarian county of Floyd and the no-stoplight forested and mountainous county of Craig. Counties like Botetourt, Bedford, and Franklin are growing in population and have a strong industry presence but also retain large rural swathes and a heavy agricultural presence.

Rural characteristics abound in Region 2, but a major economic strength is the area's twenty-one institutions of higher learning, including colleges, universities, community colleges, and technical training centers. The region is bookended by the state's largest public research university—Virginia Tech in Blacksburg— and the state's largest private institution—Liberty University of Lynchburg.

Region 2 has a number of entrepreneur ecosystem assets as well as a number of deficits. Overall, firm creation in the area has declined by 24% since 1999, with a particularly significant decline during the Great

Recession (GO Virginia Region 2, 2019). Despite the presence of a major research university in Virginia Tech, Region 2 also lags peer regions in university research commercialization. A comparison of the ratio of university research to venture capital investment showed the region scoring in the bottom third among peers. It is worth noting that the more urban and urban-adjacent counties are faring better in many of these measures than the more rural localities.

Access to capital remains a challenge. While the region's entrepreneurs have some access to angel and early stage funds, the region lacks a resource dedicated to seeking out promising technologies, "de-risking" them, and putting them on a path to market. Some stakeholders have suggested a need for the region's colleges and universities to collaborate more closely around economic development and regional innovation. The growth of institutions such as Radford University, Jefferson College of Health Sciences, and Liberty University may represent more entrepreneur and innovation possibilities and the opportunity to learn more from each other, streamline approaches, and identify shared aims for regional innovation. Virginia Tech and other institutions may need incentives or outside impetus to spur regionally focused commercialization and entrepreneur activities.

While the innovation landscape and technology-based entrepreneurs are important to the region, the overall entrepreneur climate is much more varied. Food and tourism-related businesses remain a stable presence. A number of asset-based initiatives seek to support regional small businesses in the outdoors, agriculture, arts, and other locally significant strengths. For example, the Roanoke Regional Partnership developed an economic strategy focused on the outdoors sector and related businesses, including outfitters, other retail, restaurants, manufacturers, and enterprises supporting outdoor recreation.

The Region 2 GO Virginia Council has invested in a number of projects to enhance the entrepreneur ecosystem and address weaknesses. For instance, to address the access to capital challenge, Region 2 has supported a Capital Ecosystem Development project led by a newer organization, the Valleys Innovation Council (VIC). The project helped understand and describe the various sources of capital in the region through surveys and interviews with entrepreneurs and investors in the region. The project created a capital access plan to better connect businesses and entrepreneurs with investors throughout the region. Since that time, Region 2 has supported the role of the Valleys Innovation Council as a key ecosystem champion and has tasked the organization with coordinating efforts to grow the entrepreneur and innovation ecosystem across the region. Region 2 also supported the growth and expansion of a regional accelerator (Regional Acceleration and Mentorship Program or RAMP) to assist technology-based start-ups.

Parts of the region lacked access to small business assistance services, so GO Virginia supported an expansion of the Roanoke Small Business Development Center (SBDC) to serve five municipalities in the New River Valley, much of that area is rural. Likewise, Region 2 supported two projects led by the Advancement Foundation focused specifically on helping identify and support high-growth-potential entrepreneurs in more rural places, from Alleghany to Pulaski.

Taken as a whole, these and other projects represent a concerted effort to strengthen the region's entrepreneur ecosystem. In addition, there have been several other developments in the region over the past two years. Virginia Tech and Carilion, a major hospital system headquartered in Roanoke, have created a $15 million venture capital fund that will help start-ups take root around the research institute. They expect to spin off more lab discoveries into new businesses, and they anticipate that other businesses will develop around the campus to support the additional faculty and students. Coworking and incubator spaces in the region have developed or expanded, including in Botetourt County, Roanoke City, the City of Lynchburg, Salem, Roanoke County, Blacksburg, and others. In the spring of 2021, VIC announced an organizational merger with the Roanoke-Blacksburg Technology Council (RBTC) and RAMP, which indicates a willingness for existing organizations to collaborate in new ways. VIC is now coordinating groups of entrepreneur support organizations in each of the Region 2 MSA/subregions (Lynchburg, Roanoke-Alleghany, and New River Valley) and helping those groups better support start-ups.

The current situation is evolving, but there are some noticeable positive trends. A once-fragmented ecosystem is becoming more connected, in part thanks to GO Virginia and the role of VIC in supporting subregional entrepreneur coalitions. GO Virginia and other support has helped lynchpin ecosystem organizations grow and become more established.

There have been recent projects to identify and support high potential emerging industries and technologies. The recently approved Blockchain Ecosystem Catalyst project led by Virginia Tech is one such example. Higher education institutions are partnering more with regional efforts for technology, talent, and entrepreneur development.

Some ongoing challenges do remain. A 2017 study of the Roanoke-Blacksburg Entrepreneur Ecosystem cited concerns of entrepreneur diversity and inclusion across race, ethnicity, gender, income, and geography (Cowell, Lyon-Hill, and Tate 2018). To date, there have been few efforts to advance more inclusive entrepreneurship efforts in a substantive way in Region 2. Ecosystem resources remain centralized and more visible and accessible in the urban hubs than in more predominantly rural places.

Case Study #2: The Region 9 Entrepreneur Ecosystem

GO Virginia Region 9 encompasses a nine-county region that spans central Virginia communities from Warrenton in the north to Nelson County in the south. Much of the region borders Virginia's Route 29, and Charlottesville (population 47,226) serves as the region's largest urban center. The region is home to several smaller towns, such as Culpeper, Warrenton, and Orange, but, in general, most parts of Region 9 are rural.[1]

Thanks to the local presence of the University of Virginia (UVA), Charlottesville has emerged as a nationally recognized center for innovation and entrepreneurship. UVA's Darden School of Business regularly ranks among the top entrepreneurship programs, and other UVA schools and programs, especially in the life sciences, also have global reputations for effective technology transfer and commercialization. The Charlottesville community is nationally recognized as a good place for start-ups, ranking especially high in areas like angel capital investments and for growth in technology-related businesses. In fact, Charlottesville ranked eleventh among 201 smaller metro areas in the 2020 Milken Institute Best Performing Cities assessment (Lin, Lee, and Wong 2020).

While exciting opportunities have emerged in and around UVA, community leaders long recognized that other parts of Region 9 were not well integrated into the local ecosystem emerging around Charlottesville. For

---

1. GO Virginia Region 9 includes the City of Charlottesville, and the following counties: Albemarle, Culpeper, Fauquier, Fluvanna, Greene, Louisa, Madison, Nelson, Orange, and Rappahannock.

example, the original Region 9 Growth and Diversification plan noted that:

> Currently, Region 9's entrepreneur ecosystem is strong with regard to student and faculty innovations at UVA, but thin and fragmented elsewhere in the region. It does not adequately support new businesses or help existing businesses to scale throughout the region. Most programs are operated on limited budgets that constrain their capacity to assist entrepreneurs. Often, managers of these programs lack the background to provide meaningful assistance to quickly growing companies. (GO Virginia Region 9, 2017, 7)

A related deeper dive into regional innovation assets noted low impacts of start-ups on regional development in technology industries and also noted that networking and business opportunities were difficult to access outside of Charlottesville or Fauquier County (TEConomy Partners, 2018).

Armed with this analysis, regional GO Virginia leaders invested in two initiatives to enhance the regional ecosystem. An initial effort focused directly on Charlottesville and Albemarle County, developing a plan to build a Venture Hub facility in or near downtown Charlottesville. A second effort assessed ecosystem building efforts in the region's surrounding counties (GO Virginia Region 9, 2020). The GO Virginia leadership team opted to fund two projects to ensure that rural ecosystem development efforts were front and center in regional economic development discussions.

Phase 1 of this work produced a business plan for a Charlottesville-based "Venture Hub" facility, designed to serve three purposes:

1. As a gateway to help connect people with existing entrepreneurship resources and encourage the creation of resources as the need arises.
2. As an accelerator for high-growth, traded sector start-ups to include programming such as entrepreneurs-in-residence, mentoring, networking, venture accelerator, start-up incubator, speaker series, and so forth.
3. To support a narrative that promotes central Virginia as a center for entrepreneurship.

A team of local partners began fundraising and planning for the Venture Hub beginning in late 2019, and efforts to develop the new facility remain underway. While the Venture Hub facility and programming offer great promise, the project team also recognized that the region's rural entrepreneurs needed access to more specialized support closer to home. While many local business owners were willing to travel to the Venture Hub on occasion, support networks and programs were needed in locations outside of downtown Charlottesville. Regional leaders hoped to develop a stronger set of programs and work spaces that operated both in Charlottesville, the region's business center, and in other communities across Region 9. This was the primary focus of the project's second phase.

This Phase 2 rural ecosystem work built on several important characteristics of the central Virginia economy. First, distance to markets and to support services poses a challenge for rural business owners who lack the time to travel to network meetings and other events, especially during business hours. Second, many of Region 9's rural entrepreneurs operate outside of the tech sectors that dominate ecosystem-related discussions in Charlottesville. Food and agriculture-related ventures are especially important in central Virginia, which is widely recognized for its assets related to organic foods, wine, beer, cider, and other food products. These companies often have different needs and concerns than life science or other tech firms affiliated with UVA programs. Third, rural communities view ecosystem building in a more holistic manner where local firms serve as community anchors. Ecosystem development is not just about helping companies grow; it has wider economic development purposes as well. It is about building companies and building communities at the same time. Last, rural entrepreneurs in central Virginia still face thorny infrastructure challenges. Broadband connections are often poor, and talent attraction/retention is challenging due to housing shortages and other factors.

Region 9's rural ecosystem strategy contains several key components. Creating local "hubs" for rural entrepreneurs is a top priority. Local business owners have long expressed interest in easier access to networks and support services but were often unable to travel into Charlottesville or other urban centers for these events. The Region 9 plan recommends the creation of a "home for entrepreneurs" in every county. This "home" could take many forms but is intended to serve as a community meeting space/coworking space where business owners, freelancers, and others could work, interact, and do business together. These locations could take many forms, and preliminary county planning had designated different types of spaces for this function, including existing private coworking spaces, private offices, or extra space in existing government facilities. The spaces would also be linked into a regional network, including the central Venture Hub facility, via a regional coworking passport program where entrepreneurs could access space and programs in every county. This proposal was modeled on similar passport programs operating in Colorado, Florida, Indiana, and Minnesota.

This space would also serve as an access point for business service providers, such as the Small Business Development Center network. The report also recommended the hiring of two business navigators focused on helping rural business owners access needed support and services. Ultimately, these navigators would operate within the wider regional Venture Hub network connecting the central facility in Charlottesville with county-level business hub spaces. A related initiative calls for a regulatory review of county-level rules, in areas like zoning and planning, to ensure that they are as "entrepreneur friendly" as possible.

Recognizing the connection between ecosystem building and community building, the strategy also envisions a major expansion of youth entrepreneurship training across Region 9. This initiative builds on strong local programs already operating in the region, especially in Culpeper and Fauquier Counties. It envisions a regional network to offer youth training, business plan competitions, career coaching, and other support, with an intention to build an entrepreneur mindset among local youth, support talent retention, and build a stronger entrepreneur business culture in central Virginia.

A final recommendation seeks to further develop the region's promising food and agriculture sector. Central Virginia has developed a burgeoning reputation for excellence in areas like beer, wine, and organic foods, and food and agriculture start-ups are among the region's fastest growing sectors. The plan recommends expansion of a fledgling Food Enterprise Center in Culpeper County as a first step toward a more robust commitment to support local food and agriculture-related start-ups. This rural ecosystem strategy was completed in March 2020, and further implementation has been on hold due to the COVID-19 pandemic.

Promising Lessons from Regions 2 and 9

Both Region 2 and Region 9 illustrate the complexity of understanding and building entrepreneur ecosystems. As such, the primary value of this chapter's contribution may be to identify some key questions for future exploration and to sound a note of caution about intra-regional equity across urban and rural areas.

One question raised by the GO Virginia initiative concerns how to define the borders and bounds of an ecosystem and whether those borders and bounds may be externally imposed. In these instances, the regional geography is a constructed one, imposed by the state. Each region had some portions of its geography that were accustomed to working together and functioning as a shared ecosystem and some areas that were less central or even apart from the previous naturally forming ecosystems. For instance, a previous study of the Roanoke-Blacksburg entrepreneur ecosystem in Region 2 was funded by the Kauffmann Foundation (Cowell, Lyon-Hill, and Tate 2018). The research found that the perceptions of experiences of entrepreneurs within a given ecosystem can vary depending on their familiarity with and sense of connectivity to the key ecosystem-building entities.

Both Region 2 and Region 9 also include both urban and rural locations, and the need for the more rural and peripheral communities to feel connected to the larger ecosystem remains a concern. Region 9's focus on a rural entrepreneurship strategy is commendable. Region 9 recommends multiple ecosystem hubs or nodes throughout its localities while Region 2 focuses on strengthening the ecosystems around its three subregional urban hubs and spreading those resources out to the periphery. In addition, Region 2 offers assistance across the region through an intermediary organization, the Valleys Innovation Council.

Some of the key questions and possibly promising lessons include:

- **How do we account for regional variations in entrepreneur ecosystem building?** This question points to a need for local customization: How do regions design and align business support programs to match local needs, preferences, and practices? Both regions are attempting different approaches and offer varied strategies for different localities. This seems important to note. The most effective programs likely are those that design place-specific responses instead of simply importing models from other regions. It may be particularly important to adapt strategies and activities to the types of businesses and industry expertise found close to home.

- **How do we structure ecosystems that engage people in both urban and rural locations across a particular regional geography?** The lesson here suggests a need for widespread engagement. By definition, rural places have fewer people—and fewer entrepreneurs—than more densely populated urban centers. Effective support programs and entrepreneur networks often require a certain scale and size to provide needed services and networks for local entrepreneurs. The question becomes how to leverage these economies of scale to engage as many residents as possible across larger regional geographies. Activities and programs must be open to all in principle (they don't turn people away) and in practice and spirit (they actively reach out to involve those less engaged). This may mean that some resource providers will find their customer base to be quite diverse, from technology entrepreneurs to food business operations to a working parent developing their side hustle. Regional assets and programs must be able to meet entrepreneurs where they are and adjust their offerings to fit specific and varying needs.
- **How do we remedy a relative scarcity of experienced high-growth entrepreneurs?** This speaks to the need to engage existing entrepreneurs as leaders and to build bridges to knowledge and resources outside the region. Concerning the latter point, the COVID-19 epidemic has actually created opportunities here. RAMP in Region 2 has created a pool of virtual mentors and coaches across the country, available to lend their expertise to Region 2 start-ups via remote technologies. The experienced start-ups have much to share and often the best entrepreneur support organizations are not only led by entrepreneurs but also find ways to actively engage in dialogue with current entrepreneurs of all types. Established entrepreneurs

also serve important functions as role models, mentors, and coaches for new and aspiring business owners.
- **How do we find and support entrepreneurs with potential, especially in more rural places?** The lesson here is to leave few stones unturned in growing the future entrepreneur pipeline. In each region, talent attraction and retention are a concern and there are a finite number of existing high-potential small businesses. This places a premium on reaching out to youth and considering innovative ways to help younger and less experienced entrepreneurs of all ages. This may mean the introduction of school-based partnerships, mentoring programs, and other initiatives that expose youth to entrepreneurship as a career option.
- **When geography is a challenge, how do we help more rural entrepreneurs experience some of the benefits of networking and connectivity?** This question concerns the need to create more spaces for entrepreneurs to connect. In a previous study Twitter analytics and social network analysis mapped where entrepreneurs connect (Cowell, Lyon-Hill, and Tate 2018). Those spaces included chamber of commerce events, coffee shops, and libraries. Both rural and urban places benefit from having a number of physical homes for entrepreneurship and innovation. This can be dedicated spaces or networking events. The spaces can be formal or informal but do need to be accessible and widely known and publicized.
- **How do we harness the power of local anchors and actors to connect with and support local entrepreneurs?** This question underscores the importance of engaging anchor institutions. Anchor institutions are universities, colleges, hospitals, and other entities that tend to have a long-term "rooted" presence in their local communities and economies. Anchor institutions also are enduring, significant contributors to the local community whether as part of their mission, as an employer, through capital investments, through partnerships and programming, or other connections to local and regional businesses, customers, or suppliers. The presence of a

large entity in a community is significant, but the focus and literature on these entities as "anchors" suggests that intentional strategies must be employed to maximize their role as anchor institutions and more effectively maximize their local impacts and significance.

In the case of entrepreneurship, entities such as Virginia Tech and the University of Virginia are in the midst of pivots to better maximize their anchor institution potential. Anchor institutions may require a mix of incentives and motivation to realize their economic potential. Other institutions can also play an "anchor" role. Carilion Virginia Western Community College helped establish and grow RAMP, the first accelerator program in the region. While the COVID-19 pandemic has slowed the development and implementation of the projects discussed above, both regions remain focused on the goal of building effective and inclusive ecosystems that are open to all types of entrepreneurs and to partners from all communities. They have embraced strategies that are tailored but inclusive, building on strong technology assets, such as Virginia Tech's technology strengths and UVA's life sciences assets, while also offering opportunities for rural entrepreneurs as well.

Policy recommendations based on these experiences focus on helping other regions and states develop and implement effective entrepreneurship strategies in order to spur rural development and build closer urban-rural connections.

For Local Leaders and Economic Development Professionals

Step one for local leaders is simple: Embrace entrepreneurship as a core part of the region's economic development portfolio. At the broadest level, this embrace involves using the bully pulpit available to elected officials and other leaders to talk about why entrepreneurs matter to local prosperity and to encourage more local people to consider entrepreneurship as a career option. Further actions would involve support for low-cost strategies, such as local awards programs or efforts to support more small business–friendly rules and regulations.

Step two is to think regionally and support initiatives and investments that enhance regional ecosystems while checking to be sure the gains are shared across more rural and more urban locations within a region.

This step necessitates the cultivation of a regional mindset and an awareness of rural-urban interdependencies. The Advancement Foundation's GAUNTLET program in Region 2 is an example. The GAUNTLET has become Virginia's largest business program and competition, combining a ten-week business development program with a competition that connects budding entrepreneurs to resources and funding. In 2020, participants won over $300,000 in cash and in-kind awards as well as other resources such as low-interest loan funds, matching grants, and industry coaches and advisors. Local governments actively support the program through economic development office staff time, other in-kind support, and direct funding in some instances.

Further local action might include investments to fund start-ups, provide technical assistance, and other activities. As localities move in these directions, it is especially important for rural leaders to reach out to each other, to more urban counterparts, and to area anchor institutions and intermediaries via partnerships that bring in new resources, new perspectives, and access to new business opportunities.

Rural communities should also access expertise and resources from national partners such as the Kauffman Foundation and its related programs, including the One Million Cups networking program that already operates in numerous communities around the US (including Fairfax County, Prince William County, Richmond, and Virginia Beach). Rural ecosystem builders will then benefit from emerging networks that connect ecosystem champions and help share new ideas and best practices. Examples include Rural RISE, a network for rural ecosystem builders, and the Global Entrepreneurship Network. Finally, rural ecosystem leaders must also ensure that local entrepreneurs are connected to outside resources and business opportunities. Developing these types of regional connections was a key part of Region 9's plans for a shared co-working network across the nine-county region.

For State Agencies

The GO Virginia initiative pursued several approaches that have proved highly effective and worth considering in similar state or regional initiatives. At the most basic level, GO Virginia helped regional and local leaders "do their homework" via state-backed investments in research and assessment so that every region was benchmarked to assess its ecosystem-related assets and gaps. These assessments helped regions hit the ground running and develop specific programming and investments that addressed program gaps and capitalized on opportunities. For example, Region 9's entire rural strategy grew directly from data that highlighted ecosystem challenges in the region's more isolated communities. In addition to funding critical early research, GO Virginia also encouraged specialization and local customization of programming. Each GO Virginia region is developing entrepreneurship-related programming, but their approaches do not follow a cookie cutter approach.

GO Virginia is designed to encourage higher wage job creation in important industry sectors and specifically excludes nontraded sector companies in areas such as tourism, agriculture, and local "main street" retail. This may be more observation than lesson, as there are positives and negatives to this type of policy focus for rural localities. For many rural places, the higher wage entrepreneur opportunities may be more common in tourism or related areas. This has meant that those communities have not been able to structure GO Virginia projects in support of entrepreneurs in those areas.

However, in some cases, the focus has challenged rural entrepreneur resource providers to consider the extent to which they work with higher potential entrepreneurs. In the New River Valley in Region 2, GO Virginia helped expand the capacity of an existing SBDC to meet an unmet need, but only if a significant percentage of the SBDC activities included a focus on higher-growth-potential start-ups. The policy implication here may be that state guidelines can encourage changes in practice at the local level, which ultimately improve the local capacity for innovation and growth.

GO Virginia has been in many ways a top-down approach, spurred by state policymakers and influential private sector leaders. However, the program has also recognized the importance of geographic differences and local customization through the establishment of regional councils and regionally specific plans and strategies. The program has sought to recognize that rural regions face different challenges than their more urban counterparts. However, the focus on intra-regional variation is also critical. There remains room for greater support of bottom-up, community-specific initiatives, with lower barriers to entry. Often this is more of a need in rural communities. GO Virginia incentivizes certain types of projects and requires substantive cross-jurisdictional collaboration, financial commitment, and clear return on investment.

For smaller, more exploratory, single-jurisdiction, and less resourced projects, GO Virginia is often less of a fit. Some state-level programs that supported this type of ecosystem building have ended or have seen their funding levels decrease in recent years, as funding was reallocated for more prominent initiatives such as GO Virginia. There do remain some other notable programs that support local ecosystems such as the Department of Housing and Community Development's Community Business Launch and the Rally Southwest Virginia programs.

Beyond Virginia, other states have initiated promising practices for supporting entrepreneur ecosystems, such as Georgia's Entrepreneur Friendly Initiative led by the Georgia Department of Economic Development. The program helps communities create a more entrepreneur-friendly environment and develop local-level entrepreneur and small business development strategies. Network Kansas's E-Communities program offers another model for supporting locally designed and managed ecosystem efforts.

For Anchor Institutions and Universities

Anchor institutions, like colleges and universities, often play central roles in ecosystem building, but they assume outsized importance in more rural regions. Their specific roles will vary, but anchor institutions hold great potential to better leverage their assets and revenues to promote local private sector development and entrepreneur activity. This might be seen in a number of ways, including offering space and facilities; directing a greater percentage of their purchasing power toward local vendors; and partnering and investing in ecosystem programs, such as accelerators, loan funds, or business assistance programs. Educational entities can create more opportunities for students and faculty to work with local entrepreneurs as interns, advisors, consultants, or workers.

Where feasible, higher education institutions should actively embrace the mission of ecosystem building and align education and training options in a way that provides support to the university community and to the wider community as well. In both cases discussed here, Virginia Tech and UVA have partnered to invest in new community-focused programs and facilities, such as VIC and RAMP in Region 2 and UVA's Catalyst

Accelerator programs in Region 9. Virginia Western, a community college in Roanoke, has played a key anchor institution role in supporting RAMP and entrepreneur learning. Liberty University, a private institution in Lynchburg, has invested in research lab spaces and equipment that are accessible to area companies and start-ups. It can also be more difficult for smaller or more rural entities to serve as anchors. In the Alleghany Highlands, Dabney Lancaster Community College has tried to spur a focus on unmanned systems through support of an incubator and a workforce training initiative. The results have been mixed, largely due to a gap in the amount of resources available and needed in the mostly rural region to truly compete and cultivate such a technology-intensive industry sector in the absence of larger private sector companies or major research universities.

In rural regions, stand-alone incubators or accelerator programs may not be available. Anchor institutions can help with the provision of shared services and spaces. In addition to the Virginia examples discussed here, other successful national models include Iowa's Pappajohn Centers program and Purdue's Firestarter programs, which include programming at Purdue's main campus and rural satellites operating in smaller communities such as Vincennes and the three-county region surrounding the Crane Naval Surface Warfare Center in south central Indiana.

Conclusion

This chapter has explored intentional efforts to enhance the entrepreneur ecosystem in two Virginia regions, each with a mix of urban and rural features. Both regions remain a work in progress, but state-level policy through the GO Virginia program is contributing to significant ecosystem enhancement in both places.

The pandemic has necessitated shifts in these regions. Resource providers are employing more distance or virtual technologies, which has lessened some of the geographic and transportation limitations but highlighted other barriers (broadband access). Small business resilience and recovery is a pressing concern nationally, but especially in rural places more reliant on tourism, which has suffered greatly during the pandemic. GO Virginia has supported economic recovery and resilience projects, including initiatives aimed at pivoting resource provision to more remote options.

The on-the-ground work of a range of actors has also been important, particularly the role of anchor institutions. Ecosystems are dynamic and complex, and this chapter focused on ways that one state program has incentivized local activity to better support entrepreneurship, and how that has impacted rural places. In considering possible lessons from these regions, this research identifies the importance of local customization and place-specific approaches; the value of widespread engagement and access to ecosystem resources; the potential of engaging local entrepreneurs as leaders and stakeholders; the necessity of growing the future entrepreneur pipeline; the benefit of creating more spaces for entrepreneurs to connect; the possibilities associated with building bridges within and across the ecosystem as well as beyond the region to outside markets and resources; and the critical role of connecting and maximizing anchor institutions.

Chapter 6

Advancing STEM Educational Opportunities for All Virginians

*Phyllis L. Newbill, Susan G. Magliaro, Kerry O. Cresawn,
Lindsay B. Wheeler, Elizabeth W. Edmondson,
Albert Byers, and Padmanabhan Seshaiyer*

The purpose of this chapter is to describe a rationale and blueprint for a strategic, multisector STEM network in Virginia to strengthen STEM literacy and STEM workforce development throughout the state. This chapter describes a multiuniversity collaborative led by Virginia Tech, a needs assessment, and evidence-based recommendations for developing and sustaining a strategic multisector STEM network in Virginia. The chapter concludes with recommendations to aid in the development of a strategic STEM network or multisector partnership to support STEM in Virginia.

Literacy and workforce competency in science, technology, engineering, and mathematics (STEM) are vital to our nation's and our state's global leadership and advancement of our citizens' quality of life. Yet STEM is more than the letters in an acronym. It is an integrated understanding, a habit of mind, a way of approaching the world—asking and answering questions, thinking critically, and using evidence to make informed decisions in everyday situations and circumstances.

Major issues, such as reductions in biodiversity, energy sustainability, emergence and reemergence of infectious diseases, vulnerabilities of the internet, clean oceans, and food demand are just a few of the grand challenges that affect our citizenry on local, regional, national, and global levels (Bybee 2018). There are benefits and trade-offs embedded within these STEM-infused issues. As such, it is paramount we help students successfully analyze, evaluate, and enact their collective response beyond their formative years and create innovative solutions to these challenges. Thus, STEM education is of critical importance now and into the foreseeable future.

STEM literacy is foundational to everyday life, and expertise across the STEM disciplines is essential to our economic growth, competitiveness, and national security (Committee on STEM Education 2018; Council on Foreign Relations 2012). STEM is important to workforce development. Virginia's STEM jobs are expected to grow by 18% in the next four years (Mickle 2020), and employers often struggle to fill skilled labor jobs (Tupponce 2013). Regions of Virginia have unequal education, employment, and income opportunities. STEM education paired with workforce development can address these inequities.

The purpose of this chapter is to describe a rationale and blueprint for a strategic, multisector STEM network in Virginia to strengthen STEM literacy and STEM workforce development throughout the state.

Equity in STEM Education

Equity in STEM education is a nationwide problem. The United States is experiencing a crisis in STEM fields due to a decrease in pursuit of STEM-related careers (DeCoito and Myszkal 2018). The National Research Council (2012) frames promoting equity in science in these ways:

> Equity in science education requires that all students are provided with equitable opportunities to learn science and become engaged in science and engineering practices; with access to quality space, equipment, and teachers to support and motivate that learning and engagement; and adequate time spent on science. In addition, the issue of connecting to students' interests and experiences is

particularly important for broadening participation in science. (28)

These same commitments to equity, access, and inclusion should apply to formal and informal STEM education and experiences across the Commonwealth's STEM network.

Like other Virginia resources, access to quality STEM programming varies from region to region across the state. Schools are inherently local institutions. In the interest of "best practices" and "generalizability," local context can get lost in the education system. It should not, however, because "much of the local economic and social realities of that place determine the opportunities and constraints of local schooling" (Biddle and Azano 2016, 316). The inherently local quality of schools is couched in the inherent need for local workforce development, especially in rural communities where the love of place is deeply ingrained in the culture (Jones and Brunner 1994). Varying characteristics of rural and urban parts of Virginia mean that different regions have different needs and resources for learners in STEM.

For example, rural schools have unique challenges for STEM education, including teacher recruitment, retention, and training; access to field trips; and access to resources (Biddle and Azano 2016). While not every rural student considering a STEM career needs to attend college, the opportunity to consider it is important. Rural high school students often lack access to information about college, including college campus visits and visits to their high school from colleges (Ardoin 2018).

Similar challenges exist in urban settings where students are the least likely to be taught by well-prepared educators, and challenges of teacher turnover and retention in STEM areas are well documented (Cochran-Smith et al. 2015; Darling-Hammond 2010). Collectively, irrespective of the geographic location, research documents the issue of securing adequately trained teachers for both urban and rural schools, both of which serve low-income communities (Ingersoll 2004).

Regional hubs with cross-sectional partnerships are critical for building sustainable workforce development processes (National Science Board 2020; Weld 2017). In a rural example, a Vibrant Virginia initiative aligned with this project and United Way of Southwest Virginia programming was designed to advance career awareness through two parallel and complementary goals: (1) to increase student internship opportunities by better connecting teachers and business leaders, and (2) to help high school teachers develop a better understanding of the employment opportunities in the region by orchestrating site visits and professional development workshops with the same employers.

In addition to a community's population density, the demographics of its population can also affect STEM equity. Virginia public schools are now over 50% minority and as such, we cannot ignore the inequities that exist in our communities across the state in providing high-impact STEM learning experiences for all students (Virginia Department of Education 2016). To increase diversity in STEM, components for success include the acquisition of knowledge, skills, and habits of mind coupled with the opportunity to put these into practice, which allow students to develop a sense of competence and progress, belonging, motivation, and self-identification within the STEM fields, including information about various requirements and future opportunities (National Academy of Sciences, Engineering and Medicine 2011).

For African Americans and Hispanics, who collectively constitute approximately 30% of the US population (and growing), their pursuits of undergraduate degrees in physical science, mathematics, and engineering have remained flat since the 2000s, hovering around 12%. African Americans and Hispanics constitute only a very small percentage (3% or less) of the current US STEM workforce in math, science, and engineering (National Center for Science and Engineering Statistics 2013). This leads to a troubling and significant gap between these underrepresented groups and majority groups, which limits their participation in many well-paid, high-growth professions and stifles our nation's benefits from diverse perspectives, talents, and creativity (PCAST 2010).

In particular, the number of students from underrepresented and underserved populations who choose careers related to STEM is significantly lower than that of their counterparts. And yet, "all students should be able to learn about the broad set of possibilities that modern life offers and to pursue their aspirations, including their occupations of interest" (National Research Council 2012, 279).

In addition to demographic factors, STEM education needs vary across the regions because of environmental variables. The Chesapeake Bay ecosystem is relevant and relatively accessible as a STEM laboratory to the most populous parts of the state. However, in the southwestern part of the state, waters drain to the Mississippi River, and Chesapeake Bay–specific curricula are less relevant. Features and challenges of karst topography—land characterized by caves and sinkholes—are not present in Richmond, Fairfax, or Hampton Roads but are important economic and environmental factors from the Shenandoah Valley to Bristol. Coal's presence in a few Virginia counties has historically dominated those economies. STEM equity includes connections to learners' experiences, both environmentally and culturally.

While rural and urban regions face unique challenges, it is important to note that "sustainable growth hinges less on a place's designation as urban or rural, and more on its economic connections" (McFarland 2018). Regional connections are important; McFarland and Grabowski (2020) found a significant association between the employment growth rate for the county in which an industry is located and whether or not that industry is identified as being regionally connected. Education ecosystems built on the same regional infrastructure can provide similar connections. Collaboration and cooperation across a STEM network allow schools in rural districts with limited resources to do more to create opportunities for learners (Weld 2017).

Achieving STEM equity in Virginia will involve understanding and coping with the intersectionality of rural-urban designations, race and ethnicity, and income to create culturally relevant STEM experiences for learners. An analysis of these factors in Virginia reveals that, contrary to prevailing stereotypes, many rural areas also have higher concentrations of African American populations. Also contrary to stereotypes, many primarily white localities are in the lowest bracket of median income. With this in mind, STEM programming based on stereotypes or assumptions that do not take these nuances into account run the risk of being irrelevant to their target audiences.

In alignment with the findings of McFarland, Grabowski, and others, the proposed Virginia STEM network model aims to (1) connect higher education institutions, K–12 schools, government agencies, and other sources of quality STEM education in the metropolitan and micropolitan regions to their neighboring rural regions by establishing regional hubs, and (2) work with stakeholders representing STEM industries to provide a platform for building their connectivity by facilitating development of industry-supported formal and informal STEM education opportunities.

STEM Networks as an Answer

In the most recent federal STEM education plan, the Committee on STEM Education (2018) identified that one of the most successful mechanisms for achieving both STEM literacy and a STEM workforce is the development of strategic multisector partnerships at the community, regional, state, and federal levels. These multisector partnerships connect preK–12 schools, informal education systems (libraries, museums, after school programs, clubs), colleges and universities, government, and employers (corporate, government, and nonprofit). The partnerships are often identified as networks of the stakeholders, and they are supported by corporate interests, state government, and/or university systems, as they serve to connect groups that often operate in isolation (Magliaro and Ernst 2018). Many STEM networks around the United States are based in the population centers and metropolitan areas. Some, such as Iowa's and Tennessee's networks, are statewide enterprises that encompass large swaths of rural territory (Magliaro and Ernst 2018). The examples of successes from other statewide networks launched the conversations that led to the university collaboration described in this chapter. As we draw upon best practices of existing STEM networks, literature also documents the challenges in deploying state-based efforts, which in part include: (a) a lack of clearly identified stable leadership, (b) an ill-defined strategic plan, (c) unnecessary bureaucracy that hinders momentum, (d) insufficient self-sustainable infrastructure, and (e) adequate and meaningful stakeholder involvement (Johnson 2012).

In the spring of 2018, five public universities (George Mason University, James Madison University, The University of Virginia, Virginia Commonwealth University, and Virginia Tech) were awarded a 4-VA grant to investigate the current STEM preK–12 outreach programming at each institution and convene key STEM national and state leaders to envision a future statewide STEM network for Virginia. Based on the literature (e.g., Weld 2017), it was known that statewide STEM networks needed to be framed by the voices of the stakeholders including those in K–12 education, informal education, higher education, workforce development, government, and corporations. As such, the team approached this work as a research investigation to provide an evidence-based foundation for future development of the potential network's vision, mission, infrastructure, operation, and activity. The projected deliverable was a white paper or blueprint for consideration by state government and educational agencies. Virginia's STEM coordinator and the Virginia Department of Education's STEM director joined the team as advisors and provided guidance related to project activities.

In the spring of 2019, Governor Northam launched the STEM Education Commission to develop a state STEM education strategic plan. The goal of this plan is to guide future learning opportunities to advance STEM literacy and workforce development. The team's advisors were coordinating the work of the commission and collaborated to ensure that the work was in support of and complementary to the commission's effort and outcome. The goal was for the blueprint to ultimately inform the development of a statewide STEM network and provide input to advance the Commonwealth's STEM strategic plan.

The research included both local and national voices. The team:

- explored other states' STEM networks to understand what is available and their missions, infrastructures, operations, and funding;
- gathered data from various stakeholders across the state and included their perspectives in final recommendations; and
- used the research on STEM education to understand these voices within the national context.

This chapter describes this collaborative led by Virginia Tech, the outcomes of the needs assessment, and evidence-based recommendations for developing and sustaining a strategic multisector STEM network in Virginia. The data were summarized into the major themes and key considerations, and then delivered to the Governor's STEM Commission in March 2020 to serve as a foundation for the blueprint of a successful and thriving STEM network in Virginia.

A needs assessment approach to this research was chosen in order to give voice to all of the major sectors involved with STEM education in Virginia. Two major needs assessment activities yielded information to frame the blueprint: (1) a pilot inventory of the current STEM education programs and collaborations that have been successful at our institutions and that might be scaled up or replicated across Virginia, and (2) a day-long STEM Summit that convened 150 STEM leaders representing multiple sectors from across Virginia and the nation in October 2019.

STEM Education Inventory

To make progress toward a database of current STEM initiatives within Virginia, a survey was administered in April and May 2019 to faculty and administrators at the five higher education institutions. The survey inventoried the outreach opportunities they were providing in K–12 education, whom they were providing it for, and the target region of the state. The goal of this survey was to understand what was already happening across the state in terms of STEM programming from universities and to field test a process that would be scaled up to survey STEM programming across all Virginia institutions of higher education.

STEM Summit

The next step was organizing the Virginia STEM Summit. The goal was to convene STEM education leaders across the Commonwealth to inform the development of a Virginia STEM network blueprint. An important step in the planning process was identifying and inviting individuals from key sectors (e.g., higher education, K–12, informal, government, and corporate) to attend. Quotas ensured a relatively balanced distribution of attendees and that the Summit would represent diverse participants and perspectives. Hosted at Virginia Commonwealth University, members of the Governor's STEM Commission were also invited and most attended.

The program blended inspiration, information sharing, and information gathering. The STEM Summit featured a keynote address by Virginia native Leland Melvin, a retired NASA astronaut. He shared his inspirational story of grace, grit, and second chances, describing the people and mechanisms that enabled him to succeed in his amazing STEM career. Then, a panel of experts in STEM education, including Dr. James Lane, Virginia superintendent of schools, Dr. Andrew Daire, Dean, VCU School of Education, Dr. Laylah Bulman, Enterprise director, LEGO Education, and Dr. Robert Corbin, director of Global Initiatives, Discovery Education. The panel fielded a range of questions about developing and sustaining a statewide STEM network. With a focus on access and inclusion, the panel offered specific ideas, concerns, strategies, and potential solutions. The clear messages from the panelists were: (a) Virginia already has many points of pride in STEM education, (b) the goal should be to build on our existing resources, and (c) there is a need to create an infrastructure to ensure that all Virginians have access to STEM education.

Participants then organized into "by sector" groups, then "cross-sector" groups to identify the key issues and priorities for STEM education in Virginia. The groups identified exemplary initiatives and associated success metrics, implementation steps, and sectors to be involved. These ideas were articulated on chart paper and posted around the room for a gallery walk. Participants reviewed and voted for their top initiatives. The STEM Summit concluded with a summative statement from Dr. Jeff Weld, executive director, Iowa Governor's STEM Advisory Council.

Following the STEM Summit, participants completed an evaluation survey that provided feedback to the research collective on the day's events. It also provided a mechanism for individuals to articulate their thoughts and share perspectives on creating and sustaining a STEM network.

The collaborative used two major data collection and analysis processes aligned with the project goals. For the first goal, inventorying STEM education initiatives across the state, the collaborative deployed a survey to build an initial STEM inventory with the intent of assessing the survey's effectiveness. Responses were analyzed in order to identify the number, type, and nature of STEM education initiatives across Virginia that institutions of higher education coordinated or partnered to implement.

For the second goal, the STEM Summit, the collaborative analyzed the responses to the open-ended evaluation questions and documents produced by attendees during the "by-sector" and "cross-sector" activities. The process identified fifteen initial themes with some overlapping features. The members of the collaborative discussed these initial/emerging ideas to create the broader overarching themes and principles, described below, that comprehensively captured attendees' perceptions.

WHAT THE SURVEY AND SUMMIT TELL US ABOUT STEM IN VIRGINIA

Results from the pilot survey of STEM initiatives and the STEM Summit are described below. Survey results revealed important information about current activities reported by the participating universities as well as about the survey itself. The STEM Summit results represent the voices across multiple sectors, and specific principles and themes emerged that provide considerations for STEM network design. Example comments from the data illustrate these themes. Integrated in each section are relevant connections to prior published work.

In brief, the pilot survey of STEM initiatives yielded eighty-two responses (i.e., different STEM activities) detailing a myriad of different types of programs in regions served by the universities involved in the project. Each university serves its surrounding region with a range of programs. Most of the programs served twenty-one to fifty people and focused on a regional or metro-area audience rather than a statewide one.

One of the main ideas that came from the STEM Summit was that "STEM is a culture, not a class" (Corbin 2019). The Virginia STEM network should focus on building a strong foundation for STEM literacy for all Virginia learners by ensuring opportunities to master basic STEM concepts (Weld 2017). According to the Virginia Department of Education (2020), "STEM literacy is the ability to identify and acknowledge science, technology, engineering and mathematics concepts and processes in everyday life." Furthermore, STEM literacy should be viewed as a "dynamic process" that transcends educational content objectives to align with learners' emotional needs, physical skills, and cognitive skills. Beyond individual growth, STEM literacy reaches to the economic, societal, and personal needs of humanity (Zollman 2012, 18). Such a perspective enables us to focus on "STEM literacy for continued learning" (Zollman 2012, 18) and promote STEM as a culture (Corbin 2019).

Most of the fastest-growing occupations require significant mathematics and science preparation (US Department of Labor and Statistics 2019). Priorities and activities of the STEM network should be informed by workforce trends to ensure alignment between "what is taught and learned with what is needed at work and in the communities" (Committee on STEM Education 2018, 9). STEM Summit participants saw value in a STEM network informed by workforce trends with regard to "creation of talent to supply a skilled workforce to companies working in Virginia" and "improving the number of children who are interested in pursuing a career in a STEM field."

Necessary Conditions for Success

Active Promotion of Equity, Access, and Inclusion

When STEM Summit participants were asked what was most important to them about creating a STEM network in Virginia, attention to issues of equity, access, and inclusion quickly surfaced, acknowledging the need for "a focus on equity and access to extend the reach into as many communities as possible." As one participant commented, creating a STEM network in Virginia is important for "the future of its children to remain and grow and thrive."

To realize this hope, the STEM network must work for all children across Virginia. Participants discussed the need to support all Virginia students through equitable access to resources, high academic standards, and opportunities to learn STEM. Learners within the STEM network should be provided equitable access to, and opportunity for, formal and informal STEM learning that is intentionally inclusive of learners of diverse backgrounds and abilities.

Attention to students' opportunity to learn STEM is necessary to promote equity, access, and inclusion across the STEM network (Tate 2001). Focused on quality STEM education for all, opportunity to learn encompasses three related constructs: time on task (i.e., engaged time, time allocated to science instruction), quality of instruction (relative to concepts assessed), and technology (including science equipment; Tate 2001). Yet, across Virginia there are disparities in opportunities to learn consisting of, for example, (a) limited time engaged in STEM due to inadequate resources or limited course offerings, (b) curricular or ability tracking that limits exposure to quality STEM instruction, and (c) little opportunity for students to interact with the tools and technologies of STEM via authentic investigations and inquiries.

Further, educational approaches need to be culturally relevant to ensure all students are motivated and challenged to learn. For example, locally focused STEM experiences germane to students' everyday lives support intrinsic inspiration to learn. One participant put it this way, "Making STEM a statewide network will even up the playing/learning/experience field for all students across the Commonwealth. Just a little touch of what some call STEM is zero compared to what other regions are accomplishing and what other students are experiencing and learning that should be available and required for all students."

Collaboration

As a second theme from the STEM Summit, participants overwhelmingly cited collaboration as a valuable component of creating and sustaining a STEM network. To be effective, collaboration relies heavily on inter-sector and inter-stakeholder group communication. For example, stakeholders from different regions and sectors (e.g., K–12 educators, K–12 administrators, postsecondary, out-of-school time, businesses, state offices) need opportunities to communicate, and where appropriate share ideas or partner with one another. Parents, community members, and students should also be included in these conversations. Importantly, communication should involve cross-sector data sharing. As one participant stated, a STEM network needs "increased opportunities for collaborations and a clearer path for direct communication among stakeholders."

"True collaboration involves equity and mutual participation" (Burbank and Kaushack 2003, 500), which aligns with the two additional characteristics that emerged as themes related to successful collaborations: (1) what it means to collaborate, and (2) the distinction between collaboration and competition. First, participants across stakeholder sectors hold differing perceptions of what it means to collaborate, and acknowledging and respecting these differences as collaborations are forged is important. For example, one participant stated, "Each stakeholder is looking at STEM through their lens" and suggested the need to make sure that all stakeholders who collaborate also benefit. Second, stakeholders should recognize key distinctions across sectors and encourage collaboration rather than competition. For a STEM network to be successful and sustained, resources need to be equitably distributed, and collaboration between stakeholders must prevail over competition. As another participant noted, "The infrastructure needs to change to allow for true STEM education. We also need to become more collaborative and less competitive." One approach to this goal may be creating state-based funding and corporate/foundation incentive structures to encourage collaborative partnerships, such as those in North Carolina, Iowa, and Oregon, to name a few. Or, more established STEM entities could support budding and smaller STEM organizations, while simultaneously recognizing all contributors' expertise. Models for this work include Virginia

Tech's liaisons with local school systems and the Science Museum of Western Virginia, and Northern Virginia Community College's NOVA SySTEMic program.

When these aspects are achieved and aligned with shared principles of a STEM network, "a statewide plan for STEM will join the many voices of STEM in one pathway moving forward. From education to careers and literacy throughout the populace, a coordinated STEM initiative will help optimize STEM efforts so that entities 'work smart' providing equity in access and supporting stakeholder needs." This sentiment of "working smart" was echoed by stakeholders from several different sectors, and the authors reiterate its importance.

Infrastructure

Another overarching theme perceived to be a prerequisite for a successful STEM network was having the infrastructure to support it. Participant responses indicate that these infrastructure components include: (1) education of all stakeholders on the purpose and value of STEM education; (2) resource development/dissemination about STEM education at all levels; (3) access to high quality STEM experiences for all students, ensuring cultural relevance for diverse audiences; and (4) identification and continued development of leaders and champions.

Several participants noted that key stakeholders (e.g., school administrators, faculty, parents) need to be supported in better understanding STEM. This is vital to having a successful STEM network with a shared vision and set of principles. For example, participants stated, "Building a culture of awareness and support for STEM within the state" and "supporting families trying to navigate the changing work environment in STEM fields" were essential. Another participant suggested, "The state department must require superintendents to participate in STEM education workshops and require that all central office supervisors receive formal training and require that all faculty participate in required hours of training on STEM education and integration into the classroom at every level and in all subjects."

A STEM network also requires broad development and dissemination of resources. Resources can be developed by stakeholders in any section (teachers, students, community, business). Suggestions in this area included "availability of resources to use in the classroom. This could be sharing of ideas between teachers, state supplied resources or curriculum or suggestions of things to look for [in quality curriculum]," "STEM career opportunities for our students to learn about," and "a one-stop warehouse where information, contacts, resources, and grant opportunities are maintained." Not only are the types of resources important, but the access to and maintenance of resources are key to effectively sustaining a STEM network.

Access is imperative to building the STEM pipeline in Virginia. All students should be able to envision themselves as having the potential to be scientists and engineers, and they should be given opportunities to develop interests in STEM (Malcolm and Feder 2016). Students should see people who look like them when they see STEM teachers, STEM mentors, and people in STEM careers. In addition, they should have access to higher education and knowledge of available STEM careers. Diversity in the STEM pipeline increases creativity that will ultimately benefit all sectors with interests in STEM not only within the state but also nationally and internationally. One participant's response comprehensively captured the need for changes to infrastructure to support equitable access:

> There are systemic barriers to strong STEM education that are inherent within the education system. Often, we try to arm students and teachers to navigate a system that has been shown to be unfriendly to women and people of color, rather than trying to change the system (fix the student vs. fix the system). There is a need to not only assess what programs and gaps exist but also to look at issues that arise due to state and district policies, implicit bias, access to quality education opportunities, recruitment/hiring/retention/promotion of STEM teachers and faculty, and more.

Another response deftly captured the need for state-level commitment to any STEM network: "Unless there is legislation, policy, and funding, it will be meaningless to call for STEM action. Unless teachers and professors view STEM as part of an effort to reprioritize basic skills and a general education, little will change overall. STEM is now and will continue to be a series of events in some schools, some programs, and some departments throughout the Commonwealth."

Strategic Recommendations

In order to develop a strategic STEM network or multisector partnership to support STEM in Virginia, the following recommendations and considerations are offered.

1. Seek consensus on "quality STEM" in terms relevant to this network. To help maintain focus on developing a plan, it is necessary to seek a consensus on what it means to provide a quality STEM experience for students. It is recommended that stakeholders use the published work on STEM education, other well-established statewide STEM networks, and voices within Virginia to frame the conversation and identify a shared language.
2. Build a culture of STEM awareness with a focus on equity, accessibility, and inclusion. Families, parents, communities, school administrators, faculty, businesses, and the workforce need to hear and value the perspectives and needs of all stakeholders regarding STEM. All voices need to be respectively heard and all sectors, racial and ethnic groups, and geographic regions be equitably represented. There are unique and overlapping needs for learners at both the rural and urban ends of the spectrum, and identifying ways to capitalize on shared solutions can benefit everyone.
3. Develop an accessible and thorough inventory of Virginia STEM activities. While the pilot STEM inventory survey provided a starting point, additional voices should also be included, that is, other regions of the state, additional colleges and universities (including community colleges, historically Black colleges and universities, and Hispanic serving institutions), and private and government sectors. Continued data collection, perhaps by survey or landscape analysis, should use the findings from the pilot survey as a guide. Ideally, this inventory would capture programs and initiatives open to all Virginians, including children, young adults, and beyond. As part of this inventory, it is also necessary to identify the economic strengths and geographic characteristics that affect the Virginia STEM

network. A more complete understanding of the network will also enable all partners to share experiences, leverage expertise, and collaborate with each other.
4. Support sustainable network infrastructure. To achieve a sustainable infrastructure, questions that will need to be answered include: (1) What do we need to sustain the STEM initiatives in Virginia? (2) Where are there deficits of programming? and (3) How can we support sustainable growth of successful programs? Three approaches that build on existing projects and resources in Virginia have been identified. First, data from the STEM inventory can help identify what already works in each region, which can be used to develop regional hubs with long-term capacity. Second, teacher professional development may also be a way to build the network and support the development and broad dissemination of curriculum materials. Stakeholders should coordinate with the VA Department of Education (VDOE) STEM initiatives that include populating, promoting, and disseminating resources via such mechanisms as Go Open, an Open Educational Resources (OER) portal. Third, leveraging existing Virginia resources (i.e., dual-enrollment, internships, outreach programs, student-conferences, virtual network, grant mechanisms such as 4-VA, VDOE) and network partners (e.g., shipbuilding, big data, healthcare, agribusiness, government, military, cybersecurity, entrepreneurship, veterinary science, mineral resources, etc.) may support the development and sustaining of the network.
5. Advance a communication plan. A Virginia STEM network needs to communicate and share resources as well as promising practices that may benefit other regions across the state. There are many possibilities for how this could be done, such as with a website, social media updates, or through regular conferences. Whatever plan is ultimately developed, it needs to be able to (1) educate all stakeholders on the purpose and value of STEM education; (2) provide resource development/dissemination about

STEM education at all levels; (3) allow for access to high quality STEM experiences for all students, ensuring cultural relevance for diverse audiences; (4) identify and support the leaders and champions who are doing this work; and (5) share and celebrate the impact of the network across the state on a regular and consistent basis.
6. Embed an evaluation plan that ensures annual assessment of network activities and operations. A process of evaluation, revision, and sustained iteration based upon data/evidence is recommended. Establishing a common baseline of mutually agreed upon metrics to track and document impact is critical. Agreed upon metrics also help ensure consistency and coherence across the state-based STEM opportunities. For this process to be meaningful to the network and its stakeholders, we recommend the plan be developed in consultation with experts in assessment and evaluation, and that the entity implementing the plan be given dedicated time to do so.
7. Commit to long-term support and sustainability. Developing this network and shifting the culture of STEM education within it will take time. Research consistently shows that implementation of an innovation takes about five years, and at least five more years for stabilizing and full operation (e.g., Fullan 2015, 2020). A long-term timeline and an operationalized phased implementation plan are necessary for these statewide efforts to come to fruition. Growing strong leaders is crucial. Similarly, financial support across the myriad of collective regional and federal avenues may be systematically and collectively pursued to help ensure sustainability for the delivery of services across the STEM network.

Essential to building a STEM culture of success in Virginia, three major themes pervaded the data in terms of values and design elements.

- First, leaders must promote equity, access, and inclusion in the availability and delivery of high quality STEM activities across the Commonwealth.

- Second, the principle of collaboration is fundamental for this culture of sharing and opportunity for all.
- Third, the infrastructure must be supported by all sectors that commit to investment and advocacy for at least ten years. The governance of the network must have a strong financial base and leadership that is recognized, sustained, and rewarded.

Looking forward, the report from the 4-VA grant was submitted to the Governor's STEM Commission, which used it as a springboard for a comprehensive STEM plan for the governor. That recently released comprehensive plan proposes that the Commonwealth of Virginia launch a statewide STEM hub network that collaborates with state leadership and post-secondary education leadership. This organization will use common language, a common STEM education rubric, common evaluation and reporting methods, and a supported curriculum to strengthen our existing collaborations, cultivate new strategic partnerships, and ensure that all Virginians can access the activities, relationships, and tools that will equip them with the knowledge, skills, and dispositions for the future.

The authors acknowledge the contributions of Rebecca M. Jones, Jennifer L. Maeng, and Angela W. Webb to an earlier version of this document. The authors also acknowledge Lisa McNair's contributions to this work.

Chapter 7

Achieving Competitive Advantage through Expanded Virginia Broadband

Erv Blythe and James Bohland

This chapter examines how Virginia's broadband infrastructure has been shaped by an alliance of companies and interest groups. The authors argue that this alliance has deterred the development of widespread broadband infrastructure, which has contributed to difficulties and has shaped the geography of lagging regions in the state. The chapter provides both a historical account of broadband's development in Virginia as well as the rapidly changing landscape of broadband policy since the COVID-19 pandemic. The authors conclude with recommendations regarding ways to enhance broadband infrastructure for lagging urban and rural areas across Virginia.

Every community and county in Virginia's rural regions have citizens and organizations passionately committed to economic revitalization and who understand that to participate in today's global economy requires access to advanced broadband networks.[1] They are painfully aware of their infrastructure deficiencies, having watched for

---

1. For a recent review of the economic impacts of broadband networks, see Whitacre and Gallardo (2020).

three decades, as their young, worker-aged citizens leave these rural areas in order to participate in the "new economy" (Ross 2018). Although there is significant national attention given to the absence of sufficient broadband infrastructure in rural areas, a similar situation also exists for many urban neighborhoods. As US representative Donna Shalala recently noted, the lack of connectivity in many urban neighborhoods is three times as large as is true in rural areas (Díaz-Balart 2020). In the case of Virginia, the lowest broadband adoption rates are not in rural communities but in Richmond (Sallet 2020).[2]

In Virginia the causes of poor connectivity in rural and urban areas have been a function of long-standing political barriers. In urban areas, however, the "invisibility" of poor service levels is a problem attributable to how unserved or underserved are determined. Historically the designation was made by data from corporate providers. With their data, a neighborhood was assumed to be served if one household in a census tract meets the minimal bandwidth established by the FCC. Or, importantly, it was designated as served if the company had the equipment at a point of service for a neighborhood, even if the equipment was not in service. For these reasons, the terms "unserved" or "underserved" are not used in the following discussion. Where the term is used as part of a policy or is a statement from others, it is noted in italics.

Like other public utilities—water, sewage, telephones, and electricity—broadband telecommunications are necessary for the health and well-being of all communities and to create an infrastructure for economic development in today's world (Drake et al. 2019). Yet, despite this necessity, Virginia's implementation of broadband networks, be it rural or urban, has been severely restricted by a morass of restrictions created by the strong influence of self-interested alliances, companies, and vested political entities. Also, inhibiting connectivity in both rural and urban communities is the lack of competitive pricing according to Holmes and Zubak-Skees (2015). As their Pew Center study notes, "Higher broadband prices don't just mean fewer dollars in Americans' wallets at the end of every month. They make it difficult for low-to-middle-income families to

---

2. As is true in all states, broadband access and quality vary significantly within a state. Thus, state averages for connectivity are meaningless.

afford fast internet service, which has become a necessity for job training, education, health care" (2).[3]

The Commonwealth Commitment 2022: Rural Thoughts for a Four-Year Plan for Universal Broadband Coverage (Blythe, Mitchell, and Jones 2018), submitted to Governor Northam in 2018 documented the stark economic realities of Virginia's regional disparities and the need for improving the state's broadband infrastructure. In the 1960s the richest communities in Virginia on a per capita basis were clustered along its southern border. Since then, across Virginia's long southern border, according to former state senator Charles Hawkins, "We have lost our corporate board rooms" (Blythe 2003). Senator Hawkins was referencing the loss of Virginia-based national manufacturing and distribution companies dependent on agriculture and forest products in the east; textile, forest, and tobacco products in the piedmont; and extraction-based industries (especially coal) in the west. Since the 1970s, a number of communities and regions of Virginia have been devastated by changes in the global economy. Today, the lowest median household incomes for counties in the Northern Virginia region are higher than the highest median household incomes in their southern county counterparts. Regional variations in other indicators of economic viability demonstrate the same patterns (Weldon Cooper Center for Public Service 2018). Populations are significantly older in Southside and the southwest and eastern regions, primarily driven by outmigration of younger populations and families. This not only presents challenges for elderly support and care but also explains why the workforce and school enrollment in these areas have been declining (Weldon Cooper Center for Public Service 2018).

This chapter examines the major role that an alliance of companies and vested interested groups have had in deterring broadband infrastructure and thus shaping the geography of depressed regions in the state. Given the rapidly changing landscape of broadband policy since the COVID-19 pandemic, our discussion has a historical context to it. Changes are underway in bringing about accessibility to broadband networks. However, some of the long-standing barriers to expansion persist. Therefore,

---

3. In the same report, a comparison of the competition of internet providers between US and French cities, including Roanoke, Virginia, shows that French cities had two to three times the number of internet providers per city even when controlling for population density (Homes and Zubak-Skees 2015).

the chapter concludes with recommendations on how the Commonwealth could enhance its rural broadband infrastructure. In response to comments and questions raised by state officials in earlier drafts, the addendum also addresses some of the more recent changes that have occurred in Virginia.

Recognizing the Critical Role of Broadband Connectivity within the Commonwealth

The absence of significant progress in connecting communities with high-speed broadband networks has not been because leaders have failed to recognize the importance of expanding the technology to these areas. For the past three decades state and federal officials, whether Democrats or Republicans, have acknowledged the importance of broadband connectivity to economic competitiveness for all communities in the state—urban and rural. Over the last two decades, every governor of Virginia, and key legislators, have talked the talk. Unfortunately, the hundreds of millions of federal and state dollars dedicated to solving this problem have not been very successful. This chapter argues that the gap between talk and successful action is because a coalition of traditional communications industries, associations, and friends has shaped policy in this domain. As a consequence, hundreds of thousands of Virginia homes and businesses as well as hundreds of communities have remained outside the global economy while similar communities in other states have moved forward, which is discussed later in the chapter.

As examples, in a 2003 press release, Governor Warner emphasized the "need to eliminate the digital divide and that broadband telecommunications to Appalachian Virginia is about commerce, education, and quality of life" (Executive Office Release 2003). In 2007, Governor Kaine established the Broadband Roundtable, which later advocated for the creation of a strategic plan to achieve "universal access" to broadband services (Commonwealth Broadband Roundtable Report 2008). Importantly, the roundtable noted that despite billions of dollars of investment by the private sector over the previous decades, numerous communities were relying on public investment to solve local broadband access deficiencies. In 2011, the Commonwealth's Broadband Advisory Council reported to Governor McDonnell that the state had "large geographic areas that remain unserved, lacking (affordable) broadband services needed to participate . . . in the global economy" (Broadband Advisory Council 2011). The same report identified expenditures totaling $150 million in federal support to developing broadband access in Virginia.

In 2018, in response to a call from Governor Northam, the nongovernmental Virginia Rural Broadband Coalition (Blythe, Mitchell, and Jones 2018) and the Virginia Association of Counties (LaRiviere 2018) submitted separate plans for developing broadband infrastructure. Both organizations were responding to the governor's call for "universal broadband connectivity for all Virginians." There were minor differences between the two plans, but there were more common elements; elements that were starkly different from previous state government–led efforts. Both plans recognized that communications infrastructure has many of the classic characteristics of a public good that are critical to individual and local community economic competitiveness and are essential to health, education, cultural, and emergency services. Both plans embodied perspectives of local community leaders that were often missed by state and federal government reports. However, their arguments for bottom up, local community-led solutions to the rural broadband problem were not implemented in large measure because a coalition of legislators and legacy communications and cable providers resisted them.[4]

Acknowledging the lack of progress in resolving the problem of inadequate network infrastructure, in July 2020, Senator Mark Warner sent an email to constituents announcing his sponsorship of the Accessible, Affordable Internet for All Act calling for a federal investment of $100 billion to build high speed internet service in unserved and underserved communities. Given the exposed frailty of the communication networks in rural and some urban communities revealed by the COVID-19 pandemic, Governor Northam obtained an increased budget of $50 million annually for fiscal years '21 and '22 for broadband deployment. These funds would be managed and dispersed by the state agency responsible for broadband policy. Under the current rules, and given the history of past state initiatives, it is highly probable that the state's broadband funds will be allocated based on the recommendations from the influential

---

4. The term legacy communications provider (LCP) is used to designate investor-owned communications providers that deploy and manage a vertically integrated communications system (and business model) designed for either broadcast television over copper, or telephone over copper. These communications providers, beginning in the 1990s, jury-rigged their networks to offer services based on the internet protocol (i.e., internet data services) over their networks.

coalitions that have been so powerful in guiding past decisions (Virginia Department of Housing and Community Development 2020).

Designing Advanced Broadband Networks

One can view a vibrant broadband infrastructure as a hierarchal network with four geographic levels:

1. Global: infrastructure with access points to most nations around the world;
2. National: (for the US) an inter-regional infrastructure linking the largest cities to the global network
3. Regional: infrastructure connecting access points from within regions (e.g., southwest, Southside, and Tidewater Virginia) to the national network; and
4. Local: town, county, and city, fiber, copper, and wireless infrastructure tying business and residential communities to the regional network.

The architecture of a broadband network, be it global or local, has several major technical elements. One critical element is the optical fiber–based internet access points (in industry parlance points of presence or POPs). Ideally, access points are in close proximity to local user communities. POPs are connected both to multipurpose optical backbone networks and to the local community network infrastructure. The local network provides the connection to businesses, nonprofit organizations, public offices, and citizens. POPs and the fiber backbones connecting them have typically been financed by public dollars or joint ventures by public and private sector entities, whereas the "last-mile" internet connections to users (consumers) have been primarily provided/installed by the private sector. The "last mile," arguably the most important element of the local infrastructure, connects users to the global internet. However, without advanced broadband infrastructure throughout the network, last-mile connections would be inadequate to support economic, personal, and regional growth.

Virginia's funding efforts within this multiscale network infrastructure have been at the regional and local levels. By a substantial margin, operating costs, technology turnover, and the most significant (political, regulatory, and capital investment) barriers to entry are in the local last-mile part of the broadband network. Any state effort to provide "universal" broadband access for internet services has to solve this problem. Importantly, responsibility for the last-mile connections in Virginia, with a few exceptions, has been reserved for incumbent or legacy private sector telecommunications companies, such as Cox, Comcast, CenturyLink, Verizon, and AT&T. Legacy providers argue that the last-mile connections in sparsely populated areas are too costly and the anchor tenants needed to recovering costs are absent. Neither claims are correct as evidenced by the successful implementations in many communities across the country. Most experts in the computing industry and network communications as well as scientists also refute those claims. Historically, legacy companies have owned and controlled the last-mile connections in the network, and thus, have determined what applications and services are offered, at what cost, to what communities, and where within those communities what specific services or bundles (TV, phone, and internet) might be offered.

Community Broadband Strategies

Deployment of different architectures for advanced communications networks at reasonable costs is possible. Therefore, the policy objective for the state and many communities should be to agree on an end goal with respect to local communication technologies and services. If the goal is to achieve enhanced consumption of existing content and have more content at faster speeds, the current technology and business models may achieve the goal. No change in technology would be required. Alternatively, if the goal is a network that enables a more viable economic future with greater opportunities for innovation, increased quality of life, and better educational and occupational opportunities, then the current network architecture and business models must be changed. Entrepreneurs who wish to create new products, services, and knowledge, particularly those requiring large amounts of data from different sources and in different formats (text, numeric, images, etc.), must have access to advanced network capabilities. These two futures are designated as a consumption future versus a production future. Importantly, while a production future will also enable a more vibrant consumption future, the reverse is not true. A network architecture and business models focused primarily on improving consumption cannot be reconfigured to a network that supports a dynamic production future. A strategy attuned to consumption is called "catching up" versus a strategy to produce a production competitive advantage "leapfrogging." Moreover, a production model for broadband is essential if communities within the Commonwealth are to gain a comparative advantage for future economic development over not only other communities in the United States, but globally.

Legacy cable and telecommunications companies are unable, because of technology limitations, and unwilling, because of their vertical business model, to construct networks with the key attributes required of a producer-oriented network. Their technologies and business models are based on the old broadcast television paradigm where every connecting party is primarily a passive receiver of information services. This model is the result of private-sector-owned and -controlled last-mile connections whose infrastructure and business modes cannot scale to support the goal of a production future.

Production Infrastructure Requirements

A network designed to support the development and production of online services and information must be reliable, reflect reasonable cost-to-price ratios for services (in the highly competitive global internet market), have scalable upload and download speeds from a minimum of 100 megabits per second to 10s of gigabits per second, and must have customer-driven network performance and availability measurement capabilities. No communities in Virginia, urban or rural, have network infrastructure that exactly match all of these requirements because their networks are incompatible with either the business model or the technology infrastructure of any of Virginia's imbedded cable television or legacy telecommunications companies. A few municipal or community-based networks, which are described later in this chapter, have the potential to meet all or most of the criteria. But, again, if Virginia communities and citizens are given adequate leverage over this infrastructure so critical to their future, it is a reachable goal.

Other states (see Utah's Infrastructure Agency) have had significant successes with broadband networks that increase "production" potentials. Yet, Virginia has lagged seriously behind in creating the networks that will serve as infrastructures for innovation (Chamberlain 2020; Kienbaum 2019). As noted above, the issue is not technology. What then? To understand why Virginia has lagged behind other states requires an understanding of the policy structure in the Commonwealth as it pertains to telecommunications and broadband deployment.

BROADBAND POLICY IN VIRGINIA: A COALITION DOMINANCE

What has evolved in Virginia is a policy assemblage that supports legacy providers to the detriment of community-oriented efforts, be they rural or urban. As a recent study by Whitacre and Gallardo (2020) documents using data from the Pew Charitable Trusts, three factors are critical to successful deployment of broadband:

1. availability of state-level funding;
2. a state-wide agency with full-time employees dedicated to broadband deployment; and
3. a lack of restrictions on municipal/cooperative broadband initiatives.

The lack of restrictions is particularly critical for leapfrogging to a new plane of deployment. While Virginia now meets the funding and administrative requirements, it is one of seventeen states that still has restrictions on municipal/cooperative initiatives (Pew 2020; Whitacre and Gallardo 2020). In 2019, the Benton Foundation recommended that states need to repeal restrictions or in lieu of that, Congress should preempt state laws that restrict municipalities and counties from deploying broadband initiatives (Sallet 2020). The argument below lays out how the persistent restrictions on municipal/cooperative options is a function of a policy coalition led by legacy providers.

An approach to understanding policy coalitions and how they function can best be explored using what Sabatier and Jenkins-Smith (1993) label the advocacy coalition framework (ACF). Refined from its initial conceptualization,[5] ACF describes a contested policy process between coalitions comprised of individuals and institutions that share common core values and have similar policy beliefs. Policy formation becomes a

---

5. This refinement involved the integration of ACF and cultural theory into the policy framework provided by Jenkins-Smith et al. (2014). The importance of values, "deep values and policy values" to the policy process represented an important refinement to the ACF model.

competitive process as coalitions vie for power within a particular policy domain, for example, broadband. The coalition membership is dynamic as it fluctuates over time based on the issue being addressed and by the emergence of disruptive external forces, for example, in the case of telecommunications, the external force might be the emergence of new technologies. Although memberships within a coalition are subject to change, at the core of each coalition member are values or beliefs that are steadfast, which means that changing core beliefs is akin to religious conversion (Jenkins-Smith et al. 2014). A coalition does not pass legislation or administer it directly, rather it consists of people and organizations who are "trusted" voices to lawmakers on policy issues.

In Virginia the ability of a coalition to achieve success in privileging their values in formal legislation is influenced significantly by the Dillon Rule "charter." Because Virginia adheres strongly to the spirit of the Dillon Rule, any initiative by local municipalities to develop community-based network systems requires full legislative approval.[6] As a consequence, well-funded coalitions within any public policy domain can block community initiatives with intensive lobbying efforts or by having allies in the policy forums that control decisions.

Coalition members in the broadband policy domain within the state have changed over time but the key players have been consistent.

State legislators: Any state funding or joint state-federal funding must be approved by the legislature. Thus, coalitions that have influence over a large number of legislators through lobbying or campaign efforts, have the ability to influence legislation in the telecommunications policy domain.

Legacy providers: Legacy providers consist of the major telecommunication companies, their associations (Virginia Cable Telecommunications Association [VCTA] and Wireless Internet Service Provider Association [WISPA]), and other

---

6. The Dillion Rule is a legal doctrine that requires any local government to secure approval from the state to institute any policy that has fiscal ramifications. There are thirty-two Dillon Rule states (versus Home Rule) in the US, but they vary significantly in terms of adherence to the ruling that municipalities are the creation of the state and thus must be governed accordingly. Virginia does not allow exemptions to this view, which is not the case in many other Dillon Rule states.

corporate entities, such as wireless companies. These groups have representation on the Broadband Advisory Council.[7]

Chief Broadband Advisor: In an attempt to streamline authority, in 2018 the legislature gave authority to the Office of Broadband in the Department of Housing and Community Development (DHCD), the Broadband Advisory Council, and a newly created Chief Broadband Advisor. All three groups claim some responsibility for broadband in Virginia. Researchers and Consultants: Individuals from different public, private, and nonprofit institutions who provide technical advice and who represent a loose coalition of "experts" whose input is called upon as needed.

Community Interests Groups: Nonprofits, citizens, journalists, and so forth that have vested interests in promoting broadband connectivity in underserved communities. Some collaborations between the nonprofits have emerged to help engage more vigorously in the broadband debates, for example, the Virginia Rural Broadband Coalition, dissolved in 2019, and the Virginia Association of Counties. An important advocate for rural Virginia broadband policy is the Virginia Tobacco Region Revitalization Commission (TRRC).

Federal Agencies: Several agencies within the federal government are important members of the broadband policy domain because of their regulatory roles in telecommunications and their role in allocating federal funds for broadband initiatives. The major agency players are the Federal Communications Commission (FCC), an independent authority of the government; the National Telecommunications and Information Administration (NTIA) under the Department of Commerce; and the Department of Agriculture (USDA). Most NTIA and FCC programs require private-public partnerships

---

7. Created in 2008 the Council is charged with providing advice to the governor and legislature on broadband initiatives and has significant leverage in shaping state broadband policies. Its composition is fixed by statute. In addition to state legislators, membership includes two associations that represent legacy providers (WISPA and VCTA); one representing the wireless coalition; one representing community interests; and another from the Center for Rural Virginia.

and award projects consistent with state government broadband policies. In Virginia NTIA has focused much of its broadband funding to projects led by legacy providers. The USDA funds broadband through its ReConnect program, and other programs through loans and grants. Notably, the USDA program does not limit funds to public-private partners, nor to legacy providers.

These key players have formed three coalitions that have contested policy decisions in the various broadband policy forums in the state. Both in terms of power over the debate and internal consistency on values and beliefs, the strongest of the three is the legacy/corporate coalition. Comprised of legacy providers; telecommunication professional associations; government officials whose core beliefs are generally consistent with legacy providers; federal agency bureaucrats; and some researchers and consultants, the coalition guides most broadband efforts.

A second coalition (community coalition) consists of local governments, nonprofits, and citizens representing communities seeking better connectivity. Their principal goal has been advocating for expansion of broadband in these areas. Because coalition member beliefs may vary significantly on some issues (e.g., education versus healthcare, production versus consumption focus, etc.), membership in the coalition is quite volatile depending on the issues and the nature of the legislation being proposed.

A third coalition (technical coalition) consists of researchers, technical experts, journalists, and consultants from a range of organizations who form a loosely connected coalition based on technical issues and strategic directions. Members in this coalition will join one of the other two depending on the particular broadband issue to provide either technical or economic advice.

Legacy/Corporate Coalition Goals and Actions

The legacy/corporate coalition shapes policy in five ways unavailable to the community coalition:

1. strong coordinated lobbying efforts;
2. political patronage at all levels of government, both state and local;

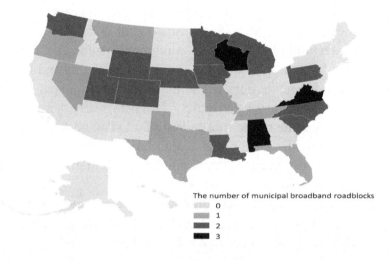

Figure 7.1. Policy barriers to municipal broadband expansion

3. control of data that "define" connectivity problems;
4. ownership and control of the last-mile infrastructure; and
5. well-funded associations of members that enable it to be active in all the councils and commissions overseeing broadband.

The legacy/corporate coalition has strongly held beliefs that they advocate for in national, state, and regional forums:

1. a commitment to asymmetrical versus symmetrical network architecture;
2. a business model based on the belief that every commodity connection must be for consumption rather than production of communication applications and services;
3. extending the life and maximizing the returns on imbedded copper-based (cable and telephone) communications infrastructure no longer capable of providing state-of-the-art broadband services; and
4. a business model that fuses network services to content in ways that limits users' options for innovative use of the network.

Many of the legacy coalition's efforts have been successful in limiting opportunities for community-based broadband initiatives and restricting the architectural platforms for community broadband. Chamberlain (2020) notes, for example, Virginia along with Alabama and Wisconsin have the most restrictive policy environments for municipal broadband initiatives in the country (see figure 7.1). Historically, Virginia's government has been one of the most allied of all state governments to the interests of the traditional dominant cable and telecommunications companies and the most resistant to community-led initiatives in this arena (Arlington Fiber Cooperative 2020).

Over time the legacy coalition helped create a number of barriers that localities must overcome if they desire to leapfrog to a production future (Arlington Fiber Cooperative 2020). These include changing the obsolete definition of broadband that does not conform to an architecture required for a "production" oriented system. Virginia defines broadband as follows: "access to high-speed internet is defined as having access to a network that can transmit data at speeds greater than 10 megabits per second download and 1 megabits per second upload"[8] (Virginia's Chief Broadband Advisor 2020), which is substantially below the obsolete FCC definition of 25 megabits per second download and 3 megabits per second upload (Pressgrove 2020). These asymmetrical definitions are a function of the legacy coalition's goal to limit government subsidies for network architectures that are beyond the capabilities of legacy providers, thus ensuring that any new deployment is controlled by existing private providers.

Local/municipal owned networks in Virginia face severe restrictions on their ability to compete with legacy providers. Although community-based, locally controlled communications entities exist nationally that have advanced symmetrical infrastructure and services at significantly lower prices than legacy provider offerings, Virginia policy makes these models very difficult to implement. For example, Virginia dictates that community/municipal broadband networks are not allowed to set prices lower than prices charged by incumbent providers (Code of Virginia 56–484.7.1).

---

8. With these speeds it would be difficult to maintain an efficient teleconference system such as Zoom or Google Chat across many users.

Localities are not allowed to subsidize the development of locally controlled infrastructure.[9] However, historically both the federal[10] and our Virginia state government have effectively subsidized expansion of legacy providers' closed network architectures and business models. Virginia state government, to a degree that sets it apart from more future oriented states, sustains its legacy communications providers through laws and administrative actions that favor legacy providers and that constrain local governments, and even state-based electric utilities, attempting to address local broadband needs.[11]

If locally controlled systems propose to offer bundled services (telephone, data, and cable television), they must guarantee through a feasibility study that the locally controlled network will be profitable within one year of installation (Code of Virginia 15.2–2108.6). This standard policy is not feasible for most providers, public or private.

Perhaps more damaging to advancing broadband networks was the state's adoption of the legacy providers' own definition of *underserved* areas.[12] This created misleading data (maps) designed to identify who is "served" and "not served" with adequate broadband communications. This flawed data significantly constrained the ability of Virginia communities to compete for $100s of millions in federal funds available to mitigate communications infrastructure deficiencies (Chambers 2018).

---

9. Code of Virginia 56-484.7:1 Offering of communications services, see section C. Code of Virginia 56-265.4:4 Certificate to operate as a telephone utility, see section B 3. Code of Virginia 15.2-2108.6 Feasibility study of providing cable television services, see sections C and D.

10. Of the many references that could be cited, federal support of CenturyLink in Virginia, totaling millions of dollars, and its failure to deliver promised services is especially egregious (Engebretson 2020). Yet the Commonwealth of Virginia continues to reward CenturyLink ($2,276,110) as a welcomed partner in its latest broadband infrastructure grants. (See Office of the Governor Press Release on March 18, 2021, "Governor Northam Announces $20.1 Million to Strengthen Broadband Infrastructure in 17 Localities.)

11. Code of Virginia 56-484.7:1 Offering of communications services. Code of Virginia 56-265.4:4 Certificate to operate as a telephone utility. Code of Virginia 15.2-2108.6 Feasibility study of providing cable television services. Code of Virginia 56-585.1:8 Provision of Broadband Capacity to Unserved Areas of the Commonwealth by Certain Electric Utilities.

12. The definition is communicated and maintained through the department of DHCD's and Commonwealth Connect sponsored site at Virginia Tech titled Virginia Broadband Availability Map and Integrated Broadband Planning and Analysis Toolbox. The map includes layers for underserved, and unserved, with the definitions that were provided to Virginia Tech's Center for Geospatial Information Technology. https://broadband.cgit.vt.edu/IntegratedToolbox/#toolPane.

Virginia officials blamed the FCC for these deficiencies but worked hard to prevent alternative, customer-based measures of broadband availability and speed, insisting that "only Virginia's established communications providers can provide this information on services levels and quality."[13] CenturyLink used this "census block" data to compete for $10s of millions of dollars in Federal Communications Commission's Connect America Funds over the last several years. But few citizens in Virginia communities benefited from this investment or obtained the promised broadband services (Engebretson 2020).

CAN COMMUNITY BROADBAND INITIATIVES IN VIRGINIA BE SUCCESSFUL?

Given the barriers posed by existing policies attributed to the legacy broadband coalition, can rural communities successfully navigate a "leapfrog" strategy? While Virginia's broadband initiatives are constrained, there are exceptional, potential breakthrough efforts in Virginia for providing advanced communications access to the home and businesses.

The Orange County Broadband Authority recently outlined a thirty-six-month plan to deliver fiber optic connections providing advanced broadband service to 75% of county residents (Poole 2020).

The Roanoke Valley Broadband Authority recently announced its intention to expand from its business model, currently limited to the provision of advanced broadband services to government, businesses, and education institutions. The authority recently announced its plans to offer optical fiber network connections to residences in its region, potentially competing with current legacy systems: Cox Communications in Roanoke City and County, and Comcast in Salem (Chittum 2020).

The customer-owned Citizens Telephone Cooperative based in Floyd County has been one of the most responsive and active communications providers in the state by keeping county residents competitive with advanced broadband access. It announced in 2019 that it will install over 1,700 miles of fiber optic infrastructure by 2021. The project by the Citizens Cooperative is notable in that Floyd County is extremely rural

---

13. Conversation with Deputy Secretary of Technology with Virginia Tech Vice President of Information Technology, Erv Blythe, in April 2012 expressing displeasure with data collected by Virginia Tech via network measurement tools and from end users of broadband, which was significantly different from data collected and touted by the Secretary of Technology office and provided by communications industry providers.

and mountainous, which contradict the beliefs expressed by the legacy coalition that broadband investments in places like this would not be economically feasible. The new network will be capable of providing gigabit-level internet access to 97% of Floyd County residents (Demmitt 2019).

What is common among these examples is that the providers are either locally controlled or are customer owned. There are other locally driven, advanced broadband infrastructure initiatives in Virginia. Some are struggling, but a few are succeeding, even with the substantial burdens and obstacles created by Virginia's legacy coalition.

Recommendations

A network architecture essential for rural areas seeking competitive advantage in today's global economy should achieve six essential goals:

1. Open access: a horizontally layered network architecture that separates the physical access to the network from the delivery of services.
2. Reliability: communications services that are available, consistent, measurable, and with consumer reportable access and levels of bandwidth.
3. Competitively advantageous bandwidth: at a minimum this would be above the baseline measure used in the Federal Communications Commission's "Above Baseline" technology-neutral service tier specifying download bandwidth greater than or equal to 100 megabits per second (FCC 2020). A goal of more than a gigabit per second is feasible and achievable.
4. Symmetrical bandwidth: the architecture should support identical data transmission speeds in both directions, enabling the production of new content and business opportunities from any connected consumer. (See previous statements under "Designing Advanced Broadband Networks" on the applications and emerging technology capabilities driving this requirement.)
5. Scalability: network should have access to economically priced bandwidth that matches their increasing application service needs.

6. Cost-Effectiveness: the level of service and usage to consumers must reflect the price paid in an open, competitive market.

Currently no communities in Virginia meet all of these goals, but ignoring these goals will assign second-class status to Virginia communities and place them at a comparative disadvantage in securing a viable productive future.

Much debate at the national level concerns the correct strategy for attacking the problem of developing advanced network access and producer capabilities throughout the nation. As noted earlier, effective policies are being utilized in places not held captive by incumbent communication providers. A new day for Virginia communities is possible. To achieve that new future, the Commonwealth needs to aggressively pursue the following:

- Virginia should revisit state and federal regulations that have created outdated communications service models. To the extent possible by Virginia, providers of telecommunications services should be free from restrictions on what they provide, who they can serve, where they can provide services, and on limits to return on investment (Blythe 2003). But this can only work if coupled with two changes in current policies:[14]
    - Virginia should recognize that communications services must meet the goals outlined above and that network infrastructure is an essential public good. Therefore, local community and municipal roles in the development and deployment of the requisite infrastructure and services should be facilitated.
    - Encourage, not discourage, locally driven community business models (cooperatives, municipal utilities, nonprofit infrastructure and service providers,

---

14. This recommendation is similar to one made by Blythe (2003). Without new community and citizen-driven competition, legacy providers will not develop broadband capabilities consistent with the goals identified above.

homeowners associations) to assist in the deployment of large-scale network infrastructure based on leading-edge and, in some special cases, disruptive technologies that can radically alter the economics of, and the types and levels of service available in, regional and community broadband markets.
- Virginia should create a central broadband assistance organization that works with communities to aggregate demand and encourage regional internet traffic aggregation to advantage regional economic development and to develop incentives for private-sector participation in the provision of new broadband technologies and services. The organization should be neutral from a provider perspective.
- Design goals should maximize communications survivability; support the interconnection of multiple diverse networks; enable distributed management; facilitate scalable, cost-effective communications; and enable a wide range of end-user attachments. Network infrastructure based on the internet protocols are transforming global communications. But these goals are disruptive to the business models and infrastructure of most legacy providers. Virginia policymakers need to decide whether their primary objective is to support, preserve, and extend the business interests of the state's imbedded legacy communications providers or to serve its citizens by encouraging new disruptive technologies.
- Policies should encourage community flexibility. Recognize that we cannot anticipate the full range of network requirements for the most unique and sophisticated advisory applications. This is an important driver in the move toward open access, user-controlled networks, and an asset-based, locally controlled communications business model.
- Policies should recognize that at the physical media level, the most powerful architecture is one that enables maximum distribution and movement of information. In such an architecture, any access point has approximately the

same advantage in cost efficiency and effectiveness as any other; there is no top, there is no bottom.
- The current system of commissions and councils should be reorganized to ensure that the power of the legacy coalition is diminished and that the voices of the community coalition have a stronger role to play in the formulation of policy and the allocation of resources for broadband deployment.

Conclusion

The authors of this chapter confess to having a bias toward the creation of networks that are production-oriented, and that greater control of networks should be granted to municipalities than is currently the case. To be economically and technically feasible, the enabling communication infrastructure must reflect the full functional and economic potential of today's communications technology and be able to quickly integrate emerging new capabilities. This is not a prevailing characteristic of the nation's embedded communications infrastructure, but it is a potential advantage to an awakening in Virginia.

In order to enable a new future, state-of-the-art network capabilities must be coupled with significant investments in education, healthcare, community institutional building, and labor force development. Communities must be committed to creating a local competitive advantage that will enhance its growth potential not just in Virginia but across the nation, or indeed, the world.

Most state and local leaders see the changes in communications capabilities over the last three decades as a problem of catching up to the present. But over the next twenty years, society will see the most significant and fundamental changes in the technology underpinning our national communications infrastructure in history. The problem must be seen as a competition for the future viability of rural communities and many urban neighborhoods that are currently unable to achieve such a goal. To place Virginia communities in a comparative advantage requires deployment of broadband technologies and adoption of business models that do not restrict their opportunities to innovate and compete. Coming changes in communications capability and economics have the potential to act as extraordinary multipliers of productivity and efficiency in rural communities. For certain economy-driving information and advanced technology products, these changes will dictate what is produced, where it is produced, and who benefits. Virginia communities must have the ability to determine their own futures.

Epilogue

The editors and publisher of *Vibrant Virginia* used a process of posting chapters online, which enabled readers to review and to comment on earlier drafts of the chapter. The result is that authors are able to incorporate changes where appropriate and to address comments that are more substantive. We received a number of comments from members of the policy community in the governor's office and wish to extend our appreciation for providing some useful commentary. We addressed some comments through revisions in the body of the text. Perhaps we were insufficiently clear that our positions were not directed at the current administration, but rather, reflect a historical perspective on broadband policy in the Commonwealth. A history that we believe clearly reflects the views and values of what we have called the legacy providers of broadband. We acknowledge that the current administration has moved away from some of the more stringent positions of earlier policymakers. We also recognize that the issue of broadband has become a "hot-button" issue in today's post-pandemic/election world. The inadequacies of our network systems were boldly revealed as we were required to become more reliant on network communications during the pandemic. As a consequence, for political reasons it is understandable that officials are defensive about policy positions. Our critique is meant to provide opportunities for citizens and policymakers to recognize that we are at a critical junction in deciding our broadband future. Simply to continue forward with existing architecture and business models albeit at a faster and more expansive pace, will place many communities' future at a comparative disadvantage with others in this country and globally.

We address three substantive issues that were apparent in reading the comments.

The reviewers argue that the current process for dispersal of broadband funds used by the Office of Broadband, Virginia Telecommunications Initiative (VATI), does not restrict municipalities from securing grants. Indeed, the VATI "challenge" process does not prohibit application for funds from any source, but transparency is an issue. Under the VATI system, a community can apply for funds to expand broadband to a specific community; however, anyone can challenge the application for cause. The governor's Office for Broadband reviews the information and makes a judgment. The process is, however, closed and not open to the public. Parameters for adjudicating a challenge are not clearly specified nor is their relative importance to the final decision. External reviewers are not used to evaluate applications. Thus, if a community applies but a large private provider challenges, municipalities not only must demonstrate need but their applications must adhere to the requirements established by the legislature (see the Department of Housing and Community Development 2020). Although the current system enables a community to designate themselves as underserved rather than use either public or private data to make that determination, in the end, the Office of Broadband makes the judgment call on whether services expansion is warranted. The absence of transparency raises many unresolved questions and can leave decisions open to subjectivity.

The reviewers argue there are no restrictions on municipal/cooperative systems. Yet, in the Commonwealth Connection, 2020, a report authored by the Office of Broadband and the Chief Broadband Advisory, the following restrictions are noted (identical to those questioned in our report [Department of Housing and Community Development, 2020]).

- Service prices shall not be lower than prices charged by any incumbent provider for equivalent service.
- Services shall not be subsidized by the local community or cooperative.
- Services must be profitable within one year of installation.

In essence the Commonwealth has allowed municipalities to swim in the broadband waters, but only if they agree to carry leaded weights in their pockets.

In several areas of this chapter, the reviewers comment that no definition of underserved area nor suggest minimal architectural requirements are established by the state. Yet, in the same Commonwealth Connect report cited above, they state, "having access to high-speed internet is defined as having access to a network that can transmit data at speeds greater than 10 megabits per second download and 1 megabit per second upload" (7). As we note in our chapter, if a community wants to advance its comparative advantage those speeds will not achieve it. While minimum standards for speeds are encouraged, setting a low minimum enables providers to deflect fund applications from communities that seek higher speeds because they may already be "served" at 10 megabits, for example. If the Commonwealth wants to compete in a world where the home is the office, where schools require advanced applications for homework, where "zooming" around the world with multiple participants is feasible; a higher standard is required. Moreover, the 10 down and 1 up standard reinforces the acceptance of asynchronous architecture, restricting future production capabilities.

The Commonwealth is making progress toward addressing its gaps in broadband. What is now required, however, is to aggressively move to adopt the more "disruptive" innovations and policies in broadband technology, such as recently occurred in the state of Washington (Casper 2021). Bold moves are required to ensure that citizens in the Commonwealth can compete internationally in a world that, despite the pandemic, will be increasingly globally connected.

Part 3

Vibrancy of Place and Creative Placemaking

Chapter 8

Arts, Culture, and Community Building in Rural Virginia

Max O. Stephenson Jr., Lara Nagle, and Neda Moayerian

This chapter explores the ways community cultural development (CCD) strategies can facilitate individual and social learning in Patrick County, Virginia. The Virginia Tech Institute for Policy and Governance (VT-IPG), as well as Reynolds Homestead in Critz, Virginia, to date have employed story circles and strategic positioning methods in community workshop settings to enhance communication among actors across political-economic sectors and to illuminate the deeply held beliefs driving development decisions. The chapter highlights the role of arts and culture in the work of partner organizations in Patrick County and explores the ways in which CCD strategies may be employed for both engagement and development to support the goals of many of these civic organizations, as they have identified the role of arts and culture as central to their missions.

The principal VT-IPG community-based participatory project described in this chapter has involved collaboration with government and civic actors in Patrick County in southwest/southside Virginia (2018–present). Inspired by research interests in community cultural development (CCD), the authors have facilitated and delivered workshops with stakeholders in that jurisdiction to frame a community vision and to identify the principal opportunities and challenges likely to arise when implementing it. The relationship between CCD and individual and social learning is multifaceted. Community cultural development is a participatory process that leads those involved to question their taken-for-granted knowledge and to envision future aspirations for their community through creative means of expressing, preserving/enhancing, or changing its culture (Sonn and Quayle 2014). Christens, Hanlin, and Speers (2007) have argued that altering the social imagination through creative process is of central importance to attaining sustainable social change. Conversely, the potential to facilitate systems change "is constrained by social power—particularly the capacity to shape ideology" (Christens, Hanlin, and Speers 2007, 229). Neoliberal assumptions (i.e., viewing economic growth as the ultimate goal of any society and the free market as the most significant and just system for planning and regulating society, in contrast to reliance on social-democratic institutions and processes) sustain a market-dominated hierarchical order by weakening and/or delegitimizing democratic governance institutions as key social decision-making loci (Chomsky 1999; Harvey 2005).

In her book, In the Ruins of Neoliberalism: The Rise of Antidemocratic Politics in the West (2019), Brown examined the work of some of the most influential neoliberal thinkers, including Friedrich Hayek and Milton Friedman. According to Brown, these scholars proposed that the natural unfolding of market and traditional morality, as two primary spheres for organizing human life, will naturally produce the freest possible society. Brown also contended that advocates of this perspective have routinely demonized interventions aimed at increasing the role of democratic governance to secure an increased measure of social justice in the political economy. This penchant, now an evolved ideology and dominant public philosophy in Patrick County and across the United States in both urban and rural locales, raises the question of whether and how neoliberalism can be altered when it yields, as it has broadly and in the county, increased levels of inequality and injustice for large numbers of citizens. Many community development scholars and practitioners in recent decades have emphasized the potential role of the arts in the creation of spaces for individual and group participation in meaning-making processes and in de/reconstructing social imaginaries (Campbell et al. 2010; Sonn and Quayle 2014). As Adams and Goldbard (2002) have observed concerning the community cultural development process, community artists, singly or in teams, use their artistic and organizational skills to serve the emancipation and development of a community, whether defined by geography (e.g., a neighborhood), a common interest (e.g., members of a union), or identity (e.g., members of an indigenous group) (8).

Leighninger and Nabatchi (2015) have similarly contended that when people have a chance to, as the common saying goes, "step into the shoes of another" with empathy and reflective acuity, even a narrowly defined "other," they are more likely to engage in civil dialogue, gain new knowledge and awareness, and form stronger bonds that connect their individual interests and the public good. Meanwhile, Krauss and Morsella (2006) have argued that people constructively engage others' perspectives only after they understand the values and assumptions on which their own views and those of the individuals with whom they interact are predicated. Arts-based/CCD methods, including story circles, image theatre, and forum theatre (Boal 1995, 1998, 2002; Chinyowa 2014; Cowie 2017; Mundy and Chan 2013; Reimers 2015; Rohd 1998) can encourage that possibility.

According to Mezirow (2003), one's frame of reference influences the meaning-making process and under certain conditions, those "frames may be transformed to empower adult learners and to foster community development" (11). Based on an evaluation of experience in community development projects in a number of developing countries, Mezirow has pointed to the importance of critical reflection leading to awareness of one's guiding epistemic and even ontological assumptions, or as Freire (1970) has put this point, "conscientization" as integral and essential to such efforts. Conscientization serves as a precursor to and purveyor of individual learning and can be encouraged via "participatory action in community development projects" (Mezirow 2003, 12). That engagement in turn can serve "as preparation for active citizenship in political democracy" by encouraging an empathetic and other-regarding orientation (12). Adejumo (2010) has also drawn on Freire's (1970) work on emancipatory learning in a longitudinal study of an arts program in a low-income housing project in Columbus, Ohio. He found that community artists employed a critical pedagogy, "characterized by open dialogue and structured reflection . . . to facilitate social awareness and activism as imperatives of self-empowerment in a democratic society" (24).

In short, CCD strategies aim to raise participants' awareness of their fundamental values and assumptions and the existing communal structures of power, beliefs, and norms that shape and form those. As a result, arts-based approaches to community change may spur public dialogue that can permit those participating to negotiate shared aspirations across differences and map a shared path toward those goals. Such outcomes can be realized across the urban-rural spectrum.

COMMUNITY VISIONING AND THE SOCIAL IMAGINARY

When embarking on the journey of community visioning, even defining "community" can be a difficult and contested task, as membership for individuals or organizations can span temporal, physical/geographical, cultural, social, political, and economic contexts at once. Yet managing the complexity of a politics of identity, for example, how individuals and groups are imagining their lives, ways of knowing and being in a community, while creating and maintaining a common vision of their social life and obligations is essential to combating reductionist "Othering" that can swiftly result in the exclusion of specific views, populations, or needs. Similarly, one cannot simply assume shared values within an evolving popular majority (Young 1997). It is therefore both critical and an acute challenge to define the public good broadly for the purposes of community development and strategic planning, while seeking to ensure that the relational and kaleidoscopic groups and ties that comprise the citizenry are suitably represented in decision-making processes. Among other things, community spaces that invite a diverse membership to the table will very likely broaden the objectives of community development.

A related challenge when defining the frame for community visioning is creating explicit space to examine the fundaments of the "social imaginary" mentioned above, a term originally coined by the philosopher Charles Taylor (2002), also known as individuals' "ways of knowing" or "social identity," which is how members of a community make "sense of their environments" (Stephenson 2009, 418). These often latent, but widely shared, assumptions, beliefs, and values shape how residents make sense of their everyday realities and of the changes they may be confronting. They comprise, in short, how they view their worlds and daily lived experience. Following Stephenson (2009), and in principle if not always successfully in practice, ethical and transformative leaders can employ visioning processes as opportunities to encourage citizens to (re)visit their ways of knowing, become aware of their implications, and consider paths forward in light of the economic and social changes confronting their communities. During their community-based research in Patrick County, the authors found that this has taken the guise of local governments and civic organizations providing space to allow citizens to grapple frankly with the legacy of timber and manufacturing production now in decline, while considering the steps necessary to pursue other economic opportunities, including viticulture and tourism.

As an example of a new way of thinking for Central Appalachia, alternative energy, as a response to protracted economic decline, has been highly politicized and criticized by one political party and relevant market interests. While those claims are factually not true, they have relied for their persuasive and emotive power on residents viewing change as an attack on historically important, but dying, traditional economic drivers and the way of life they represented. Nonetheless, at a location not far from Patrick County, the largest net-metered, non-industrial solar project in the history of eastern Kentucky—the historical site of that state's coalfields—was recently established by a coalition of diverse members called the Letcher County Culture Hub based on the shared goal of addressing rising utility costs (Fink 2020).

As a project of Appalshop, an art and media maker first established in 1969, the Letcher County Culture Hub is employing community cultural and economic development strategies to educate and organize area citizens around common goals and cultural assets (Moayerian 2018). According to Fink (2020), "in a place long divided along political, religious, and cultural lines, these projects have brought residents together. As one community leader put it, 'We had always fought our own battles, and none of us got together and tried to fight the whole war'" (np). In this case, CCD professionals have pragmatically used arts-based strategies to build shared purpose while, for the most part, leaving social divisions and imaginaries where they exist. This stance echoes Mills and Brown's instrumental approach (2004). In the near term, the hope seems to be that getting citizens to see the humanity of those otherwise "Othered" as they address shared problems will break down such social divisions. In the long run, organizers appear to believe that continuing to work together in this way will ultimately result in opportunities for individuals to shift their underlying assumptions concerning community life and challenge the dominant roles of coal and coal companies in the citizenry's imagination, despite the near total decline of the industry in the county.

The Culture Hub case study suggests that such collective efforts can provide counter narratives to the dominant position afforded corporations and for-profit institutions in the public imagination by neoliberal thinking and claims in other small, rural communities, including Patrick County. Such efforts can open space for residents to reflect actively on alternatives to neoliberal assumptions amid the difficult economic changes wrought by changing technologies and globalization during recent decades (Carolan 2020; Marsden 2016). Fundamentally, enduring social change requires the creation of a new story, one that can appeal to a wide group of citizens while offering the prospect of shifting the community's future development in a more desirable direction: "A critical first step in community cultural and economic development is to unbound the imagination and un-resign the preferences of a community, through artistic and/or other creative processes" (Appalshop 2017, 2).

As noted above, the researchers have sought to use just such creative processes to bridge ideological and cultural divides in their involvement in Patrick County. This project employed arts and culture as its lens to understand the collective imaginary of the county's citizens with whom the investigators have worked and as a strategic tool to implement creative processes that produce and build a coalition around a freshly derived conception of necessary change. Such efforts call on the imaginations of all participants to reflect anew, and critically, on old assumptions and to devise new possibilities for discussion, shared deliberation, refinement, and potential adoption (Marsden 2016).

COMMUNITY VISIONING AND ENGAGEMENT IN PATRICK COUNTY

The authors' community-based research in Patrick County began with the support of a Vibrant Virginia seed grant facilitated by the Virginia Tech Center for Economic Development and Community Engagement in

2018. The researchers worked closely for this initiative with professionals from the Virginia Tech Outreach Campus Center, Reynolds Homestead, in Patrick County to provide technical assistance and capacity building to local officials and residents to encourage shared learning.

Patrick County is a 483-square-mile jurisdiction with 17,800 residents. The median age of the county's citizens is fifty and the jurisdiction's population has declined 5% since 2010 (US Census Bureau 2020). Patrick County's citizenry is approximately 92% white, 6% African American, and less than 1% of two or more races, American Indian and Alaska Native, Asian or Native Hawaiian, and Other Pacific Islander; 3% of residents are Hispanic (US Census Bureau 2020). Eighty percent of residents possess a high school degree or higher level of education; 10% have an associate's degree, 8% have earned a bachelor's degree, and 5% have a graduate or professional degree (US Census Bureau 2020). The county's approved budget for FY 2020–2021 totaled $54 million (Patrick County nd).

Patrick County's median income is $40,500, with an 18% poverty rate and a 48% employment rate (US Census Bureau 2020). According to 2020 second quarter economic data from Economic Modeling Specialists, Inc. (EMSI), a proprietary economic modeling software company, the top five industries in Patrick County were (by gross regional product, percent change in jobs from 2014–2019):

- Manufacturing ($74M, –28%)
- Government ($69M, +6%)
- Wholesale trade ($65M, +2%)
- Retail trade ($32M, +7%)
- Healthcare and social assistance ($22M; –21%)
- Agriculture, forestry, fishing and hunting ($21M; –17%)

Patrick County has historically profited from timber and wood production and floor manufacturing. It has a tourism industry featuring wineries and agritourism, outdoor recreation, covered bridges, and a history dating back to the American Revolution. While Patrick County has been a destination for retirees in the past decade, the closing of the local hospital in 2017 may slow or even stymie growth in this trend in coming years, as access to quality healthcare is an important determinant in decision-making for seniors relocating for retirement. Lack of access to high-speed internet throughout the county is also an ongoing challenge for business, healthcare, and other organizational development as well as for residents' quality of life.

Community Engagement Process

The authors' initial visit to Patrick County in September 2018 involved a fact-finding discussion with key stakeholders active in local and county government, business, and civic life to understand the county's opportunities and challenges. Based on this discussion, which identified a widespread desire to develop and unify engagement efforts across Patrick County's geographically distinct population areas, the research team partnered with The Reynolds Homestead to host a public engagement workshop in February 2019. The Virginia Tech team invited leaders and citizens from across the county's sectors and districts to contribute to exploratory visioning and goal setting. Facilitators asked participants to imagine, "What would make life better in Patrick County in the next 10 to 15 years?" Participants at the workshop (n = 23) collectively generated a diverse set of priorities addressing tourism, arts, and culture; healthcare and aging; infrastructure development, including acquisition of high-speed internet; and creating more opportunities for youth to inspire them to remain (or return following collegiate studies), live, and work in the county. Artists and cultural organizations were strongly represented at this workshop, highlighting the vibrancy of the county's artistic and cultural assets and enthusiasm for further developing them.

The research team and the community partner hosted a follow-up workshop on the Virginia Tech campus in September 2019 with county government, business, and civic organizational leaders (n = 14) to refine the initially identified priorities and develop specific objectives, strategies, and action plans for each. The program opened with a story circle exercise. Story circles have been employed as a CCD method by Roadside Theater, Junebug Productions, and the US Department of Arts and Culture, among numerous other arts organizations (ross and Rodda 2018). During a story circle, participants sit in a circle and listen deeply to one another as each participant shares a story from personal experience that addresses a theme or question posed. In this case, participants were asked to bring a sentimental object to the workshop that represented Patrick

County as "home," in an effort to personalize the discussion about making that jurisdiction a still better home for its residents in the future.

As the story circle exercise unfolded, participants evidenced a notable shift in attitude from professional objectivity to subjective feeling, a turn that helped the group realize some of the central goals of story circles, to "humanize complex issues, nurture empathy for each other, build bridges across differences, and generate local solutions" (ross and Rodda 2018, 4). The approach calls attention to a potential weakness of neoliberal, technocratic "solutions" for economic and community development: they often fall short of capturing public sentiments concerning how to advance the public good.

Local elections following this workshop resulted in a major turnover in county leadership. That fact led to an opportunity for the team, working in tandem with its civic partners, to present a strategy for community engagement to the new Board of Supervisors in March 2020. The researchers also provided a summary of the information they had gathered through previous planning and community activities, including insights gleaned from the workshops described above. They also shared a report created by graduate students for a Virginia Tech Urban Affairs and Planning master's degree course taught by Professor Todd Schenk, which focused on methods and considerations for integrating community engagement into planning processes. That analysis demonstrated the potential usefulness of the "Speak Out" model to address Patrick County's challenge of organizing engagement opportunities for its geographically and culturally varied residents.

The Speak Out engagement model (Sarkissian and Cook 2016) features a variety of engagement "stations" or stalls that collect citizen feedback and visioning goals. This strategy could be deployed throughout Patrick County during large annual events, such as the Strawberry Festival or the agricultural fair. The county's robust network of arts and cultural assets would be key to the success of Speak Out, as this approach typically employs creative, fun activities appropriate for all ages and is designed to appeal to a broader public. As CCD and participation scholars have suggested, in order to obtain increased levels of citizen engagement, Speak Out facilitators and processes must work to involve residents in identifying paths forward and not simply inform them of strategies already adopted.

Adaptations in Light of COVID-19

After the March meeting at which the study team presented its findings to the Board of Supervisors, COVID-19 severely restricted further in-person participation opportunities, such as piloting a Speak Out initiative, as well as the launch of a series of arts-based workshops designed by the Virginia Tech research group. The investigators were instead invited to a County Planning Commission meeting in May 2020 to brainstorm ways to support updates to the county comprehensive plan in the interim. Despite limited virtual engagement options, as a first step, the research group designed and distributed an online survey to representatives of civic and public organizations in the county that asked them to share the key strengths and five-year goals of their institutions, as well as what the county's government and residents could do to support their missions.

After sharing the survey's findings (n = 39) with the County Planning Commission members in July 2020, that discussion generated additional questions and opportunities for continued engagement, both for the design of additional questionnaires aimed at different economic subsectors, such as retail and wholesale businesses and agricultural organizations, as well as for the potential to conduct focus groups with members of the public to provide feedback on the draft comprehensive plan before it is formally adopted. The investigators provided participating organizations the initial survey results as a resource directory for partnership development and mission alignment.

One of the survey questions asked specifically about the role of arts and culture in each organization's work. The variety of responses to this question and the central role of the arts for many of the responding entities confirmed the research team's initial observation that Patrick County has strong cultural traditions that continue to be evidenced in its community events, partnerships, public, charitable, and nonprofit programming. Arts and cultural representatives responded that funding local fine artists and craftspeople; offering art classes and classical arts curricula; and hosting live music, theater, art festivals, exhibits, and art competitions are important activities for their organizations. Less conventional but equally creative applications of arts and culture in these organizations' work included using art therapy for victims of abuse or crime, art-making and live entertainment to improve quality of life for seniors, applying innovative designs for trail signage and other installations associated with outdoor recreation, and landscaping and gardening as place-making activities to beautify public spaces within the county.

Responding organizational representatives indicated they also coordinate member field trips to historical sites, host book clubs, and feature curricula showcasing local history, including the region's rich musical traditions dating back to its earliest Scots-Irish and African American residents. Environmental and economic development organizations noted a strong desire to be engaged with the region's arts and cultural entities in order to facilitate "ecosystem building." Respondents referenced agriculture and local foods numerous times when highlighting the area's heritage and opportunities to showcase artisan foods and crafts at local farmers' markets. Those responding to the survey also mentioned many festivals, workshops, classes, exhibitions, performances, and cultural symbols, such as historically preserved buildings. Some respondents also suggested that their organizations play an important supporting role in the community arts and cultural scene by providing space, security, funding, and/or volunteers to ensure the success of partner organizations' arts and cultural events.

Patrick County is facing a challenging economic future if current economic development limitations and population decline continue, COVID-19-related repercussions aside. Acknowledging that "purposive institutional deafness is an important neo-liberal feature," it will be essential for the county's government to respond to these challenges reflexively, by engaging multiple stakeholder groups as they develop their new comprehensive plan and by offering those residents opportunities to reflect actively on their current epistemic assumptions concerning the role of the market and of governance (Marsden 2016, 602). It will also be important for the county to legitimize a variety of community needs identified by citizens in that planning process by formally supporting funding proposals and project ideas related to them. This is one way that Patrick County officials could signal their awareness of the underlying reasons for the disproportionate lack of recovery in rural America compared with metropolitan areas following the recent Great Recession of 2007–2009 (Carolan 2020).

Ongoing local government support and participation will also be needed for CCD-related processes if these are to support broad-based potential for positive social change (Moayerian 2018; Sonn and Quayle

2014). Integrating this dialogue into the network of arts and cultural activities described above, employing creative engagement strategies such as a Speak Out initiative, and continuing CCD interventions could offer an even more supportive, productive context for county stakeholders to work together and move forward.

ECONOMIC AND POLITICAL INFLUENCES SHAPING THE SOCIAL IMAGINARY ALONG THE URBAN-RURAL CONTINUUM

Scholars have defined the urban-rural continuum and/or divide according to several metrics, such as density and population size, workforce and commuter patterns, and cultural values. Dewey (1960) surveyed the literature sixty years ago and found scholars defining urban-rural according to several social distinctions such as heterogeneity, literacy, anonymity, mobility, division of labor, secularism, complexity, sophistication, liberalism, interdependency, and tolerance, among other characteristics. Dewey (1960) also noted that many communities defied the prevailing urban-rural dichotomous stereotypes of the time. Similar exceptions to an urban-rural binary characterized by specific, supposedly fixed features can be identified today along lines of race, income, political affiliation, even along such subjective measures as "simplicity" or "authenticity" (Ingraham 2020).

Economic Influences

The authors have considered the urban-rural continuum in light of the ongoing impacts of neoliberal assumptions on rural areas that are not growing, or are declining, economically (Carolan 2020). In this regard, it now appears incontrovertible that, "consolidation of ownership over the means of production and the metabolic rift cultivated by rural resource extraction for largely urban consumption has left many rural communities depopulated and poor" (Ashwood 2018, 717). As Ashwood (2018) has argued, "by sounding like it is about individual rights and hard work, neoliberal politics rhetorically answers such animosity [of rural residents], while actually enacting, and even further empowering, the actual problem: corporate-state profiteering" (726). This is to say, whether citizens are conscious of it or not, it is too simple to want "less government" just because residents may have seen government officials and agencies not acting in their favor in the past (due to unequal corporate-state partnerships, for example). One key question, and one with which Patrick County is now wrestling, is "why anyone would [continue in the face of current conditions to] want less of the government, rather than more of the right kind of government" (Ashwood 2018, 719)? This reflects one of the core philosophical distinctions between neoliberalism and social-democratic reforms.

Rural and urban areas alike have confronted sweeping changes wrought by broad scale economic globalization since the 1960s. There are enormous challenges for nearly all sectors of the American economy: the movement of economic activity to lowest labor cost areas internationally; deindustrialization as a result of competition, and increased competition in many other areas of economic activity as suppliers looked to supply chains across the globe to serve their customers; and, more generally, the globalization of trade in virtually all goods and services (Serra and Stiglitz 2008; Stiglitz 2002, 2006; Taylor 2002, 2004). But they have hit rural areas especially hard in recent decades and those populations have also disproportionately accepted neoliberalism's normative claims concerning the controlling role of the market in their local political economies. The combination has made it difficult for local governments to respond aggressively to changed economic conditions in many rural locations. While widespread acceptance of neoliberal thinking and values has been important to the evolution of localities such as Patrick County, it is but a part of the story of these jurisdictions. A large share of the situation confronting many such communities must also be understood in political terms.

Political Influences

Beginning with the presidential campaign of 1964, one of the nation's two major political parties, the GOP, took a strong stance against recently enacted and contemplated national civil rights laws and companion social changes occurring or in prospect in the US and thereafter sought to capitalize on the social anxieties created by globalization and civil rights shifts in the suburbs and rural areas. This was done in particular by overtly appealing to those disaffected by those changes. In 1968, Richard Nixon railed against those calling for continued social change in favor of full civil rights for African Americans and women and appealed to the racism and racial animus of a supposedly "silent majority" (the "Southern Strategy") on the basis of law and order. Thus, Nixon signaled to rural and Southern voters, especially, that he and his party would seek to preserve existing social hierarchies (e.g., racial exclusion and hierarchy) and ways of living (Maxwell 2019; Maxwell and Shields 2019).

Indeed, to capitalize electorally on the anxiety, stress, and economic and social decline occurring in many rural towns in the wake of intensifying global competition, especially those communities that were single resource- or industry-dependent, while currying populations' angst regarding civil rights law changes, the GOP mobilized voters in affected suburbs and especially rural areas on the basis of their willingness to scapegoat others for those changes. This "deep story" involves the scapegoating of "Others," especially African Americans and minorities who the Republican Party has alleged are "line-cutters" receiving public (government) support, as the fortunes of white rural community dwellers have declined (Hochschild 2018).

GOP purveyors of neoliberal governance tenets and the deep story have worked assiduously for decades to delegitimize democratic governance institutions and reduce the budgets of the same by such arguments and via tax cuts. While both urban and rural locations have confronted globalization, it is the rural areas, especially those with single-locus economies, whose populations have adopted the deep story and find themselves thereby supporting a political party dedicated to supporting financial elites and their perceived interests, paired with an ideology that refuses to assist them as they face declining demand by firms for what their labor forces and economies have to offer (Cox Richardson 2020; MacLean 2017).

Within this paradox, some stakeholders within the community express an unwillingness to support the government, and, in fact, cast public and participatory governance aside in favor of the market as the ultimate arbiter of justice and distribution in their communities. Yet, the marketplace has left them behind with unclear options available for change to bolster their remaining populations (Silva 2019; Wuthnow 2018). It has also saddled these jurisdictions with polarized citizenries whose residents continue to support efforts that are working against their collective capability to pursue shared, joint action along a common purpose or purposes

(Stephenson et al. 2020). As the most recent leader of the GOP, President Donald Trump's dystopian rhetoric and categorical lies embodied this political strategy and its absolutism, animus, Othering, and overt racism. In the presidential election of 2020, 78.51% of Patrick County residents voted for Donald Trump, compared to the statewide rate of 44% (VA Department of Elections 2021).

In short, in the authors' experience working in one hard-hit rural southwest/southside Virginia county, the often alleged rural-urban divide cannot be understood in purely economic terms. If these rural economies can offer value to firms and urban populations, there seems little doubt that both companies and urban residents will employ their (rural) labor forces and buy their goods and services (as they do now, but to a declining degree) (Walcott 2011). Rather, it is also a self-imposed social divide in which some (though certainly not all) people living in rural areas that are no longer producing a commodity the market values or that can compete globally (flooring and furniture products in Patrick County, for example) have elected to blame others as creators of that condition rather than address it head on and mobilize their populations and employ their governments as the vehicles and arbiters of common claims directly as they do so. Because governments are responsible for the steps most necessary to secure increased competitiveness, this scenario is doubly unfortunate (Williams 2002; Young 2020).

Conclusion

For residents in southwest/southside Virginia and throughout the state, the social imaginary is a powerful driver that underpins their shared understanding of how they belong and how they can create change through their individual and collective stories (Kirakosyan 2017) as well as the roles they perceive as appropriate for individuals and organizations of all stripes in the community development process. The authors have and hope to continue to employ CCD in Patrick County to illuminate first, citizens' shared assumptions concerning the role of the market and democratic institutions in their political economy, and second, their shared humanity across differences. The researchers have operated under the assumption that social change is unlikely and any meaningful shift in the urban-rural relationship is improbable unless citizens themselves come to perceive the implications for their ways of life of continuing to accept neoliberal and deep story assumptions.

In the case of Patrick County, the newly elected local government has an opportunity to work with the multipronged activities of civic organizations and agencies, employing CCD methods where appropriate, to define a widely shared vision for the future of the county, and more importantly, to organize and represent the many subgroups of its population to work together to realize that vision. A key piece to achieving these aims will be transparency in local government and a commitment to participating, without fear of the pluriverse of organizations that are working through arts and culture to re-interpret the social imaginary (Pickren 2018).

Lastly, community asset gaps are common in both urban and rural areas, though arguably compounded in Patrick County by decades of economic decline and political polarization as outlined above. Cross-sector collaborations are needed more than ever to address those needs, with CCD providing a functional toolkit for knowledge translation and applied community visioning among local government, the private sector, and civic organization actors. Citizen consciousness of the assumptions that have yielded the present imbroglio and a process by which to change those claims are essential. That process has begun, in the authors' view, in Patrick County and CCD can continue to be employed to encourage and deepen it as it continues.

This work was funded partially by a Vibrant Virginia seed grant administered by the Virginia Tech Center for Economic and Community Engagement (2018–2019), by the Virginia Tech Center for Peace Studies and Violence Prevention (2019–2020), as well as by the Virginia Tech Institute for Policy and Governance (VT-IPG). The authors have no conflicts of interest to disclose. Correspondence concerning this chapter should be addressed to Max Stephenson, Jr., Professor and Director, Virginia Tech Institute for Policy and Governance, 201 W. Roanoke Street, Blacksburg, VA, 24061, United States. Email: mstephen@vt.edu

Chapter 9

Enhancing Place through Public Art in the Metropolitan Exurbs

Conaway Haskins

This chapter explores the Southside Community Gateway Project in the Tri-Cities region of Virginia. Through the lens of creative placemaking, the author documents the initiative, including its history, current state, and local impact. It uses the Gateway Project case to illuminate how small cities, as well as the suburban and peri-urban communities that surround them, can use public art to advance economic development.

The Southside Community Gateway Project (Gateway Project) is an initiative launched in 2017 by the nonprofit Cameron Foundation to use public art to enhance several strategically important highway intersections in the Tri-Cities region of Virginia. The foundation partnered with municipal governments in three of the localities that it serves—the cities of Hopewell and Petersburg and the county of Prince George—to jointly fund and select the artwork installations. This initiative garnered significant coverage in the local press, and though it appears to be generally well received, the response to the process and final product among residents of some communities has been mixed with regard to cost, placement, and design aesthetics (Thomas 2018).

What follows is a qualitative exploration of the Gateway Project that documents and assesses its history, current status, and local impact. The overarching purpose of this research is to illuminate the Gateway Project as a case study of how small cities and the suburban and peri-urban communities that surround them can use public art to advance economic development, a strategy known as creative placemaking (Markusen and Gadwa 2010), within the setting of small cities and their surrounding suburbs. Due to the limitations on conducting field research resulting from the COVID-19 pandemic, this study is not intended to serve as a definitive review of the Gateway Project; rather it is hoped that the findings herein will inspire and contribute to additional inquiries in the future.

Virginia's Tri-Cities Region

Located along and at the confluences of the Appomattox and James Rivers, the area of study is known colloquially as "The Tri-Cities region" of Virginia. Though it comprises the southern tier of the larger Richmond Metropolitan Statistical Area, the area has carved out a distinct regional identity over several centuries (Crater PDC 2020). This is reflected in that the area has its own regional planning and economic development agencies that are separated from those serving the larger, more urbanized northern tiers of Richmond (Crater PDC 2020). According to the regional commission serving the area, the Tri-Cities region had a total estimated population of 602,333 in 2020 (Crater PDC 2021).

Nearly 350,000 of those people reside in Chesterfield County, the largest locality in the Tri-Cities region and the broader Richmond Metropolitan Statistical Area (MSA) in terms of land mass and population. Traditionally, only the southern portions of Chesterfield County, those adjacent to the cities of Colonial Heights, Hopewell, and Petersburg, are considered to be part of the Tri-Cities region. Along with those localities, the core Tri-Cities communities are the counties of Dinwiddie, Prince George, Surry, and Sussex (see figure 9.1). That strong and complex regional identity, effectively a region within a region, would apparently emerge as a key element for how the locations for the public art installations were chosen. The primary geographic region for this study has a

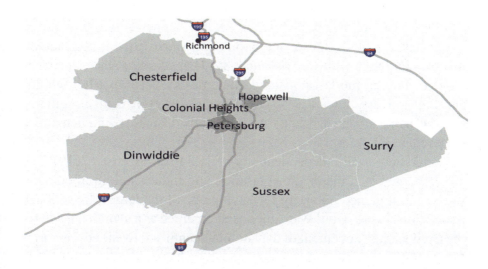

Figure 9.1. Virginia's Gateway Region, 2016

population of around 250,000. Ultimately, the Gateway Project would focus on three of the seven primary communities: the cities of Hopewell and Petersburg and the county of Prince George.

According to the US Census Bureau's (2020) measures of population density, land usage, and population clustering, Hopewell is considered 100% urban, Petersburg is considered 97.9% urban, and Prince George is considered 53.4% rural. The cities of Hopewell and Petersburg are both adjacent to Prince George County, which—despite the expressed concerns about having distinctive identities—adds a classical city-suburban dynamic to the project. Although they may be closely connected by rivers and roadways, these three communities have as many differences as they do commonalities. These differences would be reflected in the public statements about the construction of public art installations in each place.

Hopewell is an independent city of 22,596 (US Census 2019). This area was home to precolonial Native American tribes, and the British colonists formally established it as "Bermuda City" in 1613, making its location the oldest continuously inhabited English-speaking settlement in the United States. Its location at the confluence of the James and Appomattox Rivers has made it an attractive location for industrial plants, so much so that city leaders developed a marketing campaign in the mid-twentieth century promoting it as the "Chemical Capital of the South" (Foster 2005).

After years of steady population decline, Hopewell has had a relatively stable, slightly increasing population since 2010. It is a racially diverse city (51% white, 43% Black, 8% Hispanic) that faces the challenge of having modest household incomes ($39,156 per household) and high poverty rates (20%) (US Census 2019). It is also regularly listed as being among Virginia's most "fiscally distressed" municipalities (Mavredes 2018).

Petersburg is an independent city of 31,346 (US Census 2019). The area emerged as a major transportation and industrial hub in colonial times, and it gained notoriety for having one of the largest freed Black populations in pre–Civil War America. It emerged as a significant site for the Civil Rights movement of the late-nineteenth and twentieth centuries (Shorr 2005). Since the mid-1980s, Petersburg has suffered from a number of economic crises and natural disasters, which have devastated its landscape and hallowed out its sociocultural environs (Schneider 2016).

As a possible nod to its antebellum and civil rights history, it now has the highest concentration of African American residents of any locality in Virginia (79% Black, 16% white, 4% Hispanic). Petersburg has faced a steady population decline for more than four decades, and it has one of the lowest family incomes ($33,927 per household) and highest poverty rates (27.5%) in the state (US Census 2019). It was also on the brink of municipal bankruptcy in recent years and is generally considered Virginia's most "fiscally distressed" municipality (Mavredes 2018).

Prince George County is a mixed rural-suburban county of 38,082 (US Census 2019). Formed in 1703 from the original settlements of the Virginia Company, it has steadily transitioned from an agricultural-based economy to being a hub for military and industrial logistics facilities. The county has three interstate highways transecting it (I-85, I-95, and I-295), and it is home to Fort Lee, the headquarters of several US Army logistics and transportation functions (Crater PDC 2020).

Prince George is a solidly white-majority, middle-class community (61% white, 33% Black, 5% Hispanic) that has seen steady growth since the early twentieth century. It has one of the highest family incomes in the Richmond MSA ($49,877 per household) and relatively low poverty (8%) compared to the more urbanized areas in the Tri-Cities and Virginia (US Census 2019). It is considered to be a growing community with a relatively stable, well-managed municipal government (Mavredes 2018).

The Gateway Project

The Gateway Project was initiated and driven by the Cameron Foundation. Founded in October 2003, Cameron is a 501c3 nonprofit philanthropy based in the small Southern city of Petersburg, Virginia. Formed from the sale of a regional public hospital to a larger corporate healthcare company, the organization's mission is "to transform the Tri-Cities and surrounding counties into a healthy, vibrant and economically vital region by strategically leveraging resources for community impact" (Cramer 2020). Its service area was inherited from the original charter of the public hospital and includes the cities of Petersburg, Colonial Heights, and Hopewell, along with the counties of southern Chesterfield, Dinwiddie, Prince George, and Sussex. Its footprint consists of the area traditionally considered to be the core Tri-Cities region.

Although this kind of public art effort was relatively new to the Tri-Cities area, it was familiar territory for Cameron Foundation CEO, J. Todd Graham. A native of Petersburg, Graham holds a master's degree in urban planning from Harvard's Graduate School of Design and has more than thirty years of experience in nonprofit and foundation management across the US. He returned to the Greater Richmond region in 2011 to initially run another local foundation before being hired in 2012 as the second CEO in Cameron's history (Cameron Foundation 2012).

In the years immediately prior to returning to Virginia, Graham served as CEO of the Iowa West Foundation (IWF) from 2003–2011. As head of this philanthropic grantmaking organization based in the city of Council Bluffs, Iowa, he led a major push for public art planning in the area where that organization is headquartered. Council Bluffs is a small/mid-sized city of just over 62,000 located in the Omaha, Nebraska, metro area. It experienced modest population and economic growth in the 2000s (US Census 2019).

In 2004, IWF announced that it would make an initial $9 million investment in public art to help transform the image of the community. This resulted in the installation of six sculptures as the first phase of "Iowa West Public Art" a community-based public art program (Staff Report, Daily Nonpareil 2007). This effort recruited nationally recognized public artists to design pieces at six different locations in the area.

The first site IWF selected was at an interstate highway interchange, and Graham made bold statements about the rationale for the siting as well as the potential impact. He told the local newspaper that, "An initial public art master plan viewed the entire city of Council Bluffs as a sculpture park. We are optimistic about the potential impact of the public art on tourism, arts-related businesses and economic development. The improved quality of life will bring more than visitors—we hope it will attract new residents and new businesses to our community" (Staff Report, Daily Nonpareil 2007).

Graham and his IWF team worked with citizens, government officials, and consultants to draft the master plan, and after seven years, over twenty public art displays were located across the Council Bluffs area with plans in the works for thirty more. By 2011, the local arts council (Bluff Arts Council) worked with city officials to propose a formal Public Art Commission to manage the existing sites, engage community stakeholders in the development of future sites, and execute those art projects selected to move forward (Ronk et al. 2011). That entity began operating in 2012, but by then, Graham had departed for Virginia to take a CEO position with the Robins Foundation, a philanthropic grantmaking organization based in Richmond.

In 2012, he was recruited away from the Robins Foundation by the board of the Cameron Foundation. Effectively, he had returned to his hometown to bring his practice of professional philanthropy to bear on the community. According to local stakeholders, under Graham's leadership, Cameron began consideration of supporting public art projects in the Tri-Cities to enhance placemaking within its service territory. It was thought that the efforts in Council Bluffs—a small, mid-sized city in a larger metropolitan region—could serve as a model paralleling the Tri-Cities' status as a subregion set within the broader Richmond metropolitan area (personal communication 2020).

In July 2015, having awarded over $71 million to some 260+ government, nonprofit, and faith-based organizations in an eleven-year period, Cameron issued a statement to the press indicating that it would now work "to bring together stakeholders to tackle large, systemic problems in the region, instead of just waiting on proposals for grant funding from area organizations" (Small 2015a). As the foundation's CEO, Graham explained that this new focus on "proactive grantmaking" would have a greater impact on the quality of life in the region. Unlike many of its previous 868 grant awards, future funding would focus on "visible, high impact projects that transform the community and/or address social determinants of health," and proposals would be solicited on an invitation-only basis (Small 2015a). Embedded within the statement was a reference to how this newfound approach would soon manifest—the Southside Community Gateway Project.

Under the auspices of these new priorities, Cameron's leadership convened officials in each locality to ascertain ways to "beautify entrances to the cities and counties, and to highlight individual features" (Small 2015a) as a way to spur economic development. During their exploration process, Cameron staff discovered that the localities had considered "gateway" projects for several years but lacked the funding and other resources to execute a plan. Harkening to his Iowa experience, Graham's initial vision was for a region-wide "unifying" project, but that was rejected by each community. As he stated to the press, "We found out that these small communities in the Southside are very distinctive and they wish to maintain that distinctive identity" (Small 2015a). After these conversations, the foundation moved forward to plan projects in three of the communities in its footprint—Hopewell, Petersburg, and Prince George.

According to anonymous informants, despite the insistence by community leaders that each community had its unique issues, the ties binding Cameron's support was that the Gateway Project could draw more visitors to the region. Although no formal evaluation of the project was planned, the informants noted that in each community, Cameron was able to have new conversations with local officials with whom they had not previously collaborated. Among foundation and government staff, there was also a sense that this project would expose residents from across the region to larger-scale public art. While gallery, museum, and school-based fine art works are accessible across the communities, and there is a tradition of performing arts, the region has a more limited history of public art. In fact, a search of popular national public arts databases turns up a listing of the Hopewell project as the only one noted in the Tri-Cities region (Western States Arts Federation 2020). Because there is veritably no history of such installations in the region prior to the Gateway Project, it is truly a gateway on multiple levels (personal communications 2020).

One other commonality among the three localities is that these gateway installations were executed via their municipal Capital Improvement Plan (CIP) processes, not via their Comprehensive Planning processes or through the formation of a Cultural Plan. Although there is an arts council serving the broader Richmond metropolitan region as well as a local arts council for the Tri-Cities area neither of these entities was directly engaged in the Gateways Project according to anonymous informants (personal communications 2020). Indeed, in both Petersburg (Covil 2018) and Prince George (Campbell 2017), where the proposed installations were designed by architects and engineers, public input occurred mostly via meetings of ad hoc "steering committees" consisting of local elected officials, municipal staffers, and Cameron leaders, and then subsequent public meetings about the CIP processes. These efforts appear to be aligned with customary processes for economic development projects. In Hopewell, because the installation was slated to be designed by a nationally renowned artist, a more formal committee was formed consisting of several city council representatives, the head of a local nonprofit arts organization, a private citizen, and Graham; the committee's recommendation was accepted in full by a majority of city council members and was moved forward (Vogelsong 2016).

Initial public estimates were that each art installation would cost roughly $1 million. The expressed plan was for Cameron to provide grant funding for half of the costs with the localities assuming the other half (Small 2015b). Hopewell and Prince George were each slated for one major project while in Petersburg, the most fiscally and socially distressed of the communities, plans were made for two projects. The presence of other public-space initiatives such as a regionwide Appomattox River Master Trail system and a proposed development of artists' lofts in downtown Petersburg—projects spearheaded and/or significantly funded by Cameron—were seen as mutually beneficial assets (personal communication 2020). Cameron CEO Graham described these prospective gateways as the "cornerstone" of the foundation's new strategy (Small 2015b).

The Installations

In Hopewell, artist Ralph Helmick designed a fifty-one-foot-tall stainless steel sculpture shaped into the letter H; he named it "The Return." The artwork was installed at the city's western limits in the median between the eastbound and westbound lanes of US Route 10 (see figure 9.2). It is located near the point where the Appomattox River flows into the James River before heading east toward the Atlantic coast. The piece dramatically welcomes, or bids farewell to, travelers along this major highway.

Figure 9.2. "The Return" in Hopewell, VA

In comments to a local newspaper, Helmick, who is based in Boston and has completed over fifty public artworks, described his inspiration thus, "Driving around Hopewell at night, I saw the factories all lit up. It was just really quite remarkable, and so I decided to employ visual language . . . based on scaffolding" (Gibson 2018). The sculpture is approximately 20 feet wide, over 6 feet deep, and constructed of nearly

Figure 9.3. "Washington Street Bridge Gateway" in Petersburg, VA

4,500 linear feet of stainless steel. It has a brushed finish, is estimated to weigh 14,000 pounds, and together, the sculpture and base stands 65 feet high. Twelve floodlights illuminate it at night (Stebbins 2018).

In Petersburg, a team from Chroma Design, a landscape architecture firm based in Boulder, Colorado, took inspiration from the "extensive wrought iron architectural work going back to the seventeenth century" found throughout the city to craft a modern interpretation in the form of red arches attached to the Washington Street Bridge over Exit 52 of I-95 (Lamson 2020) (see figure 9.3). Near the northern terminus of I-85, over 80,000 vehicles are reported to pass under this bridge each day.

The installation—titled "Washington Street Bridge Gateway" by the designers—features arches that are fourteen-feet high and cover the entire 300-foot span of the bridge (see figure 9.3). They are fabricated from steel tubes, and this project included a refurbishment of the bridge by removing signs, cleaning and staining the concrete, refinishing the steel girders, and adding four white 4000 K LED floodlights at the base of each arch (Lamson 2020). The final project cost was $1.8 million, which far exceeded the initial estimate, and the Virginia Department of Transportation agreed to provide additional funding to accompany the city's and Cameron's contribution (Covil 2018).

In Prince George, a team from Chroma Design again served as the designers of "The Gardens at Exit 45" (see figure 9.4). The inspiration

Figure 9.4. "The Gardens at Exit 45" in Prince George County

for this project was found in "colonial garden spires" and the result is two forty-seven-foot-tall steel and blue glass sculptures that serve as a "threshold" for the nearby commercial destinations (Campbell 2017). County officials say that this I-95 interchange had once served as a major tourism hub for the area, but it had declined economically over time.

An estimated 40,000 cars per day pass by this exit ramp, and although plans initially called for the planting of 139 trees, 363 shrubs, and nearly 3,000 perennials along the exit ramp (Campbell 2017), the final project featured 27 evenly spaced English Oaks and other smaller plantings of shrubs and grasses for a 32,000-square-foot total area (Chroma Design 2018). This project was explicitly designed with economic development at the forefront and fits within the county's destination marketing plans. Further attention is drawn to them by the inclusion of color-changing LED lights that visually illuminate the spires at night. As one county official noted, "Every so often, everyone needs to put on a coat of paint and refresh and we saw this as an opportunity that came out of our November 2013 plan that we had done, saying that streetscape is an item that needs to be addressed" (Campbell 2017).

As noted earlier, the Gateway Project was conceived by the Cameron Foundation's CEO and staff who subsequently convinced three local governments to approve, and share installation and ongoing management costs of, the public art. Per Cameron representatives, the foundation funded these under its Community and Economic Development portfolio, not its Arts and Culture portfolio. Its internal grants management system subsequently notates it as such, and when a team of consultants were recently engaged to review and make recommendations for the future of its Arts and Culture grantmaking, they were not expressly advised to examine the Gateway Project (personal communication 2020).

At present, it is not yet known whether Cameron and/or the localities plan to conduct an evaluation of the Gateway Project. It is possible that they view these installations as infrastructure projects whose economic development impact is immediate and implicit—each provides for a distinct addition to the local landscape and are viewed by thousands of travelers each day. As Markusen and Gadwa-Nicodemus (2019) note, creative placemaking efforts have an inherent "conceptual fuzziness" that leads to debates across the field on proper indicators and evaluation frameworks to measure their effectiveness and impact. However, in assessing these projects, it is useful to draw upon themes from established and emergent public arts literature that navigates the intersection of fine arts and economic development.

The Gateway Project connects to Senie's (2003) work about public art's audiences, interpretation, and appreciation because the installations are highly visible. There is nothing "hidden in plain sight" about these exhibits due to their physical presence and the media publicity surrounding them. The project reflects Bishop's (2012) concerns about the "spectacle" elements of public arts engagement with the public's perceptions. It is physically imposing on the landscapes of the communities, and it is somewhat democratically derived because the public sector and nonprofit sector—which represent the citizenry and civil society—were the key drivers of the project. The Gateway Project exemplifies the creative placemaking themes explored by Frenette (2017) in that the three sculptures were inspired by local commercial landscapes (Hopewell's factory-centric skyline), ubiquitous local imagery (the wrought iron fencing found around Petersburg), and the local landscaped flora (colonial gardens throughout Prince George).

On my initial field visits to the Tri-Cities, I maintained a healthy skepticism of whether these projects were good usages of limited public and philanthropic dollars. This region has suffered multidecadal economic and social malaise, and it seemed that $4 million in local government and foundation funding could be better spent on basic services. I was aware of the concerns expressed by residents in local news media articles (Thomas 2018), as well as the Hopewell project being the subject of an online prank that was reported by media outside of the region as far as Charlotte, North Carolina (Price 2019). However, after discussions with experts in the field, conversations with local stakeholders, reflexive research on the region's history, and exploring the history of how the Gateway Project developed, examining the scholarly literature, and conducting multiple visits to each site to consider them individually, I now have a better-informed perspective that has noticeably shifted my views toward the Gateway Project.

In Hopewell, when viewing "The Return" at multiple points in the day (see figure 9.5), I was struck by how it does reflect the spirit of Hopewell, for better or worse. Coming into the city eastbound on Route 10 during the day, the sculpture initially appears to be part of the city's industrial

Figure 9.5. "The Return"

skyline before coming into clearer view as a distinct entity into itself. Approaching it closer, it becomes easier to make out that it is a piece of art. At first, I was struck by how inaccessible it is to pedestrians—its placement is in the median of a busy four-lane highway with no crosswalks or platform to allow visitors to view it up close on foot.

Although it is located near the riverside marina and park, and close to a hotel and restaurants, it does not blend into the backdrop of those. It effectively lays down a marker for the city's industrial heritage amid other nonindustrial natural and built environs. Yet, in reflecting on the intentions of Cameron and the local government officials, this is purposeful. The sculpture is designed to be seen primarily by car travelers not engaged by local residents for recreation. The H-shape artwork represents Hopewell to the external and internal audiences from afar.

In Petersburg, it was clear that the "Washington Street Bridge Gateway" is an auto-centric artwork (see figure 9.6). The choice of the arches makes sense in light of the city's architectural history, but admittedly, before I knew of this inspiration, the choice of red metal arches seemed like a random decision by the designers. Located over a section of one of the busiest interstate highways in the country, the sculpture comes into view—and leaves—rather quickly whether traveling northbound or southbound on I-95.

The bright red coloring obviously draws attention to it so that fast-driving motorists can see it, and possibly develop a curiosity about what

Figure 9.6. "Washington Street Bridge Gateway"

it is and what it represents. Its location on an exit ramp makes it possible to view it from afar at high speeds on the interstate or up close at slower speeds of the city street. Again, this is a car-centric artwork designed to engage drivers, even if only briefly. Though there are sidewalks along Washington Street that allow pedestrians to walk across the bridge, this is not space that is friendly to walkers. The sidewalk is rather narrow, and walkers are required to navigate across the on- and off-ramps with no stoplights or crosswalks—this is a major exit and entry-point, and I detected a palpable sense of danger when thinking of walking back and forth across the bridge. Whether sitting against the backdrop of the daytime sky, or illuminated against the darkness of the night sky, the artwork is distinctive and draws attention to the city.

In Prince George, there were several notable elements about "The Gardens at Exit 45" (see figure 9.7). The metal and blue glass spires fit remarkably well into the built landscape of hotels, gas stations, and restaurants. In fact, the coloring of the glass seems to match the coloring of the roof of the hotel that sits across the street from it. The two spires sit inside a well-landscaped garden, which has plantings that are similar to those found around the commercial and residential sites nearby. Despite its size and depth, in contrast to the other two gateways, "The Gardens" has a surprisingly muted effect. It complements the existing landscape by offering an artistic upgrade, but it does not seem out of place.

Figure 9.7. "The Gardens at Exit 45"

Additionally, it is apparent that county officials and private property owners have committed to keeping the surrounding area maintained as it was relatively free of trash, had road signs and commercial signage that appeared clean and modern, and the road itself had been recently paved and lined. Unlike the Hopewell and Petersburg sites, it is possible for pedestrians to access the sculpture, but the imposing form and openness of the space would create an environmental deterrent to certain kinds of activities. I found that the best location to view it was from the parking lot of one of the hotels as I could get relatively close to the sculpture and interact with its aesthetic, but not close enough to touch it. Essentially, it represents what it was intended to—the revitalizing travel corridor of a county that is navigating the transition from a pastoral rural community to a vibrant suburb.

Conclusion

In the end, the Gateway Project does what it sets out to do. It provides distinctive, highly visible public art that symbolizes life in this region of small cities and transitioning suburbs that is still attempting to find its place in a broader metropolitan area and the global economy. As with many such efforts, it clearly attempts to "serve an iconic placemaking function" (Zitcer and Almanzar 2020) while demonstrating an awareness of the need to "cater to multiple constituencies" (Doss 2006) whose pleasure with it may wax and wane over time.

To the extent that public art and creative placemaking intersect with inherently contested spaces, it is unlikely that any consensus will emerge in each community—or the Tri-Cities region as a whole—about the purported success of the project. However, in some ways, this may not matter. These are three seemingly permanent public artworks that will reflect and shape the landscapes of these cities, and the region, for years to come. Only with the benefit of time will we be able to truly assess their composite impact.

That being said, this project does showcase the need for more scholarly research into the dynamics of public art and creative placemaking in small cities and rural regions. Such inquiries could entail approaches such as more extended and formalized observations, intercept surveys, analysis of social media impressions, and so on. As noted earlier, scholars and practitioners are aware of these gaps, and it is hoped that this review of this specific initiative can serve as a case study upon which additional scholarship can be pursued.

Chapter 10

Creating Vibrant Main Streets
throughout Virginia

John Accordino and Kyle Meyer

This chapter offers a thorough description of recent efforts to rediscover the value of place in our historic cities and towns and how some of them are building on that foundation to become important economic nodes in their regions. Through their rich descriptions of Main Street revitalization efforts across the Commonwealth, the authors demonstrate how strong places can be the foundation for strong regions in a vibrant Virginia. They conclude by discussing some of the important ways that public policy might reinforce and build upon this energy by incentivizing and supporting collaborative initiatives that incorporate all communities in a region and by providing the tools necessary to strengthen them.

CITIES AND TOWNS IN REGIONS VS. CRESCENT AND HORSESHOE

Contemporary descriptions of Virginia often use the metaphors of a thriving Urban Crescent, characterized by dynamic knowledge-sector and services employment, as well as government and military jobs, on the one hand, and a lagging, desperately poor Rural Horseshoe, characterized by declining manufacturing, mining, and agriculture jobs, on the other hand.¹ Although there is truth in this characterization, it is an exaggeration that presents the state as two undifferentiated masses, failing to recognize the particular assets and challenges of the regions, cities, and towns within them. Many of the challenges commonly associated with the Horseshoe and not the Crescent actually have a different geographic distribution than these two shapes suggest. Poverty, digital exclusion, and health disparities, to take just a few examples, plague a number of communities in the Crescent area, whereas some communities in the Horseshoe do not suffer these problems significantly.²

Most important, thinking in terms of Urban Crescent and Rural Horseshoe obscures a path toward a more vibrant Virginia—as a commonwealth of regions, anchored by strong cities and towns, that is, by places. Places are geographic spaces invested with human meaning, identity, and ultimately capital and economic functions. Until recent decades, we thought of our commonwealth in terms of regions and the places that anchor them. However, as our economic structure changed in the second half of the twentieth century, we lost some traditional connections between place and economic activity and we failed to appreciate that place is still a vital component of a vibrant economy, not just a residual category. A focus on places and the regions they anchor, however, can help us to see the possibilities for urban-rural collaboration and economic vitality within each region. Fortunately, we are now coming to value place and regional collaboration more than in years past. Understanding what we

---

1. The Urban Crescent stretches from Northern Virginia along I-95 through Richmond and then east along I-64 to Hampton Roads. It owes its growth largely to the build-up of America's national defense infrastructure of the Pentagon and various commands, bases, and installations, before, during, and after World War II, as well as the interstate highway system, beginning in 1956. Today, the Urban Crescent boasts not only defense-related employment, but also various features of a "postindustrial" economy, such as software and systems development, information technology, federal, state, and local government, tourism, advanced manufacturing, and logistics. The Rural Horseshoe, along with the Eastern Shore, is the area outside the Crescent. It has been known largely for agricultural products, mining (in southwestern Virginia), and manufacturing. In recent decades, the Horseshoe, especially in the southwest and Southside, as well as on the Eastern Shore, has suffered declining employment and working-age population, due largely to the automation and globalization of its traditional industries.
2. Bagchi (2019) shows that problems of digital exclusion—lack of internet connectivity, equipment, and skills—are as prevalent in low-wealth parts of urban areas as they are in some rural areas. Bagchi (2019) notes that health disparities and the challenge of providing healthcare via telehealth, while challenged by geographic distance in rural areas, are also challenges in urban areas because of other sources of health disparities.

are accomplishing this way can help us to see the possibilities for more accomplishments and bring them into being.

This chapter tells one part of that story—how we have rediscovered the value of place in our historic cities and towns and how some of them are building on that foundation to become important economic nodes in their regions. To some, revitalized historic downtowns in a twenty-first-century economy may seem to be just nostalgic sideshows, where high-paid workers in the modern economy or wealthy tourists and retirees patronize lower-paid retail, service, accommodation, entertainment, and gastronomy workers. Yet coupled with regionally sourced food and beverages, downtown housing, recreation, and other amenities and linked spatially and programmatically to other economic sectors (e.g., for business conventions or colleges and schools), such a downtown can be a significant contributor to a regional economy and catalyze further development. Moreover, in a growing number of cities and towns, place-based revitalization is also building a foundation for new activities in small-scale manufacturing, business services, IT, and related industries, located in, near, or coupled with their historic centers. This is not a summative evaluation; the story is still unfolding. Yet in the examples found in this chapter we can see how strong places can be the foundation for strong regions in a vibrant Virginia, and we can see how public policy might reinforce and build upon this energy.

DEVELOPMENT AND DECLINE

From the early days of European colonization, city, town, and countryside throughout Virginia developed together as integrated economic systems. Activities requiring face-to-face interaction were located in cities. Agriculture and other uses that required more land were located outside of cities. The cities' centrality made them the natural locations for marketing, storage, processing, packing, manufacturing, and transshipment (via water, roads, and railways) of the produce of surrounding areas. As they grew, they supplied their regions with retail goods and consumer services, finance and legal services, government, and higher education. Factories and processing centers developed first in cities and towns near rail and waterways and often cheek by jowl with the shops and government functions of the downtown. Central cities were the incubators of small, innovative businesses that would move to the urban periphery as they grew larger and needed more space. Cities and towns were the nodes in their regions' economies and they gave their regions an identity and a brand. But it was a symbiotic relationship—neither country nor city could exist without the other.[3]

Industrialization and urban expansion in the nineteenth and early twentieth centuries occurred gradually along roads and railways and remained close to the cities. Expansion after World War II was dramatic and far-reaching, however, as the interstate and beltways facilitated suburban resettlement of residents, industrial facilities, and shopping. By the 1970s, smaller cities and towns, even those serving as county seats, were becoming "hollowed out" as manufacturing, retail, services, and residents moved out to new settlements served by new highways.

As their traditional functions moved out to suburban beltways and corridors, central cities and towns found themselves looking for a new raison d'être for their downtowns. Up to this point in history, there had been no question of the economic value of the centrality that had evolved naturally through the symbiotic relationships of towns and cities with their surrounding regions. Although the new roads passed through or encircled the city, the city itself now appeared to be an anachronism, not an asset. Traditional downtown uses, such as government, post offices, and hospitals expanded into the suburbs and sometimes closed facilities in town. No one was championing entrepreneurship or face-to-face interaction in urban business districts as a way to stimulate innovation. Other than experimental communities, such as Reston, Virginia, no one was building for the "walkable city" or what would become known as the "new urbanism"—compact, walkable, mixed-use communities. Instead, many seemed to want the freedom that the automobile, the highway, the shopping mall, and the suburban subdivision with private backyards promised.[4]

---

3. Although Virginia's cities and their surrounding regions became well integrated in the course of the nineteenth and early twentieth centuries, they, of course, also traded with other regions for goods and services that they did not produce, as part of a so-called system of cities in the national economy.
4. Declines in the region's basic industries exacerbated these challenges in the cities and towns of Southside and southwest Virginia, while growth in government, military and tertiary sector employment softened them, somewhat, in cities like Richmond and Norfolk.

Phase I: Revitalizing Historic Cities and Towns

Central city and downtown revitalization, when it began about 1980, did not happen because new economic uses required a central city or downtown location. In fact, it was driven initially by topophilia (love of place)—fond memories of the vibrant downtown streets and neighborhoods people had enjoyed in their youth, or the appreciation of a history that could be captured only in the built environment that remained after the functions that had been housed in it had disappeared (Gibson 2009). As residents of South Boston, a small city in southern Virginia, recalled in 2014, "As a youngster, I remember the downtown was very vibrant. On Friday nights you were dressing up to go downtown. . . . I have a love of downtown and I want to see it prosper. . . . I used to go to downtown business association meetings with my dad. From that point forward, I've been interested in this issue. . . . The restoration of the downtown feeling is what I like! I love seeing stuff come back" (Accordino and Fasulo 2015, 56–57). Not everyone shared this attachment to historic downtowns, but by 1980 five factors had come together to breathe new economic life into them.

Historic Preservation Interests

Until the 1940s preserving historical memory through the built environment was an activity limited mostly to the preservation of monuments or other notable places. But the postwar development boom that demolished historic structures swelled the ranks of preservation advocates to become a force in American politics, leading first to the creation of the National Trust for Historic Preservation in 1949 and then to the National Preservation Act in 1966 (Mackintosh 1986).[5] The report that led to the National Preservation Act recognized the value of place, calling for a "new preservation" that would "look beyond the individual building and individual landmark and concern itself with the historic and architecturally valued areas and districts which contain a special meaning for the community" (Mackintosh 1986, 207–8).

---

5. Virginia created a Department of Historic Resources and a Landmarks Register in 1965 to identify and manage the state's historic assets and determine ways to preserve them (Virginia Department of Historic Resources 2020).

Funding Historic Preservation

The National Trust developed ways to determine the historic significance of buildings and districts, protect them from demolition, and finance the costs of historic rehabilitation and adaptive reuse. The most powerful financing tool has been the Federal Rehabilitation Tax Credit, passed by Congress in 1976. It allows owners of income-producing properties to deduct 20% of qualified rehabilitation expenditures from their income taxes. In 1996 Virginia passed its own version of the historic tax credit, offering a tax write off of 25% of qualified rehabilitation expenditures (in addition to the federal credit).[6] Historic tax credits have helped revitalize downtowns throughout Virginia, producing positive impacts that have multiplied throughout the Virginia economy (Accordino and Fasulo 2014).[7]

Development of a Viable Strategic Approach—The National Main Street Program

In 1980, the National Trust established a program that looked beyond the individual building to the district—the National Main Street Program. Its initial targets were the downtown commercial districts of historic towns and small cities suffering from business closures. In the mid-1990s the program was introduced in neighborhood commercial districts of large cities as well (Robertson 2004). To emphasize its mission of rebuilding place and community by infusing historic districts with new economic uses, it adopted the moniker: Economic development in the context of historic preservation. In practice, this meant that a community pursuing the Main Street Approach® to downtown revitalization would focus on four elements:

1. Economics: strengthening economic assets and diversifying the business mix.

---

6. In practice, rehabilitators of historic properties have syndicated and "sold" the tax credits to wealthy individuals looking to shelter income.
7. Virginia consistently ranks among the top five states in the use of historic tax credits, and other states have experienced the same strong positive economic multiplier effects from the private investment in historic buildings as Virginia has.

2. Design: getting Main Street in top physical shape.
3. Organization: getting all stakeholders working toward the same goals.
4. Promotion: selling the image and promise of Main Street to the community.

The National Main Street Center[8] worked with states and nonprofits to establish statewide programs to provide technical assistance to local governments and Main Street communities to assess their markets and craft revitalization strategies. As of 2020, there are forty-four state coordinating programs, over 1,200 Main Street designated communities, and many more program affiliates that are not full-fledged members (Staley 2020). The National Main Street Center sets guidelines and provides technical assistance, mostly through statewide organizations, and statewide organizations add their own assistance to localities.[9] The Virginia Main Street Program was established in 1985 in the Department of Housing and Community Development. As of 2021, Virginia has thirty designated communities and ninety affiliates.

Powerful Partnerships

The goal of revitalizing historic city and town centers has attracted many public- and private-sector supporters. In Virginia, at least ten different state agencies are involved in downtown revitalization. The main ones include the Department of Housing and Community Development, Department of Historic Resources, Economic Development Partnership, Tobacco Region Revitalization Commission, Tourism Corporation, Department of Environmental Quality, and Department of Agriculture and Consumer

---

8. The National Main Street Center is an independent subsidiary of the National Trust for Historic Preservation.
9. Although each locality goes through its own process to become an active Main Street community, key elements include outreach from the statewide office to local officials and other interested parties to attend training sessions held around the Commonwealth. Interest emerges from downtown officials, property and business owners, and other local stakeholders. The state offers planning grants to help localities take a step toward a full-scale revitalization program and gradually localities gain the skills and the critical mass of interested stakeholders to move toward applying for Main Street Community status, which brings more technical assistance.

Services. At the local government level, the executive's office, as well as departments of economic development, public works, planning and development, parks and recreation, and public safety provide physical improvements and services. The private sector is involved through development professionals—developers, architects, financial consultants, skilled crafts persons, and most important, local business and property owners, as well as residents. Because of its franchise-like structure and rules, the Main Street Approach® has been able to bring these entities together and draw forth public resources, private capital, and volunteer hours (Accordino and Fasulo 2015).[10]

Attracting Markets

Important as the organizing, business development, and placemaking elements have been to the revitalization of historic downtowns, they would not have brought success in the early years of revitalization without a population interested in visiting and in purchasing goods and services there. Revitalized historic downtowns have attracted two types of markets—the local and regional consumer market, and the regional, national, and international tourist and recreation market. The local and regional market has several components. In Harrisonburg, for example, it consists of residents living within a twenty-minute drive, daytime workers in and near the district, and shoppers coming from as far as West Virginia to shop downtown and at big-box stores nearby (Dono 2020). To attract shoppers, Main Street communities took steps to reintroduce them to legacy businesses such as restaurants, theaters, and bakeries, and to new, independent businesses, such as cafes, restaurants, artisans, and art galleries.

In many historic downtowns, institutions that had been there for many years but which had not engaged with the downtown began to do so after revitalization took hold. Soon after Harrisonburg Downtown Renaissance commenced operations in 2003 it reached out to James Madison University, which is located on the edge of the downtown, but which had no relationship to it. The Main Street Program's overture resulted in a

---

10. Of course, not everyone finds the rules easy to follow. Cash-strapped communities, especially after an initial period of revitalization activity, sometimes leave the program to save the cost of an executive director and other program expenses.

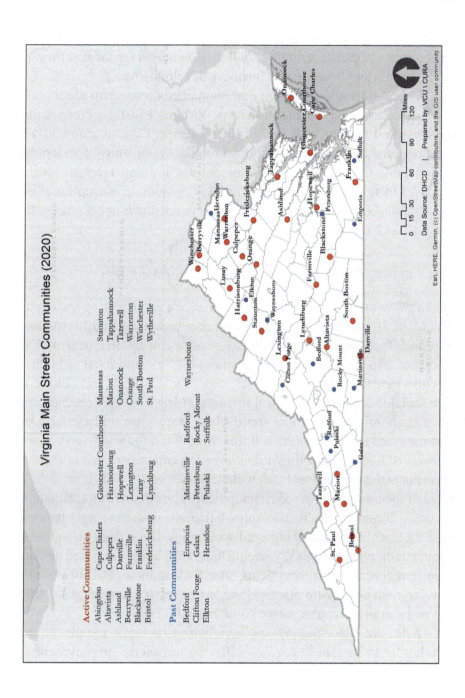

Figure 10.1. Virginia Main Street communities

collaborative partnership with the university that built a boutique hotel and conference center, bringing students downtown for the first time and leading to further housing and business development.

The second market segment that revitalized downtowns attract is the nonlocal tourist and recreation market. Virginia's historic communities have worked closely with the Virginia Tourism Commission and with their regional tourism organizations to make the downtown a stop on a regional tour for shopping, entertainment, and lodging. Heritage tourism is a $7.7 billion industry in Virginia, with economic multiplier effects throughout the state economy that exceed twice that number (Accordino and Fasulo 2017).

Assessing the Value and Limits of Downtown Revitalization

Historic downtown revitalization has achieved a good track record overall. The Main Street Program, in particular, because it is a highly structured approach that blends state and local government involvement with the efforts of experts, property and business owners, and local volunteers, has also generated jobs, businesses, capital investment, and other positive social, economic, and fiscal impacts, at less cost per job than some other economic development approaches. Many case studies and scholarly analyses have demonstrated this. Moreover, the positive economic impacts of historic downtown revitalization emerge not just at the local level but at the regional and statewide levels as well.[11] This is an endorsement of focused, place-based development as an effective tool, although it certainly does not mean that downtown revitalization can single-handedly lead the transformation of regional economies. But it does mean that we should think more holistically, seeing tools such as cluster-based development, entrepreneurship ecosystems, workforce training, and infrastructure development along with placemaking as one set of interrelated activities, not as separate concerns, as we sometimes do.[12]

To be sure, placemaking can be difficult to achieve and the momentum harder to sustain in regions suffering protracted employment and

---

11. A small sample of these studies includes Accordino and Fasulo (2015); Bias (2015); LeBlanc (2011); Ozdil (2007); Place Economics (2013, 2014, 2018); Robertson (1999, 2004); Staley (2020); and Stover and Associates (2020).

population losses. After early successes, such communities sometimes succumb to calls to shift resources to other concerns, which stops progress on revitalization. (Those that maintain their efforts, however, often continue to improve, albeit at a slower pace.) In very small communities or in communities suffering from deep-seated mistrust, collaboration may be hard to sustain (Accordino and Fasulo 2014). Success takes longer or may have less potential in communities where the demand for goods and services has been captured completely by chain stores outside the downtown (Bias, Leyden, and Zimmerman 2015). Moreover, downtown revitalization that remains focused on retail may reach a limit to its effectiveness, especially in the new age of internet-based retail.

With issues such as these in mind, in 2015 the National Main Street Center commissioned an external evaluation of the Main Street Approach® (Clue Group 2015). Although the study found that the basic elements remain viable, it also found weaknesses. Many programs focused too much attention on promotional events and not enough on economic analysis and business development. As a result, they came to be viewed as simply downtown promoters, not place-based economic developers. To strengthen its focus on place-based entrepreneurship development, the National Main Street Center created Main Street Refresh® (Wagner 2017). Refresh® puts more emphasis on business attraction, retention, and development and less on promotion. Refresh® calls on local Main Street programs to re-study their region's market opportunities and strategically deploy their assets to capture them through place-based entrepreneurship. At the same time, the National Center began to encourage local affiliates to expand their footprint outside of historic shopping streets into older industrial districts and to embrace new economic activities in the knowledge sector and in craft-based manufacturing.

Refresh® is still new. Although no hard data exist, there is anecdotal evidence that Virginia has embraced its logic more enthusiastically than other states. Even in Virginia, however, some Main Street communities have made more progress than others have. Nevertheless, Refresh® potentially is a positive development for Main Street communities, as it encourages them to embrace new activities in today's economy. It is also

---

12. The Sacramento Rural-Urban Connections Strategy provides an excellent model for this kind of holistic regional development approach. (See Sacramento Area Council of Governments 2015.)

positive for their surrounding regions, as it positions cities and towns to play vital roles in their regional economies as centers of new entrepreneurial ecosystems, thus bringing them into a new phase of downtown revitalization.

Phase II: Entrepreneurship and Place-Based Development

Over the past decade or so, social and economic circumstances have begun to change, arguably for the better, as far as historic cities and towns are concerned. Although many Americans still prefer a suburban lifestyle, a large and growing number now favor walkable communities with public amenities and strong civic spaces over suburban subdivisions (Jones and Serpas 2016; Marohn 2019).

Developments in technology and economic organization undergird these changes in preferences. Chief among these is the "micro-technology" revolution that was just starting in 1980, when investment dollars were still flowing out of cities and towns. The microprocessor, the laptop computer, and the internet make it possible for individuals or small groups to produce great economic value in much smaller spaces than previously. Although continued automation and globalization have led to corporate downsizing and employment insecurity, they have also brought an increase in entrepreneurship in all economic sectors. One result is that there are now more small businesses in the US than ever (Axelrod 2017). Cities and towns of all sizes have shifted at least some economic development efforts toward incubating and growing businesses by building entrepreneurship ecosystems. Historic cities and towns may be able to take advantage of these trends because of their place-based assets. Virginia's communities are just beginning to do so, but the initiatives to date are promising. A few examples are described next.

Community Business Launch (CBL)

The Virginia Department of Housing and Community Development (DHCD) launched the Community Business program in 2015. To date nineteen communities have implemented it. To participate, a community completes an analysis of market opportunities and then identifies vacant spaces in commercial or industrial buildings in a downtown or neighborhood that would be suitable for entrepreneurs who could address those opportunities. It then applies for a CBL grant, most of which is for training of and distribution of grants to entrepreneurs. The communities that receive grants provide training to aspiring entrepreneurs, who then pitch their ideas to receive funds for working capital, rent or property improvements, equipment, inventory, wages, or marketing in one of the vacant buildings.

Makers on Main Street

The micro-technology revolution has also spawned small-scale manufacturing, aka making, in which a single proprietor or small business makes products in textiles, hardware, wood, metal, 3D printing, or food. One well-known example is microbrewing, but others range from custom apparel production to bicycle refurbishment to furniture fabrication. Downtowns have spaces and can provide place-based amenities and the potential for casual interaction among producers that can stimulate creativity and new business ideas. In 2020, Virginia Main Street launched a program to provide technical assistance to five Main Street communities to (1) determine the potential for small-scale manufacturing as a downtown development strategy, and (2) identify opportunities and resources for scale-up strategies. Five communities from small to large—Bristol, Page County, the Town of Farmville/Prince Edward County, the City of Norfolk, and the Middle Peninsula Alliance Region were chosen (Virginia Main Street 2020). The Town of South Hill (southern Virginia) has also embraced making by establishing a maker's market that links the historic downtown with surrounding rural areas through the Southern Virginia Food Hub. It houses a local grocery store, commercial kitchen, dairy processing room, local food deli, coffee shop, and community classroom. Area farmers and bakers use the kitchen to create a variety of value-added products, and Virginia universities teach classes in agribusiness, cooking, healthy eating, canning, sustainable farming, and other skills (Town of South Hill 2020).[13]

---

13. The universities doing the training are Virginia State University School of Agriculture and Virginia Cooperative Extension.

Innovation Centers

Colleges and universities around the Commonwealth are working with communities to advance innovation. The Dalton Idea Center in downtown Martinsville (southern Virginia) operates as a program of the Longwood University Small Business Development Center and Patrick Henry Community College. The center provides equipment, including a fabrication lab, woodworking and metalworking equipment, and hands-on instruction to help students develop and move ideas from prototype to market. The center's many success stories include a business that makes decorative emblems, wall hangings, and desk pieces for the military and for civic organizations; a wood products company that makes laser engravings; a company that makes automotive parts; one that has created a tool to help autistic children; a bookstore; and a chocolatier (Godwin 2020; Patrick Henry Community College 2020).

Tele-commuting Centers

Even though they do not have the density of high-tech employment opportunities found in large urban centers, historic towns and cities can be excellent locations for tele-commuting facilities that provide high-speed, reliable connectivity as well as business services for entrepreneurs and the amenities of the historic downtown. For example, the Staunton Innovation Hub has retrofitted spaces in a former newspaper building downtown to provide flexible co-working space for tele-commuters and freelance workers, as well as conference and meeting space, all served by high-speed internet (Staunton Downtown Development Association 2019).[14] Digital economy activities are taking root in other cities in the Horseshoe as well. For example, downtown Danville has noticed a recent uptick in tele-commuters to North Carolina, and downtown Harrisonburg reports considerable tele-commuting from its region (Dono 2020; Schwartz 2020). This appears to be a national phenomenon. In a national survey of downtown Main Street communities conducted in February 2020, Accordino and Adhikari found that 27% had added offices connected to a metropolitan core and 17% had developed new tele-commuting centers in recent years (Accordino and Adhikari, 2021). As Wagner (2020) points

---

14. The Hub's partners include the Staunton Creative Community Fund, Staunton Maker Space, Mary Baldwin University, and Skylar Innovations.

out, small cities and towns can host tele-commuters if they have the reliable, high-speed internet connections that tele-commuters need, and if they can provide the amenities and high quality of life that knowledge-sector workers desire. (See the discussion of challenges to achieving universal statewide broadband connectivity by Blythe and Bohland in this volume. See also Feld 2019.)

Traditional Businesses Linking Historic Places and Regions

Although many businesses moved from central-city locations to the suburbs or out of the region entirely during the past half century, some did not. These include government offices, colleges and universities, and manufacturing firms, especially food processors that source their materials from the surrounding region and still process them in the central locations that have served them for many decades. Well-known examples are apple processing in Winchester and poultry processing in Harrisonburg. Other examples include Amory Seafood, a large wholesaler and processor with a long history in Hampton. Discussions are underway to add retail functions to this operation to create a downtown seafood marketplace along the lines of Seattle's famous Pike Place Market. In this case, a traditional central-city business that sources its inputs from the region is a foundation for downtown placemaking efforts. Recently Seven Hills Meats converted a former pork processing plant in historic Lynchburg into a beef processing operation that sources beef from central Virginia, thus strengthening traditional links between the city and its rural hinterland (Versen 2020). Also, the dramatic growth of the craft beverage industry as well as the growing farm-to-table movement have reestablished economic linkages between historic cities and towns and rural areas throughout Virginia.

CONCLUSION

A vibrant downtown can be a key regional anchor. It can enhance the experience of a nearby location for colleges and universities, government offices, and other institutions, helping them attract and keep employees and, in the case of colleges and universities, attract students. It also plays a key role in tourism and recreation, industries that are now among the largest and most productive in Virginia. Moreover, a vibrant downtown sends a positive message, not just to residents and tourists but also to potential new residents and potential new businesses, even those seeking a location in a business park elsewhere in the region. As an entrepreneurial ecosystem hub, downtowns can serve as incubators for the economy, somewhat analogous to the way inner-city industrial areas functioned in the past. Downtown's walkable streets and small spaces can incubate new businesses and grow them to scale in the company of other small businesses, especially with the support of an entity that helps create and grow small businesses where place matters. Walkable downtowns with food establishments and other amenities can be excellent places for artisanal production, from ceramics to 3-D printing, and for small-scale manufacturers that may eventually grow and create employment opportunities. Likewise, they can be an excellent location for professional services firms, such as architects and attorneys, software designers, advertising firms, and other offices. They are a good location for tele-commuting centers linked to larger urban centers and to the global economy; even for those who tele-work out of their homes, a revitalized downtown can still provide the amenities that such persons often desire.

If we focus only on the Urban Crescent–Rural Horseshoe dichotomy we may fail to recognize historic places as anchors in the development of the Commonwealth's regional economies. And we may also fail to take steps to bring about a next phase of development beyond place-based revitalization. In the next phase, downtown revitalization and regional development become integrated elements of a collaborative, urban-rural system, analogous to the way cities and their regions functioned a century and more ago. Indeed, stronger urban-rural collaboration within regions may enable communities to more effectively address seemingly intractable economic and social challenges. Achieving this will require sustained effort, however. Although some regions are known for the collaborative way that localities and private stakeholders work together to achieve positive outcomes for the region, others still struggle with this. One barrier to collaboration is the inter-jurisdictional conflict caused by local government reliance on real property and sales taxes to finance over half of their budgets. These zero-sum revenue sources force communities to compete for the most lucrative land uses rather than focusing on how the assets of each part of the region can further the development of a collaborative regional vision; we should, therefore, find ways to reduce localities' dependence upon them (see Davis and Gough 2019).

The Commonwealth also can incentivize and support collaborative initiatives that incorporate all communities in a region. The GO Virginia program, by incentivizing inter-local cooperation for economic development, has taken a step in this direction; numerous GO Virginia projects reach across cities and rural areas (Gammel 2020). Yet more can be accomplished through urban-rural collaboration at the regional level. One model worth careful study is the Sacramento Rural Urban Connections Strategy, an initiative that draws upon the assets of city, town, and countryside to create a compelling regional economic development vision that guides public policy and private investment (Sacramento Area Council of Governments 2015; see also OECD 2013). In Virginia, initiatives like the Shenandoah Innovation Coalition appear to be strong steps toward regional collaboration linking multiple entities across the public and private sectors, with historic cities such as Harrisonburg and Staunton working closely with other localities (Shenandoah Valley Innovation Coalition n.d.). We can replicate models like these across the state and provide the tools to strengthen them. Indeed, Virginia already has many necessary ingredients to become a commonwealth of vibrant cities, towns, and regions.

We are grateful to the following persons who contributed valuable insights and information in this chapter: Charlotte Cole, Andrea Dono, Billy Gammel, Ann Glave, Angeline Godwin, Michaela Martin, Sheri McGuire, Diana Schwartz, Kathy Stewart, and Stephen Versen. Thanks also to the Vibrant Virginia *editors for their help and guidance on this chapter.*

Chapter 11

Preserving Virginia's Scenic Beauty

Leighton Powell, Lynn M. Crump, Richard G. Gibbons, Lisa Dickinson Mountcastle, Patrick A. Miller, and Jisoo Sim

This chapter provides a history and overview of scenic resources in Virginia. The authors describe early scenic preservation efforts, the development of new programs to promote scenic beauty and engage the public, and the creation of a new scenic recognition tool that will allow rural and urban citizens to identify the scenic places that they consider most special. They conclude by highlighting the benefits of this new project, future goals, and viewshed implications for both rural and urban settings.

> Heaven and earth never agreed to frame a better place
> for man's habitation than Virginia.
> —Captain John Smith

When you hear the phrase "vibrant Virginia," what comes to mind? Depending on where you live, you might envision pastoral landscapes, charming towns, and hamlets; rolling forests, mountains, and valleys; or coastal and Chesapeake Bay landscapes. These

Figure 11.1. Dogwood Lane

extraordinary scenic resources contribute so much to quality of life for all Virginians.

The urban-rural divide for scenic resources has a different history when compared to, say, economic or social factors. There is an interesting story to be told of rural-urban interaction over time. Starting in the early 1800s, poets in Europe began capturing the scenic experience of rural landscapes for urban residents living in industrializing cities. This later carried over to the US with the development of National Park lodges. In the 1900s, there was yet another shift with the advent of the environmental movement. Scenery was still in rural areas—often in the West and mostly on public lands—but often it was being managed to mitigate the impacts of resource extraction, not for beauty's sake.

As a result, these scenic resources were available to urban residents who visited these lands, but most urban visitors did not know the status of the lands being managed to protect scenic value. Because of strong concerns for individual property rights, little attention was given at the time to urban scenic areas.

Today, new tools are being developed for preservation of scenic landscapes both rural and urban. The scenic viewshed register is envisioned as a way for all citizens to identify the local landscapes that are most significant and to encourage every Virginian to visit and enjoy these scenic vistas that contribute so much to Virginia's physical, mental, and economic well-being.

This chapter provides an overview of scenic resources in Virginia in three parts: (1) early recognition and public concern; (2) the development of new programs to promote scenic beauty and engage the public; and (3) the creation of a new scenic recognition tool—the first of its kind in the US—that will allow rural and urban citizens to identify the scenic places that they consider most special. A concluding section notes the new project's benefits, future goals, and viewshed implications for both rural and urban settings.

Early Programs for Scenic Resource Recognition and Preservation in Virginia

Virginia's sense of place is reflected in its extraordinary variety of landscapes throughout the Commonwealth. Its natural resources are a recognized value in the Constitution of Virginia, and the value of its scenery is identified in the Code of Virginia in Title 10.1—Conservation, General Provisions.

Scenic resources are identified in the Virginia Code in the Scenic Rivers Act Chapter 10.1-400, the Real Estate Section 58.1-3230 for special classifications, and the Transportation Section Title 33.2 for Virginia Byways and Scenic Highways. These code sections reflect the state's longtime interest in the recognition, protection, and management of scenic resources for the use of Virginians and visitors to the state.

Decades ago, there was interest and concern at the federal level directed at studying the use of public lands for outdoor recreation. In 1935, President Franklin D. Roosevelt launched the Work Progress Administration (WPA), later renamed the Work Projects Administration, which led to the creation of national parks and parkways to provide jobs for workers and a respite for weary citizens. Four of these federal parkways are in Virginia, including the Blue Ridge and Colonial Parkways, both designed by landscape architect Stanley Abbott.

Two decades later, in 1957, Congress established the National Outdoor Recreation Resources Review Commission to examine outdoor recreation and other purposes on public lands and water areas of the US. The result of the study was a twenty-seven-volume report that outlined the supply, needs, and methods for advancing outdoor recreation programming.

From this effort came the Land and Water Conservation Fund (LWCF) in 1965, which led to the requirement of a State Comprehensive Outdoor Recreation Plan, or SCORP, for each state to gain access to these funds. That same year, President Lyndon B. Johnson convened the first—and, to date, only—White House Conference on Natural Beauty. In his opening remarks to the delegates describing the conference's purpose, President Johnson said, "This is why I have called for a new conservation: to restore as well as to protect, to bring beauty to the cities as well as to keep it in the countryside, to handle the waste products of technology as well as the waste of natural resources." He added that he would be greatly disappointed if each state representative did not carry this message back to the governor and legislative body. Luckily for Virginia, State Senator FitzGerald Bemiss of Richmond attended the White House Conference and participated in the discussion of many good ideas. Returning home from Washington, DC, State Senator Bemiss established the Virginia Outdoor Recreation Study Commission.

The modern renaissance in Virginia's outdoor planning and park development began in 1965 with the publication of the first Outdoor Recreation Plan, called Virginia's Common Wealth, authored by landscape architect John Simonds.

The plan recommended the creation of numerous agencies and programs, including the Virginia Department of Historic Resources, the Virginia Byways Program, the Virginia Outdoors Foundation and its corresponding land-use tax credit program, and the Commission of Outdoor Recreation. The commission managed the development and implementation of the recommendations for Virginia's great outdoors as well as the process for the acquisition of LWCF monies.

Virginia's Common Wealth stated that "potential recreation and conservation areas, natural, cultural and landscape resources to Virginia scenery and scenic areas and aesthetic values are important" (Simonds 1965). It also directed the state to "identify areas of superior, distinctive, unusual, or unique scenery that [are] not protected or developed for public recreation use, including scenic streams or other water bodies" (ibid). This began a renewed focus on scenic resources that continues to this day.

Virginia's Scenic Programs

The Commission on Outdoor Recreation recommended the establishment of two state programs to identify and manage specific scenic resources for the benefit of the public: Virginia Byways and Virginia Scenic Rivers.

Virginia Byways

The Byways program began in Virginia in 1966 with the General Assembly's passage of enabling legislation. The program focuses on existing roads that have relatively high aesthetic or cultural values or that lead to or exist within areas of historical, natural, or recreational significance. Recommendations for Virginia Byway designation are initiated by citizens in the localities. Virginia Byways represent an exceptional example of regional landscapes that possess reasonable protection of their aesthetic and cultural values. Byways offer motorists the opportunity to bypass major roads and instead enjoy a leisurely motoring experience while accessing local historic, cultural, and recreational sites.

The Virginia Department of Transportation (VDOT) and the Department of Conservation and Recreation (DCR) co-manage the Byways program. Approximately 3,500 miles of roads are designated as Virginia Byways. Additional sections qualify but have not yet been designated at this time. Included within Virginia's program are five National Scenic Byways®, of which three are All-American Roads®, the highest designation of National Scenic Byway. A National Scenic Byway® is a road recognized by the US Department of Transportation for possessing one or more of the following six "intrinsic qualities": archeological, cultural, historic, natural, recreational, and scenic.

Virginia Scenic Rivers Program

In 1970 Governor Linwood Holton signed legislation creating the Virginia Scenic Rivers program—the only state program that specifically identifies and protects scenic resources. Scenic River designation is a bottom-up process that is initiated at the local level. Citizens can request Scenic River designation, but it is the local governing body that issues the request for a river evaluation study and, if the river qualifies, passes a required resolution of support for designation and identifies a local legislator to carry the legislation in the Virginia General Assembly.

The Virginia Scenic Rivers program identifies, recognizes, and provides a level of protection to rivers with significant scenic, historic, recreational, and natural values. Designation allows for the continuation of all riparian uses while providing a stronger voice in the planning and implementation of federal and state projects that might affect the river.

DCR administers the Scenic Rivers program and supports the Byways program. Another of DCR's duties—related to parks and outdoor recreation—is to include scenic areas in the system of outdoor recreation facilities. Virginia Code Section 10.1-201 authorizes the DCR department director to acquire properties of scenic beauty. Section 10.1-203 deals with the establishment, protection, and maintenance of the Appalachian Trail and permits agreements with landowners and others to acquire properties to preserve its natural scenic beauty.

This has resulted in the preservation of some viewsheds and park resources from incompatible commercial development. It allows for the purchase of buffer areas to protect important visual resources and the coordination of public projects such as roads, bridges, and power lines to minimize the visual impact on a park or scenic area.

Other DCR code-driven responsibilities for scenic assets include:

- the development of a statewide comprehensive recreation and land conservation plan that includes scenic areas;
- the establishment, maintenance, protection, and regulation of a statewide system of trails that includes those of "significant scenic . . . qualities"; and
- the protection of the scenic beauty of the Appalachian National Scenic Trail.

The comprehensive plan for state outdoor recreation and conservation, called the Virginia Outdoors Plan, is revised every five years and includes recommendations for state park planning. According to the Virginia State Code, each Virginia state park is required to have a master plan that is updated every ten years and documents the natural and physical attributes of the properties. Included in this, when appropriate, is information concerning viewsheds or scenic resources. The planning and siting of facilities, including trails, are executed to take advantage of the best viewshed. State park plans that include scenic attributes include Grayson Highlands, Wilderness Road, Natural Bridge, Sky Meadows, Seven Bends, and Chippokes, to name a few.

Figure 11.2. McAfee Knob Clouds

These programs represented significant progress in Virginia's ability to preserve and protect its exquisite scenic resources, but more was needed. In 2000, Virginia's Advisory Council on Intergovernmental Relations (ACIR) issued a report titled "The Impacts of Aesthetics on the Economy and Quality of Life in Virginia" that stated the need for additional scenic preservation programs and tools. It noted that many rural and urban vistas or viewsheds are not part of the Scenic Byways or Scenic Rivers programs despite meriting consideration. The report, though, left unanswered two questions: Who would create these new tools and programs, and how would they benefit Virginia's extraordinary scenic beauty to the greatest extent possible?

SCENIC VIRGINIA AND THE PROMOTION OF SCENIC PRESERVATION IN THE COMMONWEALTH

Scenic Virginia was founded in 1998 after the Virginia General Assembly granted the billboard industry the right to cut down trees in front of billboards along highways on state rights-of-way. (Never mind that most of these trees were fully mature and predated the billboards by many years.) Having successfully opposed the legislation the year before, Richmonder Hylah H. Boyd and a group of dedicated citizens—many affiliated with the Garden Club of Virginia—realized that the need existed for a full-time voice to advocate for the Commonwealth's rural and urban scenic assets with elected officials and the public.

Boyd and her group undertook a two-year campaign of engagement focused on outreach and fundraising. In 2000, Scenic Virginia hired its first executive director, Leighton Powell, who is still with the organization as of the summer of 2021. Following the lead of parent organization Scenic America, Scenic Virginia's early efforts focused on opposition to unsightly billboards as a means of improving visual quality and community character. During a meeting of the board of trustees in 2002, Powell suggested that Scenic Virginia pivot its mission to focus on the promotion and preservation of scenic beauty. This new stance, she noted, would offer a positive message that should resonate with every Virginian. Who, she asked, is opposed to scenic beauty?

The board voted enthusiastically in support of this new outlook, and Scenic Virginia began looking for new ways to engage Virginians in the preservation, protection, and enhancement of the scenic beauty of the Commonwealth. Early advocacy included promoting the Virginia Byways and the Virginia Scenic Rivers programs as well as encouraging historic preservation colleagues to preserve the viewsheds of historic sites to maintain their sense of place.

In 2003, Scenic Virginia served as the statewide coordinator of the multiyear, multiagency effort to bring the National Scenic Byways® (NSB) program to the Commonwealth. The NSB program showcases special rural and urban roadways, marketing them to national and international tourists who enjoy "taking in the scenic view."

Scenic Virginia also began assisting citizens in urban and rural localities wanting to preserve significant vistas and views and did so by stressing the point that scenic resources are critical to the physical, mental, and economic health of Virginia. The organization's unofficial motto became "Beauty is good for business, and Beauty is essential for the soul" to stress that businesses that can locate anywhere seek rural and urban places with a high quality of life to attract the best workforce.

One pivotal period for Scenic Virginia was in 2007 when the nonprofit worked with supporters to advocate for the preservation of the historic panorama known as "the View That Named Richmond." The View, which overlooks the James River from the historic neighborhood of Church Hill in the city's East End, is a cherished vista with an international connection: It is identical to a view of the River Thames from Richmond Hill in

Figure 11.3. James River

Richmond-upon-Thames, where Richmond, Virginia, founder William Byrd II had spent time as a boy.

The British view has an unusual history. At the end of the nineteenth century, as development from London began encroaching on the more rural areas of the River Thames, the English found their beloved view, which was featured prominently in art and books, threatened. The resulting uproar became known as "the Great Indignation" and is considered

Figure 11.4. Thames River

the first successful environmental movement in the United Kingdom. Parliament responded in 1902 by enacting the Richmond, Petersham, and Ham Open Spaces Act, forever preserving the view.

Although physically similar to the English view, Richmond, Virginia's historic panorama is an urban viewshed. The James River flows through the center of the city, and views of the James are particularly cherished because so many have been lost to development, including, unbelievably, what was once the Commonwealth's most significant vista: the view from Thomas Jefferson's capitol down to the James River, sacrificed to inappropriate and ill-considered development that forever despoiled that special place.

Development threats to the View That Named Richmond began after a private company purchased the riverfront parcel that sits squarely in the viewshed. The group trumpeted the economic benefits of a proposed high-rise building and requested that the site be designated for development in the Downtown Plan. Local elected officials very often embrace proposed development and its potential economic benefits over conservation measures. In this case, citizens made it clear that they would not back down. They showed up en masse at countless meetings and public hearings to argue that the best use of the riverfront parcel would be a view-saving linear park. In the end, the Downtown Plan listed the primary preferred use as "Park with Development" included as a secondary option. The plan also urged the City of Richmond to acquire the site, an action not taken years earlier because city officials were not aware of the public's passion for the special scenic resource.

The planning process to reach that point took two years and untold hours of public hearings, citizen meetings, and coalition-building. In the end, the sheer amount of time and energy invested in preserving this significant, internationally important Virginia vista led Leighton Powell and the Scenic Virginia Board to realize three significant points:

- Virginians care about urban viewsheds as well as rural. In response, Scenic Virginia made a point of featuring a Cities and Towns category in its new Virginia Vistas Photo Contest and seeking out urban honorees for the annual Scenic Awards event.
- Existing programs did not go far enough, and new tools must be developed to guide the preservation of scenic resources.

- Scenic Virginia must share its experience of working to preserve the View as a cautionary tale for citizens in rural and urban localities so that they might be spared the years of time and effort needed to preserve much-loved local scenic vistas.

Around this same time, Scenic Virginia trustee Richard G. Gibbons attended the Blue Ridge Parkway's Seventy-fifth Anniversary Symposium. There, Gibbons and fellow landscape architects celebrated the beauty of the Parkway, bemoaned the absence of scenic preservation tools, and discussed the need to recognize and preserve Virginia's most significant scenic viewsheds.

The recognition of the need for new scenic tools marked a turning point in Scenic Virginia's evolution and a new maturity among Virginians in understanding the relationship between scenic resources and their environs.

It had taken thirty or forty years to arrive at this point—to realize that a state trail is not just a path for walking or hiking but is also what is seen and experienced while there. This new, thoughtful approach needed to be reflected in the Virginia Outdoors Plan to demonstrate that while scenic resources are critical to quality of life, they cannot be fully appreciated unless they are factored into what surrounds them.

In 2011 Scenic Virginia convened a panel of esteemed state and national viewshed experts and landscape professionals to ask, "Are additional tools needed? Would a new Virginia Viewshed Register serve a useful purpose?"

In response, Scenic Virginia tasked its in-house Viewshed Committee's board members, advisory board members, and staff with researching existing scenic preservation programs in the US to help Virginians identify the places they love best and take steps to ensure their preservation. Realizing that such a program did not exist in the US, the Viewshed Committee set about to create one.

A New Tool for Scenic Preservation: The Virginia Viewshed Project

In developing its first-of-its-kind program, Scenic Virginia's Viewshed Committee determined that its primary goals should be ambitious and three-fold:

- It should engage the public in a meaningful way and assist citizens in conveying to local elected officials, planners, and others that these local scenic places are valued by the citizenry.
- It should increase "scenic" as a primary goal of land preservation and contribute toward developing a Scenic GIS layer for Virginia's land conservation map.
- It must prove that the characteristics of a scenic landscape can be quantified in a manner that will produce consistent results (i.e., are not subjective).

Scenic Virginia envisioned the resulting Virginia Viewshed Project as a multipronged effort to identify, evaluate, and provide public designation to the Commonwealth's most beloved rural and urban vistas and scenic lands. The Viewshed Committee felt confident that it could develop a statewide program to engage the public, and several conservation colleagues across Virginia had begun compiling scenic preservation data that could easily be incorporated into a statewide Scenic GIS layer.

The most daunting problem was determining how a small statewide conservation nonprofit could prove—in a scientific manner—that the characteristics of a scenic viewshed are not subjective. This goal was also clearly the most significant of the three and must be accomplished. And as it happened, an incredible opportunity arose that would transform the entire project. In January 2018 Dr. Patrick A. Miller, professor and former head of Virginia Tech's Landscape Architecture Department, contacted Scenic Virginia to express Tech's interest in participating in the statewide Viewshed Project. Scenic Virginia enthusiastically accepted the offer. Discussions ensued about what form that help might take.

During one conversation, Leighton Powell lamented the longtime absence of a Scenic category in state land preservation programs, referencing the statement from Virginia officials that scenic beauty is subjective. A light went off, and Miller immediately recognized the potential for groundbreaking work: Virginia Tech would refute the misguided notion that beauty is subjective by demonstrating that the characteristics of a scenic viewshed can be quantified scientifically—something that had never been done.

Miller and Jisoo Sim, then a PhD candidate in architecture, undertook an exhaustive, year-long review of existing research and literature related to scenic resources. Two databases were employed for the literature review. The Virginia Tech team created the first one from keyword searches for the following terms: scenic value, scenic beauty, scenic quality, visual quality, visual resource management, visual assessment, landscape preference, and landscape quality. The search produced 853 articles published in journals and books between 1969 and 2018. The Tech team also included abstracts for the articles contained in the database.

Next, using the same keywords, the Virginia Tech team mined the database created by Dr. Andrew Lothian of Scenic Solutions, which contains 1,854 publications published between 1936 and 2014. While more extensive—it includes articles and more diverse types of publications published over a longer period—it does not include abstracts. Lothian's database is available on his Scenic Solutions website at https://scenicsolutions.world/.

Miller and Sim used both databases to compile a literature review that would become the groundwork for the Viewshed Register framework and protocols. This document represented a major step forward in the recognition of scenic resources, as the existing scenic resource data had never been searched and sorted in this manner. Scenic Virginia's Viewshed Committee studied the literature review and immediately recognized the important implications of the work. For the first time, it would be possible to develop a defensible decision framework for identifying and assessing the characteristics of a scenic viewshed, and they asked Virginia Tech to create one.

The Virginia Tech team agreed and determined that the framework must possess the following three characteristics:

- be understandable (i.e., make sense);
- produce consistent, reproducible, and measurable results; and
- provide a means of engaging the public in the scenic designation process.

First, though, the Virginia Tech team needed to agree on a definition of "viewshed." They determined that it is the 360-degree area that is seen

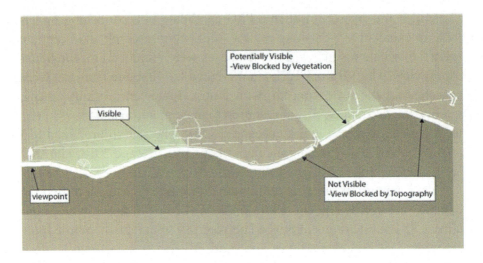

Figure 11.5. Viewshed schematic

from a specific spot, called a viewpoint; and they noted that portions of the area might not be visible from the viewpoint due to being blocked by vegetation, topography, or other objects. Miller and Sim also established that a "defined viewshed" is the specified portion that can be seen from a particular viewpoint and that is identified by its view direction, view width, and view distance.

The Virginia Tech team outlined two desired outcomes for its project: (1) to engage urban and rural citizens in identifying treasured local vistas, and (2) to develop protocols for assessing scenic viewsheds to determine if they merit placement on a Scenic Register.

The Tech team soon discovered that the scenic quality of a viewshed goes beyond its physical characteristics and content. They reviewed thousands of photos submitted to Scenic Virginia's annual photo contest and realized that these possessed certain scenic qualities not found in other areas of the US. In response, the team expanded the existing definition of Scenic Quality to include cultural, ephemeral, and urban content. Equally important, they realized that a viewshed contributes to a broader sense of place that could be measured by its public concern. The Tech team's final achievement was the development of draft protocols measuring Scenic Quality and Public Concern for the nomination, evaluation, and designation of scenic landscapes for inclusion in a new statewide Virginia Viewshed Register. At last, the report was ready for critical analysis.

As Virginia Tech began conducting its research in 2018, two other statewide efforts unfolded that would have an impact on the Viewshed Project. First, DCR, in preparation for the next edition of the Virginia Outdoors Plan, conducted a statewide Scenic Survey to gauge the importance of Scenic to Virginia citizens. The results revealed that 89% of Virginians surveyed considered Scenery and Scenic Views as either Very Important or Somewhat Important. The 2018 edition of the VOP included those survey results, establishing that Virginia's citizens care deeply about Virginia's scenic resources.

Second, that spring, newly elected Virginia governor Ralph Northam announced the launch of a land conservation initiative called ConserveVirginia. Employing a new data-driven approach to prioritizing land conservation, his new program compiled nearly twenty sets of information to identify the top 10% of lands that should be protected and preserved.

As with past programs, the first iteration of ConserveVirginia did not include a Scenic category. Given that Virginia Tech's research was moving forward with great success, Scenic Virginia updated the administration that a new report was forthcoming that demonstrated that Scenic is defensible as a category. Land trusts and other conservation partners from across the state also asked that Scenic be included.

The governor's team listened and agreed to add a Scenic Preservation category to ConserveVirginia. This represented a hard-won victory for scenic preservationists and acknowledged for the first time that scenic assets are significant and identifiable.

Scenic preservation organizations have committed to helping Virginia broaden and expand the new Scenic Preservation category. In return, the Natural Resources Secretariat has confirmed that scenic views and areas designated to the new Virginia Viewshed Register will be added to the ConserveVirginia Scenic Preservation data layer.

NEXT STOP: LOCAL ENGAGEMENT

Armed with Virginia Tech's results and viewshed experts' certification of the process, Scenic Virginia has begun developing a public outreach plan to Virginia's counties, cities, and towns. To engage rural and urban citizens at the local level, the most pressing question will be, "What views, vistas, and scenic places do you care about most, and what would you be devastated to lose?"

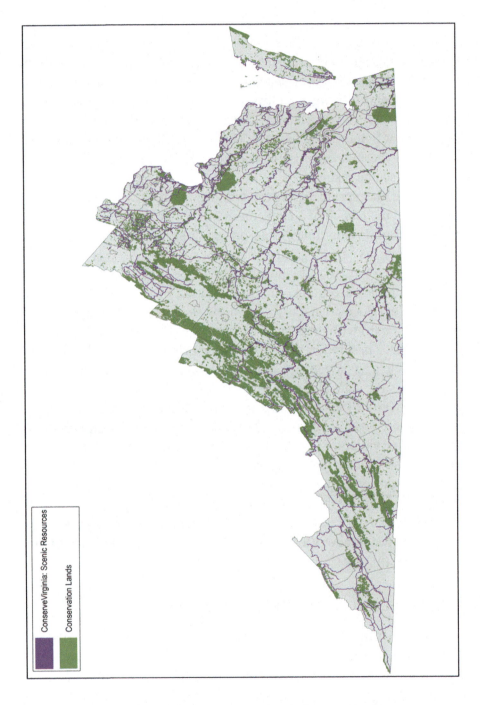

Figure 11.6. The Conserve Virginia Scenic Preservation Map

Scenic Virginia and its partners will assist citizens in each locality with developing their list as well as identifying ways to ensure that important scenic places are not lost. As citizens identify their most cherished resources, they can encourage their inclusion in the local Comprehensive Plan.

This public recognition will allow Virginians across the state to head off future development conflicts, benefiting citizens, local elected officials, planning staff, businesses, and developers. Scenic preservation solutions might include acquiring land in the viewshed, creating a new overlay district, or crafting new local ordinances that allow for development while maintaining recognized viewsheds.

Scenic Virginia and its partners look forward to announcing the first group of scenic views and lands designated to the new Virginia Viewshed Register. Scenic Viewshed designation will bestow statewide public recognition on the Commonwealth's views and vistas that score highest in Scenic Quality and Public Perception and Concern. The hope is that the project will inspire Virginians to speak up about their most treasured scenic places, potentially ensuring that the Commonwealth's most significant scenic beauty is preserved for the generations that follow. Other important outcomes include the following:

- Scenic Inventory/GIS Layer: The Viewshed Project will result in a Statewide Scenic Inventory, which can then be used—at last—to create a robust scenic GIS layer for guiding future land preservation priorities beyond the tenure of Governor Ralph Northam.
- Assistance to Land Trusts: Virginia's land trust community has been overwhelmingly positive about the creation of a scenic resources database that could serve as the "rigorous process" identified in IRS Tax Code Section 170h. These organizations will be able to use the new Scenic Inventory and GIS layer to assist citizens wanting to receive tax benefits for the donation of scenic conservation easements.
- Outreach to a Younger Audience: The goal of the Virginia ViewFinders website is to increase participation by Millennials and Gen Z, who represent the next generations of scenic preservationists. On the project website, outdoor enthusiasts can submit the shots of scenic beauty

captured as they paddle, ride, hike, and participate in other activities. The images display in a photo gallery, and the public can vote on whether the image is scenic or not. The locations appear on a separate webpage as points on a Google Map, allowing Scenic Virginia—and others—to track and explore Virginia's most popular scenic places.

Scenic Virginia and its partners are exploring additional projects to enhance the public's understanding of the value of scenic resources—both in the Commonwealth and beyond. These include the following:

- Economic Impact of Scenic Resources: There has never been a report produced that defines the economic value of the Commonwealth's scenic beauty in rural and urban areas. Citizens instinctively understand that scenic beauty benefits business development, tourism, civic pride, and quality of life. Having that scenic beauty economically quantified would help citizens expand the case for increased scenic preservation in their localities.
- Virginia Scenic Resources Advisory Board: The Virginia Scenic Rivers Advisory Board was disbanded in 2009 and folded into the Virginia Board of Conservation and Recreation (BCR). There, a Scenic Resources subcommittee was created, but it does not have full authority. Scenic Virginia and its partners hope that the Viewshed Project will refocus attention on the physical, communal, emotional, and economic value of scenic beauty and that the administration and General Assembly will create a new state body to oversee Virginia's three scenic resource programs: Rivers, Byways, and Viewsheds.
- Planning and Design Standards for Renewables: The passage of the Virginia Clean Economy Act during the 2020 General Assembly session made clear that the Commonwealth will see an increase in the development of alternative energy sources such as solar and wind. Scenic preservation groups will advocate for the development of statewide standards for planning and mitigation to reduce visual impacts—and potentially increase economic

benefits—to those visual resources considered most special by citizens.
- National Scenic Viewshed Register: Scenic Virginia's parent organization, Scenic America, has embraced the Virginia Viewshed Register project and recognizes its national implications. Scenic America's goal will be to help US citizens across the country identify and recognize their most beloved urban and rural scenic places.

Conclusion

The year 2020 was an unprecedented time for public appreciation of scenic beauty. As the COVID-19 pandemic limited social interaction and gatherings, Scenic Virginia heard time and again that the Commonwealth's incredible scenic resources were providing a much-needed tonic for the mind, body, and spirit of those seeking solace in an uncertain world. While not the optimal way to remind Virginians about the economic, physical, and emotional benefits of scenic beauty, the COVID-19 pandemic nevertheless opened people's eyes to the importance of scenic beauty in their lives.

The year 2020 also exposed inequities regarding public access to scenic beauty and its benefits. Although every Virginian should have the opportunity to experience nature on a daily basis, the fact remains that many do not. There are ways to address this. While working to save the View in Richmond, Scenic Virginia recognized that developing a linear park on the riverfront parcel in the viewshed would preserve the treasured historic panorama while providing desperately needed access to nature for lower-income families in Richmond's East End. Moving forward, Scenic Virginia will continue to seek out win-win solutions of this type that address inequity while preserving scenic beauty.

In April 2021 years of work on this project culminated in the thrilling announcement that the Capital Region Land Conservancy, a Richmond land trust and Scenic Virginia colleague, would acquire the riverfront parcel in the viewshed of the View. CRLC plans are to place the land under a View-saving conservation easement to prevent high-rise development and eventually offer the parcel to the City of Richmond for inclusion in its magnificent James River Park System to increase recreation opportunities for all Richmonders.

Scenic Virginia and its supporters hope that, post-pandemic, this renewed recognition of the value of a Scenic designation will continue, resulting in enhanced citizen participation as the Viewshed Project rolls out to Virginia's rural and urban localities. Recent advances in technology—both in identifying and capturing scenic beauty where it happens, as well as the ability to host citizen meetings virtually—greatly increase the potential for engagement.

Despite the many challenges that lie ahead, conservation groups in the Commonwealth remain enthusiastically optimistic about the future. There is broad support for the Viewshed Project as well as a recognition that it represents a giant step forward in identifying and preserving special places. It is time. Noted architect Frank Lloyd Wright once remarked, "If you foolishly ignore beauty, you will soon find yourself without it. . . . But if you invest in beauty, it will remain with you all the days of your life." The Virginia Viewshed Project is such an investment and will benefit the rural and urban citizens of the Commonwealth for years to come.

Part 4

Vibrant, Healthy, and Connected Communities

Chapter 12

Supporting Refugee, Migrant, and Community Partnerships

Rebecca J. Hester, Katrina M. Powell, and Katherine Randall

Between 2017 and 2019, a pilot study was conducted to investigate the ways that refugee resettlement in rural Virginia is similar to or different from refugee resettlement in other areas of the state and the country. This project sought to understand how rural communities in the United States support refugee resettlement through robust and meaningful forms of integration. Because of federal mandates, all refugees must become economically self-sufficient within months of arriving in the United States, regardless of their literacy skills, fluency in English, or employment history. However, the research findings indicate that these federal and state policies are written in ways that assume refugees have access to a large number of services and resources commonly available in urban areas. By focusing on rural communities, this chapter adds complexity to the on-going discussion of what constitutes the successful integration of resettled refugees and outlines actions to facilitate such integration across the rural-urban divide. Based on the results of this pilot study in rural southwest Virginia, the co-authors founded the Virginia Consortium for Refugee, Migrant, and Displacement Studies, a statewide group of academic researchers, service providers, nonprofits, and volunteer groups working with resettled populations.

Between 2017 and 2019, the co-authors conducted a small pilot study to investigate the ways that refugee resettlement in rural Virginia is similar to or different from refugee resettlement in other areas of the state and the country. Most of the published research on refugee resettlement focuses on integration in urban areas in Europe with large-scale resettlement or on refugee camps. By contrast, this project seeks to understand how rural communities in the United States support refugee resettlement through robust and meaningful forms of integration. In particular, this chapter focuses on southwest Virginia, where the co-authors have been conducting research with refugees, who because of federal mandates must become economically self-sufficient within months of arriving in the United States, regardless of their literacy skills, fluency in English, or employment history.

Our research findings indicate that all refugees, no matter where they are resettled, must comply with federal and state policies that are written in ways that assume they live in and have access to the large number of support services and community resources that are more commonly available in urban areas. Since both support services and economic opportunities are limited in rural southwest Virginia, refugees and the agencies and volunteers working with them face more challenges than their urban counterparts to comply with resettlement policies. These challenges have only been exacerbated by the dual forces of the pandemic and administrative orders that lowered the admission cap of resettled refugees from 85,000 in 2016 to 15,000 in 2020. The follow-on effect of setting the admissions cap so low was a gutted social services infrastructure, which responded by laying off employees and reducing their programming. The lack of social, political, and economic infrastructures to facilitate resettlement has implications at the individual, local, and regional level both for refugee populations and for the rural communities where they have settled. By examining resettlement in rural spaces in Virginia, this research project contributes to understanding barriers to meaningful integration, especially economic integration for refugees, and informs policy by examining both sides of the integration coin—the people seeking refuge and the communities in which they integrate.

While much has been written about the integration of refugees, this research indicates that the complexities of refugee integration and the nuanced challenges that refugees face, especially when they are resettled in rural communities, are not sufficiently explored. As a result, there is a false sense of a monolithic experience of refugees both worldwide and in the United States. Extant research most often considers the experiences of refugees in highly resourced environments where economic opportunities and support services abound. In order for academic research to fully inform both immigration and economic policy, however, more research about how the urban-rural divide shapes resettlement experiences needs to occur. By focusing on rural communities, this chapter adds complexity to the on-going discussion of what constitutes the successful integration of resettled refugees and outlines actions that the co-authors have taken to facilitate such integration across the urban-rural divide.

First, in order to understand what makes resettled refugees successful in their new communities, more nuanced discussions of integration need to occur. The integration of persons with refugee status when they arrive in a second or third country is traditionally analyzed through lenses important to the UN Refugee Agency (UNHCR): legal rights, self-sufficiency, and belonging to a community (Ager and Strang 2004; Alba and Nee 2003; Blunt 2003; Brun and Fabos 2017; Burrows and Ramic 2017; Jimenez 2011, Marks 2014; Powell and Randall 2018; Richard and Leader 2018). Furthermore, current definitions of what constitutes "successful" integration have been contested. Critical refugee and migration studies scholars recognize that the notion of integration is value laden and geographically and politically dependent on the host community. Integration can sometimes entail granting full citizenship or it can mean mutual adaptation (Jimenez 2011).

Not only is "integration" a contested notion, research about displaced populations has yet to sufficiently recognize that they are often temporally situated and subject to contradiction as they navigate integration processes. Indeed, understanding integration as an endpoint is counter to the reality of integration as an ongoing process. While standard indicators of integration generally include language proficiency, political participation, social locale, interaction with host community members, and socioeconomic participation (Ager and Strang 2004), from a policy perspective, so-called successful refugee integration is most often focused on the economic contribution of a refugee to the host society; that is, getting a job. In response to this policy focus, service providers are compelled to emphasize economic integration above all else when working with recently resettled refugees.

Because of this focus on rapid economic integration, resettlement policies and practices often fail to fully account for the ways that refugees themselves are experiencing resettlement, including the legal difficulties they face in translating their education, certifications, and skills into a rural landscape. Nor do they account for other noneconomic contributions that refugees make to their newly adopted communities. By ignoring these experiences and potential contributions, resettlement policies fail to recognize that the economic success of refugees is contingent on other, noneconomic aspects of their lives. Findings from our pilot study revealed this failure and highlighted the complexities, contradictions, and paradoxes in the resettlement policies and practices governing newly resettled refugees. For example, the expectation that refugees will be gainfully employed within months of arriving may work against their desire to first learn the language in order to feel comfortable interacting with co-workers or navigating workplace regulations and dynamics. While from a policy perspective refugees are integrated because they are working, from a refugee perspective having a job may not be "working" for them. Indeed, insofar as they will have limited time to learn to speak and read English, having a job may hinder their meaningful integration.

For the purposes of this study, the research team distinguished between "expected" integration and "meaningful" integration. Based on current resettlement policies, refugees are "expected" to find a job within ninety days, and service providers are expected to assist them in doing so. Expected integration, then, is defined as a top-down approach wherein refugees are considered successfully resettled when they are able to earn a salary, however meager, and avoid being an economic burden on their community or the government. Meaningful integration, however, recognizes integration as a process and takes refugee standpoint and experience, including their interests, abilities, and skill, as its primary focus.

The role that refugees and migrants have played in changing the broader institutional environment through civic engagement and activism has also been the subject of much research. Studies on civic engagement have examined the role that social media and other communication strategies have played in connecting refugees and forwarding causes that are important to them (Alencar 2018; Chouliaraki 2017; Nikunen 2018). Much of the scholarship on refugee integration has focused on the broader political, cultural, and social change that has occurred as a result of communication within and between refugee communities (Cheung and Phillimore 2014) or within and between refugee-serving organizations.

An area that has received relatively little attention is displaced populations' standpoints in their experiences of available resources. Most of the literature on communication between refugees and service providers is focused on overcoming the information overload that recently resettled refugees experience (Quayyum et al. 2014), the need for language support (McKeary and Newbold 2010; Morris et al. 2009), and cultural barriers between humanitarian organizations and the populations they serve (Rowe and Patterson 2010). Little is known about the ways that refugees gain access to the knowledge they need in order to facilitate their integration into host communities. For example, while resettlement agencies help support basic needs like transportation, housing, primary education, and healthcare access, it is unclear how refugees find less basic, but no less necessary services like a hairdresser who speaks their language or a community network that shares their hobby.

A research project on meaningful integration is especially warranted during this time of high risk and uncertain legal status for many refugees and migrants in the United States. As federal policies limiting incoming migrants and deportations are increasing, the global pandemic has only exacerbated the precarious conditions of recently resettled populations. In addition, many of the evacuees from Afghanistan are being brought into the United States through humanitarian parole, a status that does not offer them the same support and benefits as a refugee. Therefore, the material reality for the forcibly displaced will likely remain dire in the coming years. This, in turn, will impact the ways that communities work with resettled populations as they integrate. Without understanding conditions for equitable, just, and meaningful integration, important dimensions of the dynamic, temporal, and complex relationships between population displacement and democracy can be missed. At a time when there is greater global population displacement than ever before, and when related growing social inequities are increasing, it is especially urgent to understand and act on the factors that lead to the meaningful integration of the forcibly displaced.

INTEGRATION AS A COMPLEX AND CONTESTED PROCESS

A contested idea within refugee and migration studies, integration most often refers to the institutional environment of the host society and the personal capacities of the settling population (Ager and Strang 2004;

Friedman and Hendry 2019; Smyth, Stewart, and de Lomba 2010; Strang and Ager 2010). The United Nations High Commissioner for Refugees (UNHCR) defines integration as a process that is "complex and gradual, comprising distinct but interrelated legal, economic, social and cultural dimensions, all of which are important for the resettled populations' ability to integrate successfully as fully included members of the host Society" (UNHCR 2014). The UNHCR encourages durable solutions for refugees by host communities that allow them to rebuild their lives. Among these durable solutions is local integration, a complex process with legal, economic, social, and cultural facets (UNHCR 2020a; UNHCR 2020b). Refugees are considered integrated in a host community when they:

- achieve outcomes within employment, housing, and education that are comparable to their host communities;
- are connected with members of a cultural, religious, or ethnic community with which they identify; and
- have a linguistic competence and cultural knowledge that allows them to confidently engage in the host society. (Ager and Strang 2004)

The Migration Policy Institute also uses five main indicators to gauge integration success: language proficiency, socioeconomic attainment, political participation, residential locale, and social interaction with host communities (Jimenez 2011).

Not only are all of these terms value-laden, but they also mask some important underlying dynamics regarding how these integration measures are to be achieved, especially in under-resourced environments. For example, while refugees often use cell phones or the internet to coordinate services and communicate with loved ones, sparse broadband coverage and limited cell phone towers in rural communities make coordination and communication difficult. Further, it is unlikely that there are many other community members who share an ethnic or linguistic background with them. If there are others from the same country of origin, it is not always the case that they will get along. Because of these dynamics and limitations, our study seeks to understand the ways that varying community resources both contribute to and complicate integration.

For the purposes of this research project, varying community resources include access to transportation and education, communication technologies, and knowledge about how to access any of these resources (Boswell

2012; Broeders 2007; Jacobsen 2017; M'charek 2017; Tazzioli 2017; Van der Ploeg 1999). Scholarship regarding these resources in relationship to refugee resettlement focuses on the national, international, and local spaces and scale of integration (Beversluis et al. 2017; Bose 2018; Wren 2003); social aspects of integration, including citizenship status, legal status, social capital, lived experience, and meaning-making (Ager and Strang 2004; Bansak et al. 2018; Bernstein and DuBois 2018; Bloemraad 2006; Strang and Ager 2010); and policy perspectives, including the relationship between policymaking, reception of refugees, and the development and implementation of policy frameworks in comparative contexts (Cheung and Phillimore 2017; Ives 2007). Building on these studies, the small pilot study discussed here illuminates the challenges of both defining and achieving "successful" integration given the material realities present within the rural communities where that integration is expected to occur.

A Pilot Study in Southwest Virginia

In order to more fully understand refugee lived experiences of integration and the access to knowledge they need in order to integrate, the research team conducted a pilot study with several nonprofits, service-provider organizations, and newly resettled refugees in southwest Virginia through focus groups and interviews. Through this collaborative study, the research team examined policy implementation in rural areas to determine whether disparities exist and in what form, concentrating on the connections and communications between rural/suburban/urban spaces. The team focused on the social networks built to accommodate newcomers in order to understand how policies impacted the lived experiences of refugees and migrants as they sought to comply with integration expectations.

Informed by a feminist standpoint (Harding 1993; Hartstock 1997), feminist oral history (Srigley, Zembrzycki, and Iacovetta 2018), and critical immigration methodologies (Faist 2012; Fedyuk and Zentai 2018; Williams 2015), the team asked how the knowledges, life experiences, and standpoints of resettled populations are implemented as they integrate into a host community. Informed by a "situated, intersectional, everyday" approach to working with mobile populations (Gigler 2004), data collection and analysis methods were designed to understand values, experiences, and priorities of refugees as a way to challenge traditional conceptions of integration. The goal was not to intervene in the actions of service providers. Rather, the goal was to explore the ways that service providers are often stymied by policies written without refugee knowledge/experience in mind. Providers are often caught in the middle, trying to assist their clients in a meaningful way while adhering to constraining policy. At stake is a better understanding of the ways vulnerable groups can access resources to facilitate their democratic inclusion into their host societies.

This pilot study built upon a number of community initiatives undertaken by the research team, including outreach events and workshops in 2017, 2018, and 2019, to build relationships with service providers and recently resettled community members. In 2018, the team compared data from these outreach events with policy analyses as well as with focus groups and interviews with service providers, volunteers, and resettled refugees in southwest Virginia (Pourchot et al. 2018; Powell and Randall 2018; Randall, Powell, and Shadle 2020). Between 2018 and 2020, the team interviewed over twenty refugees and conducted focus groups with thirty service providers.

Information Networks

The data from the interviews with resettled refugees suggest that language, health, housing, and education are key concerns of refugee resettlement experiences. Federal policy requirements that necessitate a focus on employment often supersedes these concerns, however. The Refugee Assistance Extension Act of 1985 established the Reception and Placement (R&P) period for refugees as up to ninety days postarrival. The federal government provides grants to resettlement agencies to fund caseworkers and support services during this period, "primarily for the purpose of facilitating refugee employment and achievement of self-sufficiency" (Refugee Assistance Extension Act, 1985, 13). While the concerns reflected by the refugees are not unique to them—indeed many poor, marginalized, and migrant populations experience the barriers identified by our interviewees—the ninety-day requirement for self-sufficiency demanded by US resettlement policies adds to the urgency and importance of finding a job above all else.

Table 12.1 illustrates an example of the ways the team converged policy analysis, focus groups, and interviews to understand how access to resources are a vital component in the integration of recently arriving refugees. This table reveals some of the underlying dynamics that are missed by the policy focus on economic integration.

During the pilot study, participants reported that one of the biggest challenges for expected integration is the difficulty of navigating and consolidating diffuse information networks. Service providers and volunteers lamented that most of the information they had to share was outdated, inaccessible to their clients because it was primarily stored in binders located on their desktops, or was dependent on the tacit knowledge of career service providers with comprehensive institutional memories (described as "word of mouth" in table 12.1). They argued for a "one-stop" information platform that would be easily accessible to all who needed it. Relatedly, refugees reported difficulty in knowing where to go for particular services, with whom to speak about accessing those services, and which services are useful or available to them.

While in many cases this lack of knowledge was made worse by the fact that they lived in rural communities, this was not always the case. In one instance, one woman resettling from Syria expressed a feeling of being deceived by resettlement workers because she had been told conflicting information about a housing arrangement. Because she was unable to adequately communicate with them about her situation, she and her family faced eviction. She was only able to seek legal consultation through word of mouth within her neighborhood, not through the resettlement agency. The layers of communication (service provider, landlord, neighbors) and confusing information about her rights created a lack of trust. After her family's secondary relocation to a nearby, more rural town (and a new group of service providers, including the aforementioned grassroots resettlement group), she explained, "I can trust people here. I don't feel like I'm being tricked." Had she and her family stayed in their initial relocation site, the social support and trust needed to facilitate integration would have been lacking due to poor transparency and communication practices from service providers to refugees. Having access to the kind of community-led support that a small community offers may contribute to building trust-based support that facilitates better exchange of knowledge, even if the economic opportunities are limited.

Table 12.1. From Pilot Data: Analysis Linking Policy, Information, and Integration					
Federal Code Title 45/ Subtitle B/ Chapter IV/ Part 400.81	Service provider focus group question	Service provider response	Refugee interview question	Refugee response	Findings
"The services or employment must be related to the capability of the individual to perform the task on a regular basis."	Where do you find information about jobs? Have there been times when it was difficult to place refugees in appropriate jobs?	"It's often word of mouth. I wish we could hold off putting them in a job for a little longer. That way we could help them settle in more, get them in English language classes, help them find a job that's good for them instead of the first thing to come along."	Have there been times when you weren't able to get to work and if yes, what were the most common reasons?	"I share the phone with my daughter. If she has it, I can't get a ride if my schedule changes. There is no [public] transportation and I can't pay for taxi so these times I can't go to work on time or at all."	The policy requiring regular work and within 90 days is not nuanced to consider the variety of issues they navigate, making it difficult to find transportation to work, for example, particularly in rural areas. Similarly, the layers of communication technologies to coordinate do not account for the lack of independence of many people and the everyday responsibilities (childcare, health, language classes, etc.) that affect their ability to go to work on a regular basis.

Misalignment between Policy and Experiences

The information that refugees did receive prioritized getting a job as quickly as possible. Service providers also saw this model as limiting. For example, when asked what she would like to do differently if another refugee were to be resettled in the area, one resettlement volunteer stated,

> The only thing that I would think about is . . . [the] three months of total immersion learning English before they have to go find a job. . . . I think it would make them be able to get a different job and do better when they got to the job and to communicate with us and communicate with everybody.

In her assessment, being able to learn English first, before job placement, would have been better for a particular family member. Then, the job could be better suited for that person. Another volunteer with the same organization agreed:

> To be honest, we got the adults working really fast, but I can't think of any advantages to having done that. . . . If they had delayed that by two months in none of the cases would that have made any difference long-term. When we thought we would be financially finished with them in about six months, it seemed like a big deal to get them working as soon as possible. Now that we're two years in, if we had spent those two months on English it could only have helped.

Both of the volunteers quoted here work with families in rural areas through a grassroots, all-volunteer resettlement group, which is privately funded and therefore able to provide financial support beyond the ninety-day period that is supported by the federal government. Their assessment that English instruction would have been better first is deeply informed by the kinds of jobs available in the rural area and the need for the organization's continued involvement in the lives of the refugees they support.

In this case, the federal requirement is not able to account for the nuances of resources available within particular communities or for the particular needs of different families. Language skills, job experience, job availability, time to adapt, medical needs, access to information, and the presence or absence of people from a similar background, among many other things, contribute to the ways that families are or are not able to become financially independent. In many cases, lack of available knowledge, combined with a focus on obtaining any kind of employment as quickly as possible, hindered clients' ability to find meaningful employment, to access culturally appropriate healthcare and educational services, and to find recreational opportunities for their families. In other words, lack of nuance within policy requirements hindered both their expected and meaningful integration into their host communities. As mentioned earlier, meaningful integration recognizes refugee experience as its focus. Therefore, meaningful employment, as part of meaningful integration, would be employment that is both intellectually/personally satisfying and financially sufficient.

The policy emphasis on rapid economic integration is not only harmful to resettled refugees, it also impacts the communities they move to. For example, many refugees arrive with professional certifications from their home countries, including medical, legal, and engineering degrees. Yet, because they are not given the time to re-do those certifications in the United States, they often find themselves underemployed in jobs where their education and degrees are useless. For example, it is not uncommon to find refugees with degrees in architecture and engineering driving taxis in and around Washington, DC. Not only is this morally deflating and psychologically undermining for the underemployed, it represents a missed opportunity for the communities where refugees resettle. This lost opportunity was nowhere more evident than during the COVID-19 pandemic when there was a shortage of doctors and nurses in rural communities. Although many licensed health practitioners live in rural communities, because their certifications were not issued in the United States they were not eligible to help. Recognizing this fact, several states eventually adopted emergency measures to expand the number of healthcare workers, including creating pathways for internationally trained health professionals already in the United States to be licensed and practice. A report from the Migration Policy Institute outlined the impact of this approach, "while the policies represented a unique opportunity to tap the talents of underemployed immigrants and refugees with degrees in health and medicine, they also spotlight the need to think creatively about using these professionals as a resource beyond the pandemic" (Batalova, Fix, and Fernandez-Pena 2021).

Discussion

Based on the direct interactions and interviews that the co-authors have had with resettled refugees and the organizations that support them, there are complexities at work in integration experiences that are not always captured by traditional survey data. Refugee narratives documented by the research team have generated questions about how efforts get coordinated across service organizations, how the trauma of integration compares with the trauma of their initial displacement, how their new lives might not meet their expectations, and how working with so many well-intentioned volunteers can be overwhelming.

Preliminary findings from the pilot study showed that current distribution of available resources is insufficient for facilitating refugee integration for the following reasons. First, many newly resettled community members do not have all or even most of the up-to-date information on services and resources to help refugees become economically viable citizens. Their information and communication technologies (ICTs) can consist of outdated material repositories, word-of-mouth knowledge, and tacit knowledge. Resources and information are not readily accessible or complete and are limited by the dynamic nature of nonprofit programming, ever-changing programs and staff, and linguistic accessibility. These knowledge barriers can result in a lack of trust due to the disconnect between refugee needs and the providers' inability to meet them. They can also lead to gatekeeping on the part of the providers, whether intentional or otherwise, that can make it more difficult for refugees to navigate a new community, both financially and socially.

Very little of the extant knowledge in published research is based on the lived experiences and knowledge of refugees and their own communication networks. The pilot study outcomes showed that refugee perspectives are needed to identify barriers to integration as well as new strategies for meaningful integration. When available information prioritizes rapid job placement in any available area, there is little room to explore other integration factors, such as whether and how underemployment might exacerbate trauma-related depression that many displaced people experience, or the impact of available childcare and transportation networks to facilitate women's employment. Based on these findings, the research team concluded that further study is necessary to understand the relationships between efficient and appropriate knowledge networks and meaningful integration of resettled communities.

Ongoing Research

Based on the results of this pilot study in rural southwest Virginia, the co-authors founded the Virginia Consortium for Refugee, Migrant, and Displacement Studies (VCRMDS), a statewide group of academic researchers, service providers, nonprofits, and volunteer groups working with resettled populations. The vision of the VCRMDS is that "Virginia will be an inclusive, equitable, and welcoming home to refugees, migrants, and displaced populations," and its mission is "To realize our vision through research, education, advocacy and community engagement" (Powell et al. 2020). During consortium meetings, service providers from both rural and urban areas indicated a critical need for understanding the disparities in resources that impact the ways that service providers and volunteer groups can assist newly resettled community members. As the reports from the consortium meetings suggest (Powell et al. 2019a, 2019b), and as the pilot data indicates, nonprofit workers often function as the "bridge," the cultural and linguistic connection, between resettlement policy and new community members. Consortium participants identified the social and technological networks involved in processes of "making home," and the accompanying issues that arise in well-being, employment, housing, and education. The stories about home and resettlement gathered during these preliminary activities suggested that a detailed mapping of the use and availability of communication networks would benefit both the community and service providers.

Therefore, the next step in the research is to map communication networks to reveal valuable social and economic connections and information processes. From the preliminary data, we came to understand how communities form information networks in response to basic needs, yet those networks are often not visible to the broader community and are difficult to find (Powell and Randall 2018). Further, they are not as comprehensive as the refugee community or the service providers would like. Comparing the pilot study data to focus groups with service providers in more urban areas, the co-authors understood how limited resources might impact equitable social, cultural, and employment connections. The next step, then, is to continue this work by examining how communication networks may or may not reflect knowledge dissemination, how technologies circulate information between refugees and service providers, and whether and how equitable knowledge distribution impacts meaningful integration. Based on the pilot study, we anticipate that extant communication networks do not sufficiently reflect the tacit knowledge and life experiences of refugees and surmise that, because of this, both their expected and meaningful integration into their new communities is hindered. The broader take-home point is that refugees who are resettled in rural communities, and the service agencies that work with them, have a more challenging time complying with resettlement policies than those living and working in urban areas.

Future Research and Community Partnerships

With the founding of the Virginia Consortium for Refugee, Migrant, and Displacement Studies, the statewide consortium of higher education institutions involved and interested in research with and on behalf refugees, migrants, and other displaced populations, the co-authors are working closely to refine this research and to determine the best ways to make the research available to interested stakeholders. Based on the research findings, the intent is to develop a refugee-centric information exchange platform that recognizes and reflects the interactions between people and institutions throughout the state. This platform will combine neighborhood-based application design together with regional and statewide information specific to refugee and migrant communities. The exchange platform, tentatively titled "Digital Binders," will focus on the informational needs of refugees and migrants and account for the resources available in local communities. Working across technological domains (such as web browsers, phone applications), the platform will provide access to up-to-date lists of services across the state, information about formal and informal refugee support networks in different regions of Virginia, as well as other content identified by key stakeholders, including refugees, service providers, and policymakers, that would facilitate meaningful refugee integration, including social and civic engagement throughout Virginia.

This responsive application will serve as a twenty-first-century model for other states to emulate as they seek to integrate newly arriving refugee and migrant populations. The development and dissemination of Digital Binders will work in tandem with educational programs to foster mutual, reciprocal, and sustainable exchange among resettled families, service providers, researchers, and students. While in urban areas a Digital Binder system may help navigate a high number of service providers and resources, ideally the Binders would also be a resource for those in rural communities to tap into—or establish—more community-based support networks. The Digital Binder system would facilitate access to all of the invisible, but no less important, services and opportunities that resettled populations need in order to thrive.

Finally, as a result of the research team's efforts in establishing working relationships with area service providers, a collaborative focused on employment-related initiatives with the Commonwealth Catholic Charities, the Roanoke Refugee Dialogue Group, and the Roanoke Center for Higher Education has developed. These initiatives will include (1) developing survey research with employers in Roanoke who hire immigrants and refugees in order to assess their executive training needs around diversity and equity in the workplace; (2) developing a survey for refugees to assess their workplace needs and experiences; (3) exploring possibilities for providing certification to business leaders and executives on issues related to hiring displaced populations; and (4) collaborating on providing digital badging to employees and high road employer certification to employers. In each of these activities, the VCRMDS seeks to provide mutually beneficial and reciprocal research where academic institutions partner with service providers and volunteer organizations to provide useful information that will help organizations complete their work. In continuing this work in the rural southwest Virginia area, along with developing a more comprehensive way to see and understand resource networks, the co-authors hope to inform policymakers about the particular needs and barriers that refugees in rural areas face when trying to attain self-sufficiency goals as currently outlined in federal policy. Overall, the objective of this research and of the on-going community partnerships it has facilitated is to foster connectivity and reciprocity for a vibrant Virginia.

Research for this project was supported by seed funding from the Virginia Tech Policy Destination Area grant, Virginia Tech's Office of Economic Development's Vibrant Virginia grant, and the Virginia Tech Center for Peace Studies and Violence Prevention. In addition, the VCRMDS annual meeting was supported by the Office for Inclusion and Diversity's "Advancing the Human Condition" symposium grant. The authors are grateful for this support.

Chapter 13

Responding to the Addiction Crisis through University-Community Collaboration

Mary Beth Dunkenberger, Sophie Wenzel, and Laura Nelson

Addiction and its health-related concerns are an imminent and critical area for public health interventions in communities across Virginia. This chapter highlights successful collaborations and challenges in addressing the opioid epidemic in rural and urban communities based on recent research and technical assistance work in the City of Roanoke and Pulaski County. Particular emphasis is placed on opportunities for and barriers to boundary spanning and collaboration in healthcare, economic/business, public safety, and criminal justice domains. In doing so, the authors provide a guide for how engagement and planning activities similar to those in Roanoke and Pulaski County may be replicated in other communities.

The opioid addiction epidemic spans the United States, impacting urban and rural communities at an alarming and sustained rate, resulting in profound challenges at the individual, family, and community levels. A primary goal of substance use disorder (SUD) interventions is to serve the current user in harm reduction and treatment and recovery, while also preventing the onset of use by the next generation (Lipari and Van Horn 2017). Achieving these goals requires application of targeted and multipronged strategies across jurisdictional boundaries.

The addiction crisis results from a confluence of supply and demand economics, along with an economic and social paradigm shift that left many communities and individuals vulnerable. Beginning in the late 1990s there was a remarkable uptick in the manufacture of prescription opioids, paired with an underemployed and aging postindustrial workforce looking for ways to manage economic frustration and chronic pain. In a letter to the Mayo Clinic Proceedings editor, Dr. Akshay Pendyal, describes the convergence of factors that led to the crisis:

> The past few decades have been characterized by rising unemployment, poverty, and wealth inequality due to neoliberal austerity measures and a fraying social safety net. In disadvantaged communities, social capital becomes supplanted by feelings of isolation and hopelessness. Meanwhile, the US government continues to engage in drug interdiction efforts, which, in turn, lead to the emergence of synthetic and deadly heroin alternatives in the domestic black market. The end result of these seemingly disparate processes, of course, is what we see before us today: increasing overdoses and other "diseases of despair." No discussion of the "underpinnings and evolution of the current opioid crisis" is thus complete without an account of these structural factors. (Pendyal, Srivastava, and Gold 2018, 1330)

This chapter focuses on functions of boundary spanning practices within and among rural and urban communities that support a coordinated response to the addiction crisis and that enable communities to advance social and economic vitality for all citizens. As Dr. Pendyal articulates, the current crisis resulted from a convergence of public health, economic, and law enforcement factors. Coordinated response requires proactive leadership from these sectors, among others, in coming together to assess how the crisis is impacting communities and to develop a plan for addressing it.

In her 2018 book *Dopesick: Dealers, Doctors, and the Drug Company That Addicted America*, Beth Macy succinctly states the scale of commitment that is needed in order to have a coordinated response to the addiction crisis: "America's approach to its opioid problem is to rely on Battle of Dunkirk strategies—leaving the fight to well-meaning citizens, in their fishing vessels and private boats—when what's really needed to win the war is a full-on Normandy Invasion" (24).

Context of Case Study

On November 21, 2016, the Virginia State Health Commissioner declared the opioid addiction crisis a public health emergency (Coy and Brewster 2016). Four months later, President Donald Trump took the unprecedented action of signing an executive order to establish the President's Commission on Combating Drug Addiction and the Opioid Crisis (Commission). In the initial months of the Commission's work, the president complied with a Commission request to declare the opioid crisis a public health emergency under federal law (Madras 2018). The Centers for Disease Control (CDC) estimates that more than 750,000 Americans have died since 1999 from drug overdose with two-thirds of these deaths involving opioids (CDC Wonder 2020).

In 2018 Virginia Tech's (VT) Center for Economic and Community Engagement announced Vibrant Virginia, a statewide initiative to foster "collaboration between universities and communities, with the goals of building connections between urban and rural" (Vibrant Virginia website). At that time, faculty with Virginia Tech's Institute of Policy and Governance (IPG) and Center for Public Health Practice and Research (CPHPR) had been collaborating on substance use–related projects in Virginia communities for more than five years and saw the opportunity to leverage Vibrant Virginia seed funding to better understand and advance community planning efforts to address the addiction crisis in a rural and urban locality. From this collaboration, the Supporting Healthy Families and Communities (SHFC) through Collaborative Strategies to Address the Opioid Epidemic project emerged with the support of Vibrant Virginia.

In the Commonwealth of Virginia 5.9 per 100,000 people died of a prescription opioid overdose in 2017, while 11 per 100,000 people died from heroin and/or fentanyl overdose (Virginia Department of Health (VDH) 2017). From 2012–2017 these rates shifted, revealing prescription overdose deaths in more rural regions and heroin and illicit synthetic opioid overdose deaths in urban areas. In the southwest region of the state, where Pulaski County and Roanoke City are located, the fentanyl/heroin rate was 7.5, and the prescription overdose rate was 9.0 in 2017 (VDH 2017). Additionally, the rate of infants born exposed to substances in utero in southwest Virginia are the highest rates in the state at 22.9 per 1,000 live births compared to 7.7 for the state (VDH 2017). Accompanying the higher rates of overdose and exposed infants, are sharply rising rates of Hepatitis C cases reaching 245 in southwest Virginia per 1,000 cases compared to 131 for the state (VDH 2017).

Within this context and identified area of need, the project team reached out to partners in Roanoke City and Pulaski County to assess how we might work together to support local efforts to better understand and address the root causes of the opioid epidemic. Roanoke and Pulaski County communities have been significantly impacted by the opioid crisis, although in different ways and with very dissimilar resources to address the problem. Though only separated by fifty-five miles on the I-81 corridor, the two communities have experienced the opioid epidemic in quite divergent ways. Pulaski County, a rural community, has been most dramatically impacted by fatal overdoses due to prescription opioids, while Roanoke City's fatal overdose rates have been attributed to both prescriptions and to heroin and illicit fentanyl (table 13.1).

Table 13.1. Community Characteristics (2017)			
Locality	Prescription opioids—Fatal overdose (per 100,000)	Illicit—Heroin/Fentanyl—Fatal overdose (per 100,000)	Population/Land mass (square miles)
Pulaski County	20.4	5.8	34,225/330
Roanoke City	17.1	32.1	99,600/42.85
Virginia	5.9	11	

Source: Virginia Department of Health 2017 and US Census Bureau, 2020.

As the project team engaged in the communities, two primary goals unfolded: (1) to better understand how families impacted by SUD navigate treatment and recovery; and (2) to support community coalition building and sustainability that enhances a more holistic approach to the continuum of needs for SUD treatment. Through engagement in the primarily rural setting of Pulaski and the more urban setting of Roanoke, the project team sought to gain insight into the unique nature that geographical location plays in the opioid crisis and to find community-led solutions to the problem. Ultimately, this process built upon the strengths of community coalitions by providing informed guidance through data collection and analysis, with the goal of creating cross-sector planning processes and strategies specific to community assets, resources, and needs. Vibrant Virginia seed grant funding provided the necessary resources and momentum to move the project team's existing substance abuse work in Roanoke and Pulaski from episodic to currently supporting ongoing community-engaged research and interventions.

Boundary Spanning to Understand and Improve Community Collaboratives

The theory of boundary spanning, first described by Tushman (1977), aids in conceptualizing the successes and challenges experienced while working in the Pulaski and Roanoke communities for the project period (July 2018–July 2019) and beyond. Boundary spanning is a theoretical framework that helps to describe individual and organizational behavior in multisector collaborations—particularly in collaborations that link individual organizations' existing aims and resources with external sources of information and resources to develop new aims and processes (Bryson, Crosby, and Stone, 2015). Boundary spanning theory was initially applied to business collaborations and networks and have more recently been used to better understand cross-sector interactions and organizations in the areas of policymaking, public health, and community development (Langley et al. 2017).

During the past two decades, the salience of productive knowledge exchange through boundary spanning engagement has been increasingly utilized by those who work to address "wicked problems" and complex social issues, such as the addiction epidemic (Bednarek et al. 2018). Practitioners and academics seemingly agree that solutions for wicked problems must account for many dimensions of knowing/understanding and continued learning across sectoral organizational and professional boundaries. A key function of knowledge exchange is interpersonal communication that enables institutional representatives from different organizations to understand better how each views the cause of the problem, how they access and process information on the problem, their views on potential solutions, and the feasibility of possible solutions (Bednarek et al. 2018).

The SHFC project was launched with the aspiration of bridging academic and practitioner knowledge and actions to connect population health expertise with policy and organizational assessment capabilities and to provide a foundation on which to build community-engaged collaborations and strategic approaches for the prevention, treatment, and long-term recovery of opioid and related substance use disorders.

Weerts and Sandmann (2010) situate the work of research universities as having significant and varying roles in advancing community engagement to address complex problems, describing engagement as a two-way learning process between university agents and community actors. Bednarek et al. (2018) describe the role of boundary spanning at the science and policy interface as work that enables "exchange between the production and use of knowledge to support evidence-informed decision-making in a specific context' and boundary spanners 'as individuals or organizations that specifically and actively facilitate this process. Essentially, boundary spanners dedicate their time to creating and enabling effective knowledge exchange" (1176).

Purposeful integrated leadership is critical to achieving the aims of boundary spanning work to increase shared knowledge and collective action across organizational boundaries, enabling increased linkages of organizations to their external environments (Crosby and Bryson 2010). Shared knowledge and ongoing communication across organizational differences in mission, resources, and function are critical to enable innovative, collaborative actions by increasing shared aims and removing perceived barriers to collective action (Posner and Cvitanovic 2019).

Examples and conceptualization of boundary spanning activities and impacts will be discussed in subsequent sections, which detail the specific engagement activities of the project team with community partners. Langley et al. (2019) provide a review of the scholarship of "boundary work" connecting the related concepts of boundary spanning and boundary objects in an applied perspective that helps the project team better understand successes and remaining challenges in working with community partners on addressing the addiction crisis.

> We define boundary work here as a purposeful individual and collective effort to influence the social, symbolic, material, and temporal boundaries, demarcations, and distinctions affecting groups, occupations and organizations. This definition offers a processual constructivist view of boundaries as in flux, as continually becoming and as subject to human agency, something that is not always reflected in other related concepts (e.g., boundary spanning, boundary objects), where the pre-existence of boundaries as fixed elements of structure tends to be assumed. (4)

Boundary work in the SHFC project included university agents providing the seed funding to support the work and the project team conducting the work with the support and buy-in from the community collaboratives. This boundary spanning work included facilitating group discussions, preparing summary data reports for the community collaborations, and researching evidence-based practices that could be implemented in the communities. An overview of the project's engagement in the Roanoke and Pulaski communities is provided below. It is followed by reflections on how this engagement reflects principles of boundary spanning.

UNDERSTANDING THE IMPACT OF THE OPIOID EPIDEMIC

The project team planned its research and engagement methods to create a foundation of data and research from which cross-sector organizations could come together to understand the impact of the opioid epidemic on their communities and to create collaborative plans for solutions. To understand the breadth of the issue and set a common benchmark for engagement within Pulaski County and the City of Roanoke, an initial step was to gather data on both localities, including the demographic, socioeconomic, health status, and healthcare context of each locality.

Second, the project team supported efforts in both communities to create an inventory of SUD-related services and resources available to residents. The data collection was undertaken within the social determinants of health (SDOH) approach. The SDOH considers the conditions under which people are born, grow, live, work, and age, including factors such as education, employment, housing, and food security among many others. The project team also conducted a policy review of all local and state SUD and opioid-related policies to examine how current policies and resources intersect to support community, parental, and child needs.

The outcome of these methods was an inventory of SUD programs, resources, processes, and policies that are available in and impact these communities and that provide the foundation of shared information for community stakeholders. The project team presented summary reports to Pulaski and Roanoke stakeholders in December 2018.

The project team used the data gathered and presented in the summary reports to inform interviews with key stakeholders in each community and to coordinate town hall meetings in each locality. The project team engaged:

- service providers to gain an understanding of services, policies, and the continuum of care offered across service providers;
- parents (mothers and fathers) to gain an understanding of their narrative and experience in navigating SUD;
- local and state policymakers to determine program, policy, and political barriers to treatment access and effectiveness; and
- employers to gain a deeper understanding of barriers to hiring, possible solutions to these barriers, the potential to fund treatment options, and other services.

Before proposing these activities, the project team members met with public behavioral health agencies serving the selected communities, Blue Ridge Behavioral Healthcare and New River Valley Community Services Board, and the local health departments to gain their support for the proposed work.

Rather than forming new cross-sector planning groups in each locality, the project team partnered with existing groups: the Roanoke Valley Collective Response (RVCR), a newly formed cross-sectoral partnership, and Pulaski Community Partners Coalition (PCPC), a long-standing coalition, which needed support to regain momentum on addressing the opioid epidemic.

During the time frame supported by the Vibrant Virginia funding, the project team conducted seven group interviews across both community coalitions, as well as two individual interviews with peer recovery specialists, one interview with a parent in recovery from a SUD, and one interview with a representative from the department of social services. In total, 114 community voices were represented in the gathering and analysis of data for this project (98 from Roanoke and 16 from Pulaski).

ROANOKE VALLEY COLLECTIVE RESPONSE (RVCR)

The Roanoke Valley Collective Response was formed in early fall 2018 with momentum brought about in the community by the release of Beth Macy's book, Dopesick, which chronicled the emergence of the opioid epidemic and some of the lives impacted in the Roanoke Valley. The RVCR represents stakeholders across various sectors including policy, medical, mental/behavioral health, peer recovery, researchers, faith-based community, treatment/recovery, law enforcement, EMS, social services, and public health. RVCR hosts monthly steering committee and stakeholder meetings at which participants present and discuss new information in order to address the evolving addiction epidemic.

Table 13.2. Five Areas of Inquiry and Their Scope of Work Definition Identified by RVCR

Group Name	Working Definition
Prevention and Education	Universal prevention is a means to prevent the onset of substance misuse or dependence before it begins, generally geared to general populations (e.g., programs for elementary schoolchildren). Selective prevention includes tailored services focused on higher risk populations or groups requiring specialized information (e.g., individuals dealing with chronic pain or children of parents with SUD). Indicated prevention involves intervening with people who have already been affected by SUD, building resilience, or slowing or preventing consequences from becoming worse.
Treatment	Treatment is defined as a services array provided by a range of professionals, including peer recovery specialists, with a primary focus on treating SUD, providing both acute stabilization, and ongoing treatment.

Child and family support	Child and family support is defined as services to foster healthy maintenance and preservation of the family unit with a focus on children whose parents are actively experiencing OUD/SUD and on relatives and friends who support the family through OUD- and SUD-related crises as well as during treatment and recovery.
Harm reduction and connection to care	Crisis Response and Connection to Care (CRCC) is defined as a spectrum of strategies, including protocols and processes for overdose prevention and reversal, harm reduction, and coordinated responses and connection to OUD/SUD care. A CRCC workgroup goal is to facilitate dialogue leading to solutions that promote connections to treatment while helping those individuals in active substance use or disorder who are willing to pursue significant change find pathways to treatment and needed services.
Recovery	Recovery is defined as processes of change through which individuals, families, and communities affected by SUD seek continual improvement in their health and wellness, are self-directed, and strive to reach full potential. Because recovery often involves setbacks, resilience is key. Resilience in recovery is also vital for family members. Hope, the belief that these challenges and conditions can be overcome, is the foundation of recovery.

Through several work sessions, the RVCR collected significant data on gaps, needs, resources, and next steps that were needed to address the opioid crisis but did not have dedicated capacity to analyze the data. In addition to building on the RVCR information with independent data collection, the project team conducted analysis and provided summaries of the data to the RVCR workgroups. This analysis found that there was a gap in information in the workgroup area of Child and Family Support, so the project team facilitated a data collection session to collect data specifically surrounding parental SUD and family services from the viewpoint of all five workgroups. The data from these sessions were analyzed through thematic coding and helped inform the development of Roanoke Valley region's "Blueprint to Address the Opioid Crisis" (Blueprint) (https://www.rvcollectiveresponse.org/).

The project team remains significantly involved with the RVCR, supporting the full development of the Blueprint, released in August 2020, with four team members credited with content design and the development of the Blueprint. The project team is still working within the RVCR, aligning strategies with resource needs, supporting evidence-based practice research, and assessing and advising on policy changes. Additionally, project team members have been involved in applying for and receiving funding to advance RVCR strategies.

Pulaski Community Partners Coalition (PCPC)

The Pulaski Community Partners Coalition (PCPC) formed in 2002. PCPC began with an annual community partner meeting for Pulaski County Community-Based Prevention Planning. At this meeting, it was decided that interested community partners should meet more formally through the formation of a community coalition to address substance abuse by youth and their families. The PCPC was tasked with increasing community awareness, involvement, and cooperation regarding community substance abuse issues. Since that initial meeting, members and supporters of the PCPC have met regularly, organizing, building, and expanding the coalition, as well as working toward fulfilling its mission of reducing substance abuse among youth by promoting healthy, thriving families and a safe community by connecting people, resources, and ideas.

The project team held a meeting with several PCPC members to initially discuss how PCPC could continue moving toward their goals and identify some of the challenges that arose over the years that had stalled their efforts. The research team was then invited to a PCPC meeting to facilitate focus group discussions on parental SUD and community needs to address family needs related to SUD. The project team also conducted interviews with people in recovery. The project team then analyzed the focus group and interview data and presented them to PCPC along with updated SUD local incidence data.

The summary findings and data were presented to PCPC and subsequently used to update the coalition's action plan for addressing the opioid and addiction crises. The project team offered to work with PCPC to find funding to pursue a more comprehensive community engagement and planning process to develop a detailed action plan. At this time there was discussion of developing a regional plan for the New River Valley, incorporating engagement from various community stakeholder groups. This regional effort is still pending.

Engagement with PCPC revealed that much of the group's current efforts are focused on raising awareness of the issue of SUD, rather than engagement in identifying and facilitating intervention strategies. The rural locality lacks the resources of more urban areas, particularly in the areas of transportation and breadth of treatment options for individuals and families.

Table 13.3. Themes that Emerged from Pulaski Interviews and Focus Groups	
Theme	Definition
Substance use and parenting	Research participants identified that poly-substance use among parents is a major ongoing concern, including use of marijuana and methamphetamine and opioids. This issue has been reflected by high rates of Hepatitis C and neonatal abstinence syndrome (NAS) where babies are born substance dependent. Multigenerational trauma and SUD have resulted in deficits in parenting skills and a need for more education among human service providers on adverse childhood events (ACES) as a significant contributor to comorbid mental health and behavioral health challenges. There are many challenges facing Pulaski's child welfare system resulting from ongoing high rates of SUD. While many grandparents and other relatives have stepped forward to help raise impacted children, the multigenerational issues often serve as a barrier to kinship placements of children. Law enforcement and child welfare officials are often faced with balancing providing services to keep families together and ensuring the safety of children.
Stigma/community response/role of advocacy	Stakeholder participants indicated that there are strong collaborations between human service organizations and behavioral health providers. However, the stigma surrounding SUD, and perception that the disease is a moral failing, has persisted as a barrier to resource allocation and policy development to adequately address the epidemic. The increased use of peer recovery specialists as service providers is seen as a positive step to increase access to services and reduced stigma.

Social determinants of health	Pulaski stakeholders identified significant gaps in the social determinants of health as contributing to high rates of SUD and as barriers to treatment and recovery. Significant gaps include transportation, housing, food access, early childhood education, and quality childcare.
Existing services	Research participants identified key existing services that can serve as a foundation for establishing a more complete continuum of care for SUD services. These services include support groups for grandparents raising grandkids, treatment services provided in the regional jail, drug court, alcoholic and narcotics anonymous, and services provided through the school system and in local churches. Stakeholders also identified New River Valley Community Services (NRVCS) as a key partner and specific NRVCS programs such as the 401 Peer Center, where those needing treatment and in recovery can get support from peer recovery specialists, and Special Deliveries, serving pregnant and postpartum women.
Need for services/ treatment	Stakeholders identified key areas where additional services are needed, including inpatient and outpatient treatment, employer support for treatment that may require some accommodations, services for teenagers, need for early education and childcare, and ongoing recovery supports.
Employment	Stakeholders highlighted that there is a gap in employment opportunities and a lack of a qualified workforce that can pass drug screens. There is a need for employers to work with individuals who are in recovery and have substance use–related criminal backgrounds. Pulaski stakeholders also call for increased investment in vocational preparedness for teenagers and young adults as well as basic services to build soft skills.

UNIFIED THEMES ACROSS GEOGRAPHIC LOCALITIES

Across localities, unified themes impacted the community, regardless of rural or urban context. These themes emerged through a process of collaborative thematic analysis. All qualitative data were transcribed and uploaded into Word documents. A hybrid of inductive and deductive coding was used for theme generation for all of the qualitative data. A series of potential codes to look for was determined ahead of time to help identify themes based on a preliminary data analysis. New themes that emerged during the data analysis process were coded, compiled, and summarized. Coders looked for emerging themes common to all questions, between documents and between respondent categories. Important points and themes were summarized and presented as evidence to document SUD in the communities.

Table 13.4 provides the results from a thorough analysis along with quotations and concepts to support the emergence of those themes. The six themes depicted below emerged across both localities. The three highest priority areas for both localities were community education, removing barriers to treatment, and addressing trauma and stigma surrounding SUD.

Table 13.4. Themes that Emerged in Both Rural and Urban Localities

Theme	Quotes and Concepts
Navigating emotions and trauma	"You need something in life that provides hope." "A Peer Recovery Specialist holds hope until they [the person in treatment] can receive it." "Feelings of hopelessness when in treatment." "I have experience and therefore I do know what people go through." Services should be provided by those who understand co-occuring mental illness paired with SUD lived experience.
Importance of advocacy and education	Fear of stigma and consequences of asking for help "Community champions are key." "We had to advocate by ourselves before we had peer recovery specialists." "We now have believers"-with regards to incorporating peer recovery in community
Need more community buy-in	Faith-based buy-in Inviting faith-based leaders to the table Disseminating information for resources

Parenting support	"Children are a huge motivator for change." Needs aren't being met for parents. Parenting classes helpful but often not part of treatment. Many kids are in kinship and foster care without adequate emotional/mental support; need more trauma-informed care training.
Barriers to treatment	"So many barriers to treatment it's like spitting in the wind." Transportation Food insecurity Stigma and fear of SUD still exist Safe housing Child care during treatment Inadequate treatment for recovery needs
Reentry and recovery support	Diversion programs from jail for first time offenders "Non-violent drug offenders should be given treatment options not jail." Rapid response teams should be implemented to support those who recently overdosed. Employers need to be part of the solution.

While the research team had success engaging with service providers and individuals in recovery target populations, engaging the business community proved challenging in both Pulaski and Roanoke. The Roanoke Regional Chamber of Commerce has been involved in the RVCR, and in April 2019 it hosted an event on the opioid crisis at the Roanoke Country Club. The event was well attended by chamber affiliates, service providers, and businesses; however, to date, next steps for the business/employer sector have not evolved, and the business sector has been noticeably absent at the RVCR stakeholder meetings. In an effort to involve businesses and employers, the project team developed a survey and distributed information cards, including a link to the survey at the Roanoke Chamber event. Additionally, the survey link was shared with the Pulaski Chamber of Commerce and with stakeholders who indicated that they had connections in the business community. Ultimately, the research team ended up reaching out to business owners and private sector contacts about taking the survey. These collective efforts resulted in completion of only six surveys; therefore, survey data were considered pilot data, and the project team will seek additional opportunities to engage this critical constituency.

The pilot survey indicated common themes within the business community in relation to substance use and the workforce. When asked on a five-point Likert scale how the broader community and economy are impacted by substance abuse, all respondents stated that it "greatly impacts their community." In addition, employers stated that there were not enough resources and services for employees struggling with a substance use disorder; therefore, those employers didn't know how to help them. Respondents to the survey represented finance/insurance, healthcare/social assistance, and professional/technical assistance. The employers stated that it was difficult to find reliable "employees who are substance free and can function in the workplace." One employer also stated, "we've had to fire people due to staff emotionally unable to work because of substance abuse issues at home." This statement emphasizes the impact that substance use issues have across the entire family system and not only for the person abusing a substance. Future employment engagement has been identified as a key area to foster in both Pulaski and Roanoke as community coalitions recognize the importance of supportive employment in recovery from a SUD.

Varying Themes across Geographic Localities

Although the majority of themes that arose were similar in both rural and urban contexts, there were a few themes that emerged that were unique to the geographic locality. Volunteer fatigue was a major theme that emerged in the rural setting of Pulaski. Burnout due to the need to address opioid and other drug issues with limited resources is further complicated by coalition members being strained by the many roles they serve in the community. In addition, rural communities continue to face issues with over-prescribing of opioids within private practices. Although most prescribers are working within the Prescription Drug Monitoring Program, participants stated that not all private practices do, and the people who are seeking out these drugs know where to find them.

In the urban Roanoke context, resources are not as limited and services are slightly easier to access due to more public transportation, so some of the issues that rural communities face are mitigated by more systemwide resources. Additionally, organizations that are represented in Roanoke typically are larger and better resourced and can therefore support several individuals to participate in engagement activities, ensuring that these organizations are represented on a consistent basis. RVCR has had significant momentum since its inception to garner support across sectors and maintain engagement. A paradigm shift in policy is required to implement some of the efforts the RVCR has proposed, and although there has been great success in fostering a harm-reduction model, there are still key community stakeholders who have very different perspectives on how to address harm reduction.

Key Project Outcomes and Next Steps

Engagement and partnerships with both RVCR and PCPC are ongoing as these communities continue to work toward implementing the action items identified through this research and these community efforts. Along with community partners, the project team agrees that a key next step is engaging with people who are in active substance use. The community coalitions have provided immense insight into the community system, service provision, and obstacles they face but often without the voices of those who are primarily impacted by SUD.

Many of the action items that have been identified involve better understanding of or changes to policy at the local and state levels. Future efforts will seek to better understand what strategies can be enacted within the parameters of current policy, and policy changes that need to occur. Additionally, as this work continues, efforts to implement more evidence-based practices that support a harm-reduction model will aim to foster greater community buy-in across all sectors and geographical landscapes of southwest Virginia. Future funding opportunities are continuously being explored to support the action items identified through this research.

Discussion: Vibrant Virginia + Community Coalitions = Boundary Spanning

The support of Vibrant Virginia seed funding enabled the project team to expand on existing relationships to assist Roanoke and Pulaski community agencies in addressing impacts of the opioid and addiction crisis and provided impetus for expanded and ongoing work. Here, the project team reflects on how the various roles and actions of the project team and Vibrant Virginia actors have impacted the urban and rural communities of focus.

Weerts and Sandmann (2010) use a boundary spanning lens to expand on the body of literature on community engagement by research universities, which had previously focused on broader concepts of leadership and commitments to engagement. They create a typology of varying university agent boundary spanning roles including:

- **Community-based problem solvers:** University faculty and other representatives that are socially and physically connected in the communities and whose responsibilities are primarily technical and problem focused. This work was typically carried out by professional academic staff rather than traditional tenure-track faculty who are on the front lines of leading transformative changes in the communities in which they work. These actors most often enter community-level work through application of their technical skills but require interpersonal and group facilitation skills to be successful in the formation of partnerships.
- **Technical experts:** Boundary spanners with a primary practical or content-focused area of work who are more internally aligned with the university than their community-based problem solver colleagues. These agents are more typically tenure-track faculty members possessing a high level of expertise and contribute to the partnership as subject matter experts and researchers.
- **Internal engagement advocates:** Similar to technical experts, these individuals are closely engaged with the internal functions of the university institution and most normally have traditional faculty roles within a specialized area and don't usually provide direct expertise to community partners but often support or provide the resources and infrastructure for engagement.
- **Engagement champions:** Agents who have integrated roles within the community and possess both a socioemotional

and leadership task orientation. These are different from the internal agents who allocate a preponderance of their time in campus meetings and advocate for resources for engagement; champions are more likely to have a focus on external dimensions of their work through fundraising and political activities. These actors typically hold high-level roles such as the university president, vice president, and/or dean.

The boundary spanning framework and typology presented by Weerts and Sandmann (2010) is quite useful to examine the impact of the boundary spanning work conducted through the resources of Vibrant Virginia by the project team. At the leadership level of the university, engagement champions identified resources to support the Vibrant Virginia Initiative and the seed grants. These champions have remained visible as the work of Vibrant Virginia proceeds with its second year of seed grants.

In its administration of the Vibrant Virginia Initiative, the Center for Economic and Community Engagement's faculty and staff have served as internal engagement advocates, providing the scaffolding for the funded project teams and others engaged in community work to share their progress; challenges and barriers they may encounter; and mechanisms to share results. For the exchange of ideas, information, and knowledge between the university and communities throughout the state, Vibrant Virginia has sponsored a conference series, discussion boards, and targeted engagement in specific regions.

The project team and other Vibrant Virginia project teams most often include both community-based problem solvers and technical experts, with these roles sometimes intertwined. The SHFC project team, representing faculty and graduate students from public health, public policy, and human development, supported the Roanoke and Pulaski communities and their coalitions with timely, adaptive, and responsive boundary spanning work. The work was adaptive in recognizing that connecting with existing coalitions would better serve the communities rather than stretching resources to form new coalitions.

A particular observation during the course of this project and other community-based project work is that sometimes faculty may initially become involved in community projects as technical experts and cross over to become a community-based problem solver. These community relationships were strengthened by the resources provided and the valuable work conducted in partnership with the community coalitions, where partners served as facilitators of information and knowledge exchange. The relationships continue to strengthen as new initiatives resulting from this engagement continue to multiply and flourish.

Reflections and Conclusions

This particular project reinforced the university's practice of engaging with community actors when pursuing research that impacts a community. Community actors are part of the community as professionals and as citizens and best know their needs and will be the ones ultimately responsible for implementing solutions. Working collaboratively with community partners has a beneficial place in all phases of research and technical assistance conducted by universities and their individual representatives.

Though the project team initially thought they would be leading coalition development efforts in the Roanoke area, as they began their work in August 2018, the timely emergence of the RVCR efforts shifted their role to supporting the new coalition. This change also impacted their planned processes and timeline and enlarged the area of focus from Roanoke City to the Roanoke Valley. This adaptation meant that secondary research and primary engagement had to occur concurrently rather than through a more phased approach as proposed in the original scope of work. This responsive change resulted in improved value to the information the project team collected and the information they shared, allowing improved knowledge transfer between the university representatives and the community.

Likewise, in Pulaski, the project team sought to build on the existing and ongoing work of PCPC. With limited time, staff, and fiscal support, the momentum garnered in Roanoke drew a preponderance of the project team's resources toward the momentum of the RVCR efforts. This provides an observation to be explored further regarding how the resource imbalance between rural and urban communities creates an inertia that is difficult to overcome even with target effort and plans to provide more equitable support from the university. Researchers and funders should be more intentional in recognizing inherent barriers to engagement in rural communities and allocate additional effort and resources to ensure thorough engagement practices.

Involvement in community-engaged work takes time and trust with the community and its organizations and organizational agents to make university-community collaborations possible and successful. Engaging with trusted community leaders across demographic and sectoral boundaries in rural and urban communities should be a first step for university agents to create a stable bridge to communities. Sustained boundary spanning relationships cannot begin and end with a grant funding cycle. A major consideration when conducting community-engaged research and technical assistance is that research funding may run out before the work is complete, but it is imperative to maintain the community relationships that are formed and follow through with the project outcomes to the fullest extent possible. As representatives of a land grant institution seeking to be boundary spanners, project team members must not only be agents of sound and ethical engagement practices but remain faithful stewards of their community relationships.

Finding and achieving long-term solutions to the addiction crisis will require an engaged, coordinated, and comprehensive approach between public and private entities, representing all sectors. These efforts and solutions must be adapted to the differences between our rural and urban communities, while finding and strengthening the ties that bind these communities together. Looking beyond our own organizational and geographic boundaries, achievements, and needs is vital to creating a coordinated and sustained response. This was achieved with great success in 1944 during and after the invasion of Normandy and with renewed commitment should be attainable in 2021.

Chapter 14

Local Policy Agendas and Public Health Priorities

Stephanie L. Smith, Abdulilah Alshenaifi, Elizabeth Arledge, Thomas Layou, James McConkie, Nhung Nguyen, Benjamin Packard, Aditya Sai Phutane, Md Ashiqur Rab, Amady Sogodogo, and Joanne Tang

This chapter reports on an exploratory study that highlights many diseases, risks, and other health issues that have appeared on agendas of local governing bodies across the Commonwealth of Virginia in recent years and the nature of commitments backing that status. It shows that NCDs and related risks, mental health, and broader healthy community initiatives are significant agenda items in rural and urban areas. Notable differences in the nature of commitments across urban and rural jurisdictions may point to differences in community needs, interests, and governmental capacities to address them, potentially reflecting and having implications for their economic vitality. The chapter concludes by discussing the implications of the findings and opportunities for future research.

Public health challenges related to opioid and other substance use disorders, vaping, mental and behavioral health disorders, and an aging population have emerged alongside a number of chronic and high-burden conditions, including but not limited to cardiovascular disease, cancer, diabetes, and chronic respiratory and Alzheimer's disease. All take a significant toll on families and communities. While state and local health departments play important roles in addressing such problems, so do locally elected governing bodies with the authority to enact health promoting ordinances, such as those limiting tobacco use in public spaces and those facilitating physical activity (Librett, Yore, and Schmid 2003; Rogers and Peterson 2008), with implications for the economic vitality of rural and urban jurisdictions. Good health is linked with economic growth (Bloom, Canning, and Sevilla 2004). The agenda-setting dynamics surrounding local tobacco control ordinances have received a good deal of research attention (Samuels and Glantz 1991; Shipan and Volden 2008; Traynor, Begay, and Glantz 1993), but there has been little inquiry into which and how a broader set of health conditions and diseases reach the agendas of city councils and boards of supervisors.

This chapter reports on an exploratory study that highlights many diseases, risks, and other health issues that have appeared on the agendas of local governing bodies across the Commonwealth of Virginia in recent years and the nature of commitments backing that status. It offers preliminary insights into factors that bring health issues onto the agenda in these venues and into how these agendas comport with community health priorities in urban and rural areas. Urban and rural areas are defined using 2010 US Census measures of population density (US Census 2010). The chapter aims to inform those engaged in local health policymaking and to address gaps in agenda-setting scholarship, which tends to focus on higher levels of government.

The findings largely draw from publicly accessible meeting minutes from six city councils and ten county boards of supervisors representing seven urban and nine rural areas across eight regions of Virginia during the first half of 2020. The chapter covers the five-year period between 2015 and 2019. It finds commonalities and some variation in the representation of health issues and types of commitments, with implications for rural and urban health and economic inequities. Findings concerning factors shaping the status of issues and the intersection between governmental agendas and community health priorities are more preliminary but set the stage for further inquiry.

The chapter first discusses scholarship that forms the foundation for this approach to studying health agenda setting and adaptations for research at the local level. It then describes methods of data collection and analysis, followed by a presentation of findings by jurisdiction. In the concluding sections, insights into the kinds of factors that brought health issues onto the agendas of rural and urban local governing bodies are offered, as is a discussion of the implications of the findings and opportunities for future research.

LOCAL HEALTH AGENDA SETTING

Agenda setting is understood by scholars of the policy process as a precursor to policy adoption, implementation, and evaluation (Adolino and Blake 2010). The agenda is the list of problems to which policymakers and people with whom they work are paying serious attention at any given time (Kingdon 1995). Researchers often track debates and hearings, the introduction of bills, the enactment of laws and judicial rules, and budget allocations to inform analyses of the agenda (Baumgartner, Jones, and Mortensen 2018). At the local level, announcements, reports from officials, declarations, proclamations, resolutions, budget allocations, ordinances, and other policy actions may be tracked for the same purposes.

This research draws upon a framework developed by Fox and colleagues (2011, 2015) to help gauge the depth of political commitments underpinning status indicators (table 14.1). The framework includes stated (expressed, verbal declarations), demonstrated institutional (supporting policies and organizational infrastructure), and budgetary commitments (earmarked resource allocations). Stated commitments are often largely symbolic and of limited consequence. Commitments that require the allocation of material resources are considered more objective indicators of status (Fox et al. 2011).

Problems succeed and fail in gaining traction on governmental agendas for various reasons, including evidence establishing that problems are severe, the existence of feasible solutions, political transitions, public opinion, policy entrepreneurs, advocacy coalitions, focusing events, media coverage, issue frames, norms, and several mechanisms of diffusion, among others (Baumgartner and Jones 1993; Heikkila et al. 2014; Kingdon 1995; Sabatier and Weible 2007; Stokes Berry and Berry 2018). Multiple factors are typically at work, interacting over extended periods of time to shape the trajectory of issues on agendas and through other stages of the policy process. Policy agendas are generally characterized by stability that is punctuated by periods of rapid change (Baumgartner and Jones 1993).

Table 14.1. Political Commitments and Indicators of Status on the Governmental Agenda

Political Commitments	Governmental Agenda Status Indicators
Expressed	Announcements
	Briefings/reports
	Proclamations
	Declarations
Institutional	Municipal code, ordinance, or other policy change
	Resolutions
Budgetary	Budget action

Note: Status indicators include items introduced, discussed, and acted on (voted up or down) during council and board meetings, as reflected in meeting minutes.

Policy entrepreneurs, champions who invest their time, energy, and other resources in advancing a cause, often play critical roles in bringing problems and solutions to policymakers (Kingdon 1995). Such champions can be in or out of government, hold elected or appointed positions, or can be members of interest groups or research organizations. Focusing events—sudden, uncommon, and harmful events like mass shootings, hurricanes, oil spills, and infectious disease pandemics—also prompt movement toward policy change (Birkland 1998, 2007).

Policymakers are also observed to learn from, imitate, compete with, and be coerced by other governments (Stokes Berry and Berry 2018); the four mechanisms of diffusion affected the rise of local antismoking policies prior to 2000 (Shipan and Volden 2008). A policy diffuses via learning when "decision makers simplify the task of finding a solution by choosing an alternative that has proven successful elsewhere" (Berry and Baybeck 2005, 505). Diffusion via imitation occurs when policies are copied without regard to effectiveness but rather to appear that they are keeping up with (aspirational) peers. Diffusion via competition occurs when governments are motivated to gain financial advantage—or at least not accrue disadvantage. Coercive mechanisms of diffusion involve incentives, such as grant-in-aid programs, and mandates, such as state laws prohibiting smoking in public places (Shipan and Volden 2008).

Which public health challenges are on the agendas of local governing bodies, what brings them onto the agenda, what kinds of commitments underpin their status, and how do governmental agendas comport with community priorities for health in rural and urban areas? Systematic analysis of meeting minutes from a subset of sixteen governing bodies, with rural and urban pairs representing eight regions of Virginia, was conducted in order to gain preliminary insights into these research questions. Jurisdictions were selected on the basis of geographic diversity and rural-urban contrast within each region. Prominence (e.g., Richmond, Fairfax) and data availability also factored into some selection decisions. Included are six urban cities (Richmond, Roanoke, Danville, Virginia Beach, Harrisonburg, Bristol), one urban county (Fairfax), and nine rural counties (Nelson, Appomattox, Lunenburg, Mathews, Essex, Accomack, Bland, Page, Rappahannock) (table 14.2). All regular meeting minutes available online between 2015 and 2019 were analyzed. Agendas were also cross-referenced with the minutes to document public comments and other details as needed.

Table 14.2. Descriptive Statistics for Rural and Urban Jurisdictions					
Regions	Jurisdictions	Population	Rural (%)	Total meetings	Meetings with health on the agenda (%)
Central	Richmond	204,214	0	124	69
	Nelson	15,020	100	84	5
West Central	Roanoke	97,032	0	124	47
	Appomattox	14,973	100	52	48
Southside	Danville	43,055	4.50	121	76
	Lunenburg	12,194	100	72	43
Hampton Roads	Virginia Beach	437,994	1.50	156	42
	Mathews	8,978	100	60	18

Eastern	Essex	11,151	77	60	27
	Accomack	33,164	100	60	53
Southwest	Bristol	17,835	0	116	39
	Bland	6,824	100	70	54%
Valley	Harrisonburg	48,914	0	115	7
	Page	24,042	80	57	21
Northern	Fairfax	1,081,699	1.40	86	91
	Rappahannock	7,373	100	63	59
Averages	Urban	275,820	1	120	63
	Rural	14,858	95	64	42
Ranges	Urban	17,835–1,081,699	0–1.5	86–156	39–91
	Rural	6,824–24,042	77–100	52–84	18–59

Sources: Population data and rural assessments come from the 2010 US Census (https://www2.census.gov/geo/docs/reference/ua/)

The data offer important insights into which health issues are on governmental agendas, but they do not provide a full representation. Responsibility for community health is also distributed among local, regional, and state agencies. State and federal laws, such as those restricting alcohol and tobacco use, sometimes preempt local policymaking. And community members may champion their issues in other venues.

Taking Stock of Governmental Agendas for Health in the Commonwealth of Virginia

To summarize, between 2015 and 2019, major noncommunicable diseases (NCDs, such as heart disease, stroke, and cancer) and related risks, healthy community initiatives, and mental health were among the top five issues in both rural and urban jurisdictions (figure 14.1). Addiction and injuries round out the top five in rural areas while traffic safety and vulnerable populations (primarily senior, homeless, disabled, and inmate groups) do in urban areas. Forty-five percent of all political commitments to health were expressed, 28% budgetary and 23% institutional; 4% were uncategorized. Rural jurisdictions featured a greater proportion

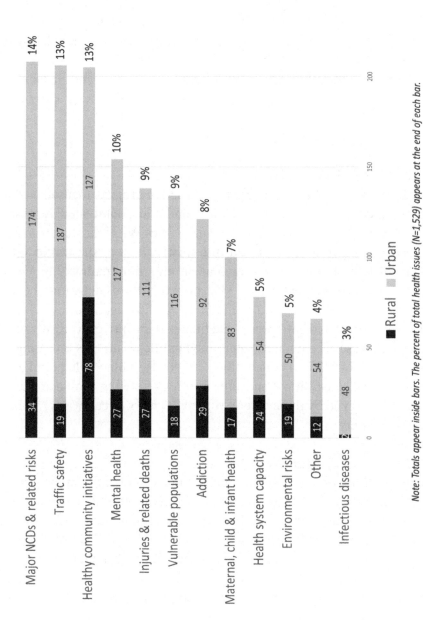

Figure 14.1. Representation of health issues in rural and urban jurisdictions

of expressed commitments and urban jurisdictions greater proportions of institutional and budgetary commitments (figure 14.2). Some of the variation observed in types of commitments reflect differences in how official meeting minutes are recorded, with some adhering to a more formal record of decisions (as in Richmond) while others include a wider range of announcements, reports, discussions, and proclamations.

Issue-specific findings are highlighted by region and jurisdiction alongside some preliminary explanatory insights in the paragraphs below.

Central Region

CITY OF RICHMOND (URBAN)

Traffic safety, consisting mostly of construction projects focused on sidewalks, bike lanes, pedestrian walkways, and trails, dominated, representing 42% of all council actions on health issues. Virginia Department of Transportation funding factored into nearly 70% of the traffic safety agenda items, pointing to coercion as an important pathway to agenda status. NCDs and related risks (13%, about two-thirds nutrition), healthy community initiatives (10%), mental health (8%), and injuries (7%) followed. Coercive and entrepreneurial financial incentives were at work in several of these. The council entertained public comments on a range of issues, with four (27%) concerning services for vulnerable populations (persons with disabilities) and four injuries related to violence leading the way, followed by three on environmental risks (clean water) and two on traffic safety.

NELSON COUNTY (RURAL)

Healthy community initiatives appeared most frequently on the governmental agenda (30%), featuring reports from the Virginia Department of Health, applications for federal funding for recreational trails development (coercion), resolutions in support of Fair Housing Month, camping and flood zone ordinances, among others. Environmental risks (16%, including water quality, waste disposal, and sanitation plans), maternal and child health (14%, school health reports, recognizing Child Abuse Awareness Month), mental health (12%, including reports on crisis intervention teams and by the Community Services Board), and addiction (8%) rounded out the top five. Accounting for more than two-thirds of

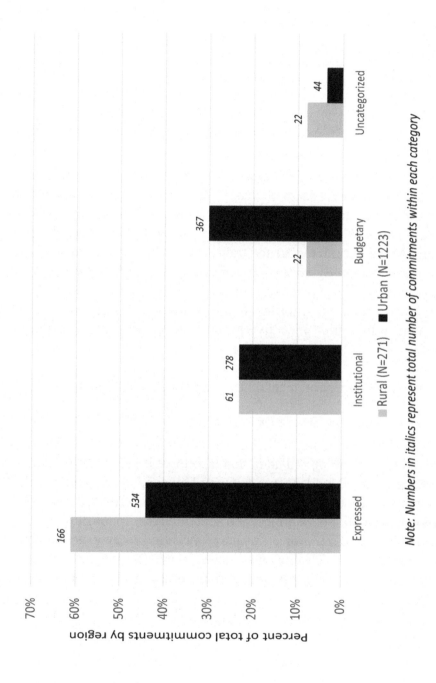

Figure 14.2. Distribution of political commitments in urban and rural jurisdictions

public comments on health issues, the board registered six on water and sanitation, four on vulnerable populations, three concerning violence-related injuries, and two each on mental health, nutrition (NCD-related risks), and broader community health issues.

West Central Region

CITY OF ROANOKE (URBAN)

Approximately 30% of the council's health actions were allocated to NCDs and related risks, with nearly 80% of these supporting nutrition programs incentivized by federal grants. Injuries and deaths related to gun violence and drug addiction each accounted for 17% of health agenda items. Mental health (13%) and traffic safety (9%) were also among the five most frequently addressed health issues. The City Council made announcements in support of National Gun Violence Awareness Day in 2017, 2018, and 2019; formed a gun violence task force in 2019; and responded to a grant incentive program (coercion) from the Virginia Department of Criminal Justice Services in 2019. The council entertained a host of public comments concerning gun violence ($N = 12$), with one additional comment on mental health and one on drug addiction.

APPOMATTOX COUNTY (RURAL)

Drug addiction appeared on the agenda most frequently (29%). The county moved to form an opioid addiction task force between 2016 and 2018 and appropriated funds (some supported by donations) to the D.A.R.E. program. Promoting healthy community initiatives (21%), the board was briefed on a major park project and supported the Appomattox Heritage and Recreation Trail project, which is incentivized by matching grants from the Federal Lands Program and the Virginia Department of Transportation. Injuries and injury-related deaths (tornado recovery and domestic violence) attracted 19% of the board's attention to all health issues. NCDs and related risks (14%, nearly all promoting exercise) and traffic safety (7%) rounded out the top five. In 2017, public comments provided an update on work to help residents affected by a February 2016 tornado.

Southside Region

DANVILLE CITY (URBAN)

Nearly a quarter of the City Council's health agenda was NCDs and related risks, with half on nutrition, exercise, and reducing obesity (many influenced by federal financial incentives) and approximately 40% on cancer awareness and fundraising events that imitate commonly organized events. Healthy community initiatives (15%, two-thirds for a bike share program and the Riverwalk Trail project, which was incentivized by funds offered by state agencies and charitable organizations) followed. Vulnerable populations (13%, primarily awareness events and funding for senior and disabled community services), addiction (10%), and environmental risks (9%), rounded out the top five. Entrepreneurial council members and imitative and coercive processes helped to bring many of these issues onto the agenda. Water quality stayed on the agenda throughout the study period due to a major coal ash spill on the Dan River in 2014, with the issue attracting five public comments. The council heard one public comment each on noise pollution and traffic safety.

LUNENBURG COUNTY (RURAL)
Primarily focused on improving healthcare infrastructure and equipment, a variety of health system capacity issues (41%) dominated the governmental agenda for health in Lunenburg County; state financial incentives were instrumental in some of these. Traffic safety (15%, with speed and alcohol selective enforcement incentivized by Department of Motor Vehicles Highway Safety Grants, work zone recognition, and mud and snow hazards receiving attention), vulnerable populations (12%, with senior resource programming incentivized by Older Americans Act funding), and mental health and injuries (9% each) rounded out the top five. Five public comments supported industrial hemp production for its therapeutic benefits, four addressed noise pollution, and three spoke to gun- and traffic-related injuries and deaths.

Hampton Roads Region

CITY OF VIRGINIA BEACH (URBAN)
Mental health was a steady presence on the agenda that drew regular budget allocations between 2015 and 2018 (28%). The issue's status rose following a mass shooting that injured four and killed twelve (not including the shooter) on May 31, 2019. One-third of all attention and resource allocations to mental health occurred after the focusing event,

including resolutions encouraging the state's general assembly to increase mental health service support, approving contracts and budget allocations for mental health service provision locally, and placing the issue on the council's 2020 agenda. With a major biomedical research and healthcare initiative spearheaded by the mayor (a policy entrepreneur), health system capacity was also high on the agenda (21%). Child health (11%) featured significant budgetary commitments incentivized by grants from the Landmark Foundation to the Department of Public Health for the Baby Care Program and from the Virginia Alcohol Beverage Control Commission for a youth leadership program. NCDs and related risks (11%, including exercise, cardiovascular disease and hypertension, cancer, nutrition, and tobacco), and addiction (10%, with budget allocations supporting prevention, recovery, and training for Naloxone use in 2017 incentivized by state funds) rounded out the five leading health issues on the governmental agenda. Two public comments were registered on a proposal to build a public fitness park.

MATHEWS COUNTY (RURAL)
Only four health issues were represented on the governmental agenda in Mathews County, with health appearing infrequently (N = 12). The majority (50%) pertained to healthy community initiatives, including discussions of community health and safety, building safety, and budget support for a new YMCA building to provide emergency shelter. A quarter covered health system capacity issues, including reports on an emergency medical dispatch program and resolutions on broadband internet as essential infrastructure for emergency services and healthcare. Environmental risks came in third with 17%. The board also received a briefing on traffic safety mitigation (8%). In 2018, a member of the public asked the board to provide safe drinking water in schools and the courthouse area.

Eastern Region

ESSEX COUNTY (MOSTLY RURAL)
Health issues came onto the agenda of the board infrequently (N = 16). Drug addiction (25%, including budget support for a regional drug court initiative) and healthy community initiatives (25%, featuring declarations of support for parks and recreation and trail development) were

the lead issues, followed by vulnerable populations (13%, addressing inmate health and nursing homes). A canned food drive announcement (addressing an NCD risk factor), approval of a mental health contract incentivized by state funding, and a tornado response briefing (injuries and injury-related deaths) filled out the agenda (6% each). One public comment urged the board to support dental and vision care.

ACCOMACK COUNTY (RURAL)
Bordering the Atlantic Ocean, Accomack County is subject to frequent and intense seasonal storms that factored into elevating the status of injuries and injury-related deaths (24%) on the board's agenda, which featured a number of emergency declarations, amended ordinances, and relief and recovery team recognition. NCDs and related risks also featured prominently (24%), led by annual allocations to nutrition programs incentivized by federal funding. Healthy community initiatives (17%, notably including yearly resolutions supporting a community health fair held at the annual Juneteenth festival), other (12%, featuring declarations of support for National Safe Boating Month), and health system capacity (7%) rounded out the governmental agenda. One public comment was registered—an invitation to a Community Opioid Forum (addiction).

Southwest Region

CITY OF BRISTOL (URBAN)
Healthy community initiatives, particularly the development of walking and biking trails, improved sidewalks, and events (5Ks) were well represented on the council's agenda (31% of health issues). NCDs and related risk factors (19%, two-thirds on amending a tobacco tax ordinance), child health (16%, including attention to child endangerment, premature birth, passenger safety, and adoption awareness), addiction (15%, with a focus on recovery support, some incentivized by new federal regulations and Substance Abuse and Mental Health Services Administration funding), and mental health services (4%) rounded out the top five health items on the governmental agenda. Five public comments were recorded, including on exercise, noise pollution, mental health, health services, and a trail project.

BLAND COUNTY (RURAL)
More than 40% of the governmental agenda focused on healthy community initiatives by facilitating physical activity. The board entertained regular updates on the Rocky Gap Greenway Project (started in 2012 with substantial funding support from the Virginia Department of Transportation and the Wythe-Bland Foundation). NCDs and related risk factors (16%, nearly half waiving fees for cancer awareness and fundraising events), vulnerable populations (12%, two-thirds proclamations recognizing Autism Awareness Month and one item approving budget to improve disabled access to polling places), environmental health (10%, including water system updates and burn bans during dangerously dry conditions), and proclamations on drug addiction and child health (8% each) rounded out the top health agenda items. A single public comment concerning cleanliness in schools was registered.

Valley Region

CITY OF HARRISONBURG (URBAN)
Traffic safety (19%), encompassing checkpoints, training, clearing roads, and managing event traffic, was the most prevalent health issue. Grant incentives (coercion) factored into about one quarter of traffic safety items. Vulnerable populations (15%) also appeared relatively frequently. Concerns for inmate health at the Middle River Regional Jail were raised four times. The council also expressed support for events raising awareness about autism, Alzheimer's disease, and senior health. Several healthy community initiatives (walk, run, bike, and parks events) (14%), NCD awareness and fundraising events with a strong emphasis on cancer (12%), and mental health service provision (9%, with budget allocations supported by Community Service Board grants) also appeared on the governmental agenda. Eighty-five public comments on health issues were recorded, with more than one-third brought by a single community member concerned with vulnerable populations, particularly the homeless, and nutrition; 60% of all public comments pertained to these two issues. Traffic safety (14%) and mental health (8%) fell into relatively distant third and fourth places.

PAGE COUNTY (RURAL)
Health issues appeared less frequently on the agenda in Page County (N = 6) than in any other jurisdiction. Traffic safety (widening or adding passing lanes and street paving) appeared twice (33%). Appearing once each, mental health (School Resource Officers training), vulnerable populations (inmate safety), healthy community initiatives (amendments to a festival ordinance discussed), and recognition of emergency medical services and volunteers rounded out the governmental health agenda. Public comments raised the following issues: traffic safety (N = 3); environmental risks (N = 3); other (N = 3, concerning unknown potential harms of solar arrays).

Northern Region

FAIRFAX COUNTY (URBAN)
The governmental agenda for health was relatively robust, with the board taking more actions of any kind in Fairfax County (N = 392) than in any other jurisdiction, with 60% in the form of expressed commitments. No single issue dominated the health agenda. Vulnerable populations appeared most frequently (14%, about half proclamations, focusing on disability awareness and services, followed by senior health and abuse). Injuries (9%, focusing on domestic violence and sexual assault awareness), and infectious diseases (9%, mostly proclamations raising awareness of immunization, disease carrying insects, and HIV/AIDS) were the next most prevalent health issues. Mental health (11.5%, mostly awareness) and child health (10.7%, with emphasis on Head Start programs) followed. There were fifteen public comments on health issues, with one-third on vulnerable populations (including immigrants, seniors, people with developmental disabilities, and those experiencing homelessness), 20% on health system capacity issues, and the remainder dispersed among domestic violence, mental health, addiction, and marijuana legalization.

RAPPAHANNOCK COUNTY (RURAL)
Mental health (27%) was the leading issue, with particular attention to bullying and counseling for students and budget appropriations to support service delivery. Healthy community initiatives were a close second (25%), with entrepreneurs from Rapp Trails helping keep a multiuse trail on the agenda. NCDs and related risks (11%, with entrepreneurs

garnering a proclamation for Food Pantry Month and Day and briefings on the county schools' Farm to Table program bringing nutrition into the spotlight) came in third. Addiction and traffic safety (9%) rounded out the top five. Public comments (N = 19, 73%) focused overwhelmingly on the multiuse trails proposal, followed by four comments on environmental health issues (15%).

Factors Shaping Council and Board Agendas for Health in the Commonwealth

Several factors that commonly influence policy agendas, including policy entrepreneurship, diffusion, and focusing events were observed. Findings provide some preliminary insights to types of factors at work based on analysis of meeting minutes, which vary considerably by jurisdiction in details captured. Causal insights are typically captured through in-depth case study research. Evidence of agenda-setting factors alongside nearly 60% of 1,529 health issue observations demonstrates the potential of this approach to complement case studies. For now, these findings provide preliminary insights into health agenda-setting dynamics in the sixteen governing bodies included in this chapter. Rural-urban dynamics appear to play limited roles in shaping differences in these jurisdictions, except in the case of coercive diffusion.

Various health issues came onto the agenda via three entrepreneurial pathways, including classical policy entrepreneurship (N = 27) and two that are underrecognized in policy process scholarship—participatory entrepreneurship (N = 219) and entrepreneurial grantmaking (N = 41). For example, functioning as classic policy entrepreneurs (Kingdon 1995), the mayor of Virginia Beach championed a biomedical research initiative that the City Council engaged several times between 2015 and 2019 and a Danville city council member urged action on the community's opioid crisis between 2018 and 2019. Policy entrepreneurs also promoted awareness of domestic violence and the opioid crisis in Appomattox County in 2017 and health systems support in Lunenburg County in 2019.

Second, individuals and organized groups engaged in participatory entrepreneurship, using venues for public participation such as hearings and comment periods to advance issues. For instance, the Rappahannock County Board of Supervisors passed a resolution in support of a multiuse trail initiative in 2017. Representatives of the Rapp Trails Coalition played strong entrepreneurial roles in 2017 and 2018, speaking on behalf of the initiative, acquiring an $800,000 grant from the Virginia Department of Transportation, and raising more than the 20% matching funds required to support the grant (Hardee 2018). The board withdrew its support for the initiative in late 2018, however.

Participatory entrepreneurship factored into the agenda in three other jurisdictions. In the City of Harrisonburg, one resident persistently spoke out to draw support for a food drive initiative and the vulnerable populations it serves—he accounted for 37% of eighty-five public comments recorded during the study period. Harrisonburg community members registered fourteen public comments that reframed a 2019 traffic safety ordinance prohibiting panhandling in medians (Section 16-6-61 Restriction of Pedestrians Within Public Rights of Way at Designated Locations) as one diminishing the ability of homeless people to acquire resources for food and shelter. A council member acknowledged their concerns, recognizing implications beyond traffic safety. The council tabled the proposal. Participatory entrepreneurship also drew attention to environmental health (Nelson), gun violence (Roanoke), and industrial hemp production (Lunenburg).

It was a surprise to observe entrepreneurial grantmaking by nonprofit organizations and charitable foundations. Grantmaking organizations used monetary incentives of $1,500 to $300,000 to persuade local governing bodies to take up a wide range of health issues, including nutrition, drug addiction, parks, recreation, and fitness. Entrepreneurial grantmaking factored into health agenda setting in four urban (Richmond, Danville, Fairfax, Virginia Beach) and three rural (Rappahannock, Appomattox, Bland) jurisdictions. Agenda-setting scholarship has largely overlooked such dynamics, though scholarship on grantmaking foundations has observed their use of soft and hard policy tools like funding (Elson and Hall 2016).

There was substantial evidence to show that coercive ($N = 218$) and imitative ($N = 347$) mechanisms of diffusion shape the health agendas of local governing bodies in Virginia; evidence of learning ($N = 2$) and competitive ($N = 3$) mechanisms of diffusion was limited. With respect to the coercive power of the state and federal governments, financial incentives ($N = 204$) outpaced legal mandates ($N = 14$). Financial incentives factored most frequently into the appearance of drug and alcohol addiction (33% of all addiction observations); traffic safety (21%); maternal and child health (20%); mental health (19%); and vulnerable populations (12%). Nearly 90% of all observations of coercion via financial incentives occurred in the six largest jurisdictions (Richmond, Fairfax County, Danville, Virginia Beach, Harrisonburg, and Roanoke). This likely reflects the capacity of large, urban governments to seek and administer such funds, raising questions about access to such resources for rural jurisdictions with significant needs and more limited economic resources.

Imitation, which entails copying others irrespective of effectiveness, was the most common form of diffusion observed. Most councils and boards made announcements, entertained briefs, and issued proclamations and declarations recognizing high-profile awareness- and fund-raising events on issues like cancer (15%), vulnerable populations (13%), infectious diseases (10%), and injuries (10%, mostly domestic violence). A small proportion (5%) imitated closer-to-home policies, programs, and projects, such as Danville's bike share initiative and consideration of a cigarette tax. Imitative diffusion was primarily connected with expressed commitments (83%), such as proclamations, and it was more common in urban than rural jurisdictions. Fairfax County accounted for 60% of all observations.

Evidence of learning from what others have found effective was limited to two cases in Rappahannock County (supporting multiuse trails and fighting opioid addiction). Competitive mechanisms were in evidence as Virginia Beach considered a proposal to create a fitness park to help the city maintain its Facebook rank as the "fittest city" in the United States and as Bland County considered its authority to tax tobacco products in efforts to prevent other jurisdictions from gaining advantage. The impacts of learning and competition as mechanisms of diffusion may be underrepresented in the meeting minutes that we analyzed.

Large- and small-scale focusing events ($N = 44$) also shaped agendas. Winter storms and hurricanes prompted the Accomack County Board of Supervisors to declare local emergencies and advance preparation and recovery plans to limit injuries and deaths. Gun-related injuries and deaths came onto the agenda following mass shootings in Dallas, Texas, in 2016 (Harrisonburg), Parkland, Florida, in 2018 (Harrisonburg and Rappahannock), and Virginia Beach in 2019 (Danville, Harrisonburg, and

Virginia Beach, with the latter also allocating attention to mental health). The Duke Energy coal ash spill in 2014 had regional impacts that shaped the Danville City Council's agenda for several years, drawing attention to water quality monitoring and remediation. Lastly, in 2016, a Zika Virus outbreak concentrated in South and Central America received attention during a briefing for the Nelson County Board of Supervisors.

Conclusion

This chapter offered preliminary insights into which and how a varied set of health issues reached the agendas of city councils and boards of supervisors in Virginia. It showed that NCDs and related risks, mental health, and broader healthy community initiatives were significant agenda items in rural and urban areas. The frequent appearance of addiction and injuries on the agenda in rural jurisdictions while traffic safety and vulnerable populations appeared more frequently in urban jurisdictions may point to differences in community needs, interests, and governmental capacities to address them, potentially reflecting and having implications for their economic vitality. The work also revealed that local governing bodies commit substantial institutional and budgetary resources to address health issues—though less costly expressed commitments comprise the greatest share.

Though limited, findings concerning factors that bring health issues onto the agenda had important implications for policymakers and for scholarship. First, coercive financial incentives factored into the health agendas of governing bodies in urban areas much more frequently than in rural areas, highlighting an important economic divide. Unless disparities in the use of state and federal grant programs are addressed in other forums, such as state health departments and community health boards, they have the potential to exacerbate urban-rural health and economic inequities. Second, while high-profile and widespread awareness- and fund-raising events often attracted expressed commitments, their roles in drawing institutional and budgetary commitments that affect systemic changes in prevention and access to treatment and care beg further investigation. Lastly, the findings raised important questions about the prevalence, roles, quality, and legitimacy of entrepreneurial grantmaking and participation in shaping local health policy agendas, and their effects on the economic vitality of communities.

Chapter 15

Improving Regional Air Service in a Rural-Metropolitan Area

Nicholas J. Swartz, Justin Bullman, and Jordan Hays

This chapter provides a detailed account of how members of the Shenandoah Valley Regional Airport and James Madison University collaborated to create the Fly SHD Community Air Service Task Force. The authors describe the task force's efforts to bolster local air service, educate residents and institutions, and improve the economic outlook of nearby urban and rural communities. The chapter includes insights from task force members who share lessons they learned through their involvement and the impacts each of them saw as a result of their collaboration. Though the focus of this chapter is on the task force's ability to galvanize regional support to enhance air service in and out of the Shenandoah Valley, the approach will likely serve as a model to other communities looking for ways to bolster and advance their own economic competitiveness.

Most people are familiar with the massive international airports like Washington Dulles or Chicago O'Hare and the myriad destinations they can go to from them. They provide a connection to the whole world, facilitating international business, immigration, and leisure travel. They amaze with jumbo jets and seemingly impossible infrastructure. All too often, however, people overlook the smaller regional airports in their own backyard. Just as interstates made long-distance travel faster and more convenient while stimulating the economy and communities along them, so too can quality local air service. Virginia residents are lucky to have numerous regional airports, as are the people and institutions who come here to do business.

On a broader scale, local air service can be an important factor in addressing the urban-rural divide. Virginia is unique among other states in that the state constitution has specifically accounted for this divide through the creation of independent cities. In fact, revisions made to the state's constitution in 1871 established all cities as independent of their surrounding or adjacent counties. This includes the separation of city and county governments as well as property taxes and services. Of the forty-one independent cities across the nation, thirty-eight are located here. The distinction is not arbitrary and allows for county governments to focus solely on the needs of rural residents and less densely populated towns while city governments address the specific needs of urban areas (Peaslee and Swartz 2014). While this model can be beneficial regarding issues like funding, urban sprawl, or conflicts of interest, it can't account for everything. Isolation and access to resources are consistent concerns in rural areas—especially in the modern, global economy—and this only serves to highlight the growing necessity of local air service.

Regional airlines provide critical links connecting communities to national and international air transport networks and the vast economic benefits that connectivity brings (Green 2017; Halpern and Brathen 2011; Ozcan 2014; Wong 2018). As the president of the Regional Airline Association, Roger Cohen, said, "In today's global economy, the only two things a community must have are an Internet connection and scheduled air service" (Kaufman 2013). As a result of the partnership among United Airlines, SkyWest, and SHD, Shenandoah Valley residents and visitors now have the benefit of reliable jet service and convenient access to United's global network of flights through two well-connected hubs (Urenko 2020).

This chapter provides a detailed account of how members of the Shenandoah Valley Regional Airport (SHD) and James Madison University came together and recruited community leaders to bolster local air service, educate residents and institutions, and improve the economic outlook of the region, both urban and rural, through the creation of the Fly SHD Community Air Service Task Force. Direct input from task force members was collected to share lessons they learned through their involvement and the impacts each of them saw as a result of their collaboration. Though the focus of this chapter is on the task force's ability to galvanize regional support to enhance air service in and out of the Shenandoah Valley, the approach used may serve as a model to other communities across Virginia, regardless of population or size, to help bolster and advance economic competitiveness in their area.

Shenandoah Valley and Local Air Service

Classified as a Primary Non-hub Commercial Service Airport by the Federal Aviation Administration, Shenandoah Valley Regional Airport provides general aviation services and commercial air service, subsidized by the Essential Air Service (EAS) program, to Harrisonburg, Staunton, Waynesboro, and surrounding areas (Shenandoah Valley Regional Airport n.d.; US Department of Transportation 2020; Virginia Department of Aviation 2018). One of sixty-six public use airports in Virginia, SHD is one of only nine Virginia airports with commercial air service (Virginia Department of Aviation 2018). According to preliminary data from the Federal Aviation Administration, SHD enplaned 17,584 passengers in 2019, the highest number in airport history and an increase of 44.38% from 2018 (US Department of Transportation 2020).

As its name suggests, the Shenandoah Valley Regional Airport is located in the Shenandoah Valley. The Shenandoah Valley is a 4,264-square-mile region between the Blue Ridge and Allegheny mountains in historic and scenic west-central Virginia. In addition to its Civil War history, the Shenandoah Valley is known for the Blue Ridge Mountains, Shenandoah National Park, the Shenandoah River, and breathtaking mountain and farm views. The Shenandoah Valley includes seven counties (Augusta, Bath, Highland, Page, Rockbridge, Rockingham, and Shenandoah), five independent cities (Buena Vista, Harrisonburg, Lexington, Staunton, and Waynesboro), and two distinct metro areas: Harrisonburg-Rockingham MSA, and Staunton-Augusta-Waynesboro MSA (Shenandoah Valley Partnership n.d.; Virginia Economic Development Partnership n.d.).

Located off Exit 235 on I-81 in Weyers Cave, SHD is conveniently located to serve communities across the Shenandoah Valley and beyond.

Situated in Augusta County—in the northwest portion of Virginia—SHD is approximately four miles northeast of the City of Staunton, twenty miles northwest of the City of Waynesboro, sixteen miles southwest of the City of Harrisonburg, and two miles southwest of the community of Weyers Cave. Passengers from all three cities—Staunton, Waynesboro, and Harrisonburg—can reach SHD in fifteen to twenty minutes by car (Shenandoah Valley Regional Airport 2017).

Two federal interstate highways—I-81 and I-64—converge in Staunton. Other significant roadways in the region include US Highways 33, 250, 340, and 256, as well as the scenic Skyline Drive and Blue Ridge Parkway. CSX and Norfolk-Southern also connect the Shenandoah Valley to major markets in the US by rail (Shenandoah Valley Partnership n.d.; Virginia Economic Development Partnership n.d.).

The fact that SHD serves multiple counties, cities, and metropolitan areas is by design. The General Assembly created the Shenandoah Valley Joint Airport Commission (now known as the Shenandoah Valley Airport Commission) in 1956 to provide air service for communities west of the Blue Ridge Mountains (1956 Acts of Assembly, c. 628). The General Assembly recognized that despite the proximity of the Shenandoah Valley to the Charlottesville-Albemarle Airport (CHO), geographic barriers made travel from the Shenandoah Valley to Charlottesville for passenger air service a challenge. Even after the completion of I-64 through Afton Gap in the early seventies, fog and ice continue to make the journey to CHO difficult for passengers who must cross the Blue Ridge. Since CHO serves communities east of the Blue Ridge, only jurisdictions west of the Blue Ridge are represented on the Shenandoah Valley Airport Commission. The commission, an independent political subdivision of the counties of Augusta and Rockingham and the cities of Harrisonburg, Staunton, and Waynesboro, considered the accessibility of the airport from each of these communities when selecting Weyers Cave as the site for SHD (Grymes n.d.).

SHD began passenger air service in 1960. During the airport's first decade, the commission replaced the farmhouse that initially housed airport operations with a terminal and extended the runway twice (Grymes n.d.). As a result of subsequent expansion over the decades, the airport now consists of 433 acres. General aviation services, representing 92% of SHD airport operations, include support services to transient corporate and private aircraft and nearly ninety locally based aircraft (Campbell

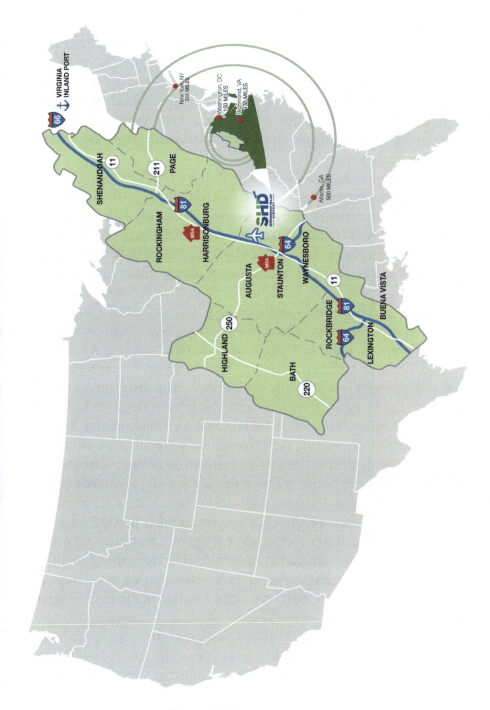

Figure 15.1. Shenandoah Valley

2019; Peters 2019). Approximately eighty airport operations occur at SHD every day with six of them being commercial air service (Peters 2019). Key elements and amenities include Runway 5-23, Taxiway A, a connector taxiway system, the commercial air carrier terminal building, the general aviation terminal building, navigational aids, automobile parking, fuel storage area, support facilities, aircraft rescue and firefighting station, aircraft tiedowns, and aircraft storage hangars (Shenandoah Valley Regional Airport 2017).

Prior to airline deregulation in 1978, the Civil Aeronautics Board determined the carriers that could fly to specific airports. Under this administrative framework, carriers had to provide two daily round trips to each city they were authorized to serve. In 1978, when Congress passed the Airline Deregulation Act (ADA), the federal government ceded control over routes, fares, and market entry of new airlines to the airline industry. This new freedom raised concerns that carriers would abandon small airports in favor of more lucrative routes and fares. Fortunately, large air carriers quickly adopted a hub-and-spoke model over point-to-point flights. In addition, Congress enacted the Essential Air Service (EAS) program to maintain a minimal level of scheduled air service for small communities served before deregulation. This law requires the US Department of Transportation (hereafter Department) to provide eligible EAS communities with access to the National Air Transportation System.

To meet this obligation, the Department generally subsidizes two round trips a day with thirty- to fifty-seat aircraft, or additional frequencies with aircraft with nine seats or fewer, usually to a large- or medium-hub airport. The Department currently subsidizes commuter and certificated air carriers to serve approximately sixty communities in Alaska and 115 communities in the lower-forty-eight contiguous states that otherwise would not receive any scheduled air service (US Department of Transportation 2017). Since 2003, after air travel fell following the 11 September 2001 terrorist attacks, SHD has been enrolled in the EAS program (Bradshaw 2017).

In the wake of 2020's COVID-19 pandemic, air carriers across the country have been met with all new lows in passenger traffic and mounting financial concerns. The CARES Act instituted in March provided $25 billion to passenger air carriers through its Payroll Support Program and another $25 billion through a combination of grants and loans, but that support ended as of 30 September 2020 (Horton 2020). Amid criticisms of how these funds were distributed and a growing number of layoffs since support expired, many are calling for a second round of relief, which may or may not come. This continued uncertainty serves to highlight the vital importance of strong partnerships and community support for local air service moving forward.

Over the years, SHD has worked with various air carriers and experienced mixed results. In November 2017, the US Department of Transportation approved SkyWest as the new carrier for SHD, with service starting April 1, 2018. SkyWest is one of the largest and most reliable regional airlines in North America with partnerships with four major carriers: United, Delta, American Airlines, and Alaska. SkyWest proposed flying fifty-passenger jets to Washington-Dulles International Airport (IAD) and Chicago O'Hare International Airport (ORD), both hubs for United. Pre-COVID, IAD offered thirty daily nonstop flights to thirty international destinations and 195 daily domestic flights to seventy-four airports. ORD is ranked first in the nation for connectivity offering 81,913 possible one-stop domestic flight connections in a three-hour window and 128+ daily direct flights to fifty international destinations at its peak. SkyWest flies a modern CRJ-200 with fifty seats and their flights are fully integrated with United systems, including tickets, baggage, customer service, and branding (Campbell, 2019). Given the remarkable resilience to date of both SkyWest and SHD, the partnership represents a huge win for the

Figure 15.2. Shenandoah Valley Regional Terminal

rural Shenandoah Valley's continued access and appeal.

While residents and tourists often seek out the Shenandoah Valley for its natural beauty and abundant recreational activities, many businesses choose the Shenandoah Valley based on its location, workforce, and low cost of doing business. Primarily rural, the Shenandoah Valley sells more agricultural products than any other region in Virginia. Four out of five of Virginia's top agricultural producing counties are located in the Shenandoah Valley. Food and beverage production in the Shenandoah Valley is four times the national average (Shenandoah Valley Partnership n.d.; Virginia Economic Development Partnership n.d.).

The location of the Shenandoah Valley is prime not only for agriculture but also for distribution. At the crossroads of I-81 and I-64, the Shenandoah Valley offers easy access to the interstate highway system and major centers of commerce in all four directions. Utilizing the interstate highway system, two-thirds of the nation's population is reachable from the Shenandoah Valley by truck in less than twenty-four hours. As a result, companies with large distribution networks like Walmart, Best Buy, Target, and Marshalls have chosen to locate their regional distribution centers in the central Shenandoah Valley (Shenandoah Valley Partnership n.d.; Virginia Economic Development Partnership n.d.).

In addition to location, businesses value the high-quality education system of the Shenandoah Valley (including eleven colleges and universities and seven career and technical centers) that adds 7,000 graduates to the workforce each year. Companies recognize the value of recruiting potential employees whose education has prepared them to enter the workforce as professionals. Companies engaged in manufacturing in the Shenandoah Valley, including Merck and The Hershey Company, have partnered with educational institutions and affiliates to create innovative workforce development programs to attract, train, and retain talent. Finally, state and local incentives further decrease the cost of doing business in the Shenandoah Valley. As a result, businesses are choosing the Shenandoah Valley for investment, expansion, and relocation. Key industries include Agribusiness, Information Technology and Professional Services, Manufacturing, and Transportation and Logistics (Shenandoah Valley Partnership n.d.).

As state and local government, nonprofits, and the private sector seek to encourage businesses in these industries and others to invest in the Shenandoah Valley, local air service is a critical selling point. As a provider of general aviation services, including corporate jet flights, the local airport may be the first contact a corporate client has with the area. If the experience or relationship is positive, the corporate client may be more likely to pursue business decisions that require them, their family, their employees, or their clients to return to the area in the future. For businesses already in the area, the general aviation services provided by the local airport offer efficiency that allows companies to focus on maintaining and growing their businesses. Meanwhile, local commercial air service improves quality of life and economic prospects for residents, making it easier for them to conduct business with long-distance partners and clients, visit friends and family, and have access to premium services, such as healthcare. As the former executive director of the Shenandoah Valley Partnership, Carrie Chenery explained,

> In this global economy where we're competing for jobs and investment not just with other states then with other countries, this air service allows us to remain competitive as a region. That competitive edge is not only for potential new companies to the Valley, but also for our existing corporate partners who rely on this market-access infrastructure for the sustainability and growth of their operations. (Bradshaw 2017)

JMU as an Anchor Institution

Recognizing the value of local air service and celebrating the success of their partnership with SkyWest, SHD leadership sought to build momentum. SHD's executive director, Greg Campbell, and director of marketing and communications, Heather Ream, took to the community, working with city and county officials, economic developers, and local stakeholders to spread the word about improvements to their services. They conducted market research, invested in advertising, and scheduled numerous speaking engagements then ultimately sought to build community partnerships through a grassroots approach that would provide them with stable, long-term support for mutual benefit.

A point of particular interest for them was not only to explore new markets but to prioritize strengthening relationships with existing markets. For years, Campbell had noted the prevalence of parking passes from Harrisonburg's James Madison University (JMU) in the lots at SHD. JMU emerged from market research as a leading source of local travelers and the single largest stakeholder for SHD's traffic. Especially given JMU's role as an anchor institution, Campbell and Ream identified them as a natural ally.

At its core, nearby Harrisonburg is a college town. In addition to JMU, it is home to Eastern Mennonite University (EMU) and American National University (ANU) within the city limits. It is also located within fifteen minutes of both Bridgewater College (BC) and Blue Ridge Community College (BRCC). Of these institutions of higher education, JMU is the largest by far and has developed into a vital anchor institution for the region. An anchor institution is place-based—tethered to its community, capable of great socioeconomic impact, and generally invested in the well-being of the surrounding area out of both mission and self-interest. Common examples include universities, hospitals, libraries, museums, churches, government installations, and so forth.

Over the last decade, JMU has distinguished itself as an anchor institution by steadily increasing its involvement in economic and community development efforts. Many of these efforts have been directly endorsed by its current leader, President Jon Alger. JMU has dedicated itself so strongly to these pursuits as to adopt the following vision statement, "To be the national model for the engaged university: engaged with ideas and the world" (James Madison University n.d.). When combined with its large number of domestic and international travelers, this commitment made JMU an ideal partner for SHD.

Campbell reached out to their colleague at the university—Dr. Nicholas Swartz, associate dean of Professional and Continuing Education (PCE) and director of the Madison Center for Community Development (MCCD). Swartz does a significant amount of his work in the realms of convening and facilitation, program start-up and incubation, and strategic planning. He often represents the university in its collaborations with local businesses, nonprofits, and economic developers. He also serves as a point of contact for outside organizations to connect with university resources.

FORMATION OF THE TASK FORCE

Every nonhub airport is expected to serve passengers across a designated geographic area, but it is inevitable that they will experience leakage—losing some of their potential customer base to nearby competitors. As expected, one of SHD's highest priorities is to capture as much of the Shenandoah Valley's air travel as possible. Knowing JMU travelers still had the potential to make a far greater impact in the airport's traffic, Campbell and Ream set a series of meetings with Swartz and his project coordinator, Justin Bullman, in March and April 2019 where they brainstormed and discussed potential options for routing more of JMU's travelers through SHD. These meetings culminated in the decision to assemble a larger team. This team would include members not only from across JMU but also the larger community, providing more diverse perspectives and broader influence. It would soon come to be known as the Fly SHD Community Air Service Task Force.

With a plan in mind, Swartz began contacting university colleagues, economic development partners, and other affiliates regarding their interest in this new venture. Fortunately, they were met with a warm reception and the first task force meeting was held on 29 May 2019. This and all subsequent meetings have been facilitated by Swartz as chair of the task force. The Fly SHD Community Air Service Task force brought together professionals from the government, nonprofit, and private sectors. Aware of the role of air service in local and regional economic development, task force members in government and nonprofit roles were eager to participate and support future growth of SHD and the region.

Based on responses to the survey issued to task force members as part of the analysis for this chapter, these government and nonprofit leaders recognized the connection between SHD's success and that of their localities, organizations, and the region. Some task force members from higher education viewed participation as an opportunity for community engagement and service. Others were motivated to participate based on the importance of the availability of accessible air travel for current and prospective faculty, staff, students, and guests of their institutions. Similarly, task force members from the business community joined based on the value of local air service to their employees, customers, and the community.

Campbell and Ream chose to be involved with the task force due to its capacity to amplify their communication and marketing strategy and increase passenger travel. The remaining members, as local residents and frequent airline travelers themselves, were motivated to join the task force based on their personal experiences with SHD and their desire to continue enjoying the benefits of local air service.

Meetings varied from bi-weekly to monthly and, during each session, the members assessed what perspectives were missing and what other contacts they could reach out to for participation. Membership grew alongside the scope of the project. The core focus on capturing JMU traffic remained throughout this first year but grew to include additional tasks for the airport's benefit. One of the most valuable additions to the task force was a dedicated JMU graduate assistant, Garland Graves, who helped coordinate task force meetings and efforts for the duration of the 2019–2020 academic year.

Among the first of their responsibilities was a nationwide search into similar community air service task forces. Their findings were used to inform best practices and generate ideas for next steps. Save for a few exceptions, information on most of these groups was sparse. Among those found, this task force was unique in the strength of its connections to higher education while another, serving Pellston Regional Airport in Emmet County, Michigan, was composed largely of retired pilots and airline representatives. Each group counted local economic development officers and local business leaders among their ranks. Goals varied from branding issues to infrastructure improvements, but without fail, each group sought to increase convenience and enplanements through additional flight frequencies to major hub airports.

MAKE-UP OF THE TASK FORCE

At the time of this writing, membership of the Fly SHD Community Air Service Task Force consists of twenty-one individuals representing eleven different organizations and sectors. Table 15.1 provides a list of current member organizations and a brief description of each.

Table 15.1. Task Force Membership	
Organization	Organization description
Blue Ridge Community College	A community college in Weyers Cave, VA, serving approximately 3,800 students.
City of Harrisonburg government	An independent city with over 50,000 people in central Shenandoah Valley.

Hotel Madison and Shenandoah Valley Conference Center	A major hotel and conference center in Harrisonburg and the official hotel of James Madison University.
Independent community volunteers	University partners and affiliates acting as independent consultants.
James Madison University	A public, comprehensive university in Harrisonburg serving 22,000 students.
Lantz Construction Company	A commercial construction firm based out of Harrisonburg that serves VA, WV, and MD.
Rockingham County government	A largely agricultural county of over 76,000. Part of the Harrisonburg-Rockingham Metropolitan Statistical Area.
Shenandoah Valley Partnership	An economic development agency servicing the entire Shenandoah Valley. Focused on business attraction and retention as well as workforce development and improvement of the economic climate.
Shenandoah Valley Regional Airport	Regional airport based out of Weyers Cave.
Shenandoah Valley Small Business Development Center	One of 29 small business development centers across Virginia's SBDC network. Focused on helping local businesses grow and improve.
Shenandoah Valley Technology Council	Nonprofit focused on the education, growth, and networking of local technology businesses.

WORK OF THE TASK FORCE

In addition to the regular meetings of the task force and the dedicated graduate assistant who was responsible for research, assisting members, coordinating tasks, and recording minutes—the most critical measure for success involved the drafting of a "master work plan." This was used to organize and track the many opportunities the task force had identified for educating JMU staff and the greater community through web page updates, promo videos, advertising packages, targeted outreach campaigns, family events, raffles, presentations, and print articles. Task force members pursued these tasks individually and in small subcommittee groups of three to five members. Each group was assigned a subcommittee chair to facilitate individual meetings and they would regularly report their progress targeting the areas found in table 15.2.

Table 15.2. Master Work Plan Categories	
Priority one	Priority two
Alumni relations	Athletic advertising
Campus advertising	Atlantic Union Bank Center
Center for Global Engagement	Conferences
Civic engagement	Family events
Educational event for administrative staff	Graduation
Local travel agents	Local civic organization meetings
Madison Magazine and promotional video	Monthly raffle
Parent relations	Weddings/Destination

The master work plan was pivotal in achieving one of the task force's first and most important successes. Even before the task force was formed, Campbell had been petitioning United for their support in establishing additional flights to and from their hub airports, Washington Dulles and Chicago O'Hare. This was largely intended to facilitate day trippers who wished to travel for work in the morning and return that evening. The extensive efforts listed in the master work plan and the considerable show of community support combined with record-setting passenger traffic recorded over several consecutive months solidified Campbell's argument. As of 4 December 2019, SHD deployed new evening flights in and out of its two hub airports, greatly increasing the convenience and flexibility offered to day trippers, vacationers, and everyone in between.

Immediately after this rollout, on 5 December 2019, JMU president Jon Alger announced SHD as the official airport of JMU. Ongoing negotiations culminated in an arrangement that prioritized air travel through SHD without strictly designating it as an exclusive option for JMU faculty and staff travel. At every turn SHD staff have only ever advocated for using their service when it makes sense logistically and financially, but this kind of support coupled with genuine policy to back it up was a clear sign of positive progress and solidified the partnership between SHD and JMU. As part of this official partnership, plans were drafted to brand large segments of the SHD commercial terminal with JMU imagery, slogans, and even a full-size "Duke Dog" mascot mannequin. At the time of this writing (summer 2021), terminal branding plans were in the final stages.

Another unique effort of the task force was the creation of a report outlining the state of SHD's physical signage on local roadways alongside a detailed comparison of their competitors. The task force conducted an in-person survey of airport signage in Weyers Cave, Charlottesville, Lynchburg, and Roanoke to include photographic images and GIS mapping. Much of SHD's signage has been identified as hard to see, insufficient, or lacking and contributes to the local airport being overlooked by locals and travelers alike. Many still confuse SHD as being a private airport like the nearby Dynamic Aviation and fail to realize they offer commercial flights. This information will be used in lobbying for improvements in existing signage and driving up awareness through visibility.

Individually, task force members value the information they learned about SHD and air travel. Prior to their involvement with the task force, many task force members were unfamiliar with SHD operations, services, and market share. During their time on the task force, members learned about SHD's history, facilities, daily operations, routes and schedule, and detailed research on passenger trends. They also learned about the history and structure of the airline industry, the role of regional airports within the national air travel system, and the economic impact of regional airports. This information prepared task force members to return to their organizations and communities and educate the public about the value of SHD to the region.

As a result of their involvement, task force members developed valuable professional and personal connections with each other. While some had previous experience working together, most had not worked closely with at least some of the other task force members in any context.

Participants gained new contacts and resources for future projects. They also came to appreciate the unique experiences, skills, and abilities each of their peers contributed. In the words of one task force member, Eddie Bumbaugh, "When carefully chosen people focus on a high-priority purpose with effective leadership, staff support, and organization, impressive strategies and outcomes are the result."

SUCCESSES AND SETBACKS

One of the task force's greatest accomplishments was its ability to facilitate a formal partnership between JMU and SHD. The task force connected SHD with key JMU leadership. Only fifteen minutes from JMU's campus in Harrisonburg, SHD is conveniently located for faculty, staff, students, and guests of the university. When JMU, the single largest source of air travel in the region, agreed to endorse SHD as "The Official Airport of James Madison University," SHD gained a powerful strategic partner and valuable marketing asset. JMU's encouragement of its faculty and staff to fly SHD whenever possible drove passenger traffic to the airport.

The task force supported targeted marketing efforts to increase awareness of SHD both on-campus and across JMU's worldwide network of parents, alumni, and friends of the university. Examples of these efforts include articles in Madison Magazine, universitywide faculty/staff emails, department-specific faculty/staff emails, print and online on-campus advertising, and an onsite airport presentation and tour for university staff who schedule faculty and staff travel. It was successful in creating enthusiastic, informed ambassadors of SHD, prepared to promote the airport to their contacts across the government, nonprofit, and private sectors. Efforts to engage the business community through one-on-one conversations with local business leaders and presentations by SHD's executive director and director of Marketing and Communications at local civic organizations have also shown early signs of success. Any success of the task force is attributable to the dedicated, well-connected people who used their platforms and connections to advance the airport.

In the same way that Campbell and Ream educated these groups, they also presented valuable information to the task force about airline operations, the airline industry, and the economic importance of local air service. These presentations informed the task force's understanding of the nature and scope of the challenges SHD faces and the ways that the community can support the airport. After the presentations, task force members had a better understanding of the ways community support can impact SHD and the region.

Task force members also brought with them the experiences and perspectives of the government entities, nonprofit organizations, colleges and universities, and businesses that employ them as well as the citizens, clients, faculty, staff, students, employees, and customers those entities serve. Due to the varied nature of their organizations and positions, members interface with many different types of potential airline travelers—from the airline savvy business traveler booking weekly international flights to the first-semester college student trying to make it home safely for Thanksgiving break. These varied perspectives, along with the personal insights of task force members as local residents and users of air service, informed the approach of the task force in the development and implementation of communication and marketing strategies.

In addition, task force members connected SHD to highly developed professional and personal networks. Task force members used these networks to circulate information about the airport to broad and targeted audiences both directly and indirectly. For example, Shenandoah Valley Partnership kept its network of twelve local development offices and 130+ private-sector businesses informed of SHD developments and facilitated an information presentation by SHD's Campbell and Ream to its members. Other task force members, in coordination with Campbell and Ream, facilitated similar presentations and on-site airport tours for target groups.

The task force was successful at building a coalition of support for SHD and establishing partnerships to support SHD as it continues to provide excellent and expanded air service to Shenandoah Valley residents. These partnerships increased passenger travel at SHD and strengthened the airport leadership's position in negotiations with commercial carriers for expanded routes. By encouraging their formalization, the task force was instrumental in the development of a model for future partnerships between SHD and other local colleges and universities, as well as major employers in the region outside higher education. As task force support grew and JMU staff advocated for the service, leaders from both organizations came together and were able to negotiate a list of expectations going forward that solidified their official partnership. Even without an exclusivity arrangement, measures include the prioritization of SHD as a travel option for JMU staff, on-site advertising of each other's brands, and the initialization of a United rewards program proved mutually beneficial. These agreements coupled with the task force's prior efforts were key to driving the partnership forward with United's full support.

Consistent support served to increase awareness of SHD's expanded commercial flight schedule to Washington Dulles and Chicago O'Hare among the business community; faculty, staff, and students of local colleges and universities; and the general public. In addition to informing the public of the new flight options, the marketing efforts of the task force emphasized the convenience, reliability, connectivity, and value of SHD and distinguished the quality of the current commercial air service provided by United and SkyWest from past service. As a result of direct interaction with SHD leadership, task force members themselves gained a deeper understanding of the role of SHD in local economic development, as well as insight into the process whereby commercial airline providers select service routes. This information prepared task force members to return to their companies, organizations, and communities as ambassadors for SHD and proponents of the type of community support necessary to sustain and expand community air service.

While task force members recognize the number of Shenandoah Valley travelers currently lost to Charlottesville or Dulles as an opportunity for growth, they also view the continued leakage of Valley passengers to other airports as a threat to the continuation of expanded service. Task force members acknowledge that outdated perceptions of SHD as unreliable or unaffordable persist despite the record built by United Airlines and SkyWest since their partnership with SHD began in 2018. Accordingly, they understand the importance of their ongoing role to engage new partners and spread the message that the passenger experience at SHD has changed for the better.

Task force members also recognize the impact that the COVID-19 pandemic has had on air travel. As a result of COVID-19, organizations and individuals have dramatically decreased their utilization of business and leisure air travel in the interest of health and cost savings. It is important now, more than ever, that SHD staff and the task force continue to explore new ways of maintaining and increasing passenger traffic. Given their small size, regional airports are likely to suffer disproportionate effects without continued support. The uncertainty of a second bailout only shifts more of that responsibility to the surrounding community, which may depend on its services more than they realize. For example, SHD provided vital, rapid transport to the out-of-state engineers and other technical experts who kept many local businesses and services running during the height of the pandemic.

While SHD has felt and will continue to feel the effects of COVID-19 on passenger demand, task force members are hopeful that when Valley passengers return to air travel they will choose to fly SHD. Passengers wary of airline travel due to concerns about COVID-19 may find SHD's smaller, less-crowded terminal less daunting than the large, crowded terminals at larger airports. Comprehensive new cleaning measures and policies, as well as the publicity and outreach focused on these efforts, may also help put travelers at ease. As the disruptions of COVID-19 prompt many to reexamine their habits and routines, SHD has an opportunity to make its case to travelers who otherwise may not have paused long enough to consider the relative merits of SHD.

Conclusion

This chapter showcased the important and powerful convening role an anchor institution can take in helping to galvanize stakeholder support to enhance economic competitiveness. The approach used for the creation and implementation of the task force can serve as a model to other localities and regions who need to garner stakeholder support and demand for enhanced and/or expanded services.

As a result of the direct work of the task force, the future of SHD is bright. Task force members are confident that SHD has the potential to recapture market share lost from competing airports and markets. If the airport successfully retains more Valley travelers, the increase in passenger demand will allow them to compete for additional routes and carriers that will only improve options for passengers to and from the Shenandoah Valley. Finally, task force members recognize the strength of SHD's leadership and its ability to create and maximize opportunities.

Many members expressed their hope that the task force would continue to build on their prior work by maintaining existing partnerships and engaging additional partners. Several expressed their desire to increase efforts to engage the business community through their connections and contacts. Others identified the continuation of targeted outreach and marketing as a priority. Most task force members expressed their desire to continue to meet periodically or quarterly.

The work of the task force is now more important than ever as businesses and consumers emerge from the COVID-19 pandemic. Task force members view their role as complementary to the already strong strategic and marketing efforts of SHD and hope that they can provide creative and effective recommendations that support SHD during this unprecedented time. Strong partnerships and community support are essential to identify and implement successful solutions to enhance a community or region. The members of the Fly SHD Community Air Service Task Force hope their work will serve as a model to other communities going forward.

Conclusion

Margaret Cowell and Sarah Lyon-Hill

Vibrancy: full of life and energy

What can we conclude about the nature of vibrancy across Virginia's urban-rural continuum? Do the wide range of historical and contemporary accounts presented in this book reveal common themes or certain challenges and opportunities that might be universal for all Virginia localities? Or is Virginia, like so many other states across the United States, a state of extremes whereby each end of the continuum seems too far afield to learn something from one another? Is a truly vibrant Virginia—home to strong, dynamic, and inclusive communities—possible, and if so, can we cultivate capacity to take advantage of emerging opportunities or at the very least embrace economic change?

We began this book with the observation that the divisive 2016 and 2020 presidential elections served as evidence of just how big the chasms have become between the haves and the have-nots, the right and the left, the urban and the rural. Moreover, we recognized the unfortunate reality that, at least in recent decades, sustainable and equitable economic growth has eluded many rural parts and some urban areas of Virginia.

Compounding these challenges is the unfortunate economic reality for those who stay in lagging regions or neighborhoods, where it is often more difficult to access the wealth-creating opportunities that generally are found in more prosperous areas. These observations raise the question of whether bridging the urban-rural divide can or should even be our goal. In essence, chapters within this book demand that we question its very title.

What then does a vibrant Virginia look like? And what will it take to engage the Commonwealth in order to expand economic vitality? As the authors in this book describe from a variety of perspectives, a vibrant Virginia is not a one-size-fits-all strategy. Indeed, vibrancy in one domain or in one place might look different from vibrancy in another. Still, the approaches elaborated within the book are not hermetically sealed from each other, many of the chapters feed into each other and are genuinely complementary. Contributions run the gamut from cases of site-specific art installations to service delivery at regional scales, and statewide networks to improve access for all. They focus on government interventions, community-university partnerships, private sector engagement, and nonprofit collaborations. While no single chapter declares a universal solution to bridge the urban-rural divide or expand economic vitality, they all contribute in some way to our nuanced understanding of the challenges we face and the opportunities that exist before us.

It is a bit daunting to extract common messages from such wide-ranging stories of vibrancy, engagement, and vitality. Yet several themes do stand out clearly and the following four will likely prove useful to scholars, practitioners, policymakers, stakeholders, and residents working diligently to cultivate strong, vibrant, and inclusive communities across the Commonwealth and beyond.

Narratives of Vibrancy Are Inherently Contested

As we hinted at in the introduction, vibrancy is a "fuzzy concept," meaning that we lack a clear definition of the term and would likely find it difficult to operationalize in the context of economic development or community engagement. In her work on fuzzy concepts, Ann Markusen (1999) called upon scholars to deliver "greater conceptual clarity, increased rigour in the presentation of evidence and a more concerted effort to render work in regional studies relevant to the daily world of politics, policy and planning" (870). While our goal in this book was never really focused on defining vibrancy in the context of economic development, we do see this book as an attempt to address Markusen's request that we engage in scholarship that is relevant to the daily world of politics, policy, and planning. Advancing scholarship in this domain requires that we engage with the concept of vibrancy and work diligently to uncover divergent perspectives on what it means for a place or community to be vibrant.

Narratives of vibrancy are the strands of material we have woven together here in Vibrant Virginia. Using narratives, contributors have offered insights into vibrancy at the scale of the block, neighborhood, community, region, and state. In these examples we see evidence of narratives and antinarratives; positive and negative narratives; and historical and future-oriented narratives. They have urged us to consider for whom the existing narrative applies, asking us to reimagine who has the right to engage in conversations about vibrancy and how we might hold and create space for people whose voices are typically not present in these conversations. Importantly, they also offer practical ideas for how we might expand upon this critical work.

If this book does nothing else, it most certainly engages with the idea that no one person would describe vibrant communities the same way. While we may offer overlapping ideas about some of the key ingredients necessary for vibrant communities, the subjectiveness of the term "vibrancy" means that it is inherently contested. We see this as a good thing, in that it not only allows for but also encourages diverse conversations whereby we center perspectives, voices, and ideas that have not always been included in conversations about community, economy, and engagement. We challenge ourselves and our readers to take up, and reflect upon, this important charge in our or their own communities.

Local Vibrancy Is Linked to Regional, State, and Even National Vibrancy

No locality is an island. As contributors have shown throughout the book, the vibrancy of a place is inherently connected to the vibrancy of the broader context in which it is located and the vibrancy of the smaller building blocks of which the place is composed. Whether it be through the positive effects of shared priorities or through the often negative effects of things like state preemption, local vibrancy is inherently linked to the vibrancy of the nested structure in which it is located.

As most policy wonks will tell you, the nested nature of localities can offer benefits and impediments. Numerous contributors to this book have noted that the ties that bind us can sometimes make things more difficult when it comes to challenges like expanding access to broadband or resettling refugee and migrant communities. However, contributors have also demonstrated that the opposite can also be true, as evidenced by the discussions of scalable and/or collaborative strategies for STEM recruitment, addiction service delivery, and community building efforts. Still, we acknowledge that this is difficult work.

Successful recovery from the pandemic, economic upheaval, regional inequalities, and racial injustice that have challenged communities across the Commonwealth in recent years will require a new era of interjurisdictional collaboration, marked by synergy rather than antagonism.

As we write this in the summer of 2021, state and local governments are engaged in conversations about how best to deploy resources received via the Biden administration's $1.9 trillion COVID-19 relief bill—the American Rescue Plan Act (ARP). Many, including the editors, see this as an opportunity to increase interjurisdictional cooperation and think creatively about inclusive long-term growth that will foster vibrancy at the local, regional, state, and national scales.

Vibrancy Benefits from the Inertia of Prior Investment (but the Opposite Can Also Be True)

Economists conceptualize inertia as path dependence. Psychologists describe emotional inertia as the degree to which emotional states are resistant to change. No matter how you frame it, it is often true that success begets success and investment begets further investment. While the odd locality may be able to buck the trend, a pragmatist will tell you that the battle to override inertia is indeed an uphill battle.

Economists have long written about how seemingly small effects can be amplified via positive feedback thereby resulting in larger advantages down the line. In that sense, even comparatively small investments can create the potential for small initial changes that lead to large-scale transformations in a system. So, the good news is that the smaller investments we read about in chapters 6 or 10 can have lasting impacts in the longer term. The bad news, however, is that for many other parts of Virginia there is a lot of catching up to do, especially when we think about the compounded gains their competitors have seen as a result of smaller investments that were made long ago.

Given the book's focus on highlighting opportunities for community stakeholders from all sectors to address regional challenges, we would be wise to re-frame this idea of investment inertia as an opportunity to accelerate good ideas and leverage competitive advantages. As Stephen Moret notes in chapter 3, localities across Virginia offer immense potential for growth both in the near and longer term. If we successfully harness the potential for positive feedback effects and capitalize on resulting inertia, then small initial competitive advantages for localities may, through positive feedback, lead to enormous differences in outcomes over time. But in order to do so, we must do more to understand the particular sequence of historical and geographical events in places where investment inertia has resulted in sustained positive feedback. Moreover, and perhaps most important, we also need to do more to understand why historical and geographical events in other places have resulted in disinvestment inertia. All eyes will be on us as we reflect on and learn from recent events that shined an important spotlight on the legacy of historical disadvantages in BIPOC and other underserved communities.

VIBRANCY IS INHERENTLY PLACE-SPECIFIC

As John Accordino and Kyle Meyer remind us in chapter 10, a Main Street strategy that works well in the Town of Farmville is not guaranteed to work in the City of Norfolk. The success of these revitalized main streets is inherently tied to the place-specific interventions and investments that have been made in each locality. Indeed, contributors to this book are universally clear in their assertion that there is no one-size-fits-all strategy to encourage vibrancy across Virginia's urban-rural continuum. True vibrancy—the kind that you can see and feel—is decidedly place-dependent. Contributing authors, especially in part III, remind us that there is much to be gained from understanding the place needs of people and firms.

Armed with this information, we can help scholars, practitioners, policymakers, stakeholders, and residents develop innovative strategies to support place-specific community and economic development that will nurture or jumpstart inclusive economic opportunities.

Virginia is no stranger to place-specific investments, including its fair share of splashy investments in its downtowns, waterfronts, and innovation districts during recent years. Some of these are noted elsewhere in this book. But what is also noted in this book are the less conspicuous investments in place, like those seen in Scenic Virginia (chapter 11) or the Southside Community Gateway Project (chapter 9). Though they generally garner less attention than the big-ticket items like Virginia Tech's Innovation Campus in Alexandria, there is much to be learned from smaller, place-specific investments about how they, too, can strengthen localities across the urban-rural spectrum and ensure that all citizens can participate in emerging economic opportunities.

We also recognize that there is a lot of work to be done. The ebb and flow of people and firms during eras of sprawl, coupled with the "back to the city" movement, have wreaked havoc on the spatial organization of localities across Virginia. It would be ill-advised to ignore the fact that the automobile remains dominant in much of Virginia and has fueled countless problems of severe spatial mismatch between affordable housing and economic opportunity, fiscal waste, and widespread environmental concerns. With these challenges in mind, we are reminded that place matters more than ever. Bridging the urban-rural divide will require policy and investment reforms that support place-specific opportunities through economic development, environmental, land use, infrastructure, and governance strategies that improve access and connectivity and foster inclusive opportunities for more Virginians in more localities.

Works Cited

Chapter 1

APA (Auditor of Public Accounts) Commonwealth of Virginia. 2017. *Amended Comparative Report of Local Government Revenues and Expenditures for the Fiscal Year Ended June 30, 2017.* http://www.apa.virginia.gov.

Cronon, W. 1991. *Nature's Metropolis: Chicago and the Great West.* New York: Norton.

Eller, R. D. 2008. *Uneven Ground: Appalachia since 1945.* Lexington: University Press of Kentucky.

Hailu, A., and C. Wasserman. 2016. *Guidelines for Using Rural-Urban Classification Systems for Community Health Assessment,* 1–26. Washington State Department of Health, https://www.doh.wa.gov/Portals/1/Documents/1500/RUCAGuide.pdf.

Halfacree, K. H. 1993. "Locality and Social Representation: Space, Discourse and Alternative Definitions of the Rural." *Journal of Rural Studies* 9(1): 23–37. https://doi.org/10.1016/07430167(93)90003-3.

Health Resources & Services Administration (HRSA) 2017. *Medically Underserved Areas/Populations (MUA/P).* US Department of Health and Human Services. https://data.hrsa.gov/data/download. Accessed 20 November 2020.

Heinemann, R. 1996. *Harry Byrd of Virginia.* Charlottesville: University of Virginia Press.

Holsinger, M., ed. 1999. "How Ya Gonna Keep 'Em Down on the Farm?" [Song]. *War and American Popular Culture: A Historical Encyclopedia.* Westport, CT: Greenwood Press.

Isserman, A. M. 2005. "In the National Interest: Defining Rural and Urban Correctly in Research and Public Policy." *International Regional Science Review* 28(4): 465–499. https://doi.org/10.1177/0160017605279000.

Orfield, M. 1997. *Metropolitics*. Washington, DC: Brookings Institution Press.

Orfield, M. 2002. *American Metropolitics*. Washington, DC: Brookings Institution Press.

Persky, J., and W. Wiewel. 2000. *When Corporations Leave Town: The Costs and Benefits of Metropolitan Job Sprawl*. Detroit, MI: Wayne State University Press.

Porter, M. 2004. *Competitiveness in Rural U.S. Regions: Learning and Research Agenda*. US Economic Development Administration. https://www.isc.hbs.edu/Documents/ced/EDA_RuralReport_20040621.pdf. Accessed 12 February 2021.

Ratcliffe, M., C. Burd, K. Holder, and A. Fields. 2016. Defining Rural at the U.S. Census Bureau.

Roanoke Times. 2021a. "Breakthrough on School Disparity." *Roanoke Times* [Unsigned editorial]. https://roanoke.com/opinion/editorial/editorial-an-astonishing-breakthrough-on-school-disparity---for-now/article_fae1ee96-6a32-11eb-9c79-1ba2841a574e.html?fbclid=IwAR1pDgItXWL2WDycJNFiRtGtXuFpVGHCUvzaIbz_nIDYVD2rJVv8F8r_2wo. Accessed 12 February 2021.

Roanoke Times. 2021b. "The Curious Reluctance of Some Northern Virginia Democrats to Help Rural Virginia." *Roanoke Times*. [Unsigned editorial]. https://roanoke.com/opinion/editorial/editorial-the-curious-reluctance-of-some-northern-virginia-democrats-to-help-rural-virginia/article_620cf20a-6a51–11eb-9730–47542c70988b.html. Accessed 16 February 2021.

Schneider, G. 2018. "Law Aimed at Helping Poor Areas of Va. Shows Power—and Limits—of Bipartisanship." *Washington Post*. https://www.washingtonpost.com/local/virginia-politics/new-law-aimed-at-helping-poor-areas-of-virginia-shows-power—and-limits—of-bipartisanship/2018/05/20/68a03cc0–5a1a-11e8–8836-a4a123c359ab_story.html. Accessed 16 February 2021.

Scott, A., A. Gilbert, and A. Gelan. 2007. *The Urban-Rural Divide: Myth or Reality?* Macaulay Institute Aberdeen.

Stoll, M., H. Holzer, and K. Ihlanfeldt. 2000. "Within Cities and Suburbs: Racial Residential Concentration and the Spatial Distribution of Employment across Sub-Metropolitan Areas." *Journal of Policy Analysis and Management* 19(2): 207–232.

U.S. Bureau of Economic Analysis. CAINC1 Personal Income Summary. 1969–2018.

U.S. Census. Historic Population Counts. 1820–2019.

Virginia Department of Housing and Community Development. 2021. GO Virginia Board. https://www.dhcd.virginia.gov/gova. Accessed 11 February 2021.

Virginia Department of Housing and Community Development (DHCD). 2020. *Report on Local Vulnerability Analysis.*

Virginia Department of Taxation. 2017. *Annual Report Fiscal Year 2017.* https://www.tax.virginia.gov.

Weitz, J. 2003. *Jobs-Housing Balance.* Chicago: Planning Advisory Service, American Planning Association.

Wilkerson, I. 2010. *The Warmth of Other Suns: The Epic Story of America's Great Migration.* New York: Vintage Books.

Wilson, W. J. 1987. *The Truly Disadvantaged.* Chicago: University of Chicago Press.

Wilson, W. J. 1997. *When Work Disappears: The World of the New Urban Poor.* New York: Knopf.

Chapter 2

Atkinson, Frank B. 2006. *Virginia in the Vanguard: Political Leadership in the 400-Year-Old Cradle of American Democracy, 1981–2006.* Lanham, MD: Rowman and Littlefield.

Bai, Matt. 2002. "Nascar-Lovin.'" *New York Times*, 15 September. https://www.nytimes.com/2002/09/15/magazine/nascar-lovin.html.

Barakat, Matthew. 2021. "Virginia Unlikely to See Major Changes in Redistricting." *Washington Post*, 22 January. https://www.washingtonpost.com/local/virginia-unlikely-to-see-major-changes-in-redistricting/2021/01/22/cb4bd74a-5cdc-11eb-a849-6f9423a75ffd_story.html.

Bascom, Jonathan. 2001. "'Energizing' Rural Space: The Representation of Countryside Culture as an Economic Development Strategy." *Journal of Cultural Geography* 19(1): 53–73. https://doi.org/10.1080/08873630109478297.

Beiler, David. 2001/2002. "Mark Warner's Five-Year Plan." *Campaigns and Elections* 22(10): 34. http://search.ebscohost.com.umw.idm.oclc.org/login.aspx?direct=true&db=f5h&AN=5675018&site=ehost-live.

Cowell, Margaret, Adam Eckerd, and Henry Smart. 2020. "The Rural Identity and the Encroaching City: Governance, Policy and Development in Northern Virginia's Wine Country." *Growth and Change* 51(1): 79–101. https://doi-org.umw.idm.oclc.org/10.1111/grow.12344.

Black, Earl, and Merle Black. 2002. *The Rise of Southern Republicans*. Cambridge, MA: Harvard University Press.

Dabney, Virgnius. 1971. *Virginia: The New Dominion*. Charlottesville: University of Virginia Press.

Dionne, E. J., Jr., Norman J. Ornstein, and Thomas E. Mann. 2017. *One Nation after Trump*. New York: St. Martin's Press.

Egan, Timothy. 2002. "Pastoral Poverty: The Seeds of Decline." *New York Times*, 8 December. https://www.nytimes.com/2002/12/08/weekinreview/the-nation-pastoral-poverty-the-seeds-of-decline.html?searchResultPosition=1.

Farnsworth, Stephen J. 2002a. "Campaigning against Government in the Old Dominion: State Taxation, State Power and Virginia's 1997 Gubernatorial Election." *Politics and Policy* 30(3): 460–480.

Farnsworth, Stephen J. 2002b. "In Virginia, Democracy Degraded." *Washington Post*, 17 November. https://www.washingtonpost.com/archive/opinions/2002/11/17/in-virginia-democracy-degraded/1e497cc9-70a0-4a8a-ab66-005dcd7c1a12/.

Farnsworth, Stephen J. 2005. "Virginia Politics, Washington-Style." *Washington Post*, 23 October. https://www.washingtonpost.com/wp-dyn/content/article/2005/10/21/AR2005102102271.html.

Farnsworth, Stephen J. 2015a. "Virginia Voters and Decentralized Governmental Power: Federal Frustration and State Satisfaction?" *Virginia Social Science Journal* 50(Spring): 81–90. https://www.virginiasocialscience.org/wp-content/uploads/2015/03/VSSJ-2015_Revised-Addendum.pdf.

Farnsworth, Stephen J. 2015b. "How Gerrymandering Cost Virginia Its Medicaid Expansion." *Washington Post*, 18 January. https://www.washingtonpost.com/opinions/how-gerrymandering-cost-virginia-its-medicaid-expansion/2015/01/16/5f8762d8–95f8–11e4–8005–1924ede3e54a_story.html.

Farnsworth, Stephen J. 2018. *Presidential Communication and Character: White House News Management from Clinton and Cable to Twitter and Trump*. New York: Routledge.

Farnsworth, Stephen J., and Jeremy R. Engel. 2018. "Ralph Northam's Excellent Timing." *Washington Post*, 7 October. https://www.washingtonpost.com/0459d64c-c33b-11e8-b338-a3289f6cb742_story.html.

Farnsworth, Stephen J., and Stephen P. Hanna. 2013. "Why Republicans Lost in Virginia—in Three Great Maps." *Washington Post* [*The Fix* blog], 12 November. https://www.washingtonpost.com/news/the-fix/wp/2013/11/12/why-republicans-lost-in-virginia-in-three-great-maps/.

Farnsworth, Stephen J., and Stephen P. Hanna. 2017a. "This One Map Shows the Republicans' Problem in Virginia." *Washington Post* (*The Monkey Cage* blog), 9 November. https://www.washingtonpost.com/news/monkey-cage/wp/2017/11/09/this-one-map-shows-the-republicans-problem-in-virginia/.

Farnsworth, Stephen J., and Stephen P. Hanna. 2017b. "Virginia's Changing Party Dynamics." *Richmond Times-Dispatch*, 12 November. https://richmond.com/opinion/columnists/farnsworth-and-hanna-column-virginias-changing-party-dynamics/article_c44b807b-2f64–57d0-b381–0e46f38ef236.html.

Farnsworth, Stephen J., and Stephen P. Hanna. 2018a. "People Vote, Acres Don't: Virginia's 2017 Election in Perspective." *Virginia Capitol Connections*, Winter. http://vccqm.org/qm_winter_2018/8/.

Farnsworth, Stephen J., and Stephen P. Hanna. 2018b. "Gerrymandering and Population Changes in Virginia." *Virginia Capitol Connections*, Spring. http://vccqm.org/qm_spring_2018/12/.

Farnsworth, Stephen J., Stephen P. Hanna, and Benjamin Hermerding. 2014. "Warner's Moderate Approach Is Falling out of Favor." *Charlottesville Daily Progress*, 23 November. https://dailyprogress.com/opinion/opinion-column-warners-moderate-approach-falling-out-of-favor/article_97a75b60–71c6–11e4-a79e-d372b81c4c52.html.

France, Katherine. 2005. "Cultivating Effective Practices in Government and Policy-Making: Summary of an Interview with Virginia Governor Mark Warner." *Policy Perspectives* 12(31 March). https://journal.policy-perspectives.org/articles/volume_12/10_4079_pp_v12i1_4130.pdf.

Gingrich, Newt. 1995. *To Renew America*. New York: HarperCollins.

Glass, Andrew, and Abby Phillip. 2009. "Curious Case of Catchy Political tunes." *Politico*, 30 July. https://www.politico.com/story/2009/07/curious-case-of-catchy-political-tunes-025589.

Graff, Garrett. 2006. "Is Mark Warner the Next Bill Clinton?" *Washingtonian*, February. https://www.washingtonian.com/2006/02/01/is-mark-warner-the-next-bill-clinton/.

Grim, Ryan, and Briahna Gray. 2018. "What the Progressive Surge in Rural America Means for the Election—And Beyond." *The Intercept*, 31 October. https://theintercept.com/2018/10/31/midterm-elections-2018-rural-progressives/.

Hanna, Stephen P., and Stephen J. Farnsworth. 2013. "Visualizing Virginia's Changing Electorate: Mapping Presidential Elections from 2000 to 2012. *The Virginia Newsletter* 89(2): 1–10.

Hebel, Sara. 2005. "A Businessman Bridges the Political Aisle." *Chronicle of Higher Education*, 25 February. http://search.ebscohost.com.umw.idm.oclc.org/login.aspx?direct=true&db=ehh&AN=16295055&site=ehost-live.

Hood, M. V., Quentin Kidd, and Irwin L. Morris. 2015. "Race and the Tea Party in the Old Dominion: Split-Ticket Voting in the 2013 Virginia Elections." *PS: Political Science and Politics* 48(1): 107–114. https://doi.org/10.1017/S1049096514001632.

Johnston, Ron, Kelvyn Jones, and David Manley. 2019. "Multilevel Modeling of Space–Time Variations: Exploring Landslide Voting Patterns at United States Presidential Elections, 1992–2016." *Geographical Analysis* 51(3): 280–313. https://doi.org/10.1111/gean.12176.

Key, V. O., Jr. 1949. *Southern Politics in State and Nation*. New York: Knopf.

Leahy, Norman. 2020. "Virginia Republicans Aren't Completely Out of the Picture." *Washington Post*, 6 November. https://www.washingtonpost.com/opinions/local-opinions/virginia-republicans-arent-completely-out-of-the-picture/2020/11/04/b073fc64-1eba-11eb-ba21-f2f001f0554b_story.html.

Lewis, Bob. 2019. "A Commonwealth Divided? Republican Rural Virginia Loses Ground to Democrats' Suburban Strongholds." *Virginia Mercury*, 11 November. https://www.virginiamercury.com/2019/11/11/a-commonwealth-divided-republican-rural-virginia-loses-ground-to-democrats-suburban-strongholds/.

Lichter, Daniel, and James Ziliak. 2017. "The Rural-Urban Interface: New Patterns of Spatial Interdependence and Inequality in America." *The Annals of the American Academy of Political and Social Science* 672(6), July. https://advance-lexis-com.umw.idm.oclc.org/api/document?collection=analytical-materials&id=urn:contentItem:5PTG-MG40–00CV-J1HT-00000–00&context=1516831.

Masket, Seth. 2017. "Rural White Voters Didn't Show Up for Virginia's Election." *Vox*, 9 November. https://www.vox.com/mischiefs-of-faction/2017/11/8/16625578/rural-whites-no-show-virginia.

McKee, Guian. 2020. "What 2020 Election Results Tell Us about America's Growing Urban-Rural Divide." *UVA Today*, 5 November. https://news.virginia.edu/content/what-2020-election-results-tell-us-about-americas-growing-urban-rural-divide.

McKee, Seth C. 2008. "Rural Voters and the Polarization of American Presidential Elections." *PS: Political Science and Politics* 41(1): 101–108. https://doi.org/10.1017/S1049096508080165.

Medvic, Stephen K. 1999. "Forging 'Debatable Ground': The Transformation of Party Politics in Virginia." In *Government and Politics in Virginia: The Old Dominion at the 21st Century*, ed. Quentin Kidd, 81–85. Needham Heights, MA: Simon and Schuster.

Monnat, Shannon, and David Brown. 2017. "More Than a Rural Revolt: Landscapes of Despair and the 2016 Presidential Election." *Journal of Rural Studies* 55: 227–236. https://doi.org/10.1016/j.jrurstud.2017.08.010.

Olivo, Antonio. 2018. "Kaine, Far Ahead in His Senate Race, Tries to Expand the Map in Virginia for Other Democrats." *Washington Post*, 8 September. https://www.washingtonpost.com/local/virginia-politics/kaine-far-ahead-in-his-senate-race-tries-to-expand-the-map-in-virginia-for-other-democrats/2018/09/08/a861a608-ac83–11e8–8a0c-70b618c98d3c_story.html.

Olivo, Antonio. 2019. "In This Suburban Democratic Primary, All 4 Candidates Are First-Generation Americans." *Washington Post*, 7 June. https://www.washingtonpost.com/local/virginia-politics

/in-this-suburban-democratic-primary-all-4-candidates-are-1st-generation-americans/2019/06/06/776d188e-87d4–11e9-a870-b9c411dc4312_story.html.

Olivo, Antonio. 2021. "After Fueling a Blue Tide, Democrats in Changing Virginia Suburb Aim High for More influence." *Washington Post*, 4 January. https://www.washingtonpost.com/local/virginia-politics/prince-william-democrats-election/2021/01/04/48d27f72–4acf-11eb-a9d9–1e3ec4a928b9_story.html.

Peirce, Neal. 2005. "Fiscal Integrity: Political Dead Letter—Or Not?" *Government Finance Review* 21(2): 63–64. https://umw.idm.oclc.org/login?url=https://www-proquest-com.umw.idm.oclc.org/trade-journals/fiscal-integrity-political-dead-letter-not/docview/229697075/se-2?accountid=12299.

Rodden, Jonathan. 2019. *Why Cities Lose: The Deep Roots of the Urban-Rural Divide*. New York: Basic Books.

Sabato, Larry J. 1977. *The Democratic Party in Virginia: Tantamount to Election No Longer*. Charlottesville: University of Virginia Press.

Samuelsohn, Darrell. 2011. "Rick Boucher Lands with D.C. Law Firm." *Politico*, 18 May. https://www.politico.com/story/2011/05/rick-boucher-lands-with-dc-law-firm-055254.

Scala, Dante, and Kenneth Johnson. 2017. "The New Rural-Urban Interface: Political Polarization along the Rural-Urban Continuum? The Geography of the Presidential Vote, 2000–2016." *The Annals of the American Academy of Political and Social Science* 672(1): 162–184, July. https://doi.org/10.1177/0002716217712696.

Schaller, Thomas F. 2006. *Whistling Past Dixie: How the Democrats Can Win Without the South*. New York: Simon and Schuster.

Schneider, Gregory S. 2018a. "In Virginia's Coal Country, a Democratic Challenger Makes His Case to Trump Voters." *Washington Post*, 31 October. https://www.washingtonpost.com/local/virginia-politics/long-shot-democrats-look-for-a-different-way-to-run-in-reddest-parts-of-virginia/2018/10/31/1baede26-d891–11e8-aeb7-ddcad4a0a54e_story.html.

Starobin, Paul. 2006. "The Man with the Golden Phone." *The Atlantic*, May. https://www.theatlantic.com/magazine/archive/2006/05/the-man-with-the-golden-phone/304777/.

Vozzella, Laura, Jenna Portnoy, and Rachel Weiner. 2014. "Warner Claims Victory over Gillespie in Virginia Senate Race."

Washington Post, 4 November. https://www.washingtonpost.com/local/virginia-politics/warner-gillespie-in-a-tight-race-in-first-wave-of-ballots/2014/11/04/80bb534a-60fd-11e4-9f3a-7e28799e0549_story.html.

Walsh, Katherine Cramer. 2012. "Putting Inequality in Its Place: Rural Consciousness and the Power of Perspective." *American Political Science Review* 106(3): 517–532.

Warner, Mark. 2001. "Mark Warner Country." [Gubernatorial Campaign Advertisement]. https://www.youtube.com/watch?v=BchLv9B_Gj8&fbclid=IwAR0rlcyZLNdcliMmavi7X5QWycyIh9faeX0S23sFUCQns68p9MLtoLY12S4.

Chapter 3

America's Rural Growth Challenge [Special issue]. 2019. *Virginia Economic Review*.

Arnosti, N., and A. Liu. 2018. "Why Rural America Needs Cities." Washington, DC: Brookings Institution, 30 November. https://www.brookings.edu/research/why-rural-america-needs-cities/.

Bosman, J. 2018. School's Closed. Forever. *New York Times*, 13 June. https://www.nytimes.com/2018/06/13/us/arena-wisconsin-schools-empty.html.

Buescher, B., and T. Duvall. 2018. *Independent Performance Assessment of Jobs*. Ohio: McKinsey and Company. https://www.jobsohio.com/assets/files/independent_performance_assessment_of_jobsohio_june_2018.pdf.

Coleman, E. 2019. "Want Better Education in Rural America? Start with Broadband." *Route Fifty*, 15 May. https://www.route-fifty.com/infrastructure/2019/05/want-better-education-rural-america-start-broadband/157034/.

Community Strategies Group. 2019. *Rural Development Hubs: Strengthening America's Rural Innovation Infrastructure*. The Aspen Institute. https://www.aspeninstitute.org/blog-posts/rural-development-hubs-report/.

Day, J. C. 2019. *Rates of Uninsured Fall in Rural Counties, Remain Higher Than Urban Counties*. US Census. https://www.census.gov/library/stories/2019/04/health-insurance-rural-america.html.

Economic Research Service. 2019. *Rural Employment and Unemployment*. US Department of Agriculture, 23 September. https://

www.ers.usda.gov/topics/rural-economy-population/employment-education/rural-employment-and-unemployment/

Fishbane, L., and A. Tomer. 2019. *Broadband Is Too Important for This Many in the US to Be Disconnected.* Washington, DC: Brookings Institution, 14 August. https://www.brookings.edu/blog/the-avenue/2019/08/14/broadband-is-too-important-for-this-many-in-the-us-to-be-disconnected/.

Gambale, G. 2009. "23rd Annual Corporate Survey and the 5th Annual Consultants Survey." *Area Development.*

Gambale, G. 2019. "33rd Annual Corporate Survey and the 15th Annual Consultants Survey, Q1." *Area Development.* https://www.areadevelopment.com/Corporate-Consultants-Survey-Results/Q1-2019/33nd-annual-corporate-survey-15th-annual-consultants-survey.shtml.

Greenblatt, A. 2018. "In Rural America, Violent Crime Reaches Highest Level in a Decade." *Governing*, July. https://www.governing.com/topics/public-justice-safety/gov-crime-rural-urban-cities.html.

Krugman, P. 2019. "Getting Real About Rural America: Nobody Knows How to Reverse the Heartland's Decline." *New York Times*, 18 March. https://www.nytimes.com/2019/03/18/opinion/rural-america-economic-decline.html.

Macy, B. 2018. *Dopesick: Dealers, Doctors, and the Drug Company That Addicted America.* Boston: Little, Brown.

Mannheimer, Z. 2020. "Google's Work from Home Extension Could Be a Boon for Rural America." *The Hill*, 1 August. https://thehill.com/opinion/technology/510123-googles-work-from-home-extension-could-be-a-boon-for-rural-america.

Moret, S. 2016. "Attainment, Alignment, and Economic Opportunity in America: Linkages Between Higher Education and the Labor Market." Publication No. AAI10158551. PhD diss., University of Pennsylvania. PQDT Open.

Perrin, A. 2019. "Digital Gap Between Rural and Nonrural America Persists." Pew Research Center: Fact Tank, 31 May. https://www.pewresearch.org/fact-tank/2019/05/31/digital-gap-between-rural-and-nonrural-america-persists/.

Porter, E. 2018. "The Hard Truths of Trying to 'Save' the Rural Economy." *New York Times*, 14 December. https://www.nytimes.com

/interactive/2018/12/14/opinion/rural-america-trump-decline.html?searchResultPosition=1.

Repp, D. 2020. "How Communities Can Attract and Retain Remote Workers." *Emsi*, 30 March. https://www.economicmodeling.com/attract-and-retain-remote-workers/.

Rheuban, K. S. 2019. "Broadband Expansion Is Crucial to Health Care Access." *Virginia Mercury*, 16 September. https://www.virginiamercury.com/2019/09/16/broadband-expansion-is-crucial-to-health-care-access/.

Saslow, E. 2019. "'Who's Going to Take Care of These People?': As Emergencies Rise Across Rural America, a Hospital Fights for Its Life." *Washington Post*, 11 May. https://www.washingtonpost.com/news/national/wp/2019/05/11/feature/whos-going-to-take-care-of-these-people/?utm_term=.0f8ab6cd931d.

Scott, K., and G. Shaw. 2020. *Reprogramming the American Dream: From Rural America to Silicon Valley—Making AI Serve Us All*. Harper Business.

Simpson, A. 2019. "As Rural Groceries Fade Away, Lawmakers Wonder Whether to Act." The Pew Charitable Trusts, 2 October. https://www.pewtrusts.org/en/research-and-analysis/blogs/stateline/2019/10/02/as-rural-groceries-fade-away-lawmakers-wonder-whether-to-act.

Swenson, D. 2019. "Most of America's Rural Areas Are Doomed to Decline." *The Conversation*, 7 May. https://theconversation.com/most-of-americas-rural-areas-are-doomed-to-decline-115343.

Tax Foundation. 2015. *Location Matters*. https://interactive.taxfoundation.org/location-matters/location-matters-2015.pdf.

Technology Engagement Center. 2019. "Unlocking the Digital Potential of Rural: Virginia." [Fact Sheet]. US Chamber of Commerce. https://americaninnovators.com/wp-content/uploads/2019/03/rural_report_factsheet_VA.pdf.

US Department of Agriculture. 2019. *A Case for Rural Broadband*. https://www.usda.gov/sites/default/files/documents/case-for-rural-broadband.pdf.

Van Dam, A. 2019. "The Real (Surprisingly Comforting) Reason Rural America Is Doomed to Decline." *Washington Post*, 24 May. https://www.washingtonpost.com/business/2019/05/24/real

-surprisingly-comforting-reason-rural-america-is-doomed-decline/.

Virginia Economic Development Partnership. 2017. *Strategic Plan for Economic Development of the Commonwealth.* https://www.vedp.org/strategicplan.

Virginia Economic Development Partnership. 2020. *Quarterly Employment Forecast as % of pre-COVID-19 Baseline.*

Vogels, E. A., A. Perrin, L. Rainie, and M. Anderson. 2020. "53% of Americans Say the Internet Has Been Essential During the Covid-19 Outbreak." Pew Research Center, 30 April. https://www.pewresearch.org/internet/2020/04/30/53-of-americans-say-the-internet-has-been-essential-during-the-covid-19-outbreak/.

Whitacre, B., and S. Deller. 2019. "Research Report: Broadband Availability Raises Market Value of Rural Houses." *Daily Yonder*, 17 July. https://dailyyonder.com/broadbands-value-rural-houses/2019/07/17/.

Zarroli, J. 2015. "How Singapore Became One of the Richest Places on Earth." NPR, 29 March. https://www.npr.org/2015/03/29/395811510/how-singapore-became-one-of-the-richest-places-on-earth.

Ziobro, P. 2019. "FedEx Goes Deep into Mississippi Delta to Find Workers." *Wall Street Journal*, 7 December. https://www.wsj.com/articles/fedex-goes-deep-into-mississippi-delta-to-find-workers-11575714601.

CHAPTER 4

Alicke, K., R. Gupta, and V. Trautwein. 2020, July 21. *Resetting Supply Chains for the Next Normal.* McKinsey and Company. https://www.mckinsey.com/business-functions/operations/our-insights/resetting-supply-chains-for-the-next-normal.

Audretsch D. B., and M. P. Feldman. 2004. "Knowledge Spillovers and the Agglomeration Economy." In *Handbook of Regional and Urban Economics*, ed. J. V. Henderson and J. F. Thisse, 4:2713–2739. https://doi.org/10.1016/S1574-0080(04)80018-X.

Barkley, D. L., M. S. Henry, and S. Bao. 1996. "Identifying 'Spread' versus 'Backwash' Effects in Regional Economic Areas: A Density Functions Approach." *Land Economics* 72(3): 336–357. https://doi.org/10.2307/3147201.

Benoit, Kenneth. 2011. "Linear Regression Models with Logarithmic Transformations." Methodology Institute, London School of Economics. https://links.sharezomics.com/assets/uploads/files/1600247928973-from_slack_logmodels2.pdf.

Cortright, J. 2006. *Making Sense of Clusters: Regional Competitiveness and Economic Development.* Washington, DC: Brookings Institution.

Dabson, B. 2011. "Rural Regional Innovation: A Response to Metropolitan-Framed Place-Based Thinking in the United States." *Australasian Journal of Regional Studies* 17(1).

Delgado, M., M. E. Porter, and S. Stern. 2014. "Clusters, Convergence, and Economic Performance." *Research Policy* 43(10): 1785–1799. https://doi.org/10.3386/w18250.

Delgado, M., M. E. Porter, and S. Stern. 2010. "Clusters and Entrepreneurship." *Journal of Economic Geography* 10(4): 495–518. https://doi.org/10.2139/ssrn.1689084.

Delgado, M., and K. Zeuli. 2016. "Clusters and Regional Performance: Implications for Inner Cities." *Economic Development Quarterly* 30(2): 117–136. https://doi.org/10.1177/0891242416637422.

Feser, E., and A. Isserman. 2009. "The Rural Role in National Value Chains." *Regional Studies* 43(1): 89–109. https://doi.org/10.1080/00343400801968429

Ganong P., and D. W. Shoag. 2017. "Why Has Regional Income Convergence in the U.S. Declined?" *Journal of Urban Economics* 102: 76–90. https://doi.org/10.1016/j.jue.2017.07.002.

Jaffe, A., M. Trajtenberg, and R. Henderson. 1993. "Geographic Localization of Knowledge Spillovers as Evidenced by Patent Citations." *Quarterly Journal of Economics* 108(3): 577–598. https://doi.org/10.2307/2118401.

Ketels, C. 2017. *Cluster Mapping as a Tool for Development.* Cambridge, MA: Harvard Business School Institute for Strategy and Competitiveness.

Lewin, P., B. Weber, and D. Holland. 2013. "Core-Periphery Dynamics in the Portland, Oregon, Region: 1982–2006." *Annals of Regional Science* 51(2): 411–432. https://doi.org/10.1007/s00168-013-0552-6.

Martin, S. 2011. "Critical Linkages: Strengthening Clusters in Urban and Rural Oregon." In *Toward One Oregon: Rural-Urban Interdependence and the Evolution of a State*. Corvallis: Oregon State University Press.

Mayer, H., and J. Provo, eds. 2007. *Farmshoring in Virginia: Domestic Outsourcing Strategies for Linking Urban and Rural Economies in the Commonwealth of Virginia*. VA Tech, Urban Affairs and Planning, April.

McFarland, C. 2018. "Bridging the Urban-Rural Economic Divide." *National League of Cities*.

Moretti, E. 2012. *The New Geography of Jobs*. New York: Houghton Mifflin Harcourt.

Myrdal, G. 1957. *Economic Theory and Underdeveloped Regions*. London: Gerald Duckworth.

Parker, K., J. Menasce Horowitz, A. Brown, R. Fry, D. Cohn, and R. Igielnik. 2018. "What Unites and Divides Urban, Suburban and Rural Communities." Pew Research Center, 22 May. https://www.pewsocialtrends.org/2018/05/22/what-unites-and-divides-urban-suburban-and-rural-communities.

Partridge, M. D., D. S. Rickman, K. Ali, and M. R. Olfert. 2008. "Lost in Space: Population Growth in the American Hinterlands and Small Cities." *Journal of Economic Geography* 8(6): 727–757. https://doi.org/10.1093/jeg/lbn038.

Rosenthal, S. S., and W. C. Strange. 2001. "The Determinants of Agglomeration." *Journal of Urban Economics* 50(2): 191–229. https://doi.org/10.1006juec.2001.2230.

Searls, K. 2011. *Pilot Study: Estimating Rural and Urban Minnesota's Interdependencies*. Minnesota Rural Partners, Inc.

Tandoh-Offin, P. 2010. "The Evolving Rural and Urban Interdependence: Opportunities and Challenges for Community Economic Development." *Journal of Geography and Regional Planning* 3(12): 339–345.

US Cluster Mapping Project, Institute for Strategy and Competitiveness, Harvard Business School. http://clustermapping.us.

Warren, A., and L. Goren. 2018, August 9. *The Rural-Urban Divide is Visible in Virginia's Recovery*. The Commonwealth Institute. https://thehalfsheet.org/post/176781393318/the-rural-urban-divide-is-visible-in-virginias.

Chapter 5

Cowell, M., S. Lyon-Hill, and S. Tate. 2018. "It Takes All Kinds: Understanding Diverse Entrepreneur Ecosystems." *Journal of Enterprising Communities: People and Places in the Global Economy* 12(2): 178–198. https://doi.org/10.1108/JEC-08201 70064.

Ewing Marion Kauffman Foundation. 2020. *Entrepreneur Ecosystem Building Playbook 3.0.* https://www.kauffman.org/ecosystem-playbook-draft-3/.

GO Virginia Region 9. 2020. *Building Stronger Entrepreneur Ecosystems in Central Virginia: Expanding Go Virginia Region 9's Rural Ecosystem.* https://www.centralvirginia.org/wp-content/uploads/2020/05/Final-Report-Central-VA-Rural-ESHIP-Report.pdf.

GO Virginia Region 9. 2017. *Go Virginia Region 9: Economic Growth and Diversification Plan.* https://www.centralvirginia.org/wp-content/uploads/2017/06/Economic-Growth-and-Diversification-Plan-Region-9-Aug-31–2017.pdf.

Lin, M. C. Y., J. Lee, and P. Wong. 2020. *Best Performing Cities 2020: Where America's Jobs Are Created and Sustained.* Milken Institute. Report. https://milkeninstitute.org/reports/best-performing-cities-2020.

Malecki, E. J. 2018. "Entrepreneurship and Entrepreneur Ecosystems." *Geography Compass.* 12:e12359. https://doi.org/10.1111/gec3.12359.

Pages, E. 2018. *Entrepreneur Ecosystems in Appalachia: Literature Review.* Report prepared for the Appalachian Regional Commission.

Stangler, D., and J. Bell-Masterson. 2015. *Measuring an Entrepreneur Ecosystem.* Report prepared for the Ewing Marion Kauffman Foundation.

TEConomy Partners. 2018. *Regional Entrepreneur Assessment Project: Region 9-Piedmont Opportunity Corridor.*

Chapter 6

Ardoin, S. 2018. *College Aspirations and Access in Working-Class, Rural Communities: The Mixed Signals, Challenges, and New Language First-Generation Students Encounter.* Washington, DC: Lexington Books.

Biddle, C., and A. P. Azano. 2016. "Constructing and Reconstructing the 'Rural School Problem': A Century of Rural Education Research." *Review of Research in Education* 40(1): 298–325. https://doi.org/10.3102/0091732X16667700.

Burbank, M. D., and D. Kauchak. 2003. "An Alternative Model for Professional Development: Investigations into Effective Collaboration." *Teaching and Teacher Education* 19(5): 499–514.

Bybee, R. 2018. *STEM Education: Now More Than Ever*. Arlington, VA: National Science Teaching Association.

Cochran-Smith, M., A. M. Villegas, L. Abrams, L. Chavez-Moreno, T. Mills, and R. Stern. 2015. "Critiquing Teacher Preparation Research: An Overview of the Field, Part II." *Journal of Teacher Education* 66(2): 109–121.

Committee on STEM Education. 2018. *Charting a Course for Success: America's Strategy for Stem Education*. Washington, DC: National Science and Technology Council.

Corbin, R. 2019. "STEM Dispositions Create Future Leaders and Innovators." Keynote session presented at the meeting of the Virginia Association of Science Teachers, Roanoke, VA.

Council on Foreign Relations 2012. *U.S. Education Reform and National Security (Independent Task Force Report, No. 68)*. New York: Council on Foreign Relations.

Darling-Hammond, L. 2010. "Recruiting and Retaining Teachers: Turning Around the Race to the Bottom in High Need Schools." *Journal of Curriculum and Instruction* 4(1): 16–32.

DeCoito, I., and P. Myszkal. 2018. "Connecting Science Instruction and Teachers' Self-Efficacy and Beliefs in STEM Education". *Journal of Science Teacher Education* 29(6): 485–503.

Fullan, M. 2015. *The New Meaning of Educational Change*, 5th ed. New York: Teachers College Press.

Fullan, M. 2020. *Leading in a Culture of Change*, 2nd ed. Hoboken, NJ: Jossey-Bass.

Ingersoll, R. M. 2004. "Why Do High-Poverty Schools Have Difficulty Staffing Their Classrooms with Qualified Teachers?" In *Renewing Our Schools, Securing Our Future—A National Task Force on Public Education; Joint Initiative of the Center for American Progress and the Institute for America's Future*. https://repository.upenn.edu/gse_pubs/493.

Johnson, C. 2012. "Implications of STEM Education Policy: Challenges, Progress and Lessons Learned." *School Science and Mathematics* 112(1): 44–55.

Jones, L., and W. E. Brunner. 1994. *Appalachian Values*. Ashland, KY: Jesse Stuart Foundation.

Magliaro, S. G., and J. Ernst. 2018. *Inventory of Statewide STEM Education Networks*. Blacksburg, VA: Center for Research in SEAD Education, Virginia Tech. https://drive.google.com/drive/u/0/folders/1OdVxPvbl7Wwbm3KYsWLzMpFSa-nxCtEM.

McFarland, C. 2018. *Bridging the Urban-Rural Economic Divide*. National League of Cities Center for City Solutions.

Malcolm, S., and M. Feder, eds. 2016. *Barriers and Opportunities for 2-Year and 4-Year Stem Degrees*. Washington, DC: The National Academies Press.

Mickle, D. 2020. "What Are the Hot Stem Jobs in Virginia." https://vpm.org/articles/4324/what-are-the-hot-stem-jobs-in-virginia.

National Academy of Sciences, Engineering and Medicine. 2011. *Expanding Underrepresented Minority Participation: America's Science and Technology Talent at the Crossroads*. The National Academy Press. https://www.nap.edu/catalog/12984/expanding-underrepresented-minority-participation-americas-science-and-technology-talent-at.

National Center for Science and Engineering Statistics. 2013. *Women, Minorities, and Persons with Disabilities in Science and Engineering*. Washington, DC: National Science Foundation.

National Research Council. 2012. *A Framework for K–12 Science Education: Practices, Crosscutting Concepts, and Core Ideas*. Washington, DC: The National Academic Press. https://doi.org/10.17226/13165.

National Science Board 2020. *Vision 2030*. Alexandria, VA: National Science Board.

PCAST (President's Council of Advisors on Science and Technology). 2010. *Prepare and Inspire: K12 Education in Science, Technology, Engineering, and Math (STEM) for America's Future*. White House Office of Science and Technology Policy (OSTP): 119.

Tate, W. 2001. "Science Education as a Civil Right: Urban Schools and Opportunity-to-Learn Considerations." *Journal of Research in Science Teaching* 38: 1015–1028.

Tupponce, J. 2013. "Going Begging: Jobs Go Unfilled Because of a Shortage of Skilled Workers." https://www.virginiabusiness.com/article/going-begging/.

US Department of Labor and Statistics. 2019. "News Release: Employment Projections 2019–2029." https://www.bls.gov/news.release/pdf/ecopro.pdf.

Virginia Department of Education. 2020. Science, Technology, Engineering, and Mathematics (STEM). http://www.doe.virginia.gov/instruction/stem/index.shtml.

Virginia Department of Education, Division of Teacher Education and Licensure. 2016. *The Shortage of Qualified Teachers in the Commonwealth of Virginia and Recommended Strategies for Addressing the Shortage.* https://rga.lis.virginia.gov/Published/2016/RD64/PDF.

Weld, J. 2017. *Creating A Stem Culture for Teaching and Learning.* Arlington, VA: NSTA.

Zollman, A. 2012. "Learning for STEM Literacy: STEM Literacy for Learning." *School Science and Mathematics* 112: 12–19.

CHAPTER 7

Arlington Fiber Cooperative. 2020. Virginia Is Currently Not for Lovers of Public Broadband: It Is Time to Change That. *Blue Virginia Newsletter*, 18 July. https://bluevirginia.us/2020/07/virginia-is-currently-not-for-lovers-of-public-broadband-its-time-to-change-that.

Blythe, E., J. Mitchell, and R. Jones. 2018. *Commonwealth Commitment 2022: Rural Thoughts for a Four-Year Plan for Universal Broadband Coverage.* Office of the Governor. Richmond, VA.

Blythe, E. 2003. *Rationale, Environment, and Strategic Considerations, Strategic Technology Infrastructure for Regional Competitiveness in the Network Economy*, vol. 1. An eleven-volume study sponsored by the Virginia Tobacco Region Revitalization Commission, Virginia Tech.

Broadband Advisory Council. 2011. *Broadband Activities in the Commonwealth*. Annual Report presented to Governor Robert F. McDonnell, the General Assembly, and the Joint Commission on Technology and Science.

Casper, J. 2021. *Washington State Removes All Barriers to Municipal Broadband*. Institute for Local Self Resilience. https://ilsr.org/washingto-staste-removes-all-barriers-to-municipal-broadband.

Chamberlain, K. 2020. "Municipal Broadband Is Roadblocked or Outlawed in 22 States." *Broadband Now*, 13 May. https://broadbandnow.com/report/municipal-broadband-roadblocks/.

Chambers, J. 2018. "Proving a Negative." *Broadband Communities Magazine*. August/September. https://www.bbcmag.com/rural-broadband/proving-a-negative.

Chittum, M. 2017. "Roanoke Council Condemns Del. Kathy Byron's Broadband Bill." *Roanoke Times*, 17 January.

Code of Virginia 56-484.7.1, Offering of communications services. https://law.lis.virginia.gov/vacode/title56/chapter15/section56484.7:1/#:~:text=Each%20county%2C%20city%2C%20town%2C,come%2C%20first%2Dserved%20basis%20to.

Code of Virginia 15.2-2108.6. Feasibility study on providing cable television services. https://law.lis.virginia.gov/vacode/title15.2/chapter21/section15.2–2108.6/.

Commonwealth Broadband Roundtable. 2008. *Final Report to Governor Timothy Kaine*. Richmond, VA.

Demmitt, J. 2019. "Floyd County to Become the Most Connected Rural Community in Virginia State Leaders Say." *Roanoke Times*, 22 April.

Department of Housing and Community Development. 2020. *Commonwealth Connect*. Report from the Office of Broadband, State of Virginia.

Díaz-Balart, J. 2020. Confronting American's Digital Divide. *Washington Post*, 30 September.

Drake, C., Y. Zhange, K. Chaiyachati, and D. Polsky. 2019. "The Limitations of Poor Broadband Internet Access for Telemedicine Use in Rural America: An Observational Study." *Annals of Internal Medicine* 171(5): 382–338.

Engebretson, J. 2020. "Frontier, CenturyLink Miss CAF-II Deployment Milestones for Rural Broadband." *Telecompetitor*, 21 January. https://www.telecompetitor.com/frontier-centurylink-miss-caf-ii-deployment-milestones-for-rural-broadband/.

Executive Office Release. 2003. "Governor Warner Urges Broadband Deployment to Appalachian Virginia," 3 March.

FCC. 2020. *Rural Digital Opportunity Fund*. Federal Communications Commission. 30 January. https://www.fcc.gov/auction/904/factsheet.

Holmes, A., and C. Zubak-Skees. 2015. "These Maps Show Why Internet Is Way More Expensive in the US Than Europe." *The Verge* (April 1): 1–15.

Jenkins-Smith, H., C. Silva, K. Gupta, and J. Ripberger. 2014. "Belief System Continuity and Change in Policy Advocacy Coalitions: Using Cultural Theory to Specify Belief Systems, Coalitions, and Sources of Change." *Policy Studies Journal* 42(4): 484–508.

Kienbaum, K. 2019. "Preemption Détente: Municipal Broadband Networks Face Barriers in 19 States." Institute for Local Self-Reliance. Community Networks, 8 August.

LaRiviere, K. 2018. *Blueprint for Broadband: Expanding Broadband into Rural Virginia*. Virginia Association of Counties, May.

Pressgrove, J. 2020. "Does the Federal Broadband Definition Reflect Real-World Need?" Government Technology, 24 June.

Poole, J. 2020. "Broadband Authority Announces Phased Countrywide Connection Plan." *Daily Progress*, 16 July.

Ross, S. 2018. "Update: Rural Population Loss Still Tied to Poor Broadband." *Broadband Communities*, August/September.

Sabatier, P., and H. Jenkins-Smith. 1993. *Policy Change and Learning: An Advocacy Coalition Approach*. Boulder: Westview Press.

Sallet, J. 2020. *Broadband for America Now*. Chicago: Benton Institute for Broadband and Society.

Virginia Broadband Advisor. 2020. *Report on Commonwealth Connect 2.0: Governor Northam's 2020 Plan to Connect Virginia*. Richmond, VA.

Warner, M. Senator 2020. A Plan for Rule Broadband. Email to constituents, 8 July.

Weldon Cooper Center for Public Service. 2018. "Data Visualizations Tell the Stories Within Virginia Demographics." Demographics Research Group in the Weldon Cooper Center for Public Service. http://demographics.coopercenter.org/visualizing-virginia/.

Whitacre, B., and R. Gallardo. 2020. "State Broadband Policy: Impacts on Availability." *Telecommunications Policy* 44: 1–17.

Chapter 8

Adams, D., and A. Goldbard. 2002. *Community, Culture, and Globalization*. New York: Rockefeller Foundation.

Adejumo, C. O. 2010. "Promoting Artistic and Cultural Development Through Service Learning and Critical Pedagogy in a Low-Income Community Art Program." *Visual Arts Research* 36(1): 23–34. https://doi.org/10.5406/visuartsrese.36.1.0023.

Appalshop. 2017. "Working Definitions of Key Economic Terms in Community Cultural and Economic Development." https://www.performingourfuture.com/.

Ashwood, L. 2018. "Rural Conservatism or Anarchism? the Pro-State, Stateless, and Anti-State Positions." *Rural Sociology* 83(4): 717–748. https://doi.org/10.1111/ruso.12226.

Boal, A. 1995, *The Rainbow of Desire: The Boal Method of Theatre and Therapy*. London: Routledge.

Boal, A. 1998, *Legislative Theatre*. London: Routledge.

Boal, A. 2002. *Games for Actors and Non-Actors*. London: Routledge.

Brown, W. 2019. *In the Ruins of Neoliberalism: The Rise of Antidemocratic Politics in the West*. New York: Columbia University Press.

Campbell, C., F. Cornish, A. Gibbs, and K. Scott. 2010. "Heeding the Push from Below: How Do Social Movements Persuade the Rich to Listen to the Poor?" *Journal of Health Psychology* 15(7): 962–971. https://doi.org/10.1177/1359105310372815.

Carolan, M. 2020. "The Rural Problem: Justice in the Countryside." *Rural Sociology* 85(1): 22–56. https://doi.org/10.1111/ruso.12278.

Chinyowa, K. 2014. "Re-imagining Boal through the Theatre of the Oppressor." In *Applied Drama/Theatre as Social Intervention in Conflict and Post-Conflict Contexts*, ed. H. Barnes and M. H. Coetzee, 2–17. Newcastle-upon-Tyne: Cambridge Scholars Publisher.

Chomsky, N. 1999. *Profit over People: Neoliberalism and Global Order*, 1st ed. New York: Seven Stories Press.

Christens, B. D., C. E. Hanlin, and P. W. Speer. 2007. "Getting the Social Organism Thinking: Strategy for Systems Change." *American Journal of Community Psychology*. https://prodduke-my.sharepoint.com/personal/jr216_duke_edu/Documents/6_8_21 Data Backup/6_8_21 Desktop/Current projects/2 Vibrant Virginia / 39(3–4): 229–238. https://doi.org/10.1007/s10464-007-9119-y.

Cox Richardson, H. 2020. *How the South Won the Civil War: Oligarchy, Democracy, and the Continuing Fight for the Soul of America.* New York: Oxford University Press.

Cowie, P. 2017. "Performing Planning: Understanding Community Participation in Planning through Theatre." *Town Planning Review* 4: 401.

Dewey, R. 1960. "The Rural-Urban Continuum: Real but Relatively Unimportant." *American Journal of Sociology* 66(1): 60–66.

EMSI. 2020. Economy Overview Data Set. [Proprietary economic and workforce data tool]. http://economicmodeling.com.

Fink, B. 2020. "How a Conservative Coal County Built the Biggest Community Solar Energy Project in East Kentucky." *Brookings*, 26 March. https://www.brookings.edu/blog/the-avenue/2020/03/26/how-a-conservative-coal-county-built-the-biggest-community-solar-energy-project-in-east-kentucky/.

Freire, P. 1970. *Pedagogy of the Oppressed.* Translated by M. B. Ramos, 30th ed. London: Continuum.

Harvey, D. 2005. *A Brief History of Neoliberalism.* New York: Oxford University Press.

Hochschild, A. R. 2018. *Strangers in Their Own Land: Anger and Mourning on the American Right.* New York: The New Press.

Ingraham, C. 2020. "The Harmful, Popular Misconceptions about Rural America." *The Washington Post*, 3 January. https://www.washingtonpost.com/business/2020/01/03/five-myths-about-rural-america/.

Kirakosyan, L. 2017. "Social Imaginaries, Shared Citizen Action, and the Meanings of 'Community.'" *Community Change* 1(1): 1–14. http://doi.org/10.21061/cc.v1i1.a.2.

Krauss, R. M., and E. Morsella. 2006. "Communication and Conflict." In *The Handbook of Conflict Resolution: Theory and Practice*, ed. M. Deutsch and P. T. Coleman, 2nd ed., 144–158. San Francisco: Jossey-Bass.

Leighninger, M., and T. Nabatchi. 2015. *Public Participation for 21st Century Democracy.* New York: John Wiley.

MacLean, N. 2017. *Democracy in Chains: The Deep History of the Radical Right's Stealth Plan for America.* New York: Viking.

Marsden, T. 2016. "Exploring the Rural Eco-Economy: Beyond Neoliberalism." *Sociologia Ruralis* 56(4): 597–615. https://doi.org/10.1111/soru.12139.

Maxwell, A. 2019. "What We Got Wrong about the Southern Strategy." *Washington Post*, July 26. https://www.washingtonpost.com/outlook/2019/07/26/what-we-get-wrong-about-southern-strategy/.

Maxwell, A., and T. Shields. 2019. *The Long Southern Strategy: How Chasing White Voters in the South Changed American Politics*. New York: Oxford University Press.

Mezirow, J. 2003. "Transformative Learning as Discourse." *Journal of Transformative Education*. https://prodduke-my.sharepoint.com/personal/jr216_duke_edu/Documents/6_8_21 Data Backup/6_8_21 Desktop/Current projects/2 Vibrant Virginia/ 1(1): 58–63. https://doi.org/10.1177/1541344603252172.

Mills, D., and P. Brown. 2004. *Art and Wellbeing: A Guide to the Connections Between Community Cultural Development and Health, Ecologically Sustainable Development, Public Housing and Place, Rural Revitalisation, Community Strengthening, Active Citizenship, Social Inclusion and Cultural Diversity*. Australia Council.

Moayerian, N. 2018. "Development, Public Participation, and Cultural War." *Community Change* 2(1): 3. http://doi.org/10.21061/cc.v2i1.a.15.

Mundy, A., and J. Chan. 2013. "Visualizing Boundaries and Embodying Conflicts: Lessons Learned from a Theatrical Professional Development Program." *Collected Essays on Learning and Teaching* 6: 41–47.

Patrick County. n.d. *Finance*. https://www.co.patrick.va.us/finance.

Pickren, W. 2018. "Psychology in the Social Imaginary of Neoliberalism: Critique and Beyond." *Theory and Psychology* 28: 575–580. https://doi.org/10.1177/0959354318799210.

Reimers, B. C. 2015. "Building a Bridge across the Conflict Theory-Practice Gap: Comprehensive Conflict Engagement in Community Contexts." *Conflict Resolution Quarterly* 4: 437.

Rohd, M. P. 1998. *Theatre for Community, Conflict and Dialogue: Hope Is Vital Training Manual*. Portsmouth, NH: Heinemann Press.

ross, j.m., and C. Rodda. 2018. *Story Circles: Deep Listening and Bridge Building on Issues That Matter.* Edited by K. Tacket. Sacramento, CA: Capital Public Radio.

Sarkissian, W., and A. Cook. 2016. "Speaking Out in Community Engagement: A Review of Fifteen Years of Refinement of the SpeakOut Model." The Social Planning and Research Council of B.C. (SPARC BC). https://www.sparc.bc.ca/wp-content/uploads/2016/12/speaking-out-in-community-engagement.pdf.

Serra, N., and J. Stiglitz. 2008. *The Washington Consensus Reconsidered: Toward a New Global Governance.* New York: Oxford University Press.

Silva, J. 2019. *We're Still Here: Pain and Politics in the Heart of America.* New York: Oxford University Press.

Sonn, C., and A. Quayle. 2014. "Community Cultural Development for Social Change: Developing Critical Praxis." *Journal for Social Action in Counseling and Psychology* 6(1): 16–35.

Stephenson, M. 2009. "Exploring the Connections among Adaptive Leadership, Facets of Imagination and Social Imaginaries." *Public Policy and Administration* 24(4): 417–435.

Stephenson, M., B. Abella-Lipsey, L. Nagle, and N. Moayerian. 2020. "Community Social Polarization and Change: Evidence from Three Recent Studies." *World* 1(1): 20–33. MDPI AG. http://dx.doi.org/10.3390/world1010002.

Stiglitz, J. 2002. *Globalization and its Discontents.* New York: Norton.

Stiglitz, J. 2006. *Making Globalization Work.* New York: Norton.

Taylor, C. 2002. "Modern Social Imaginaries." *Public Culture* 14(1): 91–124.

Taylor, C. 2004. *Modern Social Imaginaries.* Durham, NC: Duke University Press.

US Census Bureau. 2020. Patrick County, Virginia. https://data.census.gov/cedsci/profile?q=Patrick%20County,%20Virginia&g=0500000US51141.

VA Department of Elections. 2021. *2020 November General: Patrick County, Virginia.* https://results.elections.virginia.gov/vaelections/2020%20November%20General/Site/Locality/PATRICK_COUNTY/President_and_Vice_President.html.

Walcott, S. M. 2011. "The Furniture Foothills and the Spatial Fix: Globalization in the Furniture Industry." *Southeastern Geographer* 51(1): 6–30. https://doi.org/10.1353/sgo.2011.0012.

Williams, J. A. 2002. *Appalachia: A History*. Chapel Hill: University of North Carolina Press.

Wuthnow, R. 2018. *The Left Behind: Decline and Rage in Rural America*. Princeton, NJ: Princeton University Press.

Young, I. M. 1997. "Difference as a Resource for Democratic Communication." In *Deliberative Democracy: Essays on Reason and Politics*, ed. J. Bohman and W. Rehg, 383-406. Cambridge, MA: MIT Press.

Young, J. 2020. *Appalachian Fall: Dispatches from Coal Country on What's Ailing America*. New York: Tiller Press.

CHAPTER 9

Bishop, C. 2012. Participation and spectacle: where are we now? *In*: N. Thompson, ed. *Living as form: socially engaged art from 1991–2011*. New York: Creative Time Books, 34–45.

Cameron Foundation. 2012. The Cameron Foundation Names New President. [Press release]. Petersburg, VA: The Cameron Foundation.

Campbell, M. 2017. "Exit 45 Gardens Project Tip of Economic Development Iceberg for Prince George." *Prince George Journal*, 13 November.

Chroma Design. 2018. South Crater Road Gateway http://chromadesigninc.com/portfolio-item/s-crater-rd-gateway/

Covil, W. 2018. "The Petersburg Arches: Who Paid What, and Where Did the Cash Come From?" WTVR.com, 27 August. https://www.wtvr.com/2018/08/27/the-petersburg-arches-who-paid-what-and-where-did-they-cash-come-from/.

Cramer, B. 2020. "Accessing Foundation Funding for Community Development: The Cameron Foundation." Presentation to the Virginia Department of Housing and Community Development.

Crater Planning District Commission. 2020. "About Us—Crater PDC." https://craterpdc.org/about-us/.

Crater Planning District Commission. 2021. "Crater PDC Population Projections." https://craterpdc.org/our-works/gis-maps-data/gis-maps-data-population/.

Doss, E. 2006. *Public Art Controversy: Cultural Expression and Civic Debate*. Americans for the Arts. https://www.americansforthearts.org/by-program/reports-and-data/legislation-policy/naappd/monograph-public-art-controversy-cultural-expression-and-civic-debate.

Foster, R. 2005. "Kepone: The 'Flour' Factory." *Richmond Magazine*, 8 July.

Frenette, A. 2017. The Rise of Creative Placemaking: Cross-Sector Collaboration as Cultural Policy in the United States, The Journal of Arts Management, Law, and Society, 47:5, 333-345, DOI: 10.1080/10632921.2017.1391727

Gibson, K. 2018. "'Return' Comes Home." *Progress-Index*, 7 June.

Lamson, D. 2020. *Petersburg, VA Community Gateway*. Madison, WI: CODAWorx. https://www.codaworx.com/projects/petersburg-va-community-gateway-the-cameron-foundation/

Markusen, A., and A. Gadwa-Nicodemus. 2019. "Creative Placemaking: Reflections on a 21st-Century American Arts Policy Initiative." In *Creative Placemaking: Research, Theory and Practice*, ed. C. Courage and A. McKeown, 11–27. London: Routledge.

Markusen, A., and A. Gadwa. 2010. *Creative Placemaking*. Washington, DC: Mayors' Institute on City Design and the National Endowment for the Arts.

Mavredes, M. 2018. *Local Government Fiscal Distress Monitoring*. Virginia Auditor of Public Accounts. http://www.apa.virginia.gov/reports/LocalFiscalDistressMonitoring2017.pdf.

Price, M. 2019. "Town Panics at Widely Shared Image of Man Stuck Atop Its New $1.2 Million Artwork." *Charlotte Observer*, 15 February. https://www.charlotteobserver.com/news/article226346945.html.

Ronk, L., L. Yilmaz, L. Foster, and S. Beck. 2011. *Establishment of a Public Art Commission*. A Report to the Mayor and City Council, Bluffs Arts Council.

Schneider, G. 2016. "City on the Brink: Petersburg Can't Pay Its Bills and Time Is Running Out." *Washington Post*, 5 September.

Senie, H. 2003. Reframing Public Art: Audience Use, Interpretation, and Appreciation. In Art and its Publics, A. McClellan (Ed.). https://doi.org/10.1002/9780470775936.ch9

Shorr, K. 2005. "Civil War History Lesson Petersburg, Va., Embraces and Expands Its Past." *Boston Globe*, 9 March.

Small, L. 2015a. "County Approves Roughly $1 Million in Gateway Improvements." *Progress-Index*, 16 July.

Small, L. 2015b. "The Cameron Foundation Changes Strategy to Make Impact." *Progress-Index*, 27 July.

Staff Report. 2007. "Iowa West Foundation Unveils Public Art Program." *Daily Nonpareil*, 10 October.

Stebbins, R. 2018. "City of Hopewell and Cameron Foundation Celebrate Completion of Community Gateway Project at Route 10 Bridge." [Press release]. Petersburg, VA: The Cameron Foundation.

Thomas, A. 2018. "Hopewell Residents Question Price Tag for 'Unappealing' Towering Tourist Greeter." WRIC.com, 3 October. https://www.wric.com/news/taking-action/hopewell-residents-question-price-tag-for-unappealing-towering-tourist-greeter/.

US Census Bureau. 2020. County Rurality Levels 2010.

US Census Bureau. 2019. QuickFacts: United States.

Vogelsong, S. 2016. "Hopewell Council OKs Monumental H Sculpture: Public Artwork to Be Gifted to City by Cameron Foundation." *Progress-Index*, 14 September. https://www.progress-index.com/news/20160914/hopewell-council-oks-monumental-h-sculpture.

Western States Arts Federation. 2020. Public Art Archive, 1880-present [Data set]. https://www.publicartarchive.org/

Zitcer, A. and Almanzar, S. 2020. Public art, cultural representation, and the just city, Journal of Urban Affairs, 42:7, 998-1013, DOI: 10.1080/07352166.2019.1601019

CHAPTER 10

Accordino, John, and Sarin Adhikari. 2021. "Balancing Act: Preserving Historic Fabric and Enhancing Economic Vitality in Towns in the Metropolitan Periphery." *Planning Practice & Research*, 1-16, DOI: https://doi.org/10.1080/02697459.2021.1995970

Accordino, John, and Fabrizio Fasulo. 2014. *Economic Impact of Historic Rehabilitation Tax Credit Programs in Virginia*. Prepared for Preservation Virginia, Richmond, VA.

Accordino, John, and Fabrizio Fasulo. 2015. *30 Years of Impact: How the Main Street Program Has Revitalized Virginia Communities*. Prepared for Preservation Virginia, Richmond, VA.

Accordino, John, and Fabrizio Fasulo. 2017. *The Economic Impact of Heritage Tourism in Virginia*. Prepared for Preservation Virginia, Richmond, VA.

Accordino, John, and Fabrizio Fasulo. 2014. *VCC Efforts in Three Rural Communities and Accelerant Model of Community Revitalization*. Prepared for Virginia Community Capital, Richmond, VA.

Axelrod, Jason. 2017. "Incubating an Economy." In *American City and County*. http://americancityandcounty.com/economic-development/incubating-economy. Accessed October 1, 2020.

Bagchi, Ann D. 2019. "Expansion of Telehealth Across the Rural-Urban Continuum." *State and Local Government Review*. [Special Issue: Urban-Rural Divide, ed. John Accordino] 51 (4): 250–258.

Bias, Thomas K., Kevin M. Leyden, and Jeremy Zimmerman. 2015. "Exploring Policy-Maker Perceptions of Small City Downtowns in the USA." *Planning, Practice and Research* 30(5).

Clue Group. 2015. *Four Point Refresh*. [Document]. Internal Main Street National Center.

Davis, Stephanie, and Meghan Z. Gough. 2019. "Deepening Interlocal Partnerships: The Case of Revenue-Sharing Infrastructure Agreements." *State and Local Government Review* [Special Issue: Urban-Rural Divide, John Accordino, ed.] 51(4): 292–300.

Dono, Andrea. 2020. Executive Director, Harrisonburg Downtown Renaissance, personal interview, 13 August.

Feld, Harold. 2019. "Solving the Rural Broadband Equation at the Local Level." *State and Local Government Review* [Special Issue: Urban-Rural Divide, John Accordino, ed.] 51(4): 242–249.

Gallardo, Roberto. 2019. "Bringing Communities into the Digital Age." *State and Local Government Review* [Special Issue: Urban-Rural Divide, John Accordino, ed.] 51(4): 233–241.

Gammel, Billy. 2020. GO Virginia Policy Analyst, Department of Housing and Community Development, personal interview, 20 August.

Gibson, James W. 2009. *A Re-enchanted World: The Quest for a New Kinship with Nature*. New York: Metropolitan Books.

Godwin, Dr. Angeline. 2020. President, Patrick Henry Community College, personal interview, 18 August.

Jones, Christopher, and Sarah Serpas. 2016, February. *The Unintended Consequences of Housing Finance.* Regional Plan Association. https://www.strongtowns.org/journal/2016/2/12/americans-want-walkable-neighborhoods. Accessed 11 October 2020.

LeBlanc, Francois. 2011. "The Main Street Canada Approach for Small Historic Towns." *Proceedings of the Institution of Civil Engineers* 164(3).

Mackintosh, Barry. 1986. *The National Historic Preservation Act and the National Park Service: A History.* US Department of the Interior, National Park Service, History Division. https://www.nps.gov/parkhistory/online_books/mackintosh5/index.htm. Accessed 20 September 2020.

Marohn, Charles L. 2019. *Strong Towns: A Bottom-Up Revolution to Rebuild American Prosperity.* New York: Wiley.

OECD. 2013. *Rural-Urban Partnerships: An Integrated Approach to Economic Development.* http://dx.doi.org/10.1787/9789264204812-e.

Ozdil, Taner Recep. 2007. "Assessing the Economic Revitalization Impact of Urban Design Improvements: The Texas Main Street Program." PhD diss., Texas A&M University.

Patrick Henry Community College. 2020. Dalton Idea Center. https://www.patrickhenry.edu/workforce-dev/1759-dalton-idea-center. Accessed 18 August 2020.

Place Economics, Washington, DC. 2013, May. *Getting Results: The Economic Impact of Main Street Iowa, 1986–2012.* Prepared for Iowa Economic Development.

Place Economics, Washington, DC. 2018, July. *A Shared Table: A Study of the Impacts of Louisiana Main Street.* Prepared for Louisiana Office of Cultural Development.

Place Economics, Washington, DC. 2014, February. *Decades of Success: The Economic Impact of Main Street in North Carolina.* Prepared for the North Carolina Department of Commerce and North Carolina Main Street Communities.

Robertson, Kent A. 1999. "Can Small-City Downtowns Remain Viable? A National Study of Development Issues and Strategies." *Journal of the American Planning Association* 65(3).

Robertson, Kent A. 2004. "The Main Street Approach to Downtown Development: An Examination of the Four-Point Program." *Journal of Architectural and Planning Research* 21(1).

Sacramento Area Council of Governments. 2015. *Rural-Urban Connections Strategy*. https://www.sacog.org/sites/main/files/file-attachments/rucs_booklet_0.pdf. Accessed October 2018.

Schwartz, Diana. 2020. Director, Danville River District Association, personal interview, 13 August 2020.

Shenandoah Valley Innovation Coalition. n.d. *About Us*. https://svic.biz/about-us/

Staley, Rachel. 2020. *Historic Preservation and Downtown Revitalization: How Does the Georgia Main Street Program Affect the Population Size, Racial Makeup, Median Household Income, and Retail Sales of Designated Cities?* Georgia Tech School of City and Regional Planning Applied Research Papers. https://smartech.gatech.edu/handle/1853/62596. Accessed 16 November 2020.

Staunton Downtown Development Association. 2019. *2018–2019 Work Plan*. Virginia Main Street Document.

Stover, John, and Associates. 2020, June. *Main Street's Impact in Washington State, 2011–2019*. Prepared for Washington State Main Street Program.

Town of South Hill. 2020. *The Southern Virginia Maker's Market*. https:southhillva.org/visitor-information/makers-market. Accessed 24 July 2020.

Versen, Stephen. 2020. Manager, Office of Agriculture and Forestry Development, Virginia Department of Agriculture and Consumer Services, personal interview, 8 October 2020.

Virginia Department of Historic Resources. 2020, March 23. *DHR: Virginia Department of Historic Resources*. https://www.dhr.virginia.gov/historic-register/. Accessed 21 September 2020.

Virginia Main Street. 2020. *Small Scale Manufacturing*. https://virginiamainstreet.com/small-scale-manufacturing/. Accessed 24 July 2020.

Wagner, Matt. 2017, February 2. *Refreshed Main Street Approach™*. Main Street America. https://www.mainstreet.org/blogs/national-main-street-center/2017/06/13/refreshed-main-street-approach. Accessed 4 August 2020.

Wagner, Matthew. 2020, June 18. *Main Street America®. Main Spotlight: How Rural Economies Can Leverage the Rise in Remote Work.* https://www.mainstreet.org/blogs/national-main-street-center/2020/06/18/covid-19-trend-series-rural-economies-great-opport. Accessed 6 July 2020.

CHAPTER 12

Ager, A. and A. Strang. 2004. *Indicators of Integration: Final Report.* Edinburgh: Queen Margaret University College.

Alba, R. and V. Nee. 2003. *Remaking the American Mainstream: Assimilation and Contemporary Immigration.* Cambridge, MA: Harvard University Press.

Alencar, A. 2018. "Refugee Integration and Social Media: A Local and Experiential Perspective." *Information, Communication and Society* 21(11): 1588–1603.

Bansak, K., Ferwerda, J., Hainmueller, J., Dillon, A., Hangartner, D., Lawrence, D., and J. Weinstein. 2018. "Improving Refugee Integration through Data-driven Algorithmic Assignment." *Science* 359(6373): 325–329. https://doi.org/10.1126/science.aao4408

Batalova, J., Fix, M. and J.R. Fernandez-Pena. 2021. *The Integration of Immigrant Health Professionals: Looking beyond the COVID-19 Crisis.* Migration Policy Institute, April. https://www.migrationpolicy.org/research/integration-immigrant-health-professionals-beyond-covid-19.

Bernstein, H., and N. DuBois. 2018. "Bringing Evidence to the Refugee Integration Debate." Urban Institute. https://www.urban.org/sites/default/files/publication/97771/bringing_evidence_to_the_refugee_integration_debate_0.pdf Accessed 10 August 2021.

Beversluis, D., Schoeller-Diaz, D., Anderson, M., Anderson, N., Slaughter, A., and R.B. Patel. 2017. "Developing and validating the refugee integration scale in Nairobi, Kenya." *Journal of Refugee Studies* 30(1): 106–132. https://doi.org/10.1093/jrs/few018

Bloemraad, I. 2006. *Becoming a Citizen: Incorporating Immigrants and Refugees in the United States and Canada.* Berkeley: University of California Press.

Blunt, A.. 2003. "Home and Identity: Life Stories in Text and in Person." In *Cultural Geography in Practice*, ed. Alison Blunt, Pyrs Gruffudd, Jon May, Miles Ogborn, and David Pinder, 71–87. London: Arnold.

Bose, P. S. 2018. "Welcome and Hope, Fear, and Loathing: The Politics of Refugee Resettlement in Vermont." *Peace and Conflict: Journal of Peace Psychology* 24(3): 320–329. https://doi.org/10.1037/pac0000302

Boswell, C. 2012. *The Political Uses of Expert Knowledge: Immigration Policy and Social Research*. Cambridge, UK: Cambridge University Press.

Broeders, D. 2007. "The New Digital Borders of Europe: EU Databases and the Surveillance of Irregular Migrants." *International Sociology* 22(1): 71–92. https://doi.org/10.1177/0268580907070126.

Brun, C. and A.H Fabos. 2017. "Mobilizing Home for Long-Term Displacement: A Critical Reflection on the Durable Solutions." *Journal of Human Rights Practice* 9: 177–183.

Burrows, N. and J. Ramic. 2017. "Defining the Community Integration Model of Refugee Resettlement: Engaging the Community in Successful Refugee Resettlement." *Social Innovations Journal* 38.

Cheung, S. Y., and J. Phillimore. 2017. "Gender and Refugee Integration: A Quantitative Analysis of Integration and Social Policy Outcomes." *Journal of Social Policy* 46(2): 211–230. https://doi.org/10.1017/S0047279416000775

Chouliaraki, L. 2017. "Symbolic Bordering: The Self-Representation of Migrants and Refugees in Digital News." *Popular Communication* 15(2): 78–94. https://doi.org/10.1080/15405702.2017.1281415.

Faist, T. 2012. "Toward a Transnational Methodology: Methods to Address Methodological Nationalism, Essentialism, and Positionality." *Revue Européenne des Migrations Internationales* 28(1): 51–70. https://doi.org/10.4000/remi.5761.

Friedman, B., and D. G. Hendry. 2019. *Value Sensitive Design: Shaping Technology with Moral Imagination*. Cambridge, MA: MIT Press.

Fedyuk, O., and V. Zentai. 2018. "The Interview in Migration Studies: A Step Towards a Dialogue and Knowledge Co-Production?" In *Qualitative Research in European Migration Studies*, ed. R. Zapata-Barrero and E. Yalaz, 171–188. New York: Springer International.

Gigler, B. S. 2004. "Including the Excluded - Can ICTs Empower Poor Communities? Towards an Alternative Evaluation Framework

Based on the Capability Approach." *4th International conference on the capability approach* 5(7). https://ssrn.com/abstract=3171994

Harding, S. 1993. "Rethinking Standpoint Epistemology: 'What Is Strong Objectivity?'" In *Feminist Epistemologies*, ed. L. Alcoff and E. Potter, 49–82. London: Routledge.

Hartstock, N. 1997. "Comment on Hekmans' 'Truth and Method: Feminist Standpoint Theory Revisited.'" *Signs* 22(2): 375–381. https://www.jstor.org/stable/3175278.

Jacobsen, K. L. 2017. "On Humanitarian Refugee Biometrics and New Forms of Intervention." *Journal of Intervention and Statebuilding* 11(4): 529–551. https://doi.org/10.1080/17502977.2017.1347856

Jimenez, T. 2011. *Immigrants in the United States: How Well Are They Integrating into Society?* Migration Policy Institute. http://www.migrationpolicy.org/research/immigrants-united-states-how-well-are-they-integrating-society.

Luibhéid, E and L. Cantú Jr. 2005. *Queer Migrations: Sexuality, US citizenship, and Border Crossings*. Minneapolis, MN: University of Minnesota Press.

M'charek, A. 2017. "'Dead-bodies-at-the-border': Distributed Evidence and Emerging Forensic Infrastructure for Identification." In *Bodies of Evidence: Anthropological Studies of Security, Knowledge and Power,* ed. M. Maguire, U. Rao, and N. Zurawski, 145–64. Durham, NC: Duke University Press.

Marks, J. A. 2014. "Rural Refugee Resettlement: Secondary Migration and Community Integration in Fort Morgan, Colorado." UNHCR Issues in Refugee Research, Research Paper No. 269. Geneva, Switzerland.

McKeary, M., and B. Newbold. 2010. "Barriers to Care: The Challenges for Canadian Refugees and their Health Care Providers." *Journal of Refugee Studies* 23(4): 523–545. https://doi.org/10.1093/jrs/feq038

Morris, M. D., Popper, S. T., Rodwell, T. C., Brodine, S. K., and K. C. Brouwer. 2009. "Healthcare Barriers of Refugees Post-resettlement. *Journal of Community Health* 34(6): 529. https://doi.org/10.1007/s10900-009-9175-3

Nikunen, K. 2018. "Once a Refugee: Selfie Activism, Visualized Citizenship and the Space of Appearance." *Popular Communication*

17(2): 154–170. https://doi.org/10.1080/15405702.2018.1527336

Pourchot, G., K. Hassouna, K. M. Powell, K. Randall, B. Shadle, and S. Swarup. 2018. *Refugee Integration: Data for Smart Policy*. [Policy brief]. School of Public and International Affairs, Virginia Tech.

Powell, K. M., and K. Randall. 2018. "Community Workshops and Rhetorics of Home in the Stories of Persons Seeking Refuge." *albeit: Journal of Teaching and Scholarship* 5(1). https://albeitjournal.com/community-workshops-and-rhetorics-of-home/.

Powell, K. M., R. J. Hester, G. Pourchot, B. Shadle, and K. Randall. 2020. *Research, Education, and Advocacy in the Age of the Pandemic: Report of the Virginia Consortium for Refugee, Migrant, and Displacement Studies*. Second Consortium Meeting. Blacksburg: Virginia Tech.

Powell, K. M., R. J. Hester, and K. Randall. 2019a. *Refugee and Migrant Partnerships in Virginia: Fostering Connectivity and Reciprocity*. Report from the Fostering Reciprocity Symposium in Arlington, VA. Virginia Tech.

Powell, K. M., R. J. Hester, and K. Randall. 2019b. *Virginia Consortium for Refugee, Migrant, and Displacement Studies*. Report from VCRMDS inaugural meeting. Virginia Tech.

Quayyum, M. A., Thompson, K. M., Kennan, M. A., and A. Lloyd. 2014. "The Provision and Sharing of Information between Service Providers and Settling Refugees." *Information Research* 19(2). http://InformationR.net/ir/19-2/paper616.html

Randall, K., K. M. Powell, and B. Shadle. 2020. "Resisting the Trauma Story: Ethical Concerns in the Oral History Archive." *Displaced Voices: A Journal of Archives, Migration and Cultural Heritage* 1(1): 76–79. http://www.livingrefugeearchive.org/researchpublications/displaced_voices/.

Richard, A. C., and K. Leader. 2018. *A Case for Strengthening Evidence-based Understanding of Refugee Integration*. Penn State Institute for Urban Research.

Rowe, J., and J. Paterson. 2010. "Culturally Competent Communication with Refugees." *Home Health Care Management & Practice* 22(5): 334–338. https://doi.org/10.1177/1084822309353152

Smyth, G., E. Stewart, and S. de Lomba. 2010. "Critical Reflections on Refugee Integration: Lessons from International Perspectives." *Journal of Refugee Studies* 23(4): 411–414.

Srigley, K., S. Zembrzycki, and F. Iacovetta. 2018. *Beyond Women's Words: Feminisms and the Practices of Oral History in the Twenty-First Century.* London: Routledge.

Strang, A., and A. Ager. 2010. "Refugee Integration: Emerging Trends and Remaining Agendas." *Journal of Refugee Studies* 23(4): 589–607. https://doi.org/10.1093/jrs/feq046.

Tazzioli, M. 2017. "Containment through Mobility: Migrants' Spatial Disobediences and the Reshaping of Control through the Hotspot System." *Journal of Ethnic and Migration Studies 44*(16): 2764–2779. https://doi.org/10.1080/1369183X.2017.1401514

UNHCR. 2014, July. *The Integration of Refugees: A Discussion Paper.* https://www.unhcr.org/cy/wpcontent/uploads/sites/41/2018/02/integration_discussion_paper_July_2014_EN.pdf.

UNHCR. June 2020a. *Solutions.* http://www.unhcr.org/en-us/solutions.html. Accessed 15 June 2020.

UNHCR. June 2020b. *Local Integration.* http://www.unhcr.org/pages/49c3646c101.html. Accessed 15 June 2020.

Van der Ploeg, I. 1999. "The Illegal Body: 'Eurodac' and the Politics of Biometric Identification." *Ethics and Information Technology 1*(4): 295–302. https://doi.org/10.1023/A:1010064613240

Williams, K. 2015. "Life Narratives, Common Language and Diverse Ways of Belonging." *Forum Qualitative Social Research* 16(2): Art. 16. http://dx.doi.org/10.17169/fqs-16.2.2358.

Wren, K. 2003. "Refugee Dispersal in Denmark: From Macro-to Microscale Analysis." *International Journal of Population Geography 9*(1): 57–75. https://doi.org/10.1002/ijpg.273

CHAPTER 13

Bednarek, A. T., C. Wyborn, C. Cvitanovic, R. Meyer, R. M. Colvin, P. F. E. Addison, . . . and D. Hart. 2018. "Boundary Spanning at the Science–Policy Interface: The Practitioners' Perspectives." *Sustainability Science 13*: 1175–1183.

Bryson, J. M., B. C. Crosby, and M. M. Stone. 2015. "Designing and Implementing Cross-Sector Collaborations: Needed and Challenging." *Public Administration Review* 75: 647–663.

Centers for Disease Control and Prevention. CDC Wonder. 2020. http://wonder.cdc.gov/. Accessed 18 August 2020

Coy, B. and M. Brewster. 2016. "Opioid Addiction Crisis Declared a Public Health Emergency in Virginia." [News release], 21 November. https://governor.virginia.gov/newsroom/news.

Crosby, B. C., and Bryson, J. M. 2010. "Integrative Leadership and the Creation and Maintenance of Cross-sector Collaborations." *The Leadership Quarterly 21*: 211–230.

Langley, A., K. Lindberg, B. E. Mørk, D. Nicolini, E. Raviola, and L. Walter. 2019. "Boundary Work Among Groups, Occupations, and Organizations: From Cartography to Process." *Academy of Management Annals* 13: 704–736.

Lipari, R. N., and S. L. Van Horn. 2017. "Trends in Substance Use Disorders Among Adults Aged 18 or Older." In *The CBHSQ Report*. Substance Abuse and Mental Health Services Administration, US.

Macy, B. 2018. *Dopesick: Dealers, Doctors and the Drug Company That Addicted America*. Boston: Little, Brown.

Madras, B. K. 2018. "The President's Commission on Combating Drug Addiction and the Opioid Crisis: Origins and Recommendations." *Clinical Pharmacology and Therapeutics* 103(6): 943–945.

Pendyal, A., A. B. Srivastava, and M. S. Gold. 2018, September. "The Root Causes of the Current Opioid Crisis/Reply." *Mayo Clinic Proceedings* 93: 1329–1331.

Posner, S. M., and C. Cvitanovic. 2019. "Evaluating the Impacts of Boundary-Spanning Activities at the Interface of Environmental Science and Policy: A Review of Progress and Future Research Needs." *Environmental Science and Policy* 92: 141–151.

Tushman, M. L. 1977. "Special Boundary Roles in the Innovation Process." *Administrative Science Quarterly*, 587–605.

US Census Bureau. 2020. Locality Population. https://www.census.gov/.

Vibrant Virginia website. https://econdev.vt.edu/VibrantVirginia.html. Accessed August 2020.

Virginia Department of Health. 2017. http://www.vdh.virginia.gov.

Weerts, D. J., and L. R. Sandmann. 2010. "Community Engagement and Boundary-Spanning Roles at Research Universities." *Journal of Higher Education* 81: 632–657.

Chapter 14

Adolino, J. R., and C. H. Blake. 2010. "The Policy Process." In *Comparing Public Policies: Issues and Choices in Industrialized countries*, 2nd ed, 8-30. London: SAGE Publications.

Baumgartner, F. R., and B. D. Jones. 1993. *Agendas and Instability in American* Politics, 1st ed. Chicago: University of Chicago Press.

Baumgartner, F. R., B. D. Jones, and P. B. Mortensen. 2018. "Punctuated Equilibrium Theory: Explaining Stability and Change in Public Policymaking." In *Theories of the Policy Process*, ed. C. M. Weible and P. A. Sabatier, 4th ed., 55–101. London: Routledge. https://doi.org/10.4324/9780429494284.

Birkland, T. A. 1998. "Focusing Events, Mobilization, and Agenda Setting." *Journal of Public Policy* 18(1): 53–74. https://doi.org/10.1017/S0143814X98000038.

Birkland, T. A. 2007. "Agenda-Setting in Public Policy." In *Handbook of Public Policy Analysis: Theory, Politics, and Methods*, ed. F. Fischer, G. J. Miller, and M. S. Sidney, 1st ed., 63–78. London: Routledge. https://doi.org/10.4324/9781315093192.

Bloom, D. E., D. Canning, and J. Sevilla. 2004. "The Effect of Health on Economic Growth: A Production Function Approach." *World Development* 32(1): 1–13. https://doi.org/10.1016/j.worlddev.2003.07.002.

Elson, P. R., and S. Hall. 2016. "System Change Agents: A Profile of Policy-Focused Grantmaking Foundation Engagement in Public Policy." *Canadian Journal of Nonprofit and Social Economy Research* 7(2): 57. https://doi.org/10.22230/cjnser.2016v7n2a222.

Fox, A. M., Y. Balarajan, C. Cheng, and M. R. Reich. 2015. "Measuring Political Commitment and Opportunities to Advance Food and Nutrition Security: Piloting a Rapid Assessment Tool." *Health Policy and Planning* 30(5): 566–578. https://doi.org/10.1093/heapol/czu035.

Fox, A. M., A. B. Goldberg, R. J. Gore, and T. Bärnighausen. 2011. "Conceptual and Methodological Challenges to Measuring Political Commitment to Respond to HIV." *Journal of the International AIDS Society* 14: S2–S5. https://doi.org/10.1186/1758-2652-14-s2-s5.

Hardee, P. 2018. "Supervisors Decline School Trail Grant." *The Guide to Rappahannock*, 8 November. https://www.pressreader.com/usa/rappahannock-news/20181108/281479277430618.

Heikkila, T., J. J. Pierce, S. Gallaher, J. Kagan, D. A. Crow, and C. M. Weible. 2014. "Understanding a Period of Policy Change: The Case of Hydraulic Fracturing Disclosure Policy in Colorado." *Review of Policy Research* 31(2): 65–87. https://doi.org/10.1111/ropr.12058.

Kingdon, J. W. 1995. "How Does an Idea's Time Come?" In *Agendas, Alternatives, and Public Policies*, 2nd ed. New York: Longman.

Librett, J. J., M. M. Yore, and T. L. Schmid. 2003. "Local Ordinances That Promote Physical Activity: A Survey of Municipal Policies." *American Journal of Public Health* 93(9): 1399–1403. https://doi.org/10.2105/ajph.93.9.1399.

Rogers, E. M., and J. C. Peterson. 2008. "Diffusion of Clean Indoor Air Ordinances in the Southwestern United States." *Health Education and Behavior* 35(5): 683–697. https://doi.org/10.1177/1090198106296767.

Sabatier, P. A., and C. M. Weible. 2007. "The Advocacy Coalition Framework." In *Theories of the Policy Process*, ed. P. A. Sabatier, 2nd ed., 189–220. London: Routledge.

Samuels, B., and S. A. Glantz. 1991. "The Politics of Local Tobacco Control." *Journal of the American Medical Association* 266(15): 2110–2117. https://doi.org/10.1001/jama.266.15.2110.

Shipan, C. R., and C. Volden. 2008. "The Mechanisms of Policy Diffusion." *American Journal of Political Science* 52(4): 840–857. https://doi.org/10.1111/j.1540-5907.2008.00346.x.

Stokes Berry, F., and W. D. Berry. 2018. "Innovation and Diffusion Models in Policy Research." In *Theories of the Policy Process*, ed. C. M. Weible and P. A. Sabatier, 4th ed., 253–297. London: Routledge. https://doi.org/10.4324/9780429494284.

Traynor, M. P., M. E. Begay, and S. A. Glantz. 1993. "New Tobacco Industry Strategy to Prevent Local Tobacco Control." *Journal of the American Medical Association* 270(4): 479–486. https://doi.org/10.1001/jama.270.4.479.

US Census, 2010. https://www.census.gov/programs-surveys/geography/guidance/geo-areas/urban-rural/2010-urban-rural.html.

Chapter 15

Bradshaw, V. 2017, March. "An 'Essential' Service: Trump Budget Threatens Rural Airport Subsidies." *Daily News Record.* https://www.dnronline.com/news/local/an-essential-service/article_0f5dbbf4-0eaa-11e7-9eea-3f65be6445cf.html.

Campbell, G. Shenandoah Valley Airport [PowerPoint slides]. 2019, April. https://www.virginiaresources.gov/uploads/docs/1010am_CampbellCampbell_AirportsTheFrontDoorToEconomicDevelopment.pdf.

Green, R. K. 2017. "Airports and Economic Development." *Real Estate Economics* 35(1): 91–112.

Grymes, C. A. n.d. *Shenandoah Valley Regional Airport (SHD).* Virginia Places. http://www.virginiaplaces.org/transportation/shenvalleyairport.html#one.

Halpern, N., and S. Brathen. 2011. "Impact of Airports on Regional Accessibility and Social Development." *Journal of Transport Geography* 19(6): 1145–1154.

Horton, W. 2020, April 15. "How the U.S. Is Distributing Airline Bailout Funds in COVID-19 Relief Deal." Forbes. https://www.forbes.com/sites/willhorton1/2020/04/15/how-the-us-is-distributing-airline-bailout-funds-in-covid-19-relief-deal/?sh=e0f986263a1d.

James Madison University. n.d. *JMU Plans: Mission, Vision and Values.* https://www.jmu.edu/jmuplans/mission-vision-values.shtml.

Kaufman, W. 2013, May 8. "Airport Hubs Become Busier as Airlines Cut Costs." NPR. http://www.npr.org/templates/story/story.php?storyId=182337931.

Ozcan, I. C. 2014. "Economic Contribution of Essential Air Service Flights on Small and Remote Communities." *Journal of Air Transport Management* 34: 24–29.

Peaslee, L., and N. Swartz. *Virginia Government.* CQ Press, 2014.

Peters, L. 2019, September. "Valley Airport at 100% Occupancy, Needs Millions in Upgrades." *The Newsleader.* https://www.newsleader.com/story/news/2019/09/10/valley-airport-100-occupancy-needs-multi-million-dollar-upgrade/2272560001/.

Shenandoah Valley Partnership. *Market Overview.* https://theshenandoahvalley.com/market-overview/.

Shenandoah Valley Partnership. *Shenandoah Community Profile.* https://theshenandoahvalley.com/wp-content/uploads/2018/07/Shenandoah-Valley-Community-Profile.pdf.

Shenandoah Valley Partnership. n.d. *Workforce and Talent.* https://theshenandoahvalley.com/workforce/workforce-copy/.

Shenandoah Valley Regional Airport. 2017. *Airport Master Plan— 2017: Executive Summary.* https://flyshd.com/wp-content/uploads/2018/05/13124-SHD-MP-Executive-Summary-FINAL-2page-view.pdf.

Shenandoah Valley Regional Airport. n.d. *About the Airport.* Fly SHD. https://flyshd.com/about-shd/.

Urenko, C. 2020, January. "Shenandoah Regional Airport Has Most Successful Year to Date in 2019." *WHSV3.* https://www.whsv.com/content/news/Shenandoah-Regional-Airport-has-most-successful-year-to-date-in-2019–567144261.html.

US Department of Transportation. 2017. *Essential Air Service.* https://www.transportation.gov/policy/aviation-policy/small-community-rural-air-service/essential-air-service.

US Department of Transportation. 2020. *Passenger Boarding (Enplanement) and All Cargo Data for U.S. Airports.* https://www.faa.gov/airports/planning_capacity/passenger_allcargo_stats/passenger.

Virginia Department of Aviation. 2018. *Virginia Airport System Economic Impact Report: Technical Report.* https://doav.virginia.gov/contentassets/ab031db6ded94e008f22a57a3bf082d4/virginia-airports-economic-impact-technical-report-final-accessible-01may2018.pdf.

Virginia Economic Development Partnership n.d.. *Regional Profile: Shenandoah Valley.* https://www.vedp.org/region/shenandoah-valley.

Wong, J. C. Y. 2018. "Aviation Connectivity Impacts on Regional Economies in the United States." *Transportation Research Record* 2672(29): 103–113.

Conclusion

Markusen, A. 1999. "Fuzzy Concepts, Scanty Evidence, Policy Distance: The Case for Rigour and Policy Relevance in Critical Regional Studies." *Regional Studies* 33(9): 701–717.

Index

A

Accomack County, 99, 281–82, 289
ACIR (Advisory Council on Intergovernmental Relations), 221
ACS, 31, 33, 37
ADA (Airline Deregulation Act), 302
addiction, 255, 282, 284, 287–89, 291, 295
addiction crisis, 255–57, 260, 265, 271, 275, 286, 288, 290, 293
Advisory Council on Intergovernmental Relations (ACIR), 221
advocacy coalition framework (ACF), 147
African Americans, 23, 25, 28, 171, 175, 178, 184
agricultural economy in Virginia, 66
agriculture, 18, 20, 66, 102, 104–6, 171, 175, 199, 203, 209, 331, 333, 352
air carriers, 302–3
Airline Deregulation Act (ADA), 302
airports, 300, 302–3, 311–15, 361–62
  local, 305, 311
air service, 297, 299–300, 305, 307, 313, 362
  commercial, 298–99, 302
  expanded, 313
  local commercial, 305
  regional, 13, 297
Alaska, 53, 302–3

Aleutians East Borough, 90
Amazon, 1–2
  HQ2 project, 72
American Medical Association, 360
American National University (ANU), 306
anchor institutions, 2, 114–15, 118–20, 305–6, 315
anchors, 115, 119, 198, 212
  regional, 211
Annual Consultants Survey, 332
Annual Corporate Survey, 332
Appalachian regions, 26
Appalachian Virginia, 142, 341
areas
  micropolitan, 19
  nonmetro, 60–61
  nonmetropolitan, 20–21
  scenic, 218, 220
Arlington, 1–2, 5, 50–51, 338, 340, 356
arts, role of, 165, 174
arts-related businesses and economic development, 186
Ashwood, 176–77, 343
assistance, technical, 103, 105, 116, 171, 203, 209, 274–75

B

bandwidth, 155
beliefs, 42, 148, 150–51, 155, 168, 264, 338

Bemiss, 218
billboards, 221–22
Black colleges and universities, 135
Black residents, 28–29
Blacksburg-Roanoke-Lynchburg, 39
Bland, 48, 281–82, 293
Blueprint for Broadband, 342
Blue Ridge, 217, 299–300
Blue Ridge Behavioral Healthcare and New River Valley Community Services Board, 262
Blue Ridge Community College (BRCC), 72, 306, 308
Blue Ridge Crossroads Small Business Development Center, 1
Blue Ridge Mountains, 299–300
Blue Virginia, 340
Board of Conservation and Recreation (BCR), 232
boundary objects, 260–61
boundary spanners, 260, 272, 275
Bridgewater College (BC), 306
broadband, 9–10, 31, 65–66, 110, 142–43, 146–54, 156, 159–61, 331–32, 334, 340–42
access, 32, 65–67, 84, 119, 140
chief broadband advisor, 67, 149
deployment, 143, 147, 158
funding, 150, 159
gap, 10
grants, 67, 153
infrastructure, advanced, 144
investments, 155
networks, 67, 139–41, 144–46, 153
policy, 139, 141, 143, 147–49, 159
services, 142, 151
Broadband Advisory Council, 143, 149, 340
broadband connectivity, universal statewide, 211
broadband initiatives, 149
municipal/cooperative, 147, 152
Brookings Institution, 60, 324, 331–32, 335
budget allocations, 279, 288, 290

business attraction, 207, 309
business development program, 116
business leaders, 124, 252, 308, 312
business opportunities, 109, 116, 155
business owners, 111, 203, 206, 269
Byrd Organization, 44
Byways program, 219–20

C
Cambridge, 326, 347, 353–54
Cameron, 185–88, 191, 193
Cameron Foundation, 185–86, 347, 349
campaign, 8, 46–47, 222, 326
Campbell, 167, 188, 191, 300, 303, 305–7, 310, 312–13, 343, 347, 361
candidates, 45, 51–52, 87, 89, 94, 97, 227, 329
Capital Improvement Plan (CIP), 187
capital investment, 64, 69–70, 72, 106, 108, 114, 144, 206
Capital Region Land Conservancy, 233
Carilion, 107
Carilion Virginia Western Community College, 115
CECE. *See* Center for Economic and Community Engagement
CEDS (Comprehensive Economic Development Strategy), 1
census, US, 18, 20, 27, 325
census tracts, 20, 140
Center for Economic and Community Engagement (CECE), ix, 4, 257, 273, 367–69
Center for Global Engagement, 310
Center for Innovation in STEM Education, 365–66
Center for Public Administration and Policy, 365, 367–69
Center for Public Health Practice and Research (CPHPR), 257
Center for Rural Virginia, 149
Centers for Disease Control (CDC), 257, 357
Central Region, 284
CenturyLink, 145, 153–54

367

Charlottesville, 19, 23, 34, 39, 51–52, 102, 108–11, 300, 311, 314, 323, 326, 330
Chesapeake Bay, 124–25, 215
Chesterfield County, 50–51, 182
Chicago, 23, 323, 325, 342, 359
Christiansburg, 105
Chroma Design, 190–91, 347
CIP (Capital Improvement Plan), 187
cities, 25–26, 49–51, 53, 60, 104–5, 184–88, 190, 192–94, 196–200, 208–13, 224, 298, 300, 348–49, 366–67
   historic, 11, 197, 199, 203, 208, 211, 213
   small, 11, 181–82, 195–96, 201–2, 211, 336
   and urbanized counties, 21
Civil War, 23, 43, 299, 344
climate change, 11
cluster-based development, 96, 206
clusters, 9, 38, 86, 89–92, 94–97, 104, 335
   region's, 86
cluster strength, regional, 89
coalitions, 10, 38, 142–44, 147–50, 169–70, 263, 265, 270, 273, 313, 342
Code of Virginia, 152–53, 217, 341
coercion, 284, 286, 290, 294
collaborations, 125, 127, 132, 138, 207, 212, 255, 257, 259, 297, 299, 306
   urban-rural, 198, 212–13
College of Architecture and Urban Studies, 367, 369
colleges, local, 313–14
colleges and universities, 6, 72, 105, 114, 118, 123, 126, 199, 210–11, 304, 313
commitments, political, 280, 282, 285
Committee on STEM Education, 122, 126, 130, 338
Commonwealth Broadband Roundtable, 341
Commonwealth Catholic Charities, 252
Commonwealth Institute, 84, 336
Commonwealth of Virginia, 4, 7–8, 30, 59, 61, 63–64, 153, 257, 282, 323, 336

communication networks, 143, 249–51
communities
   disadvantaged, 256
   ethnic, 242
   faith-based, 263
   historic, 206
   host, 239, 241–43, 248
   inclusive, 3, 317–18
   isolated, 117
   lagging, 84, 98
   larger, 307
   local, 84–85, 114, 143, 156, 160, 251
   middle-class, 184
   migrant, 251, 320
   mixed-use, 200
   peripheral, 112
   primary, 183
   resettled, 250
   residential, 144
   small, 68, 72, 75, 78, 119, 187, 207, 245, 302
   underserved, 143, 149, 321
   urban, 4, 10, 21, 29, 38, 140, 143, 255–56, 274–75
Communities and Accelerant Model of Community Revitalization, 350
Community Business Launch (CBL), 208
community change, 168, 344–45
community coalitions, 150, 158, 259, 265, 270–71, 274
community cultural development. *See* CCD
community development, 5, 29, 39, 78, 144, 167–68, 173, 208, 325, 347, 350
   projects, 167
community engagement, 173, 180, 250, 260, 272, 307, 318, 346, 358
Community Gateway Project, 349
community health, 282, 288–89, 355
Comprehensive Economic Development Strategy (CEDS), 1
Congress, 147, 202, 217, 302
connectivity, 83–89, 91, 93–98, 112, 114, 125, 140, 298, 303, 314, 322
Connect Virginia, 342

conservation easements, 29–30
Conserve Virginia, 229
  Scenic Preservation Map, 230
consultants, 104, 118, 149–50, 186, 191
  site-selection, 68
continuum, urban-rural, 3, 17–18, 20, 39–40, 258, 262, 317, 344
Council Bluffs, 185–86
Council on Foreign Relations, 122, 338
counties, 19–20, 26–27, 29–30, 32–36, 38, 48–51, 89–93, 95–97, 104–5, 110–11, 143–44, 154, 170–75, 180–85, 299–300
  suburban, 26–27, 37
county-clusters, 89–93
county governments, 172, 298
COVID-19 pandemic, 8, 10–12, 31, 34, 57, 59–60, 76–77, 139, 141, 143, 174, 233, 314–16
Cox Communications, 154
CPHPR (Center for Public Health Practice and Research), 257
Crater Planning District Commission, 182, 184, 347
CRCC (Crisis Response and Connection to Care), 264
creative placemaking, 11, 163, 181–82, 196, 348
  in small cities, 196
Crescent, 197–98
Crisis Response and Connection to Care (CRCC), 264
Cross-sector collaborations, 180, 348, 358
Culpeper, 108, 111
culture, 10, 17, 123, 130, 133, 135, 137–38, 165–66, 170, 172, 174, 180
  entrepreneur business, 111
Custom Workforce Program, 70

D

Danville, 5, 19, 25, 51, 89, 281, 293–94
data, qualitative, 267–68
democracy, 241, 344
Democratic candidates, 41–42, 44–47, 49–51, 54, 56
Democrats, 46, 54, 142, 329–30
Department of Conservation and Recreation (DCR), 219–20, 229
DHCD (Department of Housing and Community Development), 37–38, 149, 153, 160, 203, 208, 325, 341
diffusion, 280–81, 292, 294
  mechanisms of, 279–80, 293–94
Digital Binders, 251–52
Dillon Rule, 148
displacement studies, 356, 367–69
districts, 55–56, 172, 201–2, 204
diversity, 10, 124, 134, 252–53
downtowns, 11, 68, 78, 199–204, 206–9, 212, 322

E

EAS (Essential Air Service), 299, 302
Eastern Mennonite University (EMU), 306
Eastern Region, 141, 288
Eastern Shore, 198
economic activity, 66–67, 88, 177, 198
economic development, 61, 63–64, 66–67, 74–76, 101, 170, 181–82, 186–87, 191–92, 202, 204, 318–19, 322, 334–35
  funding sources, 65
  funding sources in rural Virginia, 65
  organizations, 63, 74, 96, 175
  policies, 8–9, 83, 85, 102
  practitioners, 75, 102
  programs, 75
  regional, 69, 98, 101, 109, 157, 307
Economic Development Administration (EDA), 1, 324
economic health of Virginia, 222
economic opportunities, 8, 26, 59, 85, 169, 238–39, 245, 322
economic recovery, 8, 59–60
economic regions, 89, 93, 98
economic specializations, 84–85, 89
economies, inclusive, 3, 7
ecosystems, 102, 112, 120, 337
  regional, 109, 115

education, 35, 37, 66, 68, 124, 126, 128, 130, 133–34, 141–43, 240, 242, 244, 250, 338–40
Educational Networks, 367–68
education institutions, higher, 101–2, 108, 118, 125, 251
elections, statewide, 41, 45, 47, 54, 57
Electronic Commerce, 96–99
employees, 211, 238, 252, 270, 305, 307, 313
employers, 114, 122, 124, 126, 252, 262, 267, 269–70
employment, 22, 63–64, 89–90, 122, 242, 244, 246, 248, 250, 261, 267
employment growth, 8, 59–61, 85–88, 91–94, 125
employment opportunities, 8, 124, 212, 267
EMU (Eastern Mennonite University), 306
engagement, 113, 120, 122, 165, 167, 170, 173–74, 255, 258–61, 266, 271–74, 318–19
  civic, 240, 252
Enterprising Communities, 337
entrepreneur ecosystems, 63, 102–6, 108–9, 119, 337, 366
  building, 112
entrepreneur pipeline, 114, 120
entrepreneurs, 5, 11, 97, 103–4, 106–7, 109, 111–15, 117, 120, 209–10, 291
  local, 113–14, 116, 118, 120
entrepreneurship, 9, 39, 87–88, 101–3, 108–9, 114–15, 136, 200, 208
  participatory, 292–93
entrepreneur support organizations, 107, 113
environment, ix, 2, 41, 105, 118, 201, 340
equipment, 70, 119, 122, 140, 198, 209–10, 287
equity, 122–23, 131–32, 134–35, 138, 252
Essex, 281–82
establishment, 117, 218, 220, 348
Ewing Marion Kauffman Foundation, 102, 337
Expanded Virginia Broadband, 139

F

Fairfax, 34, 50, 52–53, 125, 281–82, 293
Fairfax County, 34, 116, 291, 294
farmshoring, 87, 336
Farnsworth, S.J., 8, 30, 41, 328, 366
Fauquier County, 109, 111
Federal Aviation Administration, 299
Federal Communications Commission (FCC), 140, 149, 154–55, 341
federal government, 55, 149, 244, 247, 293, 302
fentanyl, 258
financial incentives, 287, 293–94
Fink, 169, 344
firms, 2, 73, 86, 104, 178–79, 322
fishing, 95, 98, 171
Floyd County, 154–55, 341
Fly SHD Community Air Service Task Force, 13, 297, 299, 307–8, 316
focus groups, 243–46, 251, 265–66
Freire, 167, 344
Fullan, 137, 338
funding
  seed, 6, 253, 257, 261, 271
  state-based, 132
  state-level, 147

G

Galax, 1–2
Gateway Project, 11, 181–83, 185, 187–88, 191–92, 195
General Assembly, 70, 73, 219, 232, 300, 340
geography, 18, 88, 108, 112, 114, 139, 141, 330, 336, 361, 366
  regional, 112–13
GOP, 44, 177–79
Governance, 22, 138, 165, 175, 180, 326, 366–69
government, 23, 25, 126, 128, 149, 151, 154, 177–79, 197, 199–200, 278, 280–81, 307, 326, 328–29
governmental agendas, 278–80, 282, 284, 287–91

grantmaking, entrepreneurial, 13, 292–93, 295
grants, 63, 72, 150, 160, 209, 244, 288, 293, 302
Greater Richmond MSA, 64, 77, 185
growth, 25–27, 38, 59–60, 63–64, 66, 83–85, 87–88, 91–93, 96–98, 106–8, 198, 200, 305, 307, 309
  local, 84–85, 96

H
Hampton Roads, 1, 3, 23, 25, 29, 39, 43, 77, 125, 198, 287
Harrisonburg, 19, 23, 52–53, 204, 211, 213, 281–82, 290, 293–94, 299–301, 306, 309, 312
  city government, 308
Hartka, 61
Harvard Business School, 99, 336
Hawkins, 141
health, 140, 143, 244, 246, 249, 257–58, 261, 264, 267, 278, 281–82, 284, 287–88, 291–92, 358–59
  economic, 222
  regional, 39
  senior, 290–91
health agendas, 291, 293, 295
healthcare, 19, 42, 66, 136, 150, 158, 172, 248, 255, 288, 305
healthcare access, 84, 241
health disparities, 198
health issues, public, 34–35
healthy community initiatives, 13, 282, 284, 286–91
Henrico, 50, 52–53
heroin, 257–58
higher education, 9, 19, 126, 128–29, 134, 199, 252, 306–8, 313, 328, 332
highways, federal interstate, 300
Hispanics, 124, 135, 171, 184
historic cities and towns, 11, 197, 199, 208, 211
historic downtowns, 201, 204, 209–10
Historic Rehabilitation Tax Credit Programs, 349

historic resources, 201, 203, 218, 352
homelessness, 282, 290–91, 293
Hopewell, 11, 51, 181–85, 187–89, 192–93, 349
Hopewell project, 187, 192
Horseshoe, 197–98, 210
households, 31–32, 140, 184

I
I-64, 198, 300, 304
I-81, 20, 299–300, 304
IAD (International Airport), 297, 303
inclusion, 90, 108, 123, 128, 131, 135, 138, 191, 228, 231, 233
independent cities, five, 105, 299
industry clusters, 8–9, 39, 84–86, 89, 91–95, 98
  regional, 19, 38, 52, 83, 85, 87–89, 91, 183–84, 298, 308
influence, rural political, 42–43
infrastructure, regional, 125
infrastructure development, 172, 206
initiatives, 4, 66, 109, 111, 114, 117–19, 171, 174, 176, 181, 208, 213, 293–94
injuries, 282, 284, 286–87, 289, 291, 294–95
innovation, 11, 86, 94, 101–3, 108, 114, 117, 137, 145–46, 360, 365–66
Innovation Campus, Virginia Tech, 322
Institute of Policy and Governance (IPG), 257
integration, 12, 133, 147, 237–46, 249, 353–54, 357
  successful, 239, 243
interest groups, 139, 280
internet
  access, 31–32
  connectivity, 94, 198
  high-speed, 94, 152, 160, 172, 210
  providers, 141
internet services, 32, 145
interstate highway, 198, 304
interviews, 12, 106, 243–46, 249, 263, 265, 328, 354
investments
  federal, 143

private, 202, 213
public, 142
small, 320
Iowa West Foundation (IWF), 185
IPG (Institute of Policy and Governance), 257
IWF (Iowa West Foundation), 185

J
jail, 267, 269
James Madison University (JMU), 13, 72, 126, 204, 297–98, 305–7, 309–12, 361, 365–66, 369
James River, 182, 188, 222–24
Jenkins-Smith, 147–48, 342
job placement, 247, 250
jobs, 26, 60, 64, 83–85, 88–91, 239–40, 244, 246–48, 331, 336, 340
Johnson City, 97, 99
jurisdictions, 48–53, 98, 105, 166, 173, 177–78, 279, 281, 284, 291–94, 300
political, 47, 53

K
Kent, 351–52
Kingdon, 279–80, 292, 360
knowledge, 3, 113, 124, 134, 138, 145, 241–43, 245, 249, 260, 273
knowledge creation, 95, 99
Krugman, 59–60, 332

L
Lamson, 190, 348
lands, public, 216–17
landscapes, regional, 219
last-mile connections, 144–45
LCP (legacy communications provider), 143, 153, 157
leaders
civic, 66, 76
local, 63, 65, 73, 78, 115–16, 158
regional, 87, 110
legacy coalition, 152, 155, 158
legacy communications provider (LCP), 143, 153, 157

legacy providers, 145, 147–50, 152–53, 156–57, 159
legislature, 38, 44, 54, 56–57, 148–49, 160
Liberty University, 105–6, 119
Local and Regional Competitiveness Initiative (LRCI), 74
local businesses, 204, 306, 315
local governments, 4, 10, 148, 150, 153, 169, 177, 180, 191–92, 198, 203
localities, 21–23, 37–38, 70, 74–75, 96–97, 112, 152–53, 181–82, 187–88, 203, 212–13, 231–32, 261–62, 267–68, 319–22
location quotient, 89–90, 94–95
London, 223, 343–44, 348, 353, 355, 357, 359–60
Loudoun, 50, 52–53
low-income communities, 42, 123
LRCI (Local and Regional Competitiveness Initiative), 74
Lunenburg, 281, 287, 292–93
LWCF (Land and Water Conservation Fund), 218
Lynchburg, 19, 26, 102, 105, 107, 119, 311

M
Macy, B., 263
Madison Center for Community Development (MCCD), 306
Main Street, 203–4, 207, 209, 321, 351
Main Street America, 352–53
Main Street Program, 204, 206, 350
Manassas, 50
manufacturing, 26, 42, 65, 68, 70, 83, 96, 102, 104, 198–200, 304
maps, 23, 52–53, 96, 153, 168, 205, 327, 329, 342
marketing, 97, 99, 199, 209, 222, 305, 312, 316
Markusen, 182, 191, 348, 363
Marsden, 170, 175, 345
Martinsville, 1–2, 19, 25
Mathews County, 281, 288

Mayer, 87, 98, 336
MCCD (Madison Center for Community Development), 306
McFarland, 9, 18, 83, 88, 98, 125, 336, 339, 367
McKee, 42, 329
Medicaid Expansion, 55, 57, 327
mental health, 12, 266, 277, 282, 284, 286–87, 289–91, 294–95
mental health service provision, 288, 290
metropolitan areas, small, 39, 64
metropolitan statistical areas (MSA), 17–21, 26–27, 29–30, 34, 60–62, 64, 79, 84, 86, 105, 182, 185, 300–301
Mezirow, 167, 345
micropolitan, 17, 21, 38, 89, 93, 95
migration, 17, 25–26, 356
Migration Policy Institute, 242, 248, 353, 355
Moretti, 79, 336
municipalities, fiscally distressed, 184

N

National Main Street Center, 203, 207
National Main Street Program, 202
National Park Service, 351
National Preservation Act, 201
National Research Council, 122, 124, 339
National Scenic Byways, 219, 222
National Science Board, 123, 339
National Telecommunications and Information Administration (NTIA), 149
National Trust, 201–3
Nelson, 108, 281, 293
neoliberalism, 166, 177, 343–45
neonatal abstinence syndrome (NAS), 266
network infrastructure, 146, 156–57
Network Kansas's E-Communities program, 118
networks, 103–4, 110–11, 113, 116, 135–38, 143–46, 151–52, 155, 157–58, 160, 313
New River Valley, 12, 105, 107, 117, 265

New River Valley Community Services (NRVCS), 262, 267
New York, 23, 44, 323, 325–28, 330, 336, 338, 342–47, 350–51, 354, 360
New York Times, 325, 331–32
Northam, Governor, 127, 141, 143, 342
North Carolina Main Street Communities, 351
Northern Virginia, 3, 26, 29, 39, 43, 49–50, 64, 72, 77, 141, 198
NRVCS (New River Valley Community Services), 262, 267
NTIA (National Telecommunications and Information Administration), 149
nutrition, 284, 286–88, 290, 292–93

O

OER (Open Educational Resources), 136
Office of Broadband, 149, 159–60, 341
Office of Science and Technology Policy (OSTP), 339
Olivo, 54, 329–30
Open Educational Resources (OER), 136
opioid crisis, 34, 59, 255, 257–59, 261–64, 269, 292, 358
opioids, 257–58, 260, 265–66, 270–71, 277
opioid use disorder (OUD), 12, 264
Oregon, 4, 40, 87, 97, 132, 335–36
Orfield, 38, 324
organizations, nonprofit, 144, 293, 313
OSTP (Office of Science and Technology Policy), 339
outdoor recreation, 171, 175, 217–18, 220
outreach, 3–5, 203, 222, 231, 244, 315–16, 366
overview of scenic resources in Virginia, 217

P

Page County, 209, 291
pandemic, 2, 76–78, 119, 159, 161, 238, 249, 315, 320, 356
parks, 50, 193, 204, 220, 288, 293

partnerships, 65, 71, 114, 116, 271–72, 274, 298, 303, 305, 311, 313–14
Partridge, 85, 94, 336
passenger air service, 300
Patrick County, 10, 165–66, 169–75, 177, 179–80, 345–46
Patrick Henry Community College, 210, 351
PCE (Professional and Continuing Education), 306
pedestrians, 193–95, 293
Peer Recovery Specialist, 263, 266–68
Petersburg, 11, 72, 181–85, 187–90, 192–93, 347–49
Pew Charitable Trusts, 147, 333
Pew Research Center, 332, 334, 336
Piedmont region of Virginia, 10
Pike Place Market, 211
place-based development, 206, 208
place economics, 206, 351
placemaking, 186, 206
planning, strategic, 168, 306
planning process, 128, 173, 175, 224, 265
plans, 39, 42, 109–11, 116–17, 135–37, 143, 186–88, 191, 218, 224, 307, 311
   regional, 265
   statewide, 133
policy, 102–3, 148, 150, 157–58, 180, 243–44, 246–47, 249, 260, 262–63, 271, 319, 326, 358–59, 365–69
   state government broadband, 150
   state-level, 8, 55, 119
policy entrepreneurs, 279–80, 288, 292
policymakers, 98, 159, 252, 279–80, 295, 318, 322
politics, 30, 168, 319, 326, 328–29, 346–47, 359–60
population, 18–21, 23, 25–26, 28–29, 42, 45, 49, 52–54, 59–60, 63, 105, 175, 177–80, 182–83, 185
   aging, 34, 59, 75, 277
   changes, 23, 327
   density, 20, 141, 183, 278
   displaced, 239, 241, 250–52
   growth, 38, 42, 56, 85, 336
   working-age, 198

Porter, 38–39, 59–60, 86, 324, 332, 335
Port of Virginia , 23
postpandemic, 77–78
Povar, L., 73
predictor of growth, 91
preservation, 11, 201, 216–17, 220, 222, 224–25, 264
Preservation Virginia, 349–50
Prince George, 11, 181–85, 187–88, 190, 192, 194, 347
Prince William, 50, 52–53
priorities for STEM education in Virginia, 129
problems, wicked, 259
public art, 11, 181–82, 185–87, 191, 195–96, 348–49
   installations, 182–83, 189, 349
public health, 12, 256, 259, 263, 273, 288, 360
   challenges, 277, 281
   emergency, 257, 358
public participation, 292, 344–45
public policy, 7, 18, 197, 199, 213, 273, 324, 346, 359
Pulaski , 261, 273
Pulaski Community Partners Coalition (PCPC), 262, 265–66, 271, 274
Pulaski County, 37–38, 72, 107, 255, 258–59, 261–63, 269–70, 274

R

race, 28, 47–48, 108, 125, 171, 176, 328, 338
railways, 199–200
Randall, 239, 244, 251, 356
Rappahannock, 108, 281–82, 293–94, 360
RBTC (Roanoke-Blacksburg Technology Council), 107
Ream, 306–7, 312–13
Refugee Assistance Extension Act, 244
refugees, 237–52, 353–57, 367–69
   integration, 238, 240, 249, 354, 356–57
   narratives, 249
   perspectives, 240, 244, 249

resettlement, 12, 237–38, 243, 354
resettlement in rural Virginia, 237–38
regional airports, 13, 298, 309, 311, 315
   smaller, 298
regional connectivity, 8–9, 83, 85, 94, 98
regional economic performance, 86, 89
regional economies, 38, 84–86, 98, 199, 206, 208, 212, 362
regional hubs, 123, 136
regional job opportunities, 63
Regional Plan Association, 351
regional planning, 182, 336
regional Venture Hub network, 111
regions, 22–23, 29–30, 34–39, 59–60, 62–65, 77–79, 85–86, 88–92, 95–98, 102, 104–20, 122–24, 130–32, 135–36, 185–87, 195–200, 210–13, 281, 304–7, 311–13
   lagging, 2, 9, 13, 139, 318
   micropolitan, 34, 125
   nine-county, 108, 116
Republican candidates, 45, 47
Republicans, 43–45, 47, 54–57, 142, 178
research
   community-based, 169–70, 259, 275
   universities, 260, 272, 358
research universities, major, 106, 119
resettled refugees, successful integration of, 237, 239
resettlement, 238, 240, 250
   policies, 238, 240, 250–51
resilience, 264, 303
restaurants, 2, 106, 193–94, 204
retention, 54, 114, 123, 207, 309
revitalization, place-based, 199, 212
Reynolds Homestead, 165, 171–72
Richmond, 23, 25–26, 29, 43, 50–52, 198, 200, 223–24, 233, 281, 284, 293–94, 301, 340–41, 349–50
Richmond Hill, 222
Richmond land trust, 233
Richmond MSA, 50, 182, 184
Richmond Times-Dispatch, 327
Richmond-upon-Thames, 223
risks, environmental, 284, 287–88, 291

rivers, 183, 219–20, 232, 287
River Thames, 222–23
Roanoke, 12, 102, 107, 252, 255, 258–59, 261, 263, 269–71, 274, 281, 286, 293–94
County, 107
Roanoke-Blacksburg Entrepreneur Ecosystem, 108, 112
Roanoke City, 107, 154, 255, 258, 261, 274, 286
Roanoke Refugee Dialogue Group, 252
Roanoke Regional Chamber of Commerce, 269
Roanoke Regional Partnership, 106
Roanoke Small Business Development Center, 107
Roanoke Times, 37–38, 324, 341
Roanoke Valley, 46, 263–64, 274
Roanoke Valley Collective Response (RVCR), 262–65, 269, 271
Robins Foundation, 186
Rockingham, 299–301
Rocky Gap Greenway Project, 290
role of arts and culture, 165, 174
RUCA (Rural Urban Commuting Areas), 21
rural, 17–18, 35, 75, 93, 116, 281–82, 284, 286–91, 323, 332–33, 337
   areas, 2–3, 7–9, 12, 19–22, 41–42, 46–47, 54–57, 60–62, 84–85, 87–88, 139–40, 176–80, 198, 246–47, 278
   broadband, 39, 333, 341
   communities, 37–39, 59, 61, 66–68, 75–76, 84–85, 88–89, 97–98, 102, 116–17, 237–39, 242–43, 248, 251–52, 270
   development, 87, 98, 115
   economies, 179, 336, 353
   firms, 104
   hinterlands, 26, 38, 211
   influence, 8, 41, 54
   jurisdictions, 54, 277, 282, 285, 294–95
   localities in Virginia, 74
   locations, 65, 68, 104, 112–13, 177–78
   regions, 4, 8, 38–39, 59–60, 64, 68, 70, 72, 76–77, 101–2, 117–19, 125

residents, 20, 42, 176, 298
stakeholders, 76
voters, 42, 45, 47, 55, 329
rural communities, viability of, 10, 158
rural counties, remote, 93–95
Rural Horseshoe, 197–98, 212
Rural-urban continuum, 330, 344, 350
Rural-urban divide, 77, 336
rural Virginia, 8, 29, 41, 44, 46, 54–55, 57, 62, 64–68, 76–78, 237–38
rural Virginia broadband policy, 149

S

Sabatier, 147, 279, 342, 359–60
SBDC (Small Business Development Center), 107, 111, 309
scenery, 216–17, 229
scenic, 11, 216, 219, 226–27, 229, 231–32, 299
Scenic America, 233
Scenic Resource Recognition and Preservation in Virginia, 217
scenic resources, 11, 215–20, 222, 224–25, 227, 232
Scenic Rivers programs, 219–21
scenic value, 216, 227
Scenic Virginia, 11, 221–22, 224–26, 228–29, 231–34, 322, 368
   Board, 224, 366
   Viewshed Committee, 225, 227
School of Public and International Affairs, 356, 365–69
Science, Technology, Engineering, and Math. *See* STEM
service providers, 156, 237, 239–41, 244–45, 247, 250–52, 262, 266, 269
services, 95–96, 99, 140, 145–46, 151–52, 156–57, 160, 199–200, 204, 245–46, 251–52, 262, 264, 266–68, 270, 311, 315
   aviation, 299–300, 305
   consumer, 199, 352
   emergency, 143, 288
Shenandoah Valley, 13, 39, 125, 297–301, 304, 307, 309, 313–15, 362

Shenandoah Valley Airport Commission, 300
Shenandoah Valley Conference Center, 309
Shenandoah Valley Innovation Coalition, 213, 352
Shenandoah Valley Joint Airport Commission, 300
Shenandoah Valley Partnership, 299–300, 304–5, 309, 313, 362
Shenandoah Valley Regional Airport, 13, 297–300, 302–3, 305–7, 309–16, 361–62
SHFC (Supporting Healthy Families and Communities), 257
skills, 39, 76, 84, 88, 124, 138, 198, 203, 209, 240, 312
SkyWest, 298, 303, 305, 314
Small Business Development Center (SBDC), 107, 111, 309
small businesses, 4, 66, 115, 208–9, 212
   regional, 106
smaller metros and rural regions for growth, 64
social changes, 169–70, 177–79, 240, 346
social determinants of health, 261, 267
social network analysis, 114
Southern Virginia Food Hub, 209
South Hill, 5, 209, 352
Southside, 25, 141, 144, 187, 198, 200, 281, 286
spaces, 3, 111, 114, 118–20, 194–95, 200, 209, 319, 323, 328, 336
specialization, 26, 90, 96
stakeholders, 5–6, 120, 125–27, 132–33, 135–37, 203, 263, 267, 269, 318, 322
   local, 5, 186, 192, 203, 305
start-ups, 107–9, 113, 119
state
   agencies, 7, 18, 116, 143, 203, 282, 287
   investments in rural broadband access in Virginia, 67
   policies, 237–38
   policymakers, 117, 262

state and local leaders to work, 65
State Comprehensive Outdoor Recreation Plan, 218
state government, 126–27, 143, 152
statewide efforts, 137, 229
statewide programs, 203, 226
Staunton, 19, 104, 213, 299–301
STEM (Science, Technology, Engineering, and Math), 121–24, 129–35, 339–40
STEM education, 122–24, 126–30, 132–33, 135, 137, 338, 365–66
  opportunities, 9, 36
  in Virginia, 127, 129
STEM initiatives, 129–30, 136
STEM literacy, 122, 126, 130, 340
STEM network, 125–27, 129–34, 137
  in Virginia, 127, 131
  in Virginia to strengthen STEM literacy, 121–22
STEM Summit, 128–30, 132
STEM workforce development, 121–22
story circles, 10, 167, 172–73, 346
strategic plan, 64, 127, 142, 334
students, 3–4, 107, 109, 118, 122–24, 131–35, 137, 210–11, 307–9, 312–14, 365, 367–69
substance use disorder (SUD), 12, 255, 258, 260, 263–66, 268–71, 277
suburbs, 11, 26–27, 29, 37–38, 42, 55, 57, 101–3, 177–78, 181–82, 200
Supporting Healthy Families and Communities (SHFC), 257

T
task force, 13, 306–16
tax credits, historic, 202
taxes, 37, 72–73, 178, 202, 246, 248
technical experts, 150, 272–73, 315
technology, 95, 106, 108, 130–31, 142, 145–47, 154, 208, 246, 251, 339–40
telecommunications, 147–50
tele-commuters, 210–11
Texas Main Street Program, 351
Tidewater, 43, 144

Tobacco Region Revitalization Commission (TRRC), 69, 149, 203
tourism, 20, 42, 67, 95, 98, 117, 119, 169, 186, 198, 211
tourism-related businesses, 106
towns
  college, 306
  historic, 10, 202, 210
  small, 9, 19, 34, 102
transportation, 13, 88, 96, 219, 241–42, 246, 266–67, 269, 299, 302–4, 362
travel, 77, 110, 297, 300, 307, 310
Tri-Cities, 10, 97, 99, 181–82, 184, 186–87, 192, 196
TRRC (Tobacco Region Revitalization Commission), 69, 149, 203
Trump, President, 179, 257, 326–27
TTIP (Tech Talent Investment Program), 71–72
Tucker, S., 25
twentieth century, 25, 43–44, 66, 184, 198
  early, 23, 25, 43, 184, 200

U
United Nations High Commissioner for Refugees (UNHCR), 239, 242, 357
United States, 59, 61–62, 122, 126, 180, 183, 237–39, 241, 248, 255, 348–49, 353, 355
universities, 4, 6, 102, 105–6, 118, 126, 128, 130, 135, 209–11, 272–74, 304, 306, 312–14, 366
University of Mary Washington, 57, 366
University of Virginia (UVA), 23, 72, 108–9, 115, 118, 126, 329–30, 370
urban, 17–18, 20, 35, 282, 284, 286–87, 289–91, 336
urban areas, 2–3, 19, 22, 33, 36, 140, 198, 237–38, 250–52, 277, 281–82, 295, 298
urban cores, 19, 21, 26–27, 29, 85, 87
urban counties, 27, 37, 281, 331
urban crescent, 25, 64, 77, 197–98, 212
urbanization, 23, 62, 84

urban jurisdictions, 43, 278, 281–84, 295
urban-rural continuum, 2, 6, 13, 17–18, 22, 30–31, 36, 176, 317, 321
US Census, 18, 23, 25, 183–85, 278, 282, 331, 360
US Census Bureau, 18, 26, 28–29, 34, 171, 183, 258, 346, 349, 358
US Cluster Mapping Project, 89, 97, 99, 336
US Department of Transportation, 219, 299, 302–3, 362
US Economic Development Administration, 1, 324

V
VA Department of Education (VDOE), 136
Valleys Innovation Council, 106–7, 112
values, cultural, 176, 219
VCCS (Virginia Community College System), 70
VCRMDS (Virginia Consortium for Refugee, Migrant, and Displacement Studies), 12, 237, 250–53
VDH, 257–58
VDOE (VA Department of Education), 136
VDOT. See Virginia Department of Transportation
VEDP and Virginia's Major Employment and Investment Project Approval Commission, 73
Vibrant Virginia Initiative, 3–6, 123, 273
Viewshed Project, 229, 231–32, 234
viewshed register, 11, 216, 225, 227–29, 231
viewsheds, 220–22, 227, 232
Virginia
  counties, 88, 99, 125
  politics, 8, 41, 43, 45, 56–57, 326
  southern, 19, 23, 39, 64, 201, 209–10
  southwest, 3, 12, 19, 30, 36, 39, 52, 237–38, 243–44, 250, 258
  southwest/southside, 165, 179
  Tri-Cities region, 10, 181

Virginia Alcohol Beverage Control Commission, 288
Virginia Association of Counties, 143, 149, 342
Virginia Auditor of Public Accounts, 348
Virginia Beach, 1–2, 34, 64, 116, 281, 287, 292–95
Virginia Business-Ready Sites Program, 69
Virginia Byways, 219, 222
Virginia Cable Telecommunications Association, 148
Virginia Coalfield Economic Development Authority, 65
Virginia Commonwealth University, 126, 128, 365–66
Virginia Community College System (VCCS), 70
Virginia Consortium for Refugee, 237, 250–51, 356
Virginia Cooperative Extension, 209
Virginia Department of Aviation, 299, 362
Virginia Department of Criminal Justice Services, 286
Virginia Department of Education, 124, 130, 340
Virginia Department of Health, 257–58, 284, 358
Virginia Department of Historic Resources, 201, 218, 352
Virginia Department of Housing and Community Development, 5, 39, 78, 144, 208, 325, 367
Virginia Department of Transportation (VDOT), 190, 219, 286, 290, 293
Virginia Economic Development Partnership (VEDP), 61, 63–64, 68–71, 73–75, 78, 96, 299–300, 304, 334, 362, 367
Virginia Growth and Diversification plans, 39
Virginia homes and businesses, 142
Virginia House, 44, 54
Virginia Main Street Communities, 205
Virginia Main Street Program, 78, 203, 209, 352

Virginia Outdoors Foundation, 218
Virginia Outdoors Plan, 220, 225, 229
Virginia Rural Broadband Coalition, 149
Virginia Rural Center. *See* VRC
Virginia Rural Leadership Institute (VRLI), 76
Virginia Scenic Rivers programs, 219, 222
Virginia's Common Wealth, 218
Virginia State Board, 52–53
Virginia State Code, 220
Virginia State University, 72
Virginia STEM network, 130, 136
    model, 125
Virginia Talent Accelerator Program, 70–71
Virginia Tech (VT), ix, 3–6, 72, 106, 108, 115, 126–27, 153–54, 172, 226–29, 257, 339–40, 356, 365, 367–69
Virginia Tech
    Center for Educational Networks, 367–68
    Center for Peace Studies and Violence Prevention, 180, 253
    Center for Public Health Practice, 370
    Center for Refugee, 367–69
    Institute for Policy and Governance, 165, 180, 366–69
    Office of Economic Development, 170
Virginia Telecommunications Initiative (VATI), 159–60
Virginia Viewshed Project, 225–26, 234
Virginia Western, 119
volunteers, 175, 238, 244–45, 247, 291
votes, 46–54, 56, 232
VRC (Virginia Rural Center), 76

VTIPG (Virginia Tech's Institute for Policy and Governance), 10
vulnerable populations, 34, 282, 284, 286–87, 289–91, 293–95

W

Walsh, 42, 47, 331
Warner, 8, 41, 43, 45–54, 328, 331, 342
    campaign, 47
Washington, 19, 25–26, 46, 52, 301, 324, 331–32, 335, 337–39, 348, 351
Washington-Dulles International Airport, 303
Washington Post, 324–31, 333, 344–45, 348
Washington State Department of Health, 323
Washington Street Bridge Gateway, 189–90, 193–94
Waynesboro, 299–301
Weldon Cooper Center, 141, 342
Western States Arts Federation, 187, 349
Western Virginia, 105, 133
West Virginia, 20, 43, 72, 204
Weyers Cave, 299–300, 308–9, 311
Wireless Internet Service Provider Association, 148
work, remote, 77, 94
workers, 63, 77, 85, 118, 217
workforce development, 9, 122, 126–27, 309
    programs, 68, 84
Work Progress Administration (WPA), 217
workshops, 10, 172–73, 175, 244

*Created with www.TExtract.com.

Contributing Authors

JOHN ACCORDINO
Professor, Virginia Commonwealth University

ABDULILAH ALSHENAIFI
Ph.D. student, Center for Public Administration and Policy, School of Public and International Affairs, Virginia Tech

ELIZABETH ARLEDGE
Ph.D. student, Center for Public Administration and Policy, School of Public and International Affairs, Virginia Tech

ERV BLYTHE
Vice President Emeritus for Information Technology, Virginia Tech

JAMES BOHLAND
Emeritus Professor, School of Public and International Affairs, Virginia Tech

JUSTIN BULLMAN
Project Coordinator, Economic & Community Development, School of Professional & Continuing Education, James Madison University

ALBERT BYERS
Assistant Professor, The Center for Innovation in STEM Education, Virginia Commonwealth University

Margaret Cowell
Associate Professor, School of Public and International Affairs, Virginia Tech

Kerry O. Cresawn
Director, Center for STEM Education and Outreach, James Madison University

Lynn M. Crump
Landscape Architect–Environmental Programs Planner, Virginia Department of Conservation & Recreation

Lisa Dickinson Mountcastle
Scenic Virginia Board of Trustees

Mary Beth Dunkenberger
Associate Director, Virginia Tech Institute for Policy and Governance

Elizabeth W. Edmondson
Principal Investigator, Center for Innovation in STEM Education, Virginia Commonwealth University

Stephen J. Farnsworth
Professor and Director, Center for Leadership and Media Studies, University of Mary Washington

Richard G. Gibbons
Scenic Virginia Board of Trustees

Erica Grabowski
Senior Program Specialist, National League of Cities

Stephen Hanna
Professor of Geography, University of Mary Washington

Conaway Haskins
Vice President, Entrepreneurial Ecosystems, Virginia Innovation Partnership Corporation

Jordan Hays
Graduate Assistant, Economic & Community Development, School of Professional & Continuing Education, James Madison University

Rebecca J. Hester
Assistant Professor of Science and Technology in Society, Associate Director, Virginia Tech Center for Refugee, Migrant, and Displacement Studies

Thomas Layou
Ph.D. student, Center for Public Administration and Policy, School of Public and International Affairs, Virginia Tech

Sarah Lyon-Hill
Senior Economic Development Specialist, Virginia Tech Center for Economic and Community Engagement

Susan G. Magliaro
Professor Emeritus, Virginia Tech Center for Educational Networks and Impacts

Christiana K. McFarland
Research Director, National League of Cities

James McConkie
Ph.D. student, Center for Public Administration and Policy, School of Public and International Affairs, Virginia Tech

Kyle Meyer
Revitalization Planner, Virginia Department of Housing and Community Development

Patrick A. Miller
Professor Emeritus, College of Architecture and Urban Studies, Virginia Tech

Neda Moayerian
Non-resident Research Associate, Virginia Tech Institute for Policy and Governance

Stephen Moret
President and CEO, Virginia Economic Development Partnership

Lara Nagle
Community-Based Learning Project Manager, Virginia Tech Institute for Policy and Governance

Laura Nelson
Research Associate, Virginia Tech Institute for Policy and Governance

Phyllis L. Newbill
Outreach and Engagement Coordinator, Virginia Tech Center for Educational Networks and Impacts

Nhung Nguyen
PhD student, Center for Public Administration and Policy, School of Public and International Affairs, Virginia Tech

Benjamin Packard
Ph.D. student, Center for Public Administration and Policy, School of Public and International Affairs, Virginia Tech

Erik R. Pages
President, EntreWorks Consulting

Aditya Sai Phutane
Ph.D. student, Center for Public Administration and Policy, School of Public and International Affairs, Virginia Tech

Katrina M. Powell
Professor of Rhetoric and Writing & Director, Virginia Tech Center for Refugee, Migrant, and Displacement Studies

Leighton Powell
Director, Scenic Virginia

John Provo
Director, Virginia Tech Center for Economic and Community Engagement

Kate Seltzer
Graduate student, Philip Merrill College of Journalism, University of Maryland

Md Ashiqur Rab
Ph.D. student, Center for Public Administration and Policy, School of Public and International Affairs, Virginia Tech

Katherine Randall
Research Assistant, Virginia Tech Center for Refugee, Migrant, and Displacement Studies

Padmanabhan Seshaiyer
Professor, College of Science, George Mason University

Jisoo Sim
School of Architecture and Design, College of Architecture and Urban Studies, Virginia Tech

Stephanie L. Smith
Associate Professor, Center for Public Administration and Policy, School of Public and International Affairs, Virginia Tech

Amady Sogodogo
Ph.D. student, Center for Public Administration and Policy, School of Public and International Affairs, Virginia Tech

Max O. Stephenson, Jr.
Director, Virginia Tech Institute for Policy and Governance

Nicholas J. Swartz
Associate Dean, Economic & Community Development, School of Professional & Continuing Education, James Madison University

Joanne Tang
Ph.D. student, Center for Public Administration and Policy, School of Public and International Affairs, Virginia Tech

Scott Tate
Associate Director, Virginia Tech Center for Economic and Community Engagement

Lindsay B. Wheeler
Assistant Professor, Center for Teaching Excellence, University of Virginia

Sophie Wenzel
Associate Director, Virginia Tech Center for Public Health Practice and Research Department of Population Health Sciences, College of Veterinary Medicine

Made in the USA
Coppell, TX
29 March 2022